ILLUMINATIONS

COMPILED LECTURES ON

Shari'ah and Tasawwuf

BY

SHAYKH MUHAMMAD HISHAM KABBANI

Representing the Most Distinguished Naqshbandi Sufi Order under the direction of its world Leader Shaykh Muhammad Nazim Adil al-Haqqani

ISLAMIC SUPREME COUNCIL OF AMERICA

ISBN: 978-1-930409-52-1

Library of Congress Control Number: 2007941447

Published and Distributed by:
Islamic Supreme Council of America
17195 Silver Parkway, #201 Fenton, MI 48430
USA
Tel: (888) 278-6624
Fax:(810) 815-0518
Email: staff@islamicsupremecouncil.org
Web: http://www.islamicsupremecouncil.org

Shaykh Muhammad Nazim Adil al-Haqqani (right), world leader of the most distinguished Naqshbandi-Haqqani Sufi Order, with his representative, and author of this book, Shaykh Muhammad Hisham Kabbani.

بسم الله الرحمن الرحيم

الرَّحْمَنُ عَلَّمَ الْقُرْآنَ خَلَقَ الْإِنسَانَ عَلَّمَهُ

الْبَيَانَ

The Most Merciful has made known the Qur'ān; He Created humandkind; He Taught him eloquence.

Sūratu 'r-Raḥmān [the Merciful], 55:22

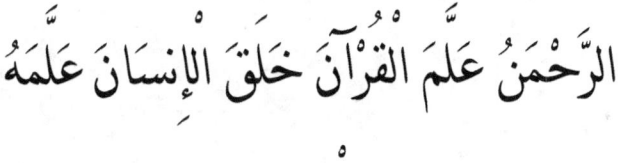

CONTENTS

Publisher's Notes 8
About the Author 10
Introduction 12
SPIRITUALITY 13
The Sufis 15
Sufism and the Perennial Conflict of Good and Evil...27
Spirituality in Modern Civilization 103
Spiritual Healing in the Islamic Tradition 151
SHARI'AH 171
What is a *Fatwa*? 173
Viewpoint: Door of *'Ijtihad'* is Open 179
Democracy According to Traditional Islamic Sources...185
Understanding Islamic Law 215
As-Salat Ritual Prayer: Its Meaning and Manner 275
Principles of Leadership in War and Peace 347
The Question of Wife-beating in Islam 439
SCIENCE AND TECHNOLOGY 477
The Importance of Technology in the Development of Islamic Countries 479
The Quran's Miraculous Eternal Relevance 493

PUBLISHER'S NOTES

This book is specifically designed for readers relatively familiar with Islamic and Sufi terms. However, to accommodate those who are not, we have often accompanied Arabic terminology with English translations.

Qur'ānic quotes are centered, highlighted in bold and italics and footnoted, citing chapter name, number and verse. The Holy Traditions of Prophet Muhammad ﷺ (known as *hadith*) are offset, italicized and footnoted referencing the bookﷺ in which they are cited. Every attempt has been made to be precise and comprehensive in citing sources.

UNIVERSALLY RECOGNIZED SYMBOLS

Muslims around the world typically offer praise upon speaking, hearing, or reading the name *"Allah"* and any of the Islamic names of God. Muslims also offer salutation and/or invoke blessing upon speaking, hearing or reading the names of Prophet Muhammad, other prophets, his family, his companions, and saints. We have applied the following international standards, using Arabic calligraphy and lettering:

ﷺ *ṣall-Allāhu ʿalayhi wa sallam* (God's blessings and greetings of peace be upon him) following the names of the Prophet ﷺ.

ﷷ *ʿalayhi 's-salām* (peace be upon him) following the names of other prophets, angels, and Khiḍr.

ﷷ *ʿalayhā 's-salām* (peace be upon her) following the name of Mary, Mother of Jesus.

ﷺ/ﷺ *raḍīy-Allāhu ʿanhu/ʿanhā* (may God be pleased with him/her) following the name of a male or female companion of the Prophet ﷺ.

ق *qaddas-Allāhu sirrah* (may God sanctify his secret) following the name of a saint.

TRANSLITERATION

To simplify reading the Arabic names, places and terms are not transliterated in the main text. Transliteration is provided in the section on the spiritual practices to facilitate correct pronunciation and is based on the following system:

Symbol	Transliteration	Symbol	Transliteration	Vowels:	
				Long	
ء	'	ط	ṭ	آ ى	ā
ب	b	ظ	ẓ	و	ū
ت	t	ع	ʿ	ي	ī
ث	th	غ	gh	Short	
ج	j	ف	f	َ	a
ح	ḥ	ق	q	ُ	u
خ	kh	ك	k	ِ	i
د	d	ل	l		
ذ	dh	م	m		
ر	r	ن	n		
ز	z	ه	h		
س	s	و	w		
ش	sh	ي	y		
ص	ṣ	ة	ah; at		
ض	ḍ	ال	al-/'l-		

ABOUT THE AUTHOR

Shaykh Muhammad Hisham Kabbani is a world-renowned author and religious scholar. He has devoted his life to the promotion of the traditional Islamic principles of peace, tolerance, love, compassion and brotherhood, while opposing extremism in all its forms. The shaykh is a member of a respected family of traditional Islamic scholars, which includes the former head of the Association of Muslim Scholars of Lebanon and the present Grand Mufti[1] of Lebanon.

In the U.S., Shaykh Kabbani serves as Chairman, Islamic Supreme Council of America; Founder, Naqshbandi Sufi Order of America; Advisor, World Organization for Resource Development and Education; Chairman, As-Sunnah Foundation of America; Chairman, Kamilat Muslim Women's Organization; and, Founder and President, The Muslim Magazine.

Shaykh Kabbani is highly trained, both as a Western scientist and as a classical Islamic scholar. He received a bachelor's degree in chemistry and studied medicine. In addition, he also holds a degree in Islamic Divine Law, and under the tutelage of Shaykh ʿAbd Allah Daghestani ق, license to teach, guide and counsel religious students in Islamic spirituality from Shaykh Muhammad Nazim ʿAdil al-Qubrusi al-Haqqani an-Naqshbandi ق, the world leader of the Naqshbandi-Haqqani Sufi Order.

His books include: *Commentary on the Chapter of Sincerity* (2007), *Universe Rising* (2007); *The Sufi Path of Self-Realization* (2006); *Keys to the Divine Kingdom* (2005); *Classical Islam and the Naqshbandi Sufi Order* (2004); *Pearls and Coral* (2005); *The Naqshbandi Sufi Tradition Guidebook* (2004); *The Approach of Armageddon? An Islamic Perspective* (2003); *Encyclopedia of Muhammad's Women Companions and the Traditions They Related*

[1] The highest Islāmīc religious authority in the country.

(1998, with Dr. Laleh Bakhtiar); *Encyclopedia of Islamic Doctrine* (7 vols. 1998); *Angels Unveiled* (1996); *The Naqshbandi Sufi Way* (1995); *Remembrance of God Liturgy of the Sufi Naqshbandi Masters* (1994).

In his long-standing endeavor to promote better understanding of classical Islam, Shaykh Kabbani has hosted two international conferences in the United States, both of which drew scholars from throughout the Muslim world. As a resounding voice for traditional Islam, his counsel is sought by journalists, academics and government leaders.

Introduction

This compilation of lectures delivered by author Shaykh Kabbani in various venues throughout the United States and in international venues, includes a presentation on spiritual Islam to HRH Prince Charles of England, a lectures delivered at before the Vice President of Indonesia and a conference in Malaysia addressing the spiritual aspects of psychology.

While in most circumstances, Naqshbandi Sufi masters do not read from a written text—rather speaking from inspiration—in order to accommodate academic norms and forms of presentation, Shaykh Kabbani has written these detailed lectures regarding Shariʿah and *Tasawwuf* to accompany what he presented orally, as inspired through his heart by his teacher Shaykh Nazim Adil al-Haqqani.

In these talks, Shaykh Kabbani presents the traditional Islamic perspectives on a number of important issues of the day, focusing on the adaptability of classical Islam to the needs of the time, exigencies of social and cultural change and the advent of new approaches and methodologies in a number of facets of life. At the same time, Shaykh Kabbani brings an unusual viewpoint to modern day issues, relating them to aspects of the psyche and an individual's spiritual state as well as societal impact and relationships and their influence on observance of Divine Law.

Shaykh Kabbani is able to present complex issues in the light of potent relevant examples from modern-day science while simultaneously relating them to the traditional understanding of classical Islam and the normative practices and unparalleled perfection found in the example of Prophet Muhammad ﷺ.

SPIRITUALITY

THE SUFIS[2]

[2] Presented to the conference "Understanding Sufism and its Potential Role in US Policy", hosted by the Nixon Center,` October 24, 2003.

THE SUFIS – ENLIGHTENED COMMUNITY BUILDERS

Sufism created community. In every age and era since the time of Prophet Muhammad, upon whom be peace, to whom all Sufis look as inspiration, role model and guide, the Sufis have sought to establish the infrastructure that, in modern parlance, would be termed privatized social welfare. It was through institutions designed not only to serve the destitute, the homeless and the ill, but whose overall purpose was to redirect the society as a whole to the goal of uplifting the people spiritually, psychologically, morally and physically, that the Sufis were able to have a immense impact on the societies in which they functioned.

The primary focus of the Sufi tradition was to establish societal order based on a hierarchical pattern of organization. Such a hierarchy governed Central Asia, South Asia, North Africa and most other areas of the Islamic world by means of Sufi societal infrastructure and institutions.

THE SUFI HIERARCHY

The primary mechanism by which Sufism exerted maximal societal impact was a sophisticated system of charities and trusts (*awqāf*). This pyramidal system was governed by a leader who directed these institutions to work to help those in most need first, followed by those at the next level of priority and so on, addressing the needs of all those in need, without leaving anyone outside the gambit of its programs. This paradigm was not dissimilar to contemporary modern day structured government-operated social programs (like public schools, hospitals, etc.) or civic society institutions. Leaders were chosen not by virtue of intelligence or political savvy, but solely by virtue of piety and wisdom, attained through disciplined participation in the Sufi school system.

The basic functional units of this infrastructure were the *khāniqah* (also known as *zāwīya* and *dergah*), buildings similar to modern hostels, but with far greater functionality and the *maljā* hospitals where all comers were treated without charge. *Khaniqahs* were places where people, both locals and travelers, could stay, eat, sleep and meet with one another. In addition to feeding and entertaining people, the institutions introduced them to Sufi customs.

Perhaps the closest parallel in westerns society to the Sufi system of societal welfare and the institutions it built would be found among the Catholic orders – particularly the Benedictine and Franciscan – many of which encountered Sufis during the Crusades and emulated them after they returned from Europe.

Unfortunately, the Wahhabis have destroyed this system of community-building. They closed the *khāniqahs* in order to eliminate the fundamental underlying principles of tolerance and openness upon which they were founded. Wahhabis sought to create a form of individualism that encouraged Muslims to reinterpret their religion according to their own whims, thereby undermining the traditional Sufi hierarchy. The result was a sort of individualistic anarchy that found differences in the most trivial aspects of religion, culture or lifestyle to be wholly unacceptable and grounds for often fierce and bitter clashes. Whenever the hierarchy established by Sufism was dismantled, disorder, confusion and anarchy took its place with inevitable result being division, destructive enmity and a downward spiral into violence.

THE SUFI APPROACH TO ADVANCEMENT

Sufism was based on the fundamental importance of the relationship between student and teacher. In Sufism, the top of the pyramid is only reached by means of education and experience. Like any important job, it requires an intensive period of internship (much as is required to become a public servant, a doctor or a lawyer). This approach to training future leaders builds integrity and relies on the test of time to confirm true leaders, those who possess insight, wisdom and divine guidance. Sufi teachings focused on the importance of self-sacrifice and the need for those well-endowed to share from what God had graced them with – whether in material wealth, learning or piety.

Sufism eliminated the anarchy of self-centeredness and cooled the rebellion of desire and egoism, enabling the accomplished Sufi to lead others. The result of this disciplined practical training was that esteemed Sufi figures were, historically, well-accomplished in the sciences of Islamic spirituality.

PRINCIPLES OF TREATING THE SELF

Islamic spirituality calls for *zuhd* (asceticism), *warā* (sincerity) and *riḍā* (acceptance of the divine decree of one's allotted share). The Sufi belief is that reason alone is not sufficient to make decisions; they believe it is also essential to understand the underlying reality of each issue one faces. To understand such realities, one must undergo physical and spiritual training exercises, much as a wrestler must do weight-training and wind-sprints, in order to prevent the anarchy and corrupt desire of the self from controlling one in the state of anger, lust or fear. Once this training is successfully accomplished, passions at the most base level will no longer control one – rather, one will control them. When this has been accomplished, decisions will no longer be based on egoism, anger or selfishness, but will be based on reason, intellect and wisdom, informed by spiritual inspiration.

To the Sufis, the whole world is in their hands, and at the same time, their hearts are in the hand of their Creator, for they observe the maxim of the Prophet's Companion, ʿAlī who said:

اعمل لدنياك كانك تعيش ابدا وعمل لاخرتك كانك تموت غدا

Work for this life as if you were going to live forever, but
work for the afterlife as if you were going to die today.

The utmost level of submission for the Sufi – and the ultimate attainment – is to "die before you die," meaning that one's heart is no longer attached to the material world, but is directed to the Divine Presence, seeking God's good pleasure, always striving to serve humanity in every possible way. Such idealism and detachment sounds almost impossible to achieve humanly, but in fact, this was achieved by countless numbers of people who flocked to the doors of the Sufi shaykhs in their retreats and hostels and trained their selves with determination and discipline.

Sufis say that a human being can be rich and ascetic at the same time, for to be ascetic, one need not be poor. Not every poor one is an ascetic, nor is every ascetic one poor. For this reason, history shows many Sufi saints were, in fact, quite wealthy, but spent their wealth in God's Way by aiding the needy, building hostels, hospitals and way stations, and by establishing trusts to promote the arts, libraries and scientific research centers.

The Sufis says, "The wise servants of God are like the earth. They accept every type of refuse to be cast upon them and yet nothing issues from them but sweetness. Both the righteous and the sinner walk upon it." The earth is characterized by strength. Whatever God Wills, the earth accepts. It has no will of its own. In this respect, the Sufis resemble the earth in that "every vile and ugly thing is cast upon" then, and they accept it. Yet, after the Sufi accepts to be such a dump, the verse continues, "nothing comes from him or her except goodness."

Such wise teachers do not treat you the same way that you treat them. Rather, they return good for evil. By this means, a counterforce comes into play by which the momentum of evil, passing through the transformative positive energy field of the advanced Sufi master, is converted into power which is rebounded to the opponent, causing a catalytic reaction which inverts the initial impulse to evil, resulting in a transfiguration of the challenger. For that reason, some of the most famous conversions in Islam came about when an opponent sought out a Sufi master seeking to harm him, yet when confronted with his own evil in the Sufi's mirror-like visage, was thus brought to contrition, repentance and redemption at the hands of the master.

THE DOCTORS OF HEARTS

With the knowledge acquired through their sincerity and piety, Sufis were able to first treat their own hearts. From this experience of self-treatment, they began to understand the illnesses of others. Through their immersion in the social life of their communities, they empathized with the feelings of pain others felt and sought the means to cure their spiritual, moral, psychological and social ills. With the wisdom and experience acquired in treating their own ills, using their understanding of culture and environment and maintaining the flexibility to accommodate the lives of all sorts of people, the Sufi leaders and healers were able to treat the people in whatever situation they found them. Sufism is not words put together in flashy phrases, nor is it theoretical knowledge; rather, it is moral character and behavior, it is the state of excellence, and it is the infrastructure of life. One of Sufism's greatest scholars, al-Junayd said, "We did not take *Taṣawwuf* from 'this one said' or 'that one said,' as the scholars did [with their *sanads* – chains of transmission and verification], but we took it by feeling the hunger of the hungry, by feeling abandoned in the desert with the homeless, by feeling the wealth of the rich in accompanying them, by feeling the pain of the ill, by feeling the pain of the injured. That is how we came to this understanding."

Thus, *Taṣawwuf* was never based on theories to be mentioned and discussed, nor on a prescription to be taken from a pharmacy. Rather *Taṣawwuf* provided a cure first tested by the doctor on himself who, after successfully deriving its benefit, was able to apply it to others in need of the same treatment. This is what made the central social role of Sufism in Muslim life acceptable to the masses, wherever it was found.

The way of the Sufi Path was one of transformation, as symbolized by the alchemical metaphor of transforming base elements, such as lead, into gold. This path of continual transformation resulted in a constant struggle to not only elevate the spiritual level of the individual, but also to raise the spiritual and material levels of the family, the tribe, the community and the nation as a whole. The French scholar Louis Massignon explains that social justice remained crucial to the ascetics' piety: "The mystic call is, as a rule, the result of inner rebellion of the conscience against social injustices, not only those of others, but primarily and particularly, against one's own faults ..."

Sufis had, and continue to play, a great role in social work, as is mentioned by Massignon and many other Orientalists. As the former stated, "The Sufis are doctors of the soul, [whose work] includes the sociology of the soul, the psychology of the soul and the mentality of the soul, and they work to cure those who have diseases in any of these aspects."[3]

THE SUFI APPROACH TO SOCIETY-BUILDING

Sufis worked to build bridges of inter-racial, inter-ethnic and cross-cultural understanding. In doing so, they differed from the Wahhabis, who tried to homogenize, standardize and eliminate all variation, in contradiction with the Qur'ānic verse:

---

[3] Massignon, Louis, *Les origines du lexique technique de la mystique mussulmanes*, p. 16, Paris, 1954

يَا أَيُّهَا النَّاسُ إِنَّا خَلَقْنَاكُم مِّن ذَكَرٍ وَأُنثَى وَجَعَلْنَاكُمْ شُعُوبًا وَقَبَائِلَ لِتَعَارَفُوا إِنَّ أَكْرَمَكُمْ عِندَ اللَّهِ أَتْقَاكُمْ إِنَّ اللَّهَ عَلِيمٌ خَبِيرٌ

O mankind! We created you from a single (pair) of a male and a female, and made you into nations and tribes, that ye may know each other (not that ye may despise (each other).[4]

As an example of this spirit, sacred education, community-building and human resource development was spread throughout Africa by the Sufi orders, creating jobs for the poor and establishing relationships between disparate communities. Especially active in such social work were the Shadiliyya and the Sanusiyya orders. The hostels founded by the shaykhs of these Sufi orders became points of convergence, bringing together different races, promoting interracial and inter-tribal marriages, and thereby, preventing wars and creating intellectual and economic opportunities for the societies in which they functioned by introducing science, business, trade, education, medicine, the arts and administrative job opportunities for people. This was accomplished by the mixing of the highly accomplished and revered Sufi teachers with the common people, the normative practice of the Sufis. To involve themselves in the lives of the common people, both rich and poor, without any thought to distinctions of ethnicity, culture or even religion – rather, considering all people members of the same human community – had an enormous impact on cultures and tribes previously isolated from, or more commonly, at war with each other.

Sufism depended on the human bonding that comes about with the commingling of peoples in a symbiotic manner, producing combinations which cut across a society's natural barriers, to generate the heat and turbulence needed to keep a

---

[4] Sūratu 'l-Ḥujurāt [The Private Apartments], 49:13.

nourishing flow of social "nutrients" moving among all the layers and stratum that make up a healthy human community. It was this tremendous spirit of egalitarianism and leveling that endeared the Sufi leaders, the *shuyukh* (literally "wise ones" or "elders"), to both the common people and the elite alike, enabling them to act as catalysts for interaction and the building of social ties in otherwise polarized and factionalized societies. This was in keeping with the tradition of the Prophet Muhammad who, upon his emigration to Medina, built the "model city," in which Jews, Christians, Muslims, Zoroastrians and idol-worshippers were able to live together in a spirit of goodness, tolerance and cooperation – a reality not unlike that of modern, democratic societies.

SUFISM AND RELIGIOUS PLURALITY

Tasawwuf, which is the essence of the true religious tradition of Prophet Muhammad and is distinguished by his high humanistic principles, is open to all religions and races. By nature, Islam is a religion open to peoples of every race. It does not differentiate between one Muslim and another. The Sufis have stretched the bounds of this principle to the point where they do not even see any difference between their religion and other faiths. They opened their doors to accept all other religions without distinction.

The Sufis call to all people, just as God sends His Mercy to all humanity, without distinguishing between those who believe in His Existence and those who do not. The renowned Naqshbandi Sufi saint Bayazid al-Bistami said, "Sufis, in general, seek God's mercy for everyone, not solely for Muslims."

In another of his famous ecstatic utterances, Bayazid, on passing a Jewish cemetery, exclaimed, "They are excused (*mădhurūn*)." What he meant here was, "O God, these people must be destined for Paradise, because they are Your creation and they did not know your last Prophet." As he passed a Muslim cemetery, he observed, "They are proud and arrogant (*maghrūrūn)* in believing they are going to Paradise and everyone else is destined for Hellfire."

Another outstanding Sufi master of the thirteenth century, Jalaluddin Rumi said, "O Muslims, what do I have to say? I do not know myself whether I am a Christian, a Jew, a Zoroastrian or a Muslim. And I do not know myself if I am eastern or western, upper or lower. And I do not know myself if I am from earth or I am from on high. And I do not know myself if I am Indian, Chinese, Bulgarian, Iraqi or Khorasani. I do not know myself if I even have an appearance or not, whether I have existence or not, if have a location or not. I do not know myself if I am a body or a soul. But what I do know is that my soul is the soul of souls. When I put my name with my Lord's, I saw the universe as one. I see One, I sing One, I know One and I read One."[5]

In his poetry, the great Sufi Ibn al-Fārid shows the commonality between all religions based on his experience with Christians, Jews, Brahmins and Muslims. He says, "I see in all of them the divisions of one fountain, and it is the attainment of the eye of sincerity to see them all as equal."

This is how the Sufi Muslims, through their rarefied understanding of the nature of society emerged as the fountainheads of religious and moral character. This was because of their openness to all different experiences in religion and human philosophy, and their harmonizing with all other spiritual influences and backgrounds, coming altogether under the perfect human university, bringing the diverse elements of society together under the commonality of the human experience without regard for the differences of culture and the happenstances of geography.

---

[5] Shams Tabriz, *Diwan,* (translated by R. A. Nicholson), p. 344.

Nicholson observed, "*Taṣawwuf* is a combination and adaptation of different philosophies and beliefs by means of which Islamic spirituality was disseminated."

The great Orientalist scholar Martin Lings said, "I am European and yet I found the safety of my soul in *Taṣawwuf*."

EMPHASIS ON ART

Through the Sufi emphasis on the figurative, art became a metaphor for the Path to the Divine, and in its various forms took on a life of their own, expressing the yearning of the seeker, the satisfaction of the benign self, and the passion of the lovers. Poetry, an art form dear to the early Arab Muslims, grew into a particularly potent vehicle for expressing the Sufi devotions. Sufism's social calling found expression in the sciences, particularly in alchemy, astronomy and in seeking to heal, through medicine, massage and natural healing methods.

As with all things, the openness of the Sufis allowed the variety and diversity of the many cultures it encountered to enter, expand and decorate the expressions of Sufi art and works of social welfare. Similarly, in the field of philosophy and intellect, the teachings of Plato, Aristotle, the Jewish sages, the Zoroastrians and the Buddhists all found a "second home" within the Sufi camp. It was in this spirit of acceptance that an eclectic milieu emerged that allowed individuality to flourish while, at the same time and under the careful guidance and wisdom of the Sufi masters, maintaining society's focus on a common, final goal.

Sufis emphasized poetry, lyrics, music, songs and chanting of many different kinds and in many different dialects. The blending of all these different dialects created even more interrelationships between communities. Thus, it is not uncommon even today to find Javanese Sufis chanting praises of the Prophet in a Yemeni dialect of Arabic, or Sufis in Afghanistan reciting Turkish poetry of love of God.

INNER PEACE, OUTER DIALOGUE

It was the emphasis on the internal struggle to purify the self of one's innermost dark characteristics that made the Sufis the foremost callers to peace. Sufis used diplomacy and wisdom to building bridges between their enemies by means of education and negotiation, rather than resorting to conflict and force of arms.

SUFISM AND THE PERENNIAL CONFLICT OF GOOD AND EVIL[6]

[6] Presented at the International Seminar on Spiritual Psychology, University of Malaya, Kuala Lumpur, Malaysia, August 23, 2007.

ABSTRACT

Evil has been a problem for mankind since the advent of the first humans on earth. Cain killed his own brother, Abel, so that his ritual sacrifice might seem more worthy in the eyes of Allah – proof that the outward forms of religiosity are not sufficient to check the negative traits of the lower self. More is required to purify the self from these evil impulses. Abel had developed this quality, as evidenced by his refusal to harm his brother even when faced with the threat of death. His was the state of purified spiritual character. That character is not developed in a vacuum, but requires a focused discipline to achieve. It is a discipline that was developed and refined by subsequent generations into a systematic path of self-analysiṭs and self-correction that became known as the "Science of the Self," or Sufism.

Sufi discipline has always played an essential role in the life of human beings. It builds upon the teachings of scholars and spiritual scientists imbued with wisdom, sagacity and the courage to stand for what is right. Such teachers were intellectually adept, able to appeal not only to the masses but to academics and people of import.

Psychologically, Sufism works to neutralize the caustic character of negative personality traits, just as a base in a chemical reaction counters the properties of an acid. The wise men and women who have mastered this path are able purify themselves in this life are able to neutralize the axes of evil that so often seek to dominate human discourse.

INTRODUCTION

The struggle between good and evil is a perennial conflict that has been ongoing throughout human history. It has been unfolding from the time of the first man and woman, Adam ﵇ and Eve, as evidenced by the dramatic showdown between their two children, Abel and Cain.[7]

Abel, who represented good, was always in conflict with his brother, Cain, who represented evil. Both sought to worship Allah ﷻ, and both were asked to render a sacrifice. However, under the influence of Satan, Cain chose as his gift the worst, most diseased sheep in his flock. Abel presented his best yearling. Abel's sacrifice was accepted, but Cain's was rejected. Out of overwhelming envy, Cain slew Abel.

Regarding this, Allah ﷻ says:

وَاتْلُ عَلَيْهِمْ نَبَأَ ابْنَيْ آدَمَ بِالْحَقِّ إِذْ قَرَّبَا قُرْبَانًا فَتُقُبِّلَ مِنْ أَحَدِهِمَا وَلَمْ يُتَقَبَّلْ
مِنَ الْآخَرِ قَالَ لَأَقْتُلَنَّكَ قَالَ إِنَّمَا يَتَقَبَّلُ اللَّهُ مِنَ الْمُتَّقِينَ

And convey unto them, setting forth the truth, the story of the two sons of Adam — how each offered a sacrifice, and it was accepted from one of them whereas it was not accepted from the other. [And Cain] said: "I will surely slay you!" [Abel] replied: "Behold, Allah accepts only from those who are conscious of Him. Even if you lay your hand on me to slay me, I shall not lay my hand on you to slay you: behold, I fear Allah, the Sustainer of all the worlds."[i]

Through this one sees Abel's purity of heart and his tolerance for his brother. More importantly, it shows his acceptance. Acceptance is a profound concept, because it goes far beyond

[7] Hābīl and Qābīl.

mere tolerance. When we say we tolerate someone, we mean that we put up with his shortcomings and faults. To accept someone is to acknowledge his right to be himself, withholding both judgment and criticism. It represents a higher state of submission to Divine Will and issues from a place of unconditional love, making it a rare quality indeed.

Allah ﷻ gave every person the right to defend himself from harm, but Abel adhered to an even higher standard. He said, "I am not extending my hand and I am not even defending myself." Here again, we see another example of utter submission to his Lord and acceptance of His Divine Will.

Abel was motivated by the same high level of faith that guided Sayyidina Ibrāhīm ؑ when he was cast into the fire by Nimrod. Jibrīl ؑ came and asked Ibrāhīm ؑ if he needed help. His reply was, "No, for truly Allah ﷻ is seeing me and will give me what I need." He was not mistaken, for Allah ﷻ then said:

قُلْنَا يَا نَارُ كُونِي بَرْدًا وَسَلَامًا عَلَى إِبْرَاهِيمَ

We said, "O Fire! be thou cool on Ibrāhīm"[8]

In this tremendous trial, Sayyidina Ibrāhīm ؑ showed the highest level of submission to Allah ﷻ, for even though he recognized Jibrīl ؑ as Allah's ﷻ messenger to the prophets, he said, "The one sending you knows what I need. I seek whatever He Wills." If Jibrīl ؑ had said, "Allah ﷻ is sending me to ensure that you are safe," then Sayyidina Ibrāhīm ؑ would have accepted. There is tremendous subtlety in this affirmation of *tawḥīd*, for keep in mind, this all occurred in the course of a great physical struggle between good and evil: the conflict between Sayyidina Ibrāhīm ؑ and Nimrod, who was the representative of Satan. Here, too, is another example of that perennial struggle.

---

[8] Sūratu'l-Anbīyā [The Prophets], 21:69.

GOAL OF THE BELIEVER: PERFECTION OF DIVINE SERVICE

Today, many Muslims believe that the purpose of Islam is to take them to Paradise and save them from Hell. In reality, this is only a secondary goal.

وَمَا خَلَقْتُ الْجِنَّ وَالْإِنسَ إِلَّا لِيَعْبُدُونِ

I have only created Jinns and men, that they may worship Me.[9]

Muhammad al-Asad, in his commentary on this verse, states:

Thus, the innermost purpose of the creation of all rational beings is their cognition (*ma'rifah*) of the existence of Allah and, hence, their conscious willingness to conform their own existence to whatever they may perceive of His will and plan: and it is this twofold concept of cognition and willingness that gives the deepest meaning to what the Qur'ān describes as "worship" (*'ibādah*). As the next verse shows, this spiritual call does not arise from any supposed "need" on the part of the Creator, who is self-sufficient and infinite in His power, but is designed as an instrument for the inner development of the worshipper, who, by the act of his conscious self-surrender to the all-pervading Creative Will, may hope to come closer to an understanding of that Will and, thus, closer to Allah Himself.

Sayyidina 'Alī ؓ said:
All goodness is found in four character traits:
aṣ-ṣamt—knowing when to keep silent
an-nuṭaq—awareness of what you speak

---

[9] Sūratu 'dh-Dhāriyāt [The Winnowing Winds], 51:56.

an-naẓr—awareness of what you observe
al-ḥaraka—awareness of where you are moving.
And he said:

> Every speech, if it is not in *dhikrullāh,* is considered *laghaw,* idle talk, of no importance. And every silence not in thinking and meditating on Allah ﷻ is considered heedlessness. And everything observed by the eyes from which one does not take an example is heedlessness. And every movement not in *taʿabudun,* worship, is useless, *faṭara.* May Your Mercy envelop someone who made his speech Your Remembrance (*nuṭuq dhikruk*) and made his silence contemplation and remembrance, and made his vision an example and made his movements worship. By that way the person will be saved from his tongue and his hand. [10]

From these examples, we see that mankind was created to worship Allah ﷻ. The Prophet ﷺ came to teach us how to accomplish that fundamental purpose.

WHAT THE PROPHET BROUGHT

Allah ﷻ sent Islam for all time:

إِنَّ الدِّينَ عِندَ اللّهِ الإِسْلاَمُ وَمَا

The Religion before Allah is Islam.[11]

هُوَ الَّذِي أَرْسَلَ رَسُولَهُ بِالْهُدَى وَدِينِ الْحَقِّ لِيُظْهِرَهُ عَلَى الدِّينِ كُلِّهِ وَلَوْ كَرِهَ
الْمُشْرِكُونَ

---

[10] *Kitāb al-lamaʿ*, pg 182.
[11] Sūrat Āli-ʿImrān [The Family of ʿImrān], 3:19.

It is He Who hath sent His Messenger with guidance and the Religion of Truth, to proclaim it over all religion, even though the Pagans may detest (it).[12]

Islam consists of two aspects: belief and practice. Its purpose is to take each individual Muslim on a personal journey towards Allah ﷻ, while at the same time creating a community in which people live together and work together as servants of Allah ﷻ, striving to establish an ideal society, living under His guidance and seeking ongoing improvement and steadfast observance of Allah's religion.

Living the religion of Islam depends on practices and actions. In the process of that journey, we face ongoing struggles between our instincts, egoistic desires and carnal lusts on the one hand, and the divine principles and good manners that the religion calls us to on the other. This struggle is continuous and like a war, in that victory or defeat are taking place at every moment. Evil may overcome the good for a time, and then good may overcome evil. Ultimately, one side overwhelms the other. The hope is that good will prevail. When the power of good surpasses that of evil, the individual soul begins to ascend through levels of knowledge that enables its possessor to prevent the ego's selfish mastery. This enables the seeker to fully comply with and fulfill Allah's Orders with alacrity. This is experienced on the seeker's journey as manifestations of virtue emerging on the horizon of the self.

The struggle, however, is long. We are torn by truth and falsehood, greed and generosity, happiness and regret – pulled towards Heaven, then goaded towards Hellfire. The only way to avoid that bad ending is to override our selfishness, our egoistic desires and our carnal lusts. Such a victory can only come through faith, *Īmān*. Allah ﷻ sent the Prophet Muhammad ﷺ so that we

[12] Sūratu 't-Tawbah [Repentance], 9:33.

might acquire this important trait, and thus advance on our spiritual journey towards Him.

Allah ﷻ said:

هُوَ الَّذِي بَعَثَ فِي الْأُمِّيِّينَ رَسُولًا مِّنْهُمْ يَتْلُو عَلَيْهِمْ آيَاتِهِ وَيُزَكِّيهِمْ وَيُعَلِّمُهُمُ الْكِتَابَ وَالْحِكْمَةَ وَإِن كَانُوا مِن قَبْلُ لَفِي ضَلَالٍ مُّبِينٍ

It is He Who has sent amongst the Unlettered an apostle from among themselves, to recite unto them His revelations, to purify them, and to instruct them in the Book and Wisdom, although they had been, before, in manifest error. [13]

Here Allah ﷻ makes clear that Sayyidina Muhammad's mission is first to teach revelation, then to purify us, then to teach us the Holy Qur'ān and wisdom. Note that *tazkīyyat an-nafs*, purification of the self, precedes learning the Holy Qur'ān and wisdom.

UMM UL-AHADITH, THE HADITH OF JIBRIL

We cite here the well-known hadith of Jibrīl ﷺ which all scholars recognize as the source of the Sunnah and the source of all hadith (*Umm as-Sunnah wa umm al-aḥādīth*). As one of the most important hadiths in Islam, it needs no additional support:

قَالَ حَدَّثَنِي اَبِي عُمَرُ بْنُ الْخَطَّابِ قَالَ بَيْنَمَا نَحْنُ عِنْدَ رَسُولِ اللَّهِ صلى الله عليه وسلم ذَاتَ يَوْمٍ اِذْ طَلَعَ عَلَيْنَا رَجُلٌ شَدِيدُ بَيَاضِ الثِّيَابِ شَدِيدُ سَوَادِ الشَّعَرِ لاَ يُرَى عَلَيْهِ اَثَرُ السَّفَرِ وَلاَ يَعْرِفُهُ مِنَّا اَحَدٌ حَتَّى جَلَسَ اِلَى النَّبِيِّ صلى الله عليه وسلم فَاَسْنَدَ رُكْبَتَيْهِ اِلَى رُكْبَتَيْهِ وَوَضَعَ كَفَّيْهِ عَلَى فَخِذَيْهِ وَقَالَ يَا مُحَمَّدُ اَخْبِرْنِي عَنِ

[13] Sūratu 'l-Jumu'ah [Congregational Prayer], 62:2.2.

الإِسْلاَمِ . فَقَالَ رَسُولُ اللَّهِ صلى الله عليه وسلم " الإِسْلاَمُ اَنْ تَشْهَدَ اَنْ لاَ اِلَهَ اِلاَّ اللَّهُ
وَاَنَّ مُحَمَّدًا رَسُولُ اللَّهِ وَتُقِيمَ الصَّلاَةَ وَتُؤْتِيَ الزَّكَاةَ وَتَصُومَ رَمَضَانَ وَتَحُجَّ الْبَيْتَ اِنِ
اسْتَطَعْتَ اِلَيْهِ سَبِيلاً . قَالَ صَدَقْتَ . قَالَ فَعَجِبْنَا لَهُ يَسْاَلُهُ وَيُصَدِّقُهُ . قَالَ فَاَخْبِرْنِي
عَنِ الإِيمَانِ . قَالَ " اَنْ تُؤْمِنَ بِاللَّهِ وَمَلاَئِكَتِهِ وَكُتُبِهِ وَرُسُلِهِ وَالْيَوْمِ الآخِرِ وَتُؤْمِنَ بِالْقَدَرِ
خَيْرِهِ وَشَرِّهِ " . قَالَ صَدَقْتَ . قَالَ فَاَخْبِرْنِي عَنِ الإِحْسَانِ . قَالَ " اَنْ تَعْبُدَ اللَّهَ
كَاَنَّكَ تَرَاهُ فَاِنْ لَمْ تَكُنْ تَرَاهُ فَاِنَّهُ يَرَاكَ " . قَالَ فَاَخْبِرْنِي عَنِ السَّاعَةِ . قَالَ " مَا
الْمَسْئُولُ عَنْهَا بِاَعْلَمَ مِنَ السَّائِلِ " . قَالَ فَاَخْبِرْنِي عَنْ اَمَارَتِهَا . قَالَ " اَنْ تَلِدَ الأَمَةُ
رَبَّتَهَا وَاَنْ تَرَى الْحُفَاةَ الْعُرَاةَ الْعَالَةَ رِعَاءَ الشَّاءِ يَتَطَاوَلُونَ فِي الْبُنْيَانِ " . قَالَ ثُمَّ انْطَلَقَ
فَلَبِثْتُ مَلِيًّا ثُمَّ قَالَ لِي " يَا عُمَرُ اَتَدْرِي مَنِ السَّائِلُ " . قُلْتُ اللَّهُ وَرَسُولُهُ اَعْلَمُ . قَالَ
" فَاِنَّهُ جِبْرِيلُ اَتَاكُمْ يُعَلِّمُكُمْ دِينَكُمْ "

From ‘Umar ؓ who said, “While we were one day sitting with the Messenger of Allah ﷺ, there appeared before us a man with a very white garment, and very black hair. No traces of journeying wee visible on him and none of us knew him. He sat down close by the Prophet ﷺ, rested his knees against his and put his palms on his thighs and said, ‘O Muhammad inform me about Islam.’ Said the Messenger ﷺ: ‘Islam is that you should testify that there is no deity save Allah and that Muhammad is His Messenger, that you should say the prayers, pay the *zakāt*, fast during Ramadan and go on Hajj to the House if you can find a way to do so.’ He said, ‘You have spoken truly.’ We were astonished at his first questioning him and telling him that he was right, but he went on to say: ‘Inform me

> about *Īmān.*' Muhammad ﷺ answered: 'It is that you believe in Allah and His angels, and his books and his messengers and in the last Day and that you should believe in the Decreeing of both good and evil.' He said: 'You have spoken truly.' Then he said: 'Inform me about *Iḥsān* [perfection of character].' The Messenger answered: 'It is that you should serve Allah as though you could see Him, for though you cannot see Him, yet He sees you.'
>
> ...
>
> Thereupon the man went off. I waited a while and then the Prophet ﷺ said: 'O 'Umar do you know who that was?' I replied: 'Allah and His Messenger know better.' He said: 'That was Jibrīl. He came to teach you your religion.'"[14]

In this hadith, the archangel Jibrīl ﷺ divided religion into three categories or main branches, from which everything else – all aḥādīth and all Sunnah – flows. He also emphasized the divisions between each branch by asking about each one separately.

The first is Islam, the practical side of the religion that includes worship, deeds and other obligations. It relates to the external aspect of the self, the body and the community. Scholars call this Shariʿah. It is the subject of 'Ilm al-*Fiqh,* the Science of Jurisprudence.

THE SECOND COMPONENT OF *DIN AL-ISLAM* - *IMAN* (BELIEF)

The second category, *Imān,* is the expression of belief through the mind and heart. This means belief in Allah ﷻ, His Messengers, His Books, the Angels, the Last Day, and Destiny. This became known to scholars as *'Ilm at-Tawḥīd,* the Science of Divine Unity, or *'Ilm al-ʿaqā'id,* the Science of Doctrine.

[14] Bukhārī and Muslim.

The meaning of *Imān* is elaborated on elsewhere in the Holy Qur'ān:

قَالَتِ الْأَعْرَابُ آمَنَّا قُل لَّمْ تُؤْمِنُوا وَلَكِن قُولُوا أَسْلَمْنَا وَلَمَّا يَدْخُلِ الْإِيمَانُ فِي قُلُوبِكُمْ وَإِن تُطِيعُوا اللَّهَ وَرَسُولَهُ لَا يَلِتْكُم مِّنْ أَعْمَالِكُمْ شَيْئًا إِنَّ اللَّهَ غَفُورٌ رَّحِيمٌ

The desert Arabs say, "We believe." Say, "Ye have no faith; but ye (only)say, 'We have submitted our wills to Allah,' For not yet has Faith entered your hearts. But if ye obey Allah and His Messenger, He will not belittle aught of your deeds: for Allah is Oft-Forgiving, Most Merciful."[15]

Here, Allah ﷻ informs the desert Arabs that they have yet to attain true belief. Rather, they have achieved the level of Islam. They became Muslims, but faith did not yet enter their hearts. Faith entails belief in the Unseen, *al-Imān bi 'l-ghayb,* and the highest level of faith is to testify to the truth of the Prophet's statements, as Sayyidina Abū Bakr did when the Quraysh confronted him saying, "Your companion claims to have ascended to heaven and returned in one night. What do you say to that?" and he replied, "The Messenger of Allah spoke the truth."

THE THIRD COMPONENT OF *DIN AL-ISLAM - IHSAN* (PERFECTION OF CHARACTER)

The third aspect of religion is known as *Iḥsān,* Perfection of Character. It combines the first category, worship, and the second, belief, to reach the State of Presence. This is why the *maqām al-Iḥsān* is described as worshipping Allah ﷻ "as if you are seeing Him." The qualifier "as if" is necessary, because in reality we

[15] Sūratu 'l-Ḥujurāt [The Private Apartments], 49:14.

cannot see Allah ﷻ. However, we can reach a level where we realize that Allah ﷻ is seeing us. That is a colossal perception, and it is sometimes termed *al-yaqīn,* certainty. One who has reached this state of perception is granted a taste of spiritual pleasure and illuminated with the light of knowledge by Allah ﷻ. The heart of the seeker is filled with His Favors and Grants.

The path to this high station of spiritual awareness has been termed by scholars the Science of Truth, *ʿilm al-Ḥaqīqat*. In the time nearest to the Prophet ﷺ, during the lives of the Sahaba, it was known as aṣ-Ṣiddiqīyya, the path of the veracious. Later, it become known as *ʿilm at-taṣawwuf,* the Science of Sufism.

We see then that Islam prescribes the behavior of a Muslim, *Īmān* relates to his beliefs and defines them, and *Iḥsān* refers to the state of the heart which determines whether his Islam and *Iḥsān* will bear fruit in this life and the next.

THE RELATIONSHIP BETWEEN SHARIʿAH AND *HAQIQAT*

Understanding the distinctions that separate these three components of religion, we can then turn to the relationship between *Fiqh,* the science of jurisprudence, and *Taṣawwuf,* the science of *Iḥsān*. To understand this relationship, it is useful to consider the example of prayer.

The science of *fiqh* teaches us that we must perform our prayer in full accordance with the rules of the Shariʿah, including all of the prescribed actions, invocations and intentions. This is known as *jassad aṣ-ṣalāt,* the body of the prayer. Included in these is the requirement to keep the heart in Allah's Divine Presence and to know that Allah is observing you during the entire prayer. The external form of the *ṣalāt* is its body, and the humility and self-effacement, *khushuʿ,* is its soul, or *rūḥ*. This is the essence of the prayer, but we know from our own experience that people sometimes perform the outward actions of *ṣalāt* without this inner awareness in their hearts. The one who performs the outward actions of *ṣalāt* without maintaining this awareness of the Divine Presence is like a zombie.

As the soul needs the body in which to live, so too does the body need the soul to give it life. The proper relationship between Shariʿah and *Ḥaqīqat* is like the relationship between body and soul. The perfect believer who has reached the state of *Iḥsān* is the one who can conjoin Shariʿah and *Ḥaqīqat*.

That is why *Imān* came directly after the five pillars of Islam in *Umm al-ḥadīth* which defined *al-aqāʿid* — the doctrine of Islam. If *Imān* is strong, then one can ascend to the third level, which is moral excellence — the state of *Iḥsān*. *Imān* is the mindset of belief, *ʿitiqād fikrī*. *Imān* is a theoretical belief that requires strong character to accept. *Imān* needs a booster. That booster is the spiritual dimension of the self.

Returning to the story of Cain and Abel, we see now that Cain was arrogant and his faith was weak. These diseases of the heart led him to kill his brother and lie to his Lord. He fulfilled Allah's Order to make a sacrifice, but his intention was impure. His story is important, for it shows us that one can perform the outward acts required by the religion and still fail to fulfill the attending obligations because those actions lack sincerity and are, therefore, not accepted.

Consider the case of one who performs his obligatory prayers, but while doing so conspires in his mind against his brother or sister. Will his prayer be accepted? A Muslim who prays and fasts but does not have a purified soul and does not have a *qalbun dhākiran,* a heart that remembers Allah ﷻ, but instead gives himself over to all kinds of pleasures and desires - one who never knew humbleness, or sincerity, or struggles in the Way of Allah – his heart is dead, although he performs his prayers. He is a Muslim in appearance, but not in reality. What is the benefit of a dry prayer that has no soul in it and no life? In such a person Islam becomes weak and faith becomes weak because there is no warmth, no *shawk*, no love, no yearning, no emotion, no fear, no compassion. That one is no different from someone who is not a Muslim.

وعن أبي هريرة قال قال رسول الله صلى الله عليه وسلم (آية المنافق ثلاث . إذا حدث كذب وإذا وعد أخلف وإذا اؤتمن خان وإن صام وصلى وزعم أنه مسلم .

(مسلم)

Abū Hurayrah ؓ narrated that the Prophet ﷺ said, "A hypocrite has three distinguishing signs; first when he talks he lies; when he makes a promise he breaks it; and when something is entrusted to him he misappropriates it. And [this is the case] even if he prays and fasts and considers himself a Muslim."¹⁶

How many Muslims today observe all five pillars, yet when they speak they lie; when they make business deals they cheat and when they enter politics they are deceitful. Such people make promises they do not keep, and they feel no remorse in eating the money of other Muslims. Such a person, even if he offers the prayers and keeps the fast, and considers himself a pious mosque-attendee, is still a hypocrite.

Abū 'l-ʿAbbās Sahl ibn Saʿad as-Saʿadī ؓ relates that a person passed by the Holy Prophet ﷺ and the Prophet ﷺ asked one of the Companions that was sitting with him: "what do you think of this man, who has just passed this way?" The companion replied, "He is one of the gentlest and by Allah if he proposes marriage with any woman, his proposal should be accepted, and if he should recommend, his recommendations should prove effective."¹⁷ And the

---

¹⁶ Bukhārī and Muslim.
¹⁷ The wording of the Ḥadīth states, *in shafaʿa yushafaʿ*. This is often mistranslated as "if he should recommend someone, his recommendation would be accepted."

Holy Prophet ﷺ kept quiet. Then another man passed by and the Prophet ﷺ asked, "What is your opinion of this man." The companion replied, "He belongs to the class of poor Muslims. If he goes for marriage his proposal will be turned down; if he were to intercede on behalf of any person, his intercession would be rejected; and if he were to speak nobody would listen to him." The Holy Prophet ﷺ said, "If everyone in the world were like the first man, this man would be better than them all."

The first person described is someone highly respected in the community. The second person described is an indigent of no apparent consequence. But the first is proud and arrogant, and full of all sorts of bad manners, while the second is humble and sincere. Although both pray, fast, give charity and do hajj, their actions will be weighed in accordance with what is in their hearts. Again, we find the same dichotomy that separated Cain and Abel.

These aḥādīth of the Prophet ﷺ, narrated by authentic sources, demonstrate that Islam requires more than just outward adherence to its five pillars. It also requires us to overcome the diseases of the ego and approach those acts of worship with sincerity and purity of heart. If we do not, all that we have done in the way of worship may come to naught and we may face disaster of Judgment Day, for Allah ﷻ said:

وَقَدِمْنَا إِلَى مَا عَمِلُوا مِنْ عَمَلٍ فَجَعَلْنَاهُ هَبَاءً مَّنثُورًا

And We shall turn to whatever deeds they did (in this life), and We shall make such deeds as floating dust scattered about. [18]

However, the correct translation is "if he should intercede, his intercession would be accepted." This description indicates that person is from the highest elite of society.

[18] Sūratu 'l-Furqān, [The Criterion], 25:22-23.

SPIRITUALITY – POWER OF THE BELIEVER

Spirituality is the most powerful weapon we can call upon in this struggle between acceptance and non-acceptance, belief or unbelief. When someone's faith becomes weak, it can ultimately reach the point of questioning the very Existence of Allah ﷻ. On the other hand, when *Īmān* increases by means of spiritual support, then the commanding self, *an-nafs al-ammāra,* becomes weaker and one begins to see increased success in the struggle against doubt.

However, spirituality, too, must be developed. While many people today like to speak about spirituality in the abstract, few discuss the practical tools of spiritual development. These include:

1) The Sunnah of the Prophet ﷺ—*as-Sunnat an-nabawīyya.*

2) Knowledge of the Qur'ān—*at-tarbīyya al-qurānīyya.*

These are the two doors to spiritual development. They are the instruments of spiritual advancement and the vehicles that lead to the purification of the self, which is the fundamental requirement for achieving the full realization of the positive potential with which Allah ﷻ has endowed human beings from birth. For, according to the Hadith:

حديث أبي هريرة رضي الله عنه أن النبي صلى الله عليه وسلم قال: "ما من مولود إلا يولد على الفطرة فأبواه يهودانه أو ينصرانه أو يمجسانه كما تنتج البهيمة بهيمة جمعاء هل تحسون فيها من جدعاء"

Abū Hurayrah reported that the Prophet of Allah ﷺ said, "Every child is born upon the natural disposition [of Islam], then it is his parents who make him Jewish, or Christian, or Magian (Zoroastrian), just as an animal delivers a perfect baby animal; do you find it maimed?"[19]

[19] Bukhārī and Muslim.

Allah ﷻ speaks of the need for self-purification in the Holy Qur'ān:

قَدْ أَفْلَحَ مَن زَكَّاهَا وَقَدْ خَابَ مَن دَسَّاهَا

Verily, the one who purified it [the self] succeeded and the one who fails corrupts it.[20]

How, then, can we learn to use these two tools? First, we need someone who can analyze these sources and deduce the principles and hidden knowledge within each to extract the methodology of self-purification. One cannot ask kindergarten students to deduce these principles and methods from the Holy Qur'ān and Hadith. This requires scholars well-versed in these areas of knowledge in order to produce an edible fruit.

Even the most learned scholars of external knowledge may not be able to plumb these depths of this subtle science. Consider the case of Imām al-Ghazālī. Although he was one of the greatest scholars in Shariʿah, he was unable to save himself from the sicknesses of his ego until he followed the way of the seekers, gnostics and ascetics whose whole lives were focused on training people to overcome such maladies of the self and raise their level of spirituality. Once Imām al-Ghazālī became a student in that school, he began to accumulate extraordinary powers, and spiritual energy until his soul was purified and Divine Light poured into his heart. Since his faith had been built up and established on a firm footing, he was able to leave all that is forbidden, ḥarām. Prior to that, despite his erudition and learning, he had always been questioning himself and questioning whatever was around him. He understood the external realities of Islam, but he needed to build up his faith.

---

[20] Sūratu 'sh-Shams [The Sun], 91:9,10.

He was able to do so by following Qur'ānic prescriptions regarding the heart and its importance, through remembrance of Allah, *dhikrullāh*, and the purification of the self, *Tazkīyyat an-nafs*. These practices and disciplines allowed him to reach a level of firmness in faith that could not be undermined by doubt; rather, the station of *Iḥsān* was pulling him up. When Allah ﷻ sees that the seeker has achieved that state where he no longer allows the lower self to pull him down, that seeker is no longer alone: the Lord is with him, observing all that he does. When that belief becomes rooted in the heart, the seeker can no longer fall into major sins.

THE SCHOOL OF *TAZKIYYA*: THE QUR'ANIC SCIENCE OF TREATING THE SELF

The practices that enabled Imām al-Ghazālī to reach this sublime state that is the goal of all seekers can be traced back to the Prophet ﷺ. They are derived from the Holy Qur'ān, as well as from his own practices and those teachings which he shared with his Companions as recorded in the Sunnah.

That school of which the Sahaba partook did not die with the passing of the Prophet ﷺ. Each of the Companions became a school from which the Ummah derived its learning of these methods and knowledge of *Tazkīyyat an-nafs*, or self-purification. With the passing of time, these schools developed and formalized their methods and created a distinct science termed the Science of *Taṣawwuf*. Just as the schools of Shariʿah was formalized in the first three centuries of Islam, so too did distinct schools of *Taṣawwuf* form to pass on this knowledge to succeeding generations of Muslims. And just as the Shariʿah did not develop outside the framework of Islam, the Qur'ān and the Sunnah, even though it branches and knowledge encompassed many areas not mentioned specifically in these sources, so too did *Taṣawwuf* develop based on the framework established by the Qur'ān and the Sunnah.

The traditional scholars of Islam understood these realities and attained these states themselves, and they began to set forth the principles, methodologies and disciplines that would allow others to follow in their footsteps so that this science would be preserved for future generations. They did this, because they heeded the warning of the Prophet ﷺ, who said:

ان رسول الله صلى الله عليه وسلم قال "ان خيركم قرني. ثم الذين يلونهم. ثم الذين يلونهم. ثم الذين يلونهم" .

The Prophet ﷺ said, "the best of you is my time then the one that follows it then the one that follows it."[21]

As Islamic civilization and culture devolved, these scholars began to see the rapid reappearance of spiritual maladies, such as love of the self, hypocrisy, showing off, lying, backbiting, hatred, envy, jealousy and countless others. They said began codifying the curricula of the science of self-purification as a means of countering this epidemic. Clearly, then, this science and the disciplines it prescribes are not something innovated, but something that has always been part of Islam and Islamic practice. Moreover, they are the only cure for the disease that has always threatened the heart of humanity since Cain first raised his hand against his brother.

A clear example of the way in which these great scholars responded to the degradation of Muslim morals and manners is that of Imām Shāfiʿī. After establishing his school of thought in Baghdad, he traveled to Cairo where he saw that the people were more corrupt and therefore modified his rulings in order to treat the illnesses he witnessed there. The medications of the heart

---

[21] Muslim.

change over time. Just as modern medical science is constantly creating new treatments for disease, so have the prescriptions of this science evolved over time. In each era, the scholars of *Tazkīyyat an-nafs* have established different treatments in order to accommodate the prevailing social, political and historical situations.

This is one example from a vast multitude of scholars, beginning immediately after the era of the Prophet ﷺ until today, who sought to establish methods for extricating human beings caught between good and evil. These luminaries established a spiritual curriculum, *ʿal-manhaj ar-rūḥīʿ*, and followed it rigorously. They transformed their faith from something theoretical and abstract into something real and practicable, *maqām al-Īmān*. In doing so, they made it part of their lives. They believed in Allah ﷻ with genuine conviction, and that conviction was constant and unshakeable. They showed Muslims by their example the importance of self-purification and demonstrated the need for such a disciplined methodology.

Their curricula formed the basis for *tarbīyyat ar-rūḥīyya,* or spiritual training. They developed a school with its own course of study, its own programs, its own methodologies and its own proofs within the context of the Qur'ān and Sunnah.

All scholars of this science know that the Qur'ān is the seal of all religious books and the last book sent by Allah ﷻ to humanity. As such, they take it as the primary medical text for treating the ailments of the self.

In the Holy Qur'ān, Allah ﷻ has emphasized the heart, the states of the heart, the situation of the heart, and the struggle against the ego and its desires. From this, these scholars learned the science of treating the heart and its maladies. They learned this science by studying the many verses in the Holy Qur'ān that discuss the purification of the self, that analyze the ego and its desires, that talk about love and fear. They also studied the many verses that describe the heart and the soul, that define love, humbleness and repentance. Their understandings were expanded by their study of those verses which focus on piety, certainty, familiarity, nearness and happiness, as well as those that discuss hypocrisy, liars, heretics and conspiracies and provide clear instruction on the avoidance of these. They also found verses on how to remember Allah ﷻ in a hidden way or in a hidden place, verses on the benefits of waking up at night to perform *qīyām al-layl* and the *tahajjud* prayer. They found many verses describing the state of *Iḥsān* and detailing the steps necessary to reach it.

These scholars found further examples in the Sunnah of the Prophet ﷺ. They studied how he taught his Companions to rid themselves of these same diseases, as exemplified by his famous statement:

قدمتم خير مقدم وقدمتم من الجهاد الأصغر الى الجهاد الأكبر مجاهدة العبد هواه.

On the authority of Jābir:

The Prophet came back from one of his campaigns saying: "You have come forth in the best way of coming forth: you have come from the smaller jihād to the greater jihād." They said: "And what is the greater jihād?" He replied: "The striving (*mujāhadat*) of Allah's servants against their idle desires."[22]

The scholar Ibn Qayyim defined 14 forms of jihād. Only one of these involves war or combat; the other 13 represent various manifestations of struggle of a person with himself, society, education and development. To struggle against the self – to control and command it – is essential to harvesting the fruits of spirituality. It is required of one who would purify himself and

[22] Al-Khaṭṭābī in his *Ṭārīkh*, Īmām Ghazālī in his *Iḥyā'* and al-'Irāqī said that Bayhaqī related it on the authority of Jābir.

become truly conscious of Allah ﷻ and fearful of His Displeasure. To do this, the seeker wages jihād against his bad desires and makes Allah ﷻ, His Prophet ﷺ and the excellent morals and manners they enjoined his goal.

THE IMPORTANCE OF REMEMBRANCE

The means that such "fighters in the Way of Allah" use to accomplish this purification is *dhikrullāh,* the Remembrance of Allah, for Allah ﷻ said:

وَاذْكُر رَّبَّكَ فِي نَفْسِكَ تَضَرُّعاً وَخِيفَةً وَدُونَ الْجَهْرِ مِنَ الْقَوْلِ بِالْغُدُوِّ وَالآصَالِ وَلاَ تَكُن مِّنَ الْغَافِلِينَ

"And do (O Muhammad) remember your Lord within yourself humbly and with awe, in a hidden manner, at morn and evening. And be not of the neglectful."[23].

To "remember your Lord in a hidden manner" indicates an inner recitation and remembrance. That is why the Holy Qur'ān is filled with verses regarding *dhikrullāh.*

The Holy Qur'ān and the Sunnah of the Prophet ﷺ represent the constitution of the Muslims. Every aspect of our existence is covered therein: morality, jurisprudence, politics, economics, social behavior and of course religion. They also cover the most important subject of all, which is the knowledge of self-purification.

While this science is essential to practicing the essence of the religion, it is far more subtle than the outward forms and is thus often ignored or overlooked. Today, we see many people studying questions of Islam and economics, we see Muslims debating *Fiqh* and reciting poetry, but almost no one is interested in learning

[23] Sūratu 'l-ʿArāf [The Heights], 7:205.

how to purify the self. Yet, *Tazkīyyat an-nafs* is what the Prophet ﷺ spent his life engaged in. And when asked by his wife 'Ā'isha ؓ, why he was so preoccupied in devotions, to the point his legs were swollen, his answer was, "And should I not be a thankful servant?"

This, then, is the science of *taṣawwuf*, from which the term "Sufism" is derived.

CRITICISMS OF SUFISM

Today, the word "Sufism" is problematic for some people because of some so-called Sufis who delved deeply into philosophy and theology and came up with things which were not accepted or not understood. This debate is beyond the scope of our discussion. Suffice it to say that Allah ﷻ mentioned *'ilm Tazkīyyat an-nafs* in the Holy Qur'ān, and whatever Allah ﷻ said must be obeyed. The Sufi scholars, including Imām al-Ghazālī and many other luminaries such as Junayd al-Baghdādī, Sulaymān ad-Dārānī, Sirr as-Saqatī, 'Abd al-Qādir Jīlānī and countless others, all imposed the condition on their students that they follow Allah's Holy Book and the Prophetic Sunnah. It is worth noting that even Ibn Taymīyya, one of the strictest scholars, accepted authentic *taṣawwuf* and even went so far as to define the three different levels of *taṣawwuf* in his renowned *Fatawā*.

Another criticism leveled at the Sufis is that they renounce the world. Often those who look at Sufism from outside imagine the Sufis to be philosophers and theologians who have turned their backs on everything to sit in their own retreats. However, the science of *taṣawwuf* in the main, while calling for asceticism, does not call for permanent withdrawal from the world. Rather, it uses the methodology of seclusion for periods of time, to help the seeker purge love of *dunyā* — his love of wealth, fame and status — from his heart. Such asceticism of the heart enables a sincere Muslim to override *dunyā* and put it under his control, moving in whatever way he likes for sake of Allah ﷻ. Such a person, if he is of good means, may use whatever he has of *dunyā* wealth in the way of Allah ﷻ, rather than using it purely for self-gratification. Such a person will spend freely in the Way of Allah ﷻ, for it has no meaning to him: "He owns the *dunyā* while the *dunyā* does not own him."

THE DIFFERENT SCHOOLS OF SPIRITUALITY

The Prophet ﷺ said:

اختلاف أمتي رحمة للناس

The differences between my nation is a mercy.[24]

We see this, too, in the schools of spirituality. The methods may change from one teacher to another, but the goal remains the same. That goal is self-purification and spiritual advancement.

Allah ﷻ said in the Holy Qur'ān:

وَالَّذِينَ جَاهَدُوا فِينَا لَنَهْدِيَنَّهُمْ سُبُلَنَا وَإِنَّ اللَّهَ لَمَعَ الْمُحْسِنِينَ

But as for those who strive hard in Our cause -We shall most certainly guide them onto ways that lead unto Us: for, behold, Allah is indeed with the doers of good.[25]

This verse mentions not one, but multiple ways for the seeker to reach his Lord. Due to this multiplicity of paths, this science developed countless methodologies, each one different than the other, and yet all constrained by Allah's Divine Law, Shariʿah. However, all these branches stem from a common trunk, a single foundation, and that is *dhikrullāh*. The goal of each is Allah ﷻ — to

---

[24] Al-Ḥāfiẓ al-ʿIrāqī, al-Ḥāfiẓ as-Sakhāwī *Maqāsid al-ḥasana* p. 49 #39 from Ibn al-Ḥājib in the *Mukhtaṣar*, al-Khaṭṭābī mentions it in the context of a digression in *Gharīb al-ḥadīth*.

[25] Sūratu 'l-ʿAnkabūt [The Spider], 29:69.

declare His Oneness and His Uniqueness and to make His remembrance.

Collectively, these paths became a means for transporting Muslims on their spiritual journey, raising believers higher and higher until they reached the state of *Iḥsān*. It is a science firmly grounded in the Hadith and the Holy Qur'ān, the science of self-purification or *ʿilm Tazkīyyat an-nafs*.

THE STRUGGLE AGAINST THE SELF

The fruit of *Tazkīyyat an-nafs* is to reach the station of perfect character, *Iḥsān*, as the Prophet ﷺ mentioned when asked by Sayyidina Jibrīl ﵇.

As we have already explained, *Iḥsān* is the highest level of *Īmān* that the seeker can develop through his quest for reality. This is what we call *al-yaqīn al-ḥaqīqī;* the reality of certainty and knowing that brings true understanding and leads to *al-Īmān ash-shuhūdī*, the true faith of witnessing the signs of Allah's Oneness everywhere. The only higher level of realization is *maqām al-Iḥsān*. At this station of perfection, the seeker realizes that Allah ﷻ is observing him in every moment. Through this realization, he is able to perfect his behavior. Then the seeker attains the genuine realization that he is observing Allah ﷻ. That is why meditation becomes a necessity, for it is through this practice that the seeker is able to reach this high level.

That is why Allah ﷻ specifically mentioned meditation, or *taffakur*, in the Holy Qur'ān:

الَّذِينَ يَذْكُرُونَ اللّهَ قِيَامًا وَقُعُودًا وَعَلَىَ جُنُوبِهِمْ وَيَتَفَكَّرُونَ فِي خَلْقِ

السَّمَاوَاتِ وَالأَرْضِ رَبَّنَا مَا خَلَقْتَ هَذا بَاطِلاً سُبْحَانَكَ فَقِنَا عَذَابَ النَّارِ

Men who celebrate the praises of Allah, standing, sitting, and lying down on their sides, and contemplate the (wonders of) creation in the heavens and the earth, (With the thought): "Our Lord! not for nothing Have You created (all) this! Glory to You! Give us salvation from the penalty of the Fire."[26]

This verse speaks of those who are focusing on their Lord intently. At the same time, Allah ﷻ is looking at them and with His Gaze, He is propelling them upward. It is of this level of spiritual attainment that the Qur'ān speaks when it says:

وَسَخَّرَ لَكُم مَّا فِي السَّمَاوَاتِ وَمَا فِي الْأَرْضِ جَمِيعًا مِّنْهُ إِنَّ فِي ذَٰلِكَ لَآيَاتٍ لِّقَوْمٍ يَتَفَكَّرُونَ

Whatever is in the heavens and in the earth will be made subject to you.[27]

Here, "heavens" refers to the realm of the spirit, while "earth" refers to the realm of the body. That power enables the seeker to leave all that Allah ﷻ has forbidden us on the physical plane and to practice all that we have been ordered in the way of physical, earthly obligations. It enables the seeker to perfect his spiritual manners. All this is achieved within the framework of *Shariʿatullāh.* In this way, the spirit is connected to the real meaning of the verses of the Holy Qur'ān and the Sunnah of the Prophet ﷺ.

Consider the example of Ḥāritha, when he was asked by the Prophet ﷺ in what state he awoke:

عن انس ان النبي صلى الله عليه وسلم قال لحارثة بن النعمان: كيف اصبحت؟ قال:

اصبحت مؤمنا حقا، قال: ان لكل حق حقيقة فما حقيقة ايمانك؟ فقال: يا نبي الله!

[26] Sūrat Āli-ʿImrān [The Family of ʿImrān], 3:191.
[27] Sūratu 'l-Jāthīya [The Crouching], 45:13.

عزفت نفسي عن الدنيا فاسهرت ليلي واظمات نهاري وكاني انظر الى اهل الجنة كيف يتزاورون فيها والى اهل النار كيف يتعاوون فيها؛ فقال: ابصرت فالزم، ثم قال: عبد نور الله الايمان في قلبه،

Anas ibn Mālik reported that the Prophet ﷺ asked Ḥāritha ibn an-Nuʿmān ؓ, "How did you find yourself this morning?" And he replied, "I found myself this morning a believer in Allah in truth." The Prophet ﷺ said, "Every statement has its verification. So, what is the verification of your faith?" Ḥāritha replied, "My soul has become averse to the *dunyā* and fled from it. So, I have made my night sleepless [i.e. through *tahajjud* and night-time *ʿibādah*] and made my day full of thirst [i.e. through constant fasting] and it is now as if I am right in front of the Throne (*ʿArsh*) of my Lord. And it is as if I am gazing upon the people of Paradise visiting each other [in joy] and as if I am gazing upon the people of the Fire trying to help each other in the Fire." The Prophet ﷺ replied, "You have gained true vision; so hold fast to it (*abṣarta, f 'alzam*)." [Speaking to Anas, he then said:] "[He is] a servant whose heart Allah has enlightened with faith."[28]

When Ḥāritha said, "I made my night sleepless and my days thirsty" it means he opposed his ego by waking up at night for prayer and working very hard during day while fasting.

When Ḥāritha said, "I woke up as if I am looking at the Throne," note that he did not relate it as if he saw it in a dream. He said, "as if I am looking up high at the Throne of Allah and as

[28] Al-ʿAskarī in his *Amthāl*, and y aṭ-Ṭabarānī in his *Kabīr*, an-Najjār and al-Bazzār with variant wordings: *ʿArāfta fa 'lzam*—"You realized so continue on what you are doing," *Kanzu 'l-ʿummāl*. #36990.

if I am looking at the people of Paradise," and "as if I am looking a the people of the Fire ..." For Ḥāritha had reached the highest level of *Īmān ash-shuhūdī*, and the Prophet ﷺ asked for proof of his claim, "for every saying there is a proof." Ḥāritha's proof was to perceive with his eyes the realities of the afterlife. Out of good manners, he said, "as if" in order not to show off his state before the master of masters, Sayyidina Muhammad ﷺ, though he had in fact achieved *yaqīn*, full certainty, of what he had witnessed.

The Heart as Key to Spiritual Improvement

The Holy Qur'ān contains at least 130 verses that mention the heart (either as *qalb* and *fūād*). Let us look within the Holy Qur'ān to see what Allah ﷻ has mentioned to us on the importance of this organ:

أَلَمْ يَأْنِ لِلَّذِينَ آمَنُوا أَن تَخْشَعَ قُلُوبُهُمْ لِذِكْرِ اللَّهِ وَمَا نَزَلَ مِنَ الْحَقِّ وَلَا يَكُونُوا كَالَّذِينَ أُوتُوا الْكِتَابَ مِن قَبْلُ فَطَالَ عَلَيْهِمُ الْأَمَدُ فَقَسَتْ قُلُوبُهُمْ وَكَثِيرٌ مِّنْهُمْ فَاسِقُونَ

Is not the time ripe for the hearts of those who believe to submit to Allah's reminder and to the truth which is revealed, that they become not as those who received the Scripture of old but the term was prolonged for them and so their hearts were hardened, and many of them are evil-livers. [29]

وَلَيْسَ عَلَيْكُمْ جُنَاحٌ فِيمَا أَخْطَأْتُم بِهِ وَلَكِن مَّا تَعَمَّدَتْ قُلُوبُكُمْ وَكَانَ اللَّهُ غَفُورًا رَّحِيمًا

[29] Sūratu 'l-Ḥadīd [Iron], 57:16.

And there is no sin for you in the mistakes that ye make unintentionally, but what your hearts purpose (that will be a sin for you). Allah is Forgiving, Merciful.[30]

لاَّ يُؤَاخِذُكُمُ اللّهُ بِاللَّغْوِ فِيَ أَيْمَانِكُمْ وَلَكِن يُؤَاخِذُكُم بِمَا كَسَبَتْ قُلُوبُكُمْ وَاللّهُ غَفُورٌ حَلِيمٌ

Allah will not call you to account for thoughtlessness in your oaths [laghaw fee aymanikkum] , but for the intention in your hearts; and He is Oft-forgiving, Most Forbearing.[31]

All of the verses that mention the heart contain clues to understanding and treating its diseases, and these are elaborated upon by the teachings of the Prophet ﷺ:

الا وان في الجسد مضغة اذا صلحت صلح الجسد كله، واذا فسدت فسد الجسد كله، الا وهي القلب.

The Prophet ﷺ said, "In the body there is a small piece of flesh; if that piece of flesh is rectified then the whole body will be rectified and if it becomes corrupt then the whole body will become corrupt, and truly that is the heart."[32]

The Prophet ﷺ emphasized the importance of the heart in this, and many other hadiths. The Holy Qur'ān's mention of the heart

---

[30] Sūratu 'l-Aḥzāb [The Confederates], 33:5.

[31] Sūratu 'l-Baqarah [The Heifer], 2:225. *Laghaw* is to swear to something loosely, such as, "I swear I did not do that." It is not a genuine oath, but rather a habit of the tongue to use Allah's Name in affirmation or negation. The Prophet ﷺ excused the Ṣaḥāba for such things. Allah ﷻ will not accept such oaths if one swears in His Name by tongue, but rejects it in one's heart. Rather, this incurs His punishment.

[32] Bukhārī and Muslim.

and its condition is so emphatic and frequent that it ties everything human beings do to the condition and state of the heart.

The heart which is enlightened is the one that will move the mind and the senses towards what is virtuous and away from all that is corrupt. Unfortunately, that is not the condition of most hearts.

THE DISEASES OF THE HEART

The Qur'ān describes the diseased heart as *marīd al-qalb,* signifying hypocrisy, doubt, suspicion, deviance, heedlessness and oppression. We shall deal with each of these conditions separately.

THE HYPOCRITICAL HEART

The most dangerous illness of the heart is hypocrisy. That is why Allah ﷻ described the munāfiqūn, hypocrites, as those who:

يَقُولُونَ بِأَلْسِنَتِهِم مَّا لَيْسَ فِي قُلُوبِهِمْ

(They) say with their tongues what is not in their hearts.[33]

This means that they conspire in their hearts, while outwardly appearing good. Such was the behavior of the hypocrites of al-Madīna with the Prophet ﷺ and his Companions. Such people are extremely dangerous, which is why Allah ﷻ warned about them many times in the Qur'ān. They were those who demonstrated their obedience to the Prophet ﷺ with one hand while stabbing him in the back with the other.

However, this disease was not limited to that time and place. There are many Muslims who stab their brothers and sisters in the back while appearing friendly to their faces. Moreover, hypocrisy

[33] Sūratu 'l-Fatḥ [Victory], 48:11.

leads to other serious illnesses, such lying, killing, harming, and cheating. Allah ﷻ said to those who have this illness:

أَفَلَا يَتَدَبَّرُونَ الْقُرْآنَ أَمْ عَلَى قُلُوبٍ أَقْفَالُهَا

Will they then not meditate on the Qur'ān, or are there locks on the hearts?[34]

The key to that lock is found in the Holy Qur'ān. However, when the heart is drowned in the ocean of sin, that key to salvation is lost. The lock of hypocrisy bars the way to the path of guidance. This is a dangerous state from which the sinner may never return to the path of truth, for the Qur'ān says:

كَذَلِكَ يَطْبَعُ اللَّهُ عَلَى قُلُوبِ الَّذِينَ لَا يَعْلَمُونَ

Thus does Allah seal the hearts of those who know not.[35]

The meaning of this verse is that Allah ﷻ will leave those who make no effort to return to right guidance to their own devices. It is for this reason that He also said:

إِنَّكَ لَا تَهْدِي مَنْ أَحْبَبْتَ وَلَكِنَّ اللَّهَ يَهْدِي مَن يَشَاءُ وَهُوَ أَعْلَمُ بِالْمُهْتَدِينَ

It is true you (O Muhammad) will not be able to guide every one whom you love; but Allah guides those whom He will and He knows best those who receive guidance.[36]

---

[34] Sūrah Muḥammad, 47:24.

[35] Sūrah Rūm [Rome], 30:59.

[36] Sūratu 'l-Qaṣaṣ [The Stories], 28:56.

THE DOUBTING HEART

Allah ﷻ said:

إِنَّمَا يَسْتَأْذِنُكَ الَّذِينَ لاَ يُؤْمِنُونَ بِاللّهِ وَالْيَوْمِ الآخِرِ وَارْتَابَتْ قُلُوبُهُمْ فَهُمْ فِي رَيْبِهِمْ يَتَرَدَّدُونَ

Only those will request exemption from you (O Muhammad) those who do not believe in Allah and the Last Day, and whose hearts are in doubt, so that they are tossed in their doubts to and fro.[37]

Those described here have an illness which causes doubts to emerge in their hearts and when they try to strive sincerely in Allah's Way they cannot because of the faltering of their hearts. That is the first disease of the heart: doubts which cause hesitation.

THE SUSPICIOUS HEART

Suspicion about the intents and motives of others is a lesser disease that causes the sufferer to imagine that other people are out to get them.

About this, Allah ﷻ said:

يَا أَيُّهَا الَّذِينَ آمَنُوا اجْتَنِبُوا كَثِيرًا مِّنَ الظَّنِّ إِنَّ بَعْضَ الظَّنِّ إِثْمٌ

O ye who believe! Avoid suspicion as much (as possible): for suspicion in some cases is a sin.[38]

This means avoid harboring bad thoughts about others, for most of such suspicion is fallacious and will lead to error.

---

[37] Sūratu 't-Tawbah [Repentance], 9:45.

[38] Sūratu 'l-Ḥujurāt [The Private Apartments], 49:12.

THE DEVIATED HEART

Those whose hearts are deviated become rude and constricted. Of them, Allah ﷻ said:

فَأَمَّا الَّذِينَ فِي قُلُوبِهِمْ زَيْغٌ فَيَتَّبِعُونَ مَا تَشَابَهَ مِنْهُ ابْتِغَاء الْفِتْنَةِ وَابْتِغَاء تَأْوِيلِهِ

But those in whose hearts is perversity follow the part thereof that is allegorical, seeking discord, and searching for its hidden meanings, but no one knows its hidden meanings except Allah.[39]

THE HEEDLESS HEART

The heedless heart is one which is asleep and unable to see. This is one of greatest problems Muslims face. There can be no true belief without the ability perceive reality and truth.

About those afflicted with this ailment, Allah ﷻ said:

وَلَا تَعْدُ عَيْنَاكَ عَنْهُمْ تُرِيدُ زِينَةَ الْحَيَاةِ الدُّنْيَا وَلَا تُطِعْ مَنْ أَغْفَلْنَا قَلْبَهُ عَن ذِكْرِنَا وَاتَّبَعَ هَوَاهُ وَكَانَ أَمْرُهُ فُرُطًا

Nor obey any whose heart We have permitted to neglect the remembrance of Us, one who follows his own desires, whose case has gone beyond all bounds.[40]

Such a heart is directed by *lahwa al-qalb*, bad desires, an illness from which most Muslims suffer.

As Allah ﷻ said:

لَاهِيَةً قُلُوبُهُمْ وَأَسَرُّوا النَّجْوَى

---

[39] Sūrat Āli-ʿImrān [The Family of ʿImrān], 3:7.

[40] Sūratu ʾl-Kahf [The Cave], 18:28.

Their hearts set on passing delights; yet they who are [thus] bent on wrongdoing conceal their innermost thoughts.[41]

THE OPPRESSIVE HEART

وعنه أن رسول الله صلى الله عليه وسلم قال أتدرون ما المفلس؟ قالوا المفلس فينا من لا درهم له ولا متاع . فقال إن المفلس من أمتي من يأتي يوم القيامة بصلاة وصيام وزكاة ويأتي وقد شتم هذا وقذف هذا . وأكل مال هذا . وسفك دم هذا وضرب هذا فيعطى هذا من حسناته وهذا من حسناته فإن فنيت حسناته قبل أن يقضى ما عليه أخذ من خطاياهم فطرحت عليه ثم طرح في النار . رواه مسلم

Sayyidina Abū Hurayrah related that the Prophet once asked his companions, "Do you know who is considered bankrupt?" The companions replied, "The bankrupt one is he who owns neither dirham nor property." The Prophet said, "The bankrupt one from among my followers is he who will come on the Day of Judgment with a good record of *ṣalāt, ṣawm* and *zakāt,* and yet he had abused someone and slandered another. He had usurped the goods of another person, he killed someone and beat yet another person. So then one person [whom he afflicted] will come and he will give him from his good deeds and another will come and take from them and if his good deeds are finished before he can fulfill what is due to them then their wrong deeds will be taken from them and thrown on him and then he will in the end be thrown in the Fire."

One would think it impossible that someone with a good record of *ṣalāt, ṣawm* and *zakāt* be spiritually bankrupt because most Muslims would describe Islam as the five pillars, believing

[41] Sūratu 'l-Anbīyā [The Prophets], 21:3.

that anyone who performs them is safe. Yet, here the Prophet ﷺ describes someone who did all these in just such a lamentable position.

This demonstrates that there is no benefit of the prayer and fasting for someone who conspired against his brother, spread harmful rumors, cheated, stole, lied or abused others. All these corrupt traits must be eliminated before those acts of worship can benefit one.

Consider another example from the Hadith:

يا خولة! رب متخوض في مال الله ومال رسوله فيما اشتهت نفسه له النار يوم القيامة.

> Khawla bint ʿAmir ﵂, the wife of Sayyidina Ḥamza ﵁ related that the Prophet ﷺ said to her, "O Khawlah! Perhaps someone may misappropriate Allah's Properties and His Prophet's properties in whatever their selves desire; for him is the Fire on Judgment Day."[42]

Today one sees how much money and wealth Muslims misappropriate from what belongs to Allah ﷻ and His Prophet ﷺ, all the while observing all five pillars of Islam fastidiously. Often those in charge of collecting the *zakāt,* though they pray and fast, misuse the Bayt al-māl and other charities designated for the poor and orphans. Because of their wrongdoing, all of their worship will be thrown in their faces. Such people are destined for the fire on Judgment Day.

These are examples of the ways in which the sickness of oppression leads people into sin, despite their adherence to the outward requirements of Islam.

The Prophet ﷺ said:

---

[42] Aṭ-Ṭabarānī in his *Kabīr.*

أخوف ما أخاف على أمتي من عالم فصيح اللسان جهول القلب

The thing I fear most for my community is a scholar with an eloquent tongue but whose heart is ignorant.

He ﷺ also said:

أخْوفُ ما أخاف على أمتي كل منافق عليم اللسان.

The thing I fear most for my community is a hypocrite eloquent of tongue but whose heart is ignorant.[43]

The Prophet ﷺ feared that people would follow religious scholars who were well-versed in the teachings of religion and adept at presenting them, but whose hearts did not reflect the status and realities of what they teach, as Allah ﷻ said:

يَا أَيُّهَا الَّذِينَ آمَنُوا لِمَ تَقُولُونَ مَا لَا تَفْعَلُونَ كَبُرَ مَقْتًا عِندَ اللَّهِ أَن تَقُولُوا مَا لَا تَفْعَلُونَ

O ye who believe! Why say ye that which ye do not? Grievously odious is it in the sight of Allah that ye say that which ye do not.[44]

Doctors and engineers cannot deduce principles of *Fiqh* or *Shariʿah,* nor can they teach the fundamentals and principles of Islam. This position is only for scholars, and scholars who are *al-ʿulamāu 'l-ʿamilīn,* those who practice what they know. Such scholars are pious and sincere men and women, working purely for Allah's sake, not for the sake of a position or a salary.

Allah said:

---

[43] Tirmidhī. Another version is "the thing I fear most for my community is every hypocrite eloquent of tongue."

[44] Sūratu 'ṣ-Ṣaff [The Ranks], 61:2

وَلَقَدْ ذَرَأْنَا لِجَهَنَّمَ كَثِيرًا مِّنَ الْجِنِّ وَالإِنسِ لَهُمْ قُلُوبٌ لاَّ يَفْقَهُونَ بِهَا

Many are the Jinns and men we have made for Hell: They have hearts wherewith they understand not... [45]

THE SEVENTEEN RUINOUS TRAITS

These ailments of the heart spawn other bad qualities in the individual.

Imām Muhammad al-Busayrī asked Shaykh Abū 'l-Ḥasan al-Kharqānī about the major ruinous traits in human character, and the latter replied that they number 17. Each of these traits resembles a great tree, for each has a trunk, which is deeply rooted, as well as primary limbs, smaller off-shooting branches, leaves and so on. Each tree is laden with an array of bad manners. The 17 negative characteristics are listed here in order their impact on the overall human character.

They are known as *al-Akhlāqu 'dh-Dhamīmah*, the ruinous traits, also known as the Tree of Bad Manners, and they are:

1. Anger (*al-Ghaḍab*)
2. Love of This World (*Ḥubbu 'd-Dunyā*)
3. Malice (*al-Ḥiqd*)
4. Jealousy (*al-Ḥasad*)
5. Vanity (*al-'Ujb*)
6. Stinginess (*al-Bukhl*)
7. Avarice (*al-Ṭama'*)
8. Cowardice (*al-Jubn*)
9. Indolence (*al-Baṭalah*)
10. Arrogance (*al-Kibr*)
11. Ostentation (*al-Riyā'*)
12. Attachment (*al-Ḥirs*)
13. Superiority (*al-'Aẓamah*)

[45] Sūratu 'l-A'rāf [The Heights], 7:179.

14. Heedlessness and Laziness (*al-Ghabāwah wa 'l-Kasālah*)
15. Anxiety (*al-Ḥamm*)
16. Depression (*al-Ghamm*)
17. The Eight Hundred Forbidden Acts (*al-Manhīyāt*)

Anger is the worst of all 17 of the ruinous traits. It may easily be said that anger is the source from which the others flow. That is why Allah ﷻ said:

وَالْكَاظِمِينَ الْغَيْظَ وَالْعَافِينَ عَنِ النَّاسِ وَاللَّهُ يُحِبُّ الْمُحْسِنِينَ

Those who control their wrath and are forgiving toward mankind; Allah loves the good.[46]

We must purify ourselves from these bad traits and rid our hearts of the underlying ailments that are their source. Outward adherence to the five pillars is not enough; we must perfect our behavior.

This requires a program of self-evaluation, purification, seclusion and establishing a practice of remembrance and contemplation under the guidance of an authorized Shaykh of Spiritual Discipline (shaykh at-tarbīyyah). In this way, the seeker is able to achieve a state in which our heart is able to receive Divine Inspiration and observe Divine Realities.

The Purified Heart

Just as the diseased heart has its ailments, the purified heart has its own qualities that manifest themselves in the life of the seeker.

These include guidance, compassion and enlightenment.

The Guided Heart

At that time the heart is purified, Allah ﷻ makes it a site of revelation and a receiver for the message of truth.

---

[46] Sūrat Āli ʿImrān [The Family of ʿImrān], 3:134.

إذا أراد الله تعالى بعبد خيرا جعل له واعظا من نفسه يأمره وينهاه.

The Prophet ﷺ said "When Allah wants good for His servant, He will give him an advisor in his heart, urging him to good and prohibiting him from wrongdoing."[47]

The Holy Qur'ān states:

مَّا جَعَلَ اللَّهُ لِرَجُلٍ مِّن قَلْبَيْنِ فِي جَوْفِهِ

Allah did not give two hearts to anyone.[48]

The meaning of this verse is that we cannot divide our heart between Allah ﷻ and this world. The heart is one, and it must be with Allah ﷻ. That why we must eradicate the ruinous traits that begin to fill our heart as we grow from infant to child, child to youth and youth to adult. We must eliminate these characteristics and open our heart so that it becomes a spring from which every individual can come and quench their thirst for knowledge.

من اخلص لله اربعين يوما ظهرت ينابيع الحكمة من قلبه على لسانه

It is related from the Prophet, "Whoever devotes himself sincerely to Allah for forty days, springs of wisdom will emerge from his heart upon his tongue."[49]

The Compassionate Heart

Allah ﷻ created human beings with social hearts. He said in the Qur'ān:

---

[47] ad-Daylamī in *al-Musnad al-Firdaws*, 30762 from Umm Salamah.
[48] Sūratu 'l-Aḥzāb [The Confederates], 33:4.
[49] Abū Na'īm.

ثُمَّ قَفَّيْنَا عَلَى آثَارِهِم بِرُسُلِنَا وَقَفَّيْنَا بِعِيسَى ابْنِ مَرْيَمَ وَآتَيْنَاهُ الْإِنجِيلَ وَجَعَلْنَا
فِي قُلُوبِ الَّذِينَ اتَّبَعُوهُ رَأْفَةً وَرَحْمَةً

Then We caused Our messengers to follow in their footsteps; and We caused Jesus, son of Mary, to follow, and gave him the Gospel, and placed compassion and mercy in the hearts of those who followed him.[50]

Thus, He put into the hearts of the believers love and mercy. That is why the Companions used to take care of their community, and even other communities, for their hearts were full of love for Allah ﷻ.

THE ENLIGHTENED HEART

There is a hadith that states:

يقول الله :ما وسعني أرضي ولا سمائي ولكن وسعني قلب عبدي المؤم

My earth and My heaven encompass Me not, but the heart of My believing servant encompasses Me.[51]

The heart of a believer can contain his Lord if it is cleansed by self-purification and is longing to contact the Divine Presence. One with such a heart is constantly yearning to obey Allah ﷻ, to serve Him and follow the Sunnah of our beloved Prophet ﷺ. Such a one longs to perform acts of supererogatory worship with as much intensity as one whose heart is given over to *dunyā* longs for the pleasures of this world.

---

[50] Sūratu 'l-Ḥadīd [Iron], 57:27.

[51] Ghazālī, *Iḥyā'*. There are disputes over the authenticity or source of this tradition and some say it is an Isrā'īlī tradition. But there is an overwhelming truth to it according to the tradition narrated by aṭ-Ṭabarānī: "The receptacles of your Lord are the hearts of His righteous servants, the most cherished, gentle and refined to Him."

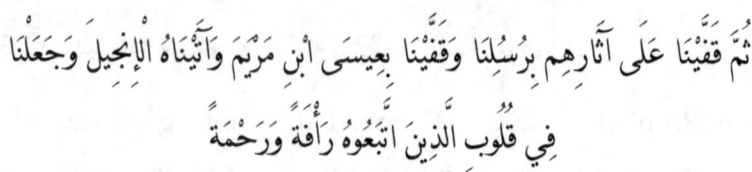

The heart has different levels and states. It is even said by the masters of the sciences of self-purification that the heart will go through ascensions that raise it higher and higher.

ان من امتي لرجالا الايمان اثبت في قلوبهم من الجبال الرواسي.

The Prophet said: Verily from my Community are men, in whose hearts the faith is like huge mountains.[52]

PRINCIPLES OF THE SCHOOL OF SPIRITUAL EDUCATION

These excellent qualities cannot be developed without a dedicated effort on the part of the seeker. They come only as the fruits of rigorous spiritual practices – practices outlined in the traditional curricula or the established schools of *ʿilm Tazkīyyat an-nafs.* Such practices cannot be learned from books; rather, they must be learned from one who has already made this journey, an authentic master of spiritual sciences who understands the maladies of the heart and knows how to cure them, a teacher in *al-madrasat ar-rūḥīyy,* the school of spiritual education.

Such schools teach the seeker how to eliminate the illnesses of the heart and the bad characteristics of the ego, and how to build in their stead good characteristics and the excellent qualities of the pure-hearted.

No doctor ever began to practice without first interning and learning from more experienced physicians in an actual medical ward. No lawyer practiced law without interning with an experienced attorney, assisting with cases and trials in order to learn that which could never be taught in the classroom or written in books. And just as there are schools of diplomacy that teach diplomats how to behave and act, there are schools that teach

[52] Ibn Jarīr. *Kanzu 'l-ʿummāl* 4573.

believers how to act in accordance with Allah's Way and how behave with their Lord, His Prophet ﷺ and with each other.

LOVE OF ALLAH AND FEAR OF ALLAH

The first principles of spiritual education are love of Allah ﷻ and fear of Allah ﷻ. These two principles must be kept foremost in the seeker's mind and heart, for they are the keys to overcoming evil and establishing good.

Allah ﷻ said:

قُلْ إِن كُنتُمْ تُحِبُّونَ اللّهَ فَاتَّبِعُونِي يُحْبِبْكُمُ اللّهُ وَيَغْفِرْ لَكُمْ ذُنُوبَكُمْ وَاللّهُ غَفُورٌ رَّحِيمٌ

Say: "If ye do love Allah, Follow me: Allah will love you and forgive you your sins: For Allah is Oft-Forgiving, Most Merciful.[53]

To love is to obey. And Allah ﷻ said:

وَأَمَّا مَنْ خَافَ مَقَامَ رَبِّهِ وَنَهَى النَّفْسَ عَنِ الْهَوَى فَإِنَّ الْجَنَّةَ هِيَ الْمَأْوَى

And for such as had entertained the fear of standing before their Lord's (tribunal) and had restrained (their) soul from lower desires, Their abode will be the Garden.[54]

وَلِمَنْ خَافَ مَقَامَ رَبِّهِ جَنَّتَانِ

But for such as fear the time when they will stand before (the Judgment Seat of) their Lord, there will be two Gardens.[55]

Fear of Allah ﷻ will prohibit the self from obeying bad desires.

---

[53] Sūrat Āli-ʿImrān [The Family of ʿImrān], 3:31.

[54] Sūratu 'n-Naziʿat [Those who drag forth], 79:40.

[55] Sūratu 'r-Raḥmān [The Most Merciful], 55:46.

Thus, love of Allah ﷻ and fear of Allah ﷻ are the two bases that will develop the means of approach to Allah ﷻ and His Prophet ﷺ, for indeed those who love and fear Allah ﷻ must also love His Prophet ﷺ, which yields obedience.

EMPTINESS AND SWEETNESS

Another principle is *taknīyya bʿada takhlīyyah,* emptiness followed by sweetness.

The purification of the self cannot be accomplished except through *takhlīyyah,* emptying oneself of bad manners. Doing so allows the Divine Sweetness to enter the heart.

Consider the example of Sayyidina Bilāl, one of the Companions of the Prophet. When he was being tortured by Umayyah ibn Khalaf, he was exclaiming *"Aḥad, Aḥad"*[56] because he had reached the station of vision where he could witness not just the Oneness of Allah ﷻ, but His Absolute Unique Oneness,[57] which is beyond any description. Sayyidina Bilāl had advanced beyond the station of witnessing Oneness[58], which would have been *"Wāḥid Wāḥid,"* to the higher level of witnessing Allah's Unique Oneness. He saw the Signs of his Creator everywhere he turned.

When a Muslim leaves the forbidden completely and eliminates all bad behaviors from his character, at that time he will be able to taste the sweetness of faith, *Īmān.* Whoever has purified his self is advancing towards the station of *Iḥsān* — perfection of character.

When we reach that level of *Iḥsān,* Allah ﷻ calls on us:

---

[56] Aḥad is one of the attributes of God defined as the Unique One.

[57] In Arabic, this is known as the station of *Aḥadīyya.*

[58] In Arabic, this is known as the station of *Waḥdānīyya.*

وَاذْكُر رَّبَّكَ فِي نَفْسِكَ تَضَرُّعاً وَخِيفَةً وَدُونَ الْجَهْرِ مِنَ الْقَوْلِ بِالْغُدُوِّ

وَالآصَالِ وَلاَ تَكُن مِّنَ الْغَافِلِينَ

And do (O reader!) Bring your Lord to remembrance in your (very) soul, with humility and in reverence, without loudness in words, in the mornings and evenings; and be not thou of those who are unheedful.[59]

At this point, there is no more illness in the heart of the seeker. There is only good behavior and reminders of obedience. At this time, he is able to remember his Lord and mention Him "*with humility and in reverence*" – with true emotion and sincere neediness. The seeker mentions Him in the morning and in the evening, calling upon his Lord and yearning for obedience to Him throughout his daily life and throughout the night.

THE METHODS OF TRAINING AND PURIFICATION OF THE SELF

1. STUDY WITH A TEACHER

وكان النبي صلى الله عليه وسلم يعرض القرآن في رمضان على جبريل عليه السلام، فكان يدارسه القرآن

On the authority of Ibn ʿAbbās ﵁: Jibrīl used to meet the Prophet ﷺ every night in Ramadan and used to study Qur'ān with him.[60]

This Sunnah proves the necessity of studying with a teacher. A qualified master is one who has already trod the path of spiritual development, who knows its ins and outs, its opportunities and

---

[59] Sūratu 'l-ʿArāf [The Heights], 7:205.
[60] Bukhārī.

pitfalls. He or she has already a veteran of the many battles required to defeat the ego and build up the heart and soul. Such a teacher knows the most effective times and places for spiritual training. A true master knows the efficacy of the verses of the Holy Qur'ān in building spiritual power, eliminating spiritual diseases and opening the heart to Allah's Divine Light. Such teachers are able to share these understandings with their students, who are in turn able to take benefit from their company. The time they spend with their teacher will allow these students to more easily purify themselves and advance more quickly on the spiritual path. Left to their own devices, these students might deviate from the *Shariʿah* or otherwise fall into error. The teacher can direct them so that their spiritual training and practices is accordance with the Divine Law, for whatever does not conform to the Shariʿah is false spirituality.

Allah ﷻ said in the Holy Qur'ān:

يَا أَيُّهَا الَّذِينَ آمَنُواْ اتَّقُواْ اللّهَ وَكُونُواْ مَعَ الصَّادِقِينَ

O ye who believe, fear Allah and keep company with those who are truthful[61]

Allah's Ancient Words are for all time, ongoing commandments from which we understand the importance of keeping company with the trustworthy. Allah ﷻ orders us to accompany them, because in doing so we see how they live – how they deal with people, how they address their companions, how they relate with their family and even how they deal with opponents; we see how they eat, sleep and drink, and how they worship based on the Sunnah of the Best of Creation ﷺ. By accompanying them, one learns all their good manners, perfections and ways of life. It is rare to find someone living their

[61] Sūratu 't-Tawbah [Repentance], 9:119.

life in such accordance with the Straight Path. Not everyone can do it, but we can all find such a trustworthy one and accompany him or her in order that we may be guided aright.

CONDITIONS FOR BEING A SPIRITUAL TEACHER

The conditions for being a teacher of spiritual discipline are rigorous:

- The shaykh must be deeply imbued with the knowledge of the religion, both external and esoteric.
- He must inherit from the Prophet ﷺ and all his predecessors the ability and Divine Support to guide his followers in the externals of the religion and its inner realities.
- He must be a scholar, well-versed in all religious obligations, such as the conditions of prescribed prayers, fasting, *zakāt* and hajj.
- He must be knowledgeable in Islamic jurisprudence and all necessary matters of the Divine Law.
- He must be a scholar in the science of monotheism and all the other conditions of faith.
- He must have the knowledge of the conditions of the state of excellence.
- He must have already purified and sanctified himself as a seeker under a guide of his own. Thus, he will have come to know the different stages of the ego, its illnesses and its defects. The guide must be fully aware of all the methods Satan uses to enter the breast and know all the ways to sanctify others and the methods to heal his followers in order to raise them up to the state of perfection.
- The shaykh must have authorization from his teacher to train his followers, authorization which must extend through a lineage of teachers all the way back to the Prophet ﷺ. As the wise person will not go to a doctor

who has no license in healing, so the seeker in this way must find a perfect guide who has received the license, the permission, from his shaykh.

يا ابن عمر ، دينك ، دينك ، إنما هو لحمك ودمك ، فانظر عمن تأخذ ، خذ الدين عن الذين استقاموا ، ولا تأخذ عن الذين قالوا

The Prophet ﷺ said:

O Ibn ʿUmar, your religion is your flesh and blood. Look at those from whom you take your religion. Take it from those who are on the right path and do not take from those who have deviated.[62]

إن هذا العلم دين فانظروا عمن تأخذون دينكم

And the Prophet ﷺ said:

This great knowledge (the knowledge of the self) is by itself the religion, so you have to know from whom you take your religion.[63]

العلماء ورثة الأنبياء

Most importantly, the Prophet ﷺ said:

The scholars of knowledge are the inheritors of the Prophets.

Ibn Khaldūn has mentioned this as one of the proofs for the necessity of following a *shaykh* in the sciences of *taṣawwuf* where he says: "To be in no need of the heir amounts to being in no need of the Prophet."[64]

---

[62] Ḥāfiẓ ibn ʿAlī, *Kanz al-ʿummāl*. Ad-Daylamī in *Musnad al-Firdaws*.

[63] Al-Ḥākim in his *Mustadrak*.

[64] Ibn Khaldūn, *Shifā' al-sā'il li tahdhīb al-masā'il* (Chapter six, on following a Sufi shaykh).

2. REMEMBRANCE OF ALLAH

The fundamental practice of self-purification is *dhikrullāh,* or the remembrance of Allah ﷻ. The purpose of this remembrance is to keep the heart awake by mentioning His Names.

In the Holy Qur'ān, there are more than 190 verses in which *dhikrullāh* was mentioned. Here we relate a representative few:

وَاذْكُر رَّبَّكَ فِي نَفْسِكَ تَضَرُّعاً وَخِيفَةً وَدُونَ الْجَهْرِ مِنَ الْقَوْلِ بِالْغُدُوِّ وَالآصَالِ وَلاَ تَكُن مِّنَ الْغَافِلِينَ

And do thou [O Muhammad) remember thy Lord within thyself humbly and with awe, below thy breath, at morn and evening. And be thou not of the neglectful.[65]

يَا أَيُّهَا الَّذِينَ آمَنُوا اذْكُرُوا اللَّهَ ذِكْرًا كَثِيرًا

O ye who believe! Remember Allah with much remembrance.[66]

فَاذْكُرُونِي أَذْكُرْكُمْ وَاشْكُرُواْ لِي وَلاَ تَكْفُرُونِ

Therefore remember Me, I will remember you. Give thanks to Me, and reject Me not.[67]

إِنَّمَا الْمُؤْمِنُونَ الَّذِينَ إِذَا ذُكِرَ اللّهُ وَجِلَتْ قُلُوبُهُمْ وَإِذَا تُلِيَتْ عَلَيْهِمْ آيَاتُهُ زَادَتْهُمْ إِيمَانًا وَعَلَى رَبِّهِمْ يَتَوَكَّلُونَ

They only are the (true) believers whose hearts feel fear when Allah is mentioned, and when the revelations of Allah are

---

[65] Sūratu 'l-ʿArāf [The Heights], 7:205.
[66] Sūratu 'l-Aḥzāb [The Confederates] 33:41.
[67] Sūratu 'l-Baqara [The Heifer],2:152.

recited unto them they increase their faith, and who trust in their Lord; [68]

The value of *dhikrullāh* is also mentioned in the hadith.

وعن عبد الله بن بشر رضي الله عنه أن رجلا قال: يا رسول الله، إن شرائع الإسلام قد كثرت علي، فأخبرني بشيء أتشبث به قال: "لا يزال لسانك رطبًا من ذكر الله".

Someone came to the Prophet ﷺ and asked, "O Messenger of Allah, I am finding that all these different rules of the religion are too difficult. Please give me something easy that I may accomplish." The Prophet ﷺ answered, "Make your tongue moist with the Remembrance of Allah."[69]

In most verses what is meant by the word *dhikr* is glorifying, exalting, and praising Allah ﷻ and sending salutations upon the Prophet ﷺ.

It is important to note that the Holy Qur'ān does not only speak of the benefits of this practice; it also warns against neglecting it:

أَفَمَن شَرَحَ اللَّهُ صَدْرَهُ لِلْإِسْلَامِ فَهُوَ عَلَىٰ نُورٍ مِّن رَّبِّهِ فَوَيْلٌ لِّلْقَاسِيَةِ قُلُوبُهُم مِّن ذِكْرِ اللَّهِ أُوْلَٰئِكَ فِي ضَلَالٍ مُّبِي

Could, then, one whose bosom Allah has opened wide with willingness towards self-surrender unto Him, so that he is illumined by a light [that flows] from his Sustainer, [be likened to the blind and deaf of heart]? Woe, then, unto those whose hearts are hardened against all remembrance of Allah! They are most obviously lost in error! [70]

---

[68] Sūratu 'l-Anfāl [The Spoils], 8:2.

[69] Aḥmad, Tirmidhī, Ibn Mājah, and Ibn Ḥibbān (*ḥasan*).

[70] Sūratu 'z-Zumar [The Groups], 39:22

BENEFITS OF DHIKR

Dhikrullāh is a means — one of many, but among the most important — to accumulate different powers of the self, *jamiʿ ṭāqat an-nafs*. These energies are derived from the light with which Allah ﷻ fills the hearts of sincere believers that we mentioned earlier. These energies are accumulated by means of *dhikrullāh*, and they are what allow the seeker to rend the veils which separate him from His Lord, granting him the power of true vision and making his heart a receiver for the Divine Emanations. The master is able to teach the seeker to keep this remembrance constant, so that the heart and tongue are always occupied with it *dhikrullāh*.

ومن فوائد الذكر أيضاً ما ذكره ابن القيم رحمه الله:

أن دور الجنة تُبنى بالذكر، فإذا أمسك الذاكر عن الذكر أمسكت الملائكة عن البناء، وأن الذكر سد بين العبد وبين جهنم فإذا كانت له إلى جهنم طريق عمل من الأعمال، كان الذكر سداً في تلك الطريق، وأن الملائكة تستغفر للذاكر كما تستغفر للتائب، وأن الجبال والقفار تتباهى وتستبشر بمن يذكر الله عز وجل عليها، وأن كثرة ذكر الله عز وجل أمان من النفاق، فإن المنافقين قليلو الذكر لله عز وجل.

قال تبارك وتعالى في المنافقين: " **وَلا يَذْكُرُونَ اللَّهَ إِلا قَلِيلا** " وأن للذكر من بين الأعمال لذة لا يُشبهها شيء فلو لم يكن للعبد من ثوابه إلا اللذة الحاصلة للذاكر، وأنه يكسو الوجة نضرةً في الدنيا ونوراً في الآخرة،

Ibn Qayyim said:

Indeed the ground floor of Paradise is built upon *dhikr*. So when the one remembering Allah stops his *dhikr* the angels stop building [the ground floor of Paradise for that servant]. And *dhikr* is truly a barrier between the servant and Hell, such that even if he is on the path to Hell because of some of his deeds, [his] *dhikrullāh* stands as a barrier in that path and verily the angels ask forgiveness for the one remembering Allah just as they do for the penitent. And verily the mountains and the plains boast and rejoice over one who remembers Allah Exalted upon their surface. And verily excessive Remembrance of Allah ﷻ is security from hypocrisy (*nifāq*), for verily the hypocrites are those who remember Allah infrequently. Allah ﷻ said regarding the hypocrites, "and they do not remember Allah except a little"[71]

Ibn Qayyim said:

And indeed Allah's remembrance obligates Allah ﷻ and His angels to bless the one remembering.

THE FLAME OF THE HEART

Ibn Qayyim said:

Surely there is a rapturous pleasure to *dhikr* among all the praiseworthy actions which nothing else resembles, such that if the servant got nothing from his *dhikr* except that ecstasy that comes to the one remembering [it would suffice him], and truly he will be dressed with a shining face in this life and with light in the Hereafter.[72]

وَمَن لَّمْ يَجْعَلِ اللَّهُ لَهُ نُورًا فَمَا لَهُ مِن نُّورٍ

for any to whom Allah giveth not light, there is no light! [73]

---

[71] Sūratu 'n-Nisā [Women], 4:142.

[72] Cited by 'Abdu 'l-'Azīz ibn Muḥammad Salmān in *Manāhil al-hisān fī durūs Ramaḍān.*

[73] Sūratu 'n-Nūr [The Light], 24:40.

When a heart is constant in remembrance it becomes illumined with a flame that always burns brightly. The strength of that flame depends on how much the seeker engages in *dhikrullāh*. When that flame appears in the heart, he is able to weigh right and wrong, discerning the good from the bad. This flame also grants contentment with everything that Allah ﷻ gives, causing anger to subside.

There is difference between soul and spirit, *rūḥ wa 'n-nafs*. The heart is the house of the soul. The spirit permeates the entire body in much the same way the nervous system does. It commands the whole body. When the soul is energized by *dhikrullāh*, that flame will expand throughout the entire body and the nervous system giving it the power to accept every condition and situation. As that flame grows, it overtakes the whole body and that person becomes truly pious and sincere. Thus, the soul and the spirit come together.

This happened to Sayyidina Khiḍr:

فَوَجَدَا عَبْدًا مِّنْ عِبَادِنَا آتَيْنَاهُ رَحْمَةً مِنْ عِندِنَا وَعَلَّمْنَاهُ مِن لَّدُنَّا عِلْمًا

They two found one of our servants that We had taught from our heavenly knowledge[74]

THE VISION OF THE PURIFIED HEART

القلب بيت الرب

It is related that the Prophet ﷺ said: "The heart is the House of the Lord."[75]

How is this possible? Because this heart becomes vast through the power of remembrance of Allah's Names and Attributes. When the spirit and the soul come together, the spirit will become

---

[74] Sūratu 'l-Kahf [The Cave], 18:65.

[75] Ibn Mājah relates a longer wording with a similar meaning.

stronger. In this way, the veils that separate the seeker from his Lord are rent and the heart is able to perceive that which cannot be seen with the eyes, as described in *hadith qudsī*:

وعن أبي هريرة قال قال رسول الله صلى الله عليه وسلم إن الله تعالى قال من عادى لي وليا فقد آذنته بالحرب وما تقرب إلي عبدي بشيء أحب إلي مما افترضت عليه وما يزال عبدي يتقرب إلي بالنوافل حتى أحبه فإذا أحببته كنت سمعه الذي يسمع به وبصره الذي يبصر به ويده التي يبطش بها ورجله التي يمشي بها وإن سألني لأعطينه ولئن استعاذني لأعيذنه وما ترددت عن شيء أنا فاعله ترددي عن نفس المؤمن يكره الموت وأنا أكره مساءته ولا بد له منه . رواه البخاري .

My servant continues to approach Me through voluntary worship until I love him. And when I love him I will be the ears with which he hears, I will be the eyes with which he sees; I will be the tongue with which he speaks, I will be the hand with which he acts, and I will be the foot with which he walks.[76]

Another hadith states:

اتقوا فراسة المؤمن، فإنه ينظر بنور الله عز وجل

The Prophet ﷺ said, "Beware of the vision of a sincere believer for verily he sees with the Light of Allah." [77]

---

[76] Bukhārī and Muslim.

[77] Narrated by Īmām at-Tirmidhī in his book of *Tafsīr* on the authority of ibn Sa'īd al-Ḥākim. Al-Bukhārī in his *Ṭārīkh*, aṭ-Ṭabarānī in his *Kabīr* and Ib Adi in his *Kāmil* from Ibn 'Umar.

This refers to the special vision that is granted to the sincere servant. An example of this is found in the story of Sayyidina ʿUmar ﵁:

ولابن مردويه عن ابن عمر عن أبيه أنه كان يخطب يوم الجمعة فعرض في خطبته أن قال «يا سارية الجبل! من استرعى الذئب ظلم». فالتفت الناس بعضهم لبعض، فقال لهم علي: ليخرجن مما قال. فلما فرغ سألوه فقال: وقع في خلدي أن المشركين هزموا إخواننا، وأنهم يمرون بجبل فإن عدلوا إليه قاتلوا من وجه واحد، وإن جاوزوا هلكوا، فخرج مني ما تزعمون أنكم سمعتموه. فجاء البشير بعد شهر وذكر أنهم سمعوا صوت عمر في ذلك اليوم. قال: فعدلنا إلى الجبل ففتح الله علينا. قال في اللآلئ: وقد أفرد الحافظ القطب الحلبي لطرقه جزءا، ووثق رجال هذه الطريق. وقال: ذكره ابن عساكر وابن ماكولا وغيرهم، وسارية له صحبة

Ibn ʿUmar ﵁ said that his father, Sayyidina ʿUmar ﵁, was delivering a sermon on Friday. In the middle of his sermon, he shouted, "*Ya Sārīyyah, al-jabal*! O Sārīyyah! [look towards] the mountain!" Then he resumed his sermon ... Some people looked at each other in dismay. Sayyidina ʿAlī ﵁ said to them, "He will likely say (something) about this statement." When the people had finished the prayer, they asked Sayyidina ʿUmar ﵁ about the incident. He said, "The idea crossed my mind that the enemy aggressors had defeated our brethren and they would run towards the mountain. Thus, if the Muslims moved towards the mountain, they would have to fight on one side only, while if they advanced, they would be destroyed. So those words escaped my mouth." After a month, a messenger came with good news. He said, "The people of the army heard Sayyidina ʿUmar ﷺ voice on that day. We all went towards the mountain and Allah made us victorious."[78]

That miracle (*karāmah*) was a sign that Sayyidina ʿUmar ﷺ had two characteristics from true faith: The Reality of Hearing, *ʿIlmu 'l-Yaqīn* and the Reality of Seeing, *ʿAynu 'l-Yaqīn*. The first characteristic is like one which Allah ﷻ gave to Sārīyya ﷺ and his troops from His Divine Attribute the Hearer, as-Samʿi. But Sayyidina ʿUmar ﷺ also could see what was occurring through the Reality of Certainty, *Haqqu 'l-Yaqīn*. Sārīyya ﷺ and his troops were only able to hear from afar. They could not see Sayyidina ʿUmar ﷺ, whereas Sayyidina ʿUmar ﷺ was seeing, hearing and speaking across the vast distance from Madina to Shām. [ii]

3. CONTEMPLATION ON ALLAH'S PRESENCE

Thus, the practice of *dhikrullāh* strengthens faith and develops the power of true vision, allowing the seeker to advance to the practice of *murāqabatillāh fī 's-sirr w 'al-ʿalānīyya* — to be able to meditate and focus upon Allah ﷻ, whether alone or in a crowd. This is important, for He said in the Holy Qur'ān:

أَلَمْ تَرَ أَنَّ اللَّهَ يَعْلَمُ مَا فِي السَّمَاوَاتِ وَمَا فِي الْأَرْضِ مَا يَكُونُ مِن نَّجْوَى ثَلَاثَةٍ إِلَّا هُوَ رَابِعُهُمْ وَلَا خَمْسَةٍ إِلَّا هُوَ سَادِسُهُمْ وَلَا أَدْنَى مِن ذَٰلِكَ وَلَا أَكْثَرَ إِلَّا هُوَ مَعَهُمْ أَيْنَ مَا كَانُوا ثُمَّ يُنَبِّئُهُم بِمَا عَمِلُوا يَوْمَ الْقِيَامَةِ إِنَّ اللَّهَ بِكُلِّ شَيْءٍ عَلِيمٌ

Do you not see that Allah doth know (all) that is in the heavens and on earth? There is not a secret consultation between three,

[78] Ibn ʿAsākir, Ibn Makūlan, Ibn al-Mardawayh and other narrations by al-Bayhaqī in *Dalā'il an-nubuwwah*, al-Lalaka'ī in *Sharḥ as-sunnah*, and al-Waqidī with variant wordings.

but He makes the fourth among them, - Nor between five but He makes the sixth,- nor between fewer nor more, but He is in their midst, wheresoever they be: In the end will He tell them the truth of their conduct, on the Day of Judgment. For Allah has full knowledge of all things. [79]

Allah ﷻ also said:

الَّذِينَ يَذْكُرُونَ اللّهَ قِيَامًا وَقُعُودًا وَعَلَىَ جُنُوبِهِمْ وَيَتَفَكَّرُونَ فِي خَلْقِ السَّمَاوَاتِ وَالأَرْضِ رَبَّنَا مَا خَلَقْتَ هَذا بَاطِلاً سُبْحَانَكَ فَقِنَا عَذَابَ النَّارِ

Those that remember Allah, standing, sitting, and on their sides contemplating about the creation of the heavens and the earth (and say): Our Lord! You did not create this in vain. Glory be to You! Preserve us from the torment of Fire.[80]

أَوَلَمْ يَنظُرُواْ فِي مَلَكُوتِ السَّمَاوَاتِ وَالأَرْضِ وَمَا خَلَقَ اللّهُ مِن شَيْءٍ وَأَنْ عَسَى أَن يَكُونَ قَدِ اقْتَرَبَ أَجَلُهُمْ فَبِأَيِّ حَدِيثٍ بَعْدَهُ يُؤْمِنُونَ

Have they not considered the dominion of the heavens and the earth, and what things Allah has created, and that it may be that their own term draws nigh? In what fact after this will they believe?[81]

قُلِ انظُرُواْ مَاذَا فِي السَّمَاوَاتِ وَالأَرْضِ وَمَا تُغْنِي الآيَاتُ وَالنُّذُرُ عَن قَوْمٍ لاَّ يُؤْمِنُونَ

---

[79] Sūratu 'l-Mujādilah [The Disputant], 58:7.
[80] Sūrat Āli-ʿImrān [The Family of ʿImrān], 3:191.
[81] Sūratu 'l-ʿArāf [The Heights], 7:185.

Say: Behold what is in the heavens and the earth! But revelations and warnings avail not folk who will not believe.[82]

وَكَأَيِّن مِّن آيَةٍ فِي السَّمَاوَاتِ وَالأَرْضِ يَمُرُّونَ عَلَيْهَا وَهُمْ عَنْهَا مُعْرِضُونَ

How many a portent is there in the heavens and the earth which they pass by with face averted![83]

أَفَلَمْ يَسِيرُوا فِي الْأَرْضِ فَتَكُونَ لَهُمْ قُلُوبٌ يَعْقِلُونَ بِهَا أَوْ آذَانٌ يَسْمَعُونَ بِهَا فَإِنَّهَا لَا تَعْمَى الْأَبْصَارُ وَلَكِن تَعْمَى الْقُلُوبُ الَّتِي فِي الصُّدُورِ

Have they not traveled in the land, and have they hearts wherewith to feel and ears wherewith to hear? For indeed it is not the eyes that grow blind, but it is the hearts, which are within the bosoms, that grow blind.[84]

Tafakkur is worship based on contemplation of Allah's creation. It involves observing the Earth, the Sun, the planets, the stars and the Moon; observing the trees, the plants, and the animals; observing the seasons and their transition from one to another. One observes the perfect cycles of water, air and energy; the perfection of the protection afforded by Earth's atmosphere, ionosphere and magnetosphere from harmful rays, meteors and energy. One observes the ants and bees, and the different ways they live and work together with intricate organization and determination. One observes the elephants, whales, birds, insects, contemplating their lives and biological diversity. One observes the microscopic world of bacteria and viruses and the still smaller

---

[82] Sūrah Yūnus [Jonah], 10: 101.
[83] Sūrah Yūsuf [Joseph], 12:105.
[84] Sūratu 'l-Ḥajj [The Pilgrimage], 22:46.

world of molecular and atomic structures in their incredible miniscule perfection.

As the seeker contemplates these wonders, he comes to the full realization that all are His amazing creation and is thereby able to authentically appreciate Allah's Oneness and Greatness. This allows the seeker to progress even deeper in his meditation, to realize the importance of keeping his heart connected to the Divine Presence and to advance even farther on his spiritual journey. In this way, he becomes an individual who is sincere in the depths of his belief and to the core of his heart. His life becomes a constant meditation on the Divine that transports him from the abyss of the ego to the deep oceans of Allah's Remembrance.

Many verses of the Holy Qur'ān encourage this practice of contemplation, and *tafakkur* is further mentioned in many hadith of the Prophet ﷺ. Indeed, there are 17 verses in the Qur'ān that explicitly use the verb *tafakkar*. There are 79 other verses containing the root *fakara,* to think or reason. And there are countless others which speak of those who have eyes, *ulī 'l-abṣār,* understanding, *uli 'l-albāb,* and reasoning, *uli 'n-nuhā.*[85] Moreover, 18 verses ask if we "see not?" (*alam yaraw, afalam yaraw, awalam yaraw*), instructing us to observe Allah's creation, generally or specifically, and take heed from these observations. There are 120 verses which ask the reader or listener if he knows (from the root: *'alama*).

Such observation allows us to remain mindful of the Presence of Allah, *murāqabah,* allowing us to truly feel that He is nearer than our jugular vein, nearer to us than our own selves.

---

[85] *uli 'l-abṣār* — those who have eyes: Sūrat Āli-'Imrān [The Family of 'Imrān], 3:13; Sūratu 'n-Nūr [The Light], 24:44; *uli 'l-albāb* — those endowed with understanding: Sūrah Ṣād, 38:43; Sūratu 'z-Zumar [The Groups], 39:21; Sūrah Ghāfir, 40:54; Sūrat Āli-'Imrān, 3:190; Sūrah Yūsuf [Joseph], 12:111. *ūli 'n-nuhā* — those who are endowed with reason: Sūrah ṬāḤā 20:54; Sūrah ṬāḤā 20:128.

There was a spiritual teacher who told all his students: "Go slaughter a chicken where no one can see you." And so they did, each returning to inform their teacher of their accomplishment save one who did not return. When the teacher found him, he asked what had happened. The student said, "How can I slaughter the chicken where no one can see me? Allah ﷻ is seeing me; the Prophet ﷺ is seeing me and my teacher is seeing me."

4. THE NIGHT VIGIL

Following the first revelation of Surat al-ʿAlaq, Allah ﷻ revealed:

يَا أَيُّهَا الْمُزَّمِّلُ قُمِ اللَّيْلَ إِلَّا قَلِيلًا نِصْفَهُ أَوِ انقُصْ مِنْهُ قَلِيلًا أَوْ زِدْ عَلَيْهِ وَرَتِّلِ
الْقُرْآنَ تَرْتِيلًا إِنَّا سَنُلْقِي عَلَيْكَ قَوْلًا ثَقِيلًا

O thou folded in garments! Stand (to prayer) by night, but not all night - half of it - or a little less, or a little more; and recite the Qur'ān in slow, measured rhythmic tones. Soon shall We send down to you a weighty Message. Truly the rising by night is most potent for governing (the soul), and most suitable for (framing) the Word (of Prayer and Praise).[86]

Allah ﷻ wanted the Prophet ﷺ to be constant in meditation and remembrance of his Lord. That is extremely difficult to do late at night when everyone is sleeping, but this is also a most efficacious time for worship as the above verse makes clear.

Waking up for night worship requires a major struggle against the ego. Thus, the seeker is encouraged to wake up and pray *Ṣalāt at-tahajjud,* the night prayer, in order to learn patience and obedience and to accompany teachers who have been practicing

[86] Sūratu 'l-Muzzammil [The Enshrouded One], 73:1-6.

that discipline and trying their best to eliminate their bad characteristics and bad manners.

5. WORSHIP AND OBEDIENCE

True servanthood is based on *al-ʿibādāt wa 't-taʿat,* worship and obedience.

As the seeker ascends through different levels of unveiling, he begins to realize that the only way to approach His Lord is through worship, for Allah ﷻ said:

قَدْ أَفْلَحَ مَن تَزَكَّى وَذَكَرَ اسْمَ رَبِّهِ فَصَلَّى

The one who attains a higher level of purification will have succeeded And remembers the name of his Lord, so prays.[87]

Let us examine this verse more closely. In it, Allah ﷻ says that, as the seeker attains to higher and higher levels, he comes to the sincere remembrance of his Lord's Name. This demonstrates that the real and authentic remembrance of Allah ﷻ is only possible once the self is purified. The one who has done this is able to truly remember his Lord, not just imitate that remembrance. The verse goes on to state *"so [he] prays."* This means that such an enlightened person feels the reality of the Divine Presence at every moment when he is performing the obligatory five prayers. From these he seeks further closeness by observing the *nawāfil,* voluntary worship.

Even today, there are among the practitioners of this science those who in every moment go and make ablution, then come and pray two *rakaʿts sunnat al-wuḍū,* then in five minutes repeat it again. They want to feel that they are doing more voluntary worship, because they know that it is pleasing to Allah, because:

الوضوء على الوضوء نور على نور

[87] Sūratu 'l-ʿAlā [The Most High], 87:14.

The Prophet ﷺ said, "Ablution over ablution is 'light upon light.'"[88]

Such people fall under Allah's Words, which he have already mentioned: "My servant continues to approach Me through voluntary worship until I love him …" Such a person becomes a subtle being who can direct others to what is correct and what is not, what is sickness and what is health.

6. GROUP REMEMBRANCE

Another important practice is to perform *dhikrullāh* in a group, forming circles such as those mentioned by Ibn Qayyim, who said:

> And verily, whoever wishes to inhabit the Gardens of Paradise in this life, he should become a member of the gatherings of *dhikr* for verily they are the Gardens of Paradise and verily the gatherings of *dhikr* are the gatherings of angels.

When people attend associations of *dhikrullāh,* they hear recitation of the Qur'ān in beautiful voices and melodies, the most beautiful praising of the Prophet ﷺ and with the *dhikrullāh,* angels surround them as mentioned in the hadith.

This is how the Prophet ﷺ was listening to the Holy Qur'ān, in a melodious way. He also used to listen to such praising and poetry by Ḥassān ibn Thābit, the likes of which made tears fall and left the listener wanting nothing from this life.

7. ABSTINENCE

Zuhd, abstinence, is to throw *dunyā* from the heart. This does not necessarily require eliminating *dunyā* from one's life, rather it requires the seeker to through it from his heart.

ورب غني شاكر أفضل من فقير صابر،

[88] Razzīn in his *Musnad*.

For that reason it is said, "It may be that a thankful wealthy person is better than a patient pauper." [89]

He who possesses little worships like the wealthy, but a pious wealthy person both worships and gives charity. For someone who has truly eliminated love of wealth from his heart, possession of great wealth will not create the disease of attachment. Instead, he will spend it in Allah's Way. The use of wealth in Allah's Way may be better by hundreds and thousands of times than a patient pauper's worship.

With the simultaneous accumulation of all positive character traits and the elimination of all negative ones, the seeker's heart begins to fill with the power needed to overcome all evil inclinations, for Allah ﷻ said:

وَالَّذِينَ جَاهَدُوا فِينَا لَنَهْدِيَنَّهُمْ سُبُلَنَا وَإِنَّ اللَّهَ لَمَعَ الْمُحْسِنِينَ

And those who strive in Our (cause), We will certainly guide them to our Paths: For verily Allah is with those who do right.[90]

This means that when we struggle against the inclinations of our lower self, Allah ﷻ will show us the way to leave those bad characteristics and behaviors behind us. Those who are accumulating pure spiritual energy will be guided in the ways that Allah ﷻ wants for them, and by means of this guidance they will reach what Allah ﷻ wants for them. Such persons are described in the Holy Qur'ān:

[89] A saying of Abū Abbās al-ʿAtā.

[90] Sūratu 'l-ʿAnkabūt [The Spider], 29:69.

مِنَ الْمُؤْمِنِينَ رِجَالٌ صَدَقُوا مَا عَاهَدُوا اللَّهَ عَلَيْهِ فَمِنْهُم مَّن
قَضَى نَحْبَهُ وَمِنْهُم مَّن يَنتَظِرُ وَمَا بَدَّلُوا تَبْدِيلًا

Among the Believers are men who have been true to their covenant with Allah. Of them some have completed their vow (to the extreme), and some (still) wait: but they have never changed (their determination) in the least.[91]

These purified ones do what Allah ﷻ wants with full knowledge of the covenant made before this worldly life, when we were in the world of souls, on the Day of Vows and Binding Promises (*Yawm al-ʿAhdi wa 'l-Mīthāq*).

8. SECLUSION

The scholars of Islam realized the importance of seclusion by studying the life of the Prophet ﷺ, and they came to understand its necessity in the spiritual journey of the seeker. That is why they made their hearts to be remote from *dunyā*.

Recall how the Prophet ﷺ used to retreat to Ghāri Hirā for many months of the year to worship and contemplate in order to be able to receive heavenly knowledge.

Allah ﷻ said:

إِنَّا سَنُلْقِي عَلَيْكَ قَوْلًا ثَقِيلًا

"Soon shall We send down to thee a weighty Message."[92]

Allah ﷻ guided the Prophet ﷺ to prepare himself in Ghāri Hirā, to guide him in his spiritual life in order that one day he

[91] Sūratu 'l-Aḥzāb [The Confederates], 33:23.
[92] Sūratu 'l-Muzammil, [The Enshrouded One], 73:5.

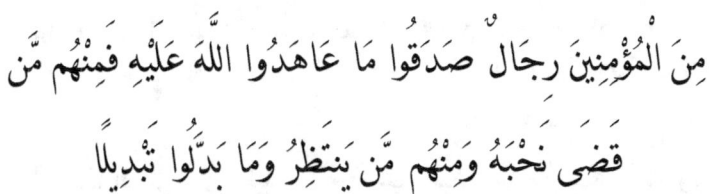

would be ready to receive that heavenly revelation. Allah ﷻ also said in the Holy Qur'ān:

لَوْ أَنزَلْنَا هَذَا الْقُرْآنَ عَلَى جَبَلٍ لَّرَأَيْتَهُ خَاشِعًا مُّتَصَدِّعًا مِّنْ خَشْيَةِ اللَّهِ وَتِلْكَ الْأَمْثَالُ نَضْرِبُهَا لِلنَّاسِ لَعَلَّهُمْ يَتَفَكَّرُونَ

"Had We sent down this Qur'ān on a mountain, verily, thou wouldst have seen it humble itself and cleave asunder for fear of Allah. Such are the similitudes which We propound to men, that they may reflect."[93]

If this revelation would have shattered a mountain, imagine what it would have done to a human being. Therefore, Allah ﷻ prepared His Prophet ﷺ through spiritual purification, *Tazkīyyat an-nafs,* in the cave, and it was there that His Revelation finally came down. It did not come down in the Prophet's house, or in the Sacred Mosque, or in a seminar, or in worship. Revelation came only in a cave after the Prophet ﷺ had completely secluded himself from worldly life. The first revelation was *iqrā*! — "*read in the name of your Lord*." Later, after the Prophet ﷺ had built up his spirituality through Allah's Guidance, Allah ﷻ allowed him to receive revelation in "normal" circumstances. Yet, despite this and despite the fact that by the end of his earthly life he was leader of a great nation, the Prophet ﷺ continued to observe seclusion, and he remained *zāhid,* ascetic and humble in his means, until the day of his passing.

CONCLUSION

The life of every human being is a struggle between good and evil. We have seen that the externalities of our religion are alone

---

[93] Sūratu 'l-Ḥashr [The Gathering], 59:21.

insufficient to grant us victory over the same evil impulses that inspired Cain to raise his hand against his brother. Rather, we must add to these the practices of the science of self-purification in order to cleanse our hearts and rid ourselves of these diseases of the spirit. Only then can we ensure that good will triumph over evil within us.

The Imāms of our pure religion cautioned against the mere thirst for knowledge at the expense of training the ego and purifying it of lust and desire for material wealth. Imām Ghazālī left the halls of learning in the midst of a prestigious career in order to devote himself to self-purification out of concern for his own soul, at the outset of which he wrote his magisterial *Iḥyā ʿUlum al-dīn* which begins with a warning to those who consider religion to consist merely in *fiqh* or jurisprudence.

Heed the words of Imām adh-Dhahabī:

> Today, in our time, the quest for knowledge and hadith no longer requires of the hadith scholar the obligation of living up to it, which is the goal of hadith … pursuing the study of hadith is other than the hadith itself.[94]

This warning stands stronger than ever today, for while thousands of young men and women run to study Islamic theology and *fiqh*, it is only a few who seek a teacher who will train them in application of this book learning and guide them along the path of self-purification that allows them to truly live it. It is for the purpose of "the hadith itself", for the purpose of living up to the Sunnah of the Prophet ﷺ whose manners were the Holy Qur'ān, according to the well-known hadith of ʿAʾisha ﵂, that the great masters of self-purification gave up the pursuit of worldly

---

[94] Dhahabī as cited in Sakhāwī, *al-Jawāhir wa al-durar fī tarjamat shaykh al-islām Ibn Ḥajar* (al-ʿAsqalani), ed. Ḥamīd ʿAbd al-Mājid and ṬāḤā al-Zaynī (Cairo: wizārat al-awqāf, al-majlis al-aʿla li al-shuʿūn al-islāmīyya, lajnah iḥyā' al-turāth al-islāmī, 1986) p. 21-22.

allurements, and placed above it the acquisition of *Iḥsān* or perfect character.

Therefore, it behooves those who today seek a solution to the perennial conflict between good and evil to return to this all-important science of the soul. With it, it is hoped that a change for the better can be affected. When that positive change occurs in the individual, its impact will spread to the level of family, then to the community and finally wider still to the entire nation. We ask Allah ﷻ to give us the guidance and inspiration to implement such a course of study and practice in a short time, for truly He is the Changer of Hearts.

Appendix: What the Scholars of Islam Said about *Tasawwuf*

The following quotations of the scholars of Islamic Divine Law regarding the precedence of the knowledge and science of *Taṣawwuf,* (Purification of the Self) are excerpted from the book *The Naqshbandi Sufi Way: History and Guidebook of the Saints of the Golden Chain.*[95]

Ibn Taymiyya (661 - 728 AH)

التصوف عندهم له حقائق وأحوال معروفة ، قد تكلموا في حدوده وسيرته وأخلاقه كقول بعضهم : " الصوفي " من صفا من الكدر ، وامتلأ من الفكر ، واستوى عنده الذهب والحجر ، " التصوف " : كتمان المعاني ، وترك الدعاوى ، وأشباه ذلك ، وهم يسيرون بالصوفي إلى معنى الصديق ، وأفضل الخلق بعد الأنبياء الصديقون ، كما قال الله تعالى:

وَمَن يُطِعِ اللّهَ وَالرَّسُولَ فَأُوْلَـئِكَ مَعَ الَّذِينَ أَنْعَمَ اللّهُ عَلَيْهِم مِّنَ النَّبِيِّينَ وَالصِّدِّيقِينَ وَالشُّهَدَاء وَالصَّالِحِينَ وَحَسُنَ أُولَـئِكَ رَفِيقًا . . .

والصواب : أنهم مجتهدون في طاعة الله ، كما اجتهد غيرهم من أهل طاعة الله ، فيهم السابق المقرب بحسب اجتهاده . . .

Taṣawwuf has realities and states of experience which Sufis talk about in their science. Some of it is that the Sufi is that one who purifies himself from anything which distracts him from the remembrance of Allah and who will be so filled up with knowledge of the heart and knowledge of the mind to the point that the value of gold and stones will

[95] Shaykh Muhammad Kabbani, KAZI, 1995

be the same to him. And *Taṣawwuf* is safeguarding the precious meanings and leaving behind the call to fame and vanity in order to reach the state of Truthfulness, because the best of humans after the prophets are the *Ṣiddiqīn*, as Allah mentioned them in the verse:

> *(And all who obey Allah and the Apostle) are in the company of those on whom is the grace of Allah: of the prophets, the sincere lovers of truth, the martyrs and the righteous; Ah! what a beautiful fellowship.*[96]

...the truth is they are striving in Allah's obedience, as others of Allah's People strove in Allah's obedience. So from them you will find the Foremost in Nearness by virtue of his striving.[97]

The miracles of saints are absolutely true and correct, by the acceptance of all Muslim scholars. And the Qur'ān has pointed to it in different places, and the Hadith of the Prophet ﷺ has mentioned it, and whoever denies the miraculous power of saints are only people who are innovators and their followers.[98]

IMAM ABU HANIFA (85 H. - 150 H)

لولا السنتان لهلك النعمان، فقد تلمذ سنتان في مجلس الامام الصادق.

"If it were not for two years, I would have perished." He said, "for two years I accompanied Sayyidina Jaʿfar aṣ-Ṣādiq and I acquired the spiritual knowledge that made me a gnostic in the Way."[99]

---

[96] Sūratu 'n-Nisā [Women], 4:69.

[97] *Majmuʿa Fatāwā Ibn Taymīyya al-Kubrā*, Vol. 11, Book of *Ṭaṣawwuf*, p. 497.

[98] *Al-Mukhtaṣar al-Fatawā*, page 603.

[99] *Ad-Durr al-Mukhtār*, vol 1. p. 43.

IMAM MALIK (95 H. - 179 H.)

يقول الإمام مالك رحمه الله تعالى : من تفقه ولم يتصوف فقد تفسق، ومن تصوف ولم يتفقه فقد تزندق ومن جمع بينهما فقد تحقق

Whoever studies Jurisprudence [*tafaqaha*] and didn't study Sufism [*taṣawwafa*] will be corrupted; and whoever studied Sufism and didn't study Jurisprudence will become a heretic; and whoever combined both will be reach the Truth.[100]

IMAM SHAFI'I (150 - 205 AH.)

قال الإمام الشافعي رحمه الله تعالى: صحبت الصوفية فاستفدت منهم كلمتين قولهم : الوقت سيف إن لم تقطعه قطعك وقولهم : نفسك إن لم تشغلها بالحق شغلتك بالباطل

I accompanied the Sufis and received from them but three words: their statement that time is a sword: if you do not cut it, it cuts you; their statement that if you do not keep your ego busy with truth it will keep you busy with falsehood; their statement that deprivation is immunity.[101]

IMAM AHMAD BIN HANBAL (164 - 241 AH.)

كان الإمام أحمد رحمه الله تعالى(قبل مصاحبته للصوفية يقول لولده عبدالله رحمه الله تعالى : (يا ولدي عليك بالحديث وإياك ومجالسة هؤلاء الذين سموا أنفسهم صوفية فإنهم ربما كان أحدهم جاهلا بأحكام دينه فلما صحب أبا حمزة البغدادي الصوفي وعرف أحوال القوم أصبح يقول

[100] 'Alī al-Adawī , vol. 2, p 195.
[101] Ibn al-Qayyim in his *Madārij al-sālikīn* (3:128) and al-Ḥāfiẓ as-Suyūṭī in his *Tā'yid al-Ḥaqīqat al-'Alīyya,* (p. 15).

لولده: يا ولدي عليك بمجالسة هؤلاء القوم، فإنهم زادوا علينا بكثرة العلم والمراقبة والخشية
والزهد وعلو الهمة

O my son, you have to sit with the People of Sufism, because they are like a fountain of knowledge and they keep the Remembrance of Allah in their hearts. they are the ascetics and they have the most spiritual power.[102]

IMAM GHAZALI (450 - 505 AH.)

ثم إني لما فرغت من هذه العلوم أقبلت بهمتي على طريق الصوفية ، وعلمت أن طريقهم إنما يتم
بعلم وعمل، وكان حاصل ععلمهم قطع عقبات النفس والنزه عن أخلاقها المذمومة وصفاتها
الخبيثة حتى يتوصل بذلك إلى تخلية القلب من غير الله تعالى وتحليته بذكر الله

I knew verily that Sufis are the seekers in Allah's Way, and their conduct is the best conduct, and their way is the best way, and their manners are the most sanctified. They have cleaned their hearts from other than Allah and they have made them as pathways for rivers to run receiving knowledge of the Divine Presence.[103]

FAKHR AD-DIN AR-RAZI (544 - 606 AH)

والمتصوفة قوم يشتغلون بالفكر وتجرد النفس عن العلائق الجسمانية ويجتهدون أن لا يخلو سرهم
وبالهم عن ذكر الله تعالى في سائر تصرفاتهم وأعمالهم

...the way of Sufis for seeking Knowledge, is to disconnect themselves from this worldly life, and they keep themselves constantly busy ...with *dhikrullāh*, in all their actions and behaviors. [104]

[102] Shaykh Amīn al-Kurdī, *Tanwīr al-Qulūb* p. 405.
[103] Īmām Ghazālī, *al-Munqidh min aḍ-ḍallāl*, p. 131.
[104] Fakhr al-Dīn al-Rāzī, *'Itiqādāt Furāq al-Muslimīn*, p. 72, 73.

IMAM NAWAWI (620 - 676 AH.)

The specifications of the Way of the Sufis are ... to keep the Presence of Allah in your heart in public and in private; to follow the Sunnah of the Prophet ﷺ ... to be happy with what Allah gave you...[105]

IBN KHALDUN (733 - 808 AH.)

وأصله أن طريقة هؤلاء القوم لم تزل عند سلف الأمة وكبارها من الحصابة والتابعين ومن بعدهم طريقة الحق

The way of the Sufis is the way of the preceding Scholars between the Companions and Predecessors of those who followed good guidance...[106]

TAJUDDIN AS-SUBKI (727 - 771 AH.)

حياهم الله وبياهم وجمعنا في الجنة نحن وإياهم وقد تشعبت الأقوال فيهم تشعبا ناشئا عن الجهل بحقيقتهم لكثرة المتلبسين بها إلى أن قال وإنهم المعرضون عن الدنيا المشتغلون في أغلب الأوقات بالعبادة .. ثم تحدث عن تعاريف التصوف إلى أن قال: والحاصل أنهم أهل الله وخاصته الذين ترتجي الرحمة بذكرهم ويستنزل الغيث بدعائهم فرضي الله عنهم وعنا بهم

May Allah praise them [the Sufis] and greet them and may Allah cause us to be with them in Paradise. Too many things have been said about them and too many ignorant people have said things which are not related to them. And the truth is that those people left the world and were busy with worship. ...They are the People of Allah, whose

105 Imām Nawawī, *Maqāsid at-tawḥīd (Letters)*, p. 20.
106 Ibn Khaldūn, *Muqaddimat ibn al-Khaldūn*, p. 328.

supplications and prayer Allah accepts and by means of whom Allah supports human beings.[107]

JALALUDDIN AS-SUYUTI (849 - 911 AH.)

إن التصوف في نفسه علم شريف، وإن مداره على اتباع السنة وترك البدع

At-Taṣawwuf in itself is the best and most honorable knowledge. It explains how to follow the Sunnah of the Prophet ﷺ and to put aside innovation.[108]

IBN QAYYIM (691 - 751 AH.)

We can witness the greatness of the People of Sufism, in the eyes of the earliest generations of Muslims by what has been mentioned by Sufyān ath-Thawrī (d. 161 AH), one of the greatest imāms of the second century and one of the foremost legal scholars. He said, "If it had not been for Abū Hishām aṣ-Ṣūfī (d. 115) I would never have perceived the action of the subtlest forms of hypocrisy in the self... Among the best of people is the Sufi learned in jurisprudence.[109]

ʿABDULLAH IBN MUHAMMAD IBN ʿABDUL WAHHAB (1115 - 1201 AH.)

My father Muḥammad ibn ʿAbdul Wahhāb and I do not deny or criticize the science of Sufism, but on the contrary we support it, because it purifies the external and the internal of the hidden sins, which are related to the heart and to the outward form. Even though the individual

---

[107] Tāj al-Dīn as-Subkī, *Muʿīd an-Naʿm* p. 190, the chapter entitled *Taṣawwuf.*

[108] al-Ḥāfiẓ Jalāl al-Dīn as-Suyūṭī, *Tā'yid al-Ḥaqīqat al-ʿAlīyya,* p. 57.

[109] Ibn Qayyim al-Jawzīyyah, *Manāzil as-Sā'irīn.*

might externally be on the right way, internally he might be on the wrong way. Sufism is necessary to correct it.[110]

IBN 'ABIDIN (1198 - 1252 AH.)

فهم لا يستمعون إلا من الإله ولا يشتاقون إلا له إن ذكروه ناحوا وإن شكروه باحوا وإن وجدوه صاحوا وإن شهدوه استراحوا

The Seekers in this Sufi Way don't hear except from the Divine Presence and they don't love any but Him. If they remember Him they cry, and if they thank Him they are happy; ... May Allah bless them.[111]

MUHAMMAD 'ABDUH (1265 - 1323 AH.)

Taṣawwuf appeared in the first century of Islam and it received a tremendous honor. It purified the self and straightened the conduct and gave knowledge to people from the Wisdom and Secrets of the Divine Presence.[112]

RASHID RIDA (1282 -1354 AH.)

لقد انفرد الصوفية بركن عظيم من أركان الدين، لا يطاولهم فيه مطاول، وهو التهذيب علماً وتخلقاً وتحققاً، ثم لما دونت العلوم في الملة، كتب شيوخ هذه الطائفة في الأخلاق ومحاسبة النفس

Sufism was a unique pillar from the pillars of the religion. Its purpose was to purify the self and to take account of one's daily behavior and to raise the people to a high station of spirituality.[113]

---

[110] ibn 'Abdul Wahhāb, *ad-Diā'at mukathaffa ḍid ash-shaykh ibn 'Abdul Wahhāb*, p. 85.
[111] *Risā'il Ibn 'Abidīn*, p. 172 & 173.
[112] *Majallat al-Muslim*, 6th ed. 1378 H, p. 24.
[113] *Majallat al-Manār*, 1st year, p. 726.

MAULANA ABUL HASAN 'ALI AN-NADAWI (1331- 1420 AH)

إن هؤلاء الصوفية كانوا يبايعون الناس على التوحيد والإخلاص واتباع السنة والتوبة عن المعاصي والظلم والقسوة ويرغبونهم في التحلي بالأخلاق الحسنة والتخلي عن الرذائل مثل الكبر والحسد والبغضاء واللم وحب الجاه وتزكية النفس وإصلاحها ويعلمونهم ذكر الله والنصح لعباده والقناعة والإيثار وعلاوة على هذه البيعة التي كانت رمز الصلة العميقة الخاصة بين الشيخ ومريديه ، إنهم كانوا يعظون الناس دائما ويحاولون أن يلهبوا فيهم عاطفة الحب لله سبحانه والحنيني إلى رضاه ورغبة شديدة لإصلاح النفس وتغير الحال.

These Sufis were initiating people on Oneness and sincerity in following the Sunnah of the Prophet ﷺ and to repent from their sins and to be away from every disobedience of Allah the Exalted. Their guides were encouraging them to move in the way of perfect Love to Allah the Exalted.

...In Calcutta India, every day more than one thousand people were taking initiation into Sufism

...by the influence of these Sufi people, thousands and thousands and hundreds of thousands in India found their Lord and reached a state of Perfection through the Islamic religion.[114]

MAULANA ABUL 'ALA MAUDOODI (1321 - 1399 AH.)

أما التصوف فيبحث عما كان في قلبه من الإخلاص وصفاء النية وصدق الطاعة عند قيامه بهذه الأعمال

[114] *Muslims in India,* p. 140-146.

Taṣawwuf searched for the sincerity in the heart and the purity in the intention and the trustworthiness in obedience in an individual's actions.[115]

[115] *Mabadi' al-Islām,* p. 17.

SPIRITUALITY IN MODERN CIVILIZATION[116]

[116] Lecture presentation before HRH Prince Charles at Temenos Academy, Nov 7, 2006.

DEFINING MODERNITY

We have been asked to address the topic of "Spirituality in Modern Civilization." Such topics are typically chosen by professors who find such combinations of concepts catchy, flashy and even a little spicy. However, when I hear the term "modern civilization" bandied about, I often wonder what it really means. After all, did people in the past consider themselves backwards, out-of-date, ancient, or behind the times? Did they consider their time uncivilized, looking towards our era as one in which they would finally be "modern?" Was not the time of our Prophet ﷺ also a "modern" one for those who were blessed to live during it? I propose that "modernity" exists in every era, depending on the circumstances of the time, and thus can be applied equally to each of them as well.

By limiting our view of modernity to the present era, we assume that previous generations were inherently discontent with their way of life. Why should this be so? Consider the amenities of water and fire. In the past people needed to go far to procure wood for fire and water to drink. They did not have a tap to get water from. For them, modernity might have meant that they had access to water at a short distance instead of having to travel for miles. Those in the Stone Age, too, considered their time to be "modern" also, as they were living in caves and using utensils carved from stones – a vast improvement over living in the wilderness with no shelter and no utensils. At least they had chairs of stone to sit on, a pot in which to cook and animal skins to keep them warm.

So, it is not only the twenty-first century or twentieth century that is modern; previous centuries were also modern in their own context. And, in many of them, Islam played a remarkable role in achieving what was then considered "modern."

THE NEED FOR SPIRITUAL TREATMENT OF PSYCHOLOGICAL ILLNESSES

Today, "modern" psychology has recently concluded that despite recent impressive advances in technology, means of production and availability of knowledge, human beings are now more out of tune with their own selves and more susceptible to damaging conditions such as neuroses, depression and other psychoses. They are also afflicted by a host of societal illnesses that seem, in many ways, unique to the "modern" era. Thus, many Western psychologists and social scientists have come to realize the importance of what they are now calling the "spiritual" aspect of the human psyche.

In doing so, they have discovered that spiritual discipline is essential in rectifying the negativity and psychoses inherent in every human being. This has led to a new emphasis in the West on treatment by spiritual means, with a focus on meditation, contemplation, seclusion and various other metaphysical exercises that are designed to assist the individual struggling with the darker aspects of his or her inner-self. Huge movements have evolved in the West, all focused on the use of spiritual discipline to treat serious psychological illnesses.

Contemporary psychology has come to view each of these illnesses as a disorder of the self that, if left untreated, eventually come to dominate the personality of the individual.

However, even with this new awareness of the spiritual dimensions of mental illness and the development of novel ways of treating such disorders, we find that such diseases of the psyche continue to spread. Moreover, we are witnessing a growing deterioration of good conduct and ethical behavior throughout our "modern" societies. Wherever you turn, you find people increasingly overcome by anger, greed, cowardice, jealousy and the other 17 major vices. These evil traits lead to harmful actions, such as lying, cheating, stealing and even violence.

These negative character traits continue to spread because all the individual therapy, group therapy and expensive treatment programs amount to nothing in the face of a world filled with unbalanced egos that – due to constant over-indulgence in material pleasures - have grown out of proportion to people's true natures. The mental health professionals tasked with treating what must be seen as a spiritual epidemic are like one man trying to stop the flow of a mighty river.

Unbridled love of this worldly life, unbalanced by moral or ethical principles, leads to an excess of desire, jealousy and envy. Envy leads to anger, and anger - when it spirals out of control - leads to aggression, violence and tyrannical behavior. Eventually, this can lead to disobedience and outward manifestations of misbehavior which directly harm others. This is true whether the individual is a common person, an educated person or the leader of a nation. If ignored, such aspects of the individual can grow, and like a cancer, spread to other aspects of the psyche, eventually destroying the individual's positive characteristics and leading him or her further into destructive patterns of behavior.

This is observed today in every level of society, to such a degree that many societies are spending massive amounts of money and resources in order to come to grips with these personality disorders that are manifesting on a large scale in their communities, towns, provinces and ultimately throughout the nation.

When this sort of psychic breakdown occurs in a leader, these bad traits are further amplified by his power to assert control and impact the lives of those around him and under him. Such negative character traits in a leader thus have momentous impact. Exacerbated by the often intense circumstances of governmental affairs, the challenges of statecraft and the pressures of the political scene, these manifestation of these traits can lead to harmful acts.

THAT ELUSIVE TERM "SPIRITUALITY"

What, then, is this concept described by the word "spirituality?"

Spirituality is something that most people believe is beyond our grasp, something dubious in need of both verification and clarification. Everyone understands when you use the term "Islam," but when you say "spirituality," everyone becomes hesitant. People exclaim, "What is that? We never heard about spirituality!" They forget, or perhaps were never aware, that Allah ﷻ mentioned this concept in Sūrat al-Kahf, as I will explain in detail later.

Take the example of a room like this one. In it, you have ordinary white lights that provide illumination, but nothing more. If you look at a theater stage, you will see that they have many different colors of lights – red, blue, green and other hues. Together, these are able to create a colorful scene that evokes a mood. If you put these lights in motion, it becomes even more scintillating. If you add neon lights and lasers, you can create a magnificent light show.

Our entire religion is called Islam. But you can decorate your Islam with various aspects which the Prophet Muhammad ﷺ showed us in order that it becomes colorful, polished, decorated and even magnificent. The religion itself is carrying within it all sorts of different effects that give it beauty, splendor and magnificence.

Let us take an example from the Qur'ān. Speaking generally, Allah says of His servants:

وَإِذَا سَأَلَكَ عِبَادِي عَنِّي فَإِنِّي قَرِيبٌ

When My servants ask thee concerning Me, I am indeed close (to them) [117]

At a higher level are those servants who strive to improve their personality, whom Allah describes by their different attributes. These attributes are like the colored spotlights on a stage, each giving new and different effects:

يَا أَيُّهَا الَّذِينَ آمَنُوا اتَّقُوا اللَّهَ وَآمِنُوا بِرَسُولِهِ يُؤْتِكُمْ كِفْلَيْنِ مِن رَّحْمَتِهِ وَيَجْعَل لَّكُمْ نُورًا تَمْشُونَ بِهِ وَيَغْفِرْ لَكُمْ وَاللَّهُ غَفُورٌ رَّحِيمٌ

O ye who believe! Remain conscious of Allah, and believe in His Prophet, [and] He will grant you doubly of His grace, and will light for you a light wherein you shall walk, and will forgive you [your past sins]: for Allah is Oft-forgiving, Dispenser of grace. [118]

Then Allah goes on to describe an even higher level:

وَعِبَادُ الرَّحْمَنِ الَّذِينَ يَمْشُونَ عَلَى الْأَرْضِ هَوْنًا وَإِذَا خَاطَبَهُمُ الْجَاهِلُونَ قَالُوا سَلَامًا

And the servants of ((Allah)) Most Gracious are those who walk on the earth in humility, and when the ignorant address them, they say, "Peace!"; [119]

There are servants who when you look at them you say, "There is so much light on his face," or "That one is so generous, always helping the poor," or "That one has such perfect good conduct and manners." Allah describes Himself by means of different Names and Attributes. Similarly, His servants can be described by different characteristics. Islam is not like a plain

---

[117] Sūratu 'l-Baqarah [The Heifer], 2:186
[118] Sūratu'l-Ḥadīd [Iron], 57:28
[119] Sūratu 'l-Furqān [The Criterion], 25:63

bowl. Rather, it is like a decorated vase - one that, when you look at it, you cannot help saying, "Oh! That is very nice."

In Surat al-Kahf, Allah mentioned,

وَاصْبِرْ نَفْسَكَ مَعَ الَّذِينَ يَدْعُونَ رَبَّهُم بِالْغَدَاةِ وَالْعَشِيِّ يُرِيدُونَ وَجْهَهُ وَلَا تَعْدُ عَيْنَاكَ عَنْهُمْ تُرِيدُ زِينَةَ الْحَيَاةِ الدُّنْيَا وَلَا تُطِعْ مَنْ أَغْفَلْنَا قَلْبَهُ عَن ذِكْرِنَا وَاتَّبَعَ هَوَاهُ وَكَانَ أَمْرُهُ فُرُطًا

And keep thy soul content with those who call on their Lord morning and evening, seeking His Face; and let not thine eyes pass beyond them, seeking the pomp and glitter of this Life; nor obey any whose heart We have permitted to neglect the remembrance of Us, one who follows his own desires, whose case has gone beyond all bounds.[120]

What Allah is saying is: "O Muhammad! Keep patient with those who gave themselves up to Me, that are doing the work of *daʿwah* – outreach and education. In the day they perform this work in public and at night they are doing *daʿwah* by sitting behind your home, O Muhammad, and praising Me and worshipping Me, calling upon Me with all My Holy Beautiful Names and Attributes. So, O Muhammad, give them a glance, give them a boost and do not ignore them when you go out of your home on the way to Fajr prayers."

Those were workers during the day and during the night. Such people are needed in order to give more attention to Islam in its perfection. Thus, those who spend their time in seeking Allah's Face are mentioned with such high regard.

[120] Sūratu 'l-Kahf [The Cave], 18:28

TREATING THE ILLNESSES OF THE PSYCHE

Islam has always given great consideration to treating the disorders of the self, to the point that the Prophet of Islam, Sayyidina Muhammad ﷺ, indicated that self-purification is one of the most essential aspects of the faith:

أخوف ما أخاف عليكم الشرك الأصغر ، فسئل عنه؟ فقال:الرياء

> He said: What I fear most for my Community is the hidden polytheism." They asked about it and he said, "It is ostentation (*ar-rīyā*)."[121]

What is meant here is that the Prophet ﷺ did not fear for his community returning to idolatry or unbelief, but rather his greatest fear was that the hidden *shirk*, about which the Prophet ﷺ is reported to have said, "Association with Allah (*shirk*) is stealthier in this community than creeping ants." In this, we see that the Prophet ﷺ feared for his community not the outward polytheism of idol-worship, for he was informed by Allah that his community was protected from that forever.[122] What he feared was the secret polytheism, which is to do something for the sake of showing-off.[123]

---

[121] Al-Ḥākim in *al-Mustadrak* (authentic).

[122] The Prophet ﷺ said, "I do not fear that you will become polytheists after me, but I fear that, because of worldly interests, you will fight each others, and thus be destroyed like the peoples of old." Bukhārī and Muslim.

[123] The Prophet ﷺ could never associate anyone with Allah, for he is Allah's most perfect servant. Nonetheless he was told to say: *I am but a man like yourselves, but the inspiration has come to me that your Allah is One*... Sūratu 'l-Kahf [The Cave], 18: 110.

The Prophet ﷺ showed his simplicity and humility by saying, "I am a human being like you, but Allah is sending His revelation to me." Although the Prophet ﷺ remains always—then and now—in Allah's Presence, even in this unequaled privilege he is utterly humble and devoid of arrogance, considering himself "like you," where that expression included all human beings seeking the means of coming closer to people, in order to make them familiar and eventually open their hearts to the truth.

Returning from a military campaign against aggressors who sought to exterminate the community of believers, the Prophet ﷺ said to his Companions:

قدمتم خير مقدم، وقدمتم من الجهاد الأصغر إلى الجهاد الأكبر: مجاهدة العبد هواه

> We are now returning from the lesser Jihād to the greater Jihād, the Jihād against the self.[124]

By this, the Prophet ﷺ meant that, while they had struggled against enemy aggressors, they were still faced with the challenge of fighting the lower ways of the inner-self. First, one must cut down vanity and make the inner-self prostrate, for one who truly submits to his Lord can no longer submit to his self. Once that state is reached, only then is prayer purely for Allah.

In the time of the Prophet ﷺ, the lesser jihād was taking place without a name. People were learning how to wage it from the Prophet ﷺ's own righteous behavior. Today, it is becoming a name without any meaning. We find many who speak of spirituality, but in reality there is no one trying to achieve it in their lives. In the time of the Prophet ﷺ, it was a concept without a name and today it is a name without a reality.

The Sahaba were practicing that reality. If one delves into the religion, we find that the Prophet ﷺ divided religion into three fundamental categories: Islam, *Imān* and *Iḥsān*. The first part is what Sayyidina Jibrīl described when he came to the Prophet ﷺ in the form of a human being, dressed in clean white clothes and in front of all his Companions began to ask him about the religion.[125]

---

[124] Ghazālī, in the *Iḥyā'*. Al-ʿIrāqī said that Bayhaqī related it on the authority of Jābir and said: There is weakness in its chain of transmission. According to Nisā'ī in *al-Kunā* is a saying by Ibrāhīm ibn Ablah.

[125] The faith of Islam, consists of three levels, as described by the Prophet ﷺ in the famous Tradition of the Archangel Jibrīl, where ʿUmar ؓ related:

While we were sitting with Allah's Messenger ﷺ one day, all of a sudden a man came up to us. He wore exceedingly white clothes. His hair was jet-black. There

If *Imān* and *Iḥsān* are not important what need did the Prophet ﷺ mention them? He described Islam as five pillars. Everyone is familiar with these: The two professions of faith, prayer, fasting, charity and hajj. But he did not stop there. He also mentioned *Īmān,* faith, thus demonstrating that there is another aspect of religion - belief. He wanted the Companions to know that not only must they accept his prophethood, but also that of those who came before him. He wanted them to have *al-Imān bi 'l-ghayb,* belief in the unseen – to accept the concept of not seeing yet believing. That is something very difficult. Today, people say, "We cannot believe in something we do not see. Without scientific discovery we cannot believe." This is a lower level of *Imān.* Furthermore, he told them to believe in the angels, in the other holy books, in the Afterlife and in Destiny. All of these are unseen.

We see then that Islam, the first component of the religion, is external and empirical: *Shahada* is pronounced; *Ṣalāt* is performed;

---

was no sign of travel on his person. None of us knew him. He went to sit near the Prophet ﷺ, leaning his knees against the knees of the Prophet ﷺ and placing his hands on his thighs.

He said, "O Muhammad! tell me about Islam (the stage of Submission)." Allah's Messenger ﷺ said, "Islam is to bear witness that there is no Allah but Allah, and that Muhammad ﷺ is the Messenger of Allah; to perform the prayer; to pay the poor-tax; to fast during Ramadan; and to make the pilgrimage to [Allah's] House if you are able to go there." The man said, "You have spoken the truth."

We wondered at him; how could he be asking the Prophet ﷺ and confirming him at the same time?

Then he said, "Tell me about *Imān* (the stage of Belief)." The Prophet ﷺ said, "*Imān* is to believe in Allah, His angels, His books, His messengers, and the Last Day; and to believe in Destiny, both its good and its evil."

The man said, "You have spoken the truth. Now tell me about *Iḥsān* (the stage of Excellence of character)." The Prophet ﷺ replied, "Excellence is to worship Allah as if you see Him, for if you do not see Him, He certainly sees you."

..Then he left and time passed. Later he [the Prophet] said to me, "O ʿUmar, do you know who that was asking questions?" I said, "Allah and His Messenger know best." He said, "He was none other than Jibrīl. He came to you to teach you your religion." Narrated by Muslim.

ṣawm is experienced; Hajj is undertaken. Thus, the five pillars are physical concepts. *Imān*, however, is a non-physical concept that requires belief without seeing.

Consider this concept in light of our understanding of physics. Every atom consists of a mass, the nucleus, and electrons spinning around it, which are energy. Similarly, a person has a body and soul, mass and energy. You cannot see the soul, the energy, but can you see the body, the mass. So:

atom = mass + energy

person = body + soul

الدين = اسلام + أيمان

Religion = Islam (physical performance of worship) + *Imān* (the spiritual dimension of the religion that cannot be seen.)

Everything consists of these two elements as shown in the hadith of Sayyidina 'Umar. Therefore, if you are able to perform the five pillars of Islam and fulfill the six pillars of *Imān*, you attain perfection, *Iḥsān*. If you balance the equation of the body and spirit, (i.e. mind and soul), it means you achieve health which is perfection in the dimension of the body and in the dimension of the spirit.

That is: Islam + *Imān* = *Iḥsān*.

The Prophet ﷺ is giving us this equation: *Iḥsān* is to worship Allah as if you are seeing Him, and if you are not seeing Him, He is seeing you. You cannot see Allah ﷻ but you can see His manifest signs. This means that, if you are able to balance the daily prayers and obligations that Allah ordered you to do, together with the spiritual struggle against the self, you will be able to see His Signs. That is why Allah said in Holy Qur'ān:

سَنُرِيهِمْ آيَاتِنَا فِي الْآفَاقِ وَفِي أَنفُسِهِمْ حَتَّى يَتَبَيَّنَ لَهُمْ أَنَّهُ الْحَقُّ

Soon will We show them our Signs in the (furthest) regions (of the earth), and in their own souls, until it becomes manifest to them that this is the Truth. [126]

In his time the Prophet ﷺ did not explain the scientific signs to his Companions. He only explained the principles and discipline of Islam because, at that time (in what was their "modern" style of life), life revolved around agriculture and animal husbandry, medicines were herbal or Prophetic, and they lived in homes of mud or tents. Since that era was incapable of understanding what we see in ours, the Prophet ﷺ only mentioned these signs in general terms without explanation. He wanted the people of later times, who possess the capacity and knowledge, to recognize the greatness of Holy Qur'ān and hadith through their scientific discoveries.

That is why today we see *'ulamā* are finding many scientific discoveries in the Holy Qur'ān and hadith. Such discoveries are the reason some people in the West to convert to Islam. Allah seeks to guide people - through any means - and one of them is through their science and technology.

If someone cleanses himself by eliminating all his internal negativity and ruinous traits he will be able to reach a level of purity of heart wherein he becomes subtle in his very being and in direct receipt of heavenly support because of the spotless qualities he attains. This is mentioned in Qur'ān:

قَدْ أَفْلَحَ مَن زَكَّاهَا

Truly he succeeds that purifies it [127]

This is why Allah says you are not a believer until you love Allah more than you love anyone:

---

[126] Sūrah Fuṣṣilat [Explained in Detail], 41:53

[127] Sūratu 'sh-Shams [The Sun], 91:9.

قُلْ إِن كَانَ آبَاؤُكُمْ وَأَبْنَاؤُكُمْ وَإِخْوَانُكُمْ وَأَزْوَاجُكُمْ وَعَشِيرَتُكُمْ وَأَمْوَالٌ اقْتَرَفْتُمُوهَا وَتِجَارَةٌ تَخْشَوْنَ كَسَادَهَا وَمَسَاكِنُ تَرْضَوْنَهَا أَحَبَّ إِلَيْكُم مِّنَ اللّهِ وَرَسُولِهِ وَجِهَادٍ فِي سَبِيلِهِ فَتَرَبَّصُواْ حَتَّى يَأْتِيَ اللّهُ بِأَمْرِهِ وَاللّهُ لاَ يَهْدِي الْقَوْمَ الْفَاسِقِينَ

Say: If it be that your fathers, your sons, your brothers, your mates, or your kindred; the wealth that ye have gained; the commerce in which ye fear a decline: or the dwellings in which ye delight - are dearer to you than Allah, or His Messenger, or the striving in His cause;- then wait until Allah brings about His decision: and Allah guides not the rebellious.[128]

This is also mentioned in the hadith of the Prophet ﷺ:

حَدَّثَنَا مُحَمَّدُ بْنُ الْمُثَنَّى، وَابْنُ بَشَّارٍ قَالاَ حَدَّثَنَا مُحَمَّدُ بْنُ جَعْفَرٍ، حَدَّثَنَا شُعْبَةُ، قَالَ سَمِعْتُ قَتَادَةَ، يُحَدِّثُ عَنْ أَنَسِ بْنِ مَالِكٍ، قَالَ قَالَ رَسُولُ اللَّهِ صلى الله عليه وسلم " لاَ يُؤْمِنُ أَحَدُكُمْ حَتَّى أَكُونَ أَحَبَّ إِلَيْهِ مِنْ وَلَدِهِ وَوَالِدِهِ وَالنَّاسِ أَجْمَعِينَ "

None of you believes until he loves me more than his children, his parents and more than every human being[129].

He will be considered a lover of the Prophet ﷺ when he loves the Prophet ﷺ even more than his very self, as in the hadith of Sayyidina 'Umar ؓ:

---

[128] Sūratu 't-Tawbah [Repentance], 9:24
[129] Muslim, Aḥmad and Ibn Dāwūd.

وقد قال له عمر رضي الله عنه انك احب الي من كل شيء الا نفسي، قال لا يا عمر فلما قال عمر رضي الله عنه والله لانت احب الي من نفسي قال الآن يا عمر تمّ أيمانك.

'Umar ﷺ said, "You are more beloved to me than all things except myself." The Prophet ﷺ said, "No, O 'Umar." 'Umar then said, "By Allah you are more beloved to me than my own self," the Prophet ﷺ replied, "Now, O 'Umar you have completed your faith."

It was also related from Anas that the Prophet ﷺ of Allah said:

عَنْ انَسِ بْنِ مَالِكٍ، قَالَ قَالَ رَسُولُ اللَّهِ صلى الله عليه وسلم "كَمْ مِنْ اَشْعَثَ اَغْبَرَ ذِي طِمْرَيْنِ لاَ يُؤْبَهُ لَهُ لَوْ اَقْسَمَ عَلَى اللَّهِ لاَبَرَّهُ مِنْهُمُ الْبَرَاءُ بْنُ مَالِكٍ "

How many a ragged dusty person possessing only the tattered clothes on his body, given no importance by anyone, if he were to swear an oath by Allah, Allah would fulfill it.[130]

The Prophet ﷺ used the phrase *"ash'ath aghbar,"* a ragged, dusty person, meaning someone to whom no one gives attention nor believes could ever be favored by Allah's Grace, saying that he may be the one who reached the level of sincere love to Allah, love to His Prophet ﷺ and love to the Community.

When one achieves this level, one will love all human beings. Love emerges when one is able to eliminate the 17 major ruinous traits that bind the human self, as Islamic scholars of the science of self-purification and struggle (*tazkīyya wa mujāhidat an-nafs*) have derived from the Qur'ān and the Sunnah. By means of the 13 forms of jihād, entailing the struggle against the self, an individual

[130] *Sunan at-Tirmidhī*, 4227.

may be able to eliminate these ruinous character traits until he achieves a state of purity and perfected character.

Among the 17 primary aspects of the human psyche that need treatment in order for Allah's servant to attain a level of purified character are:

- Anger (*ghaḍab*)
- Love of the world (*ḥubb ad-dunyā*)
- Malice (*ḥiqd*)
- Jealousy (*hasad*)
- Pride (*kibr*)
- Vanity (*aẓama*)
- Showing off (*rīyāʿ*)
- Depression(*al-ghamm*)

and the 800 prohibited actions (*al-manhīyat*).

These characteristics, as has been shown today in psychology, are in fact each a disorder of the self, which if left untreated, eventually come to dominate the personality of the individual. When this happens the person will become subject to the dangerous aspects of these traits.

So, the importance of purification in the modern era as in the past, is to purify the self, to struggle against the ego through jihād of the self, through the 13 characteristics of jihād mentioned by Ibn Qayyim al-Jawzīyyah in his *Zād al-Maʿād,* and through this struggle attain the level of enlightenment.

At that time the servant of Allah will be in accordance with the Prophet ﷺ's saying:

عَنْ أَبِي هُرَيْرَةَ قَالَ قَالَ رَسُولُ اللَّهِ صَلَّى اللَّهُ عَلَيْهِ وَسَلَّمَ إِنَّ اللَّهَ قَالَ مَنْ عَادَى لِي وَلِيًّا فَقَدْ آذَنْتُهُ بِالْحَرْبِ وَمَا تَقَرَّبَ إِلَيَّ عَبْدِي بِشَيْءٍ أَحَبَّ إِلَيَّ مِمَّا افْتَرَضْتُ عَلَيْهِ وَمَا يَزَالُ عَبْدِي يَتَقَرَّبُ إِلَيَّ بِالنَّوَافِلِ حَتَّى أُحِبَّهُ فَإِذَا أَحْبَبْتُهُ كُنْتُ سَمْعَهُ الَّذِي يَسْمَعُ بِهِ

وَبَصَرَهُ الَّذِي يُبْصِرُ بِهِ وَيَدَهُ الَّتِي يَبْطِشُ بِهَا وَرِجْلَهُ الَّتِي يَمْشِي بِهَا وَإِنْ سَأَلَنِي لَأُعْطِيَنَّهُ وَلَئِنْ اسْتَعَاذَنِي لَأُعِيذَنَّهُ وَمَا تَرَدَّدْتُ عَنْ شَيْءٍ أَنَا فَاعِلُهُ تَرَدُّدِي عَنْ نَفْسِ الْمُؤْمِنِ يَكْرَهُ الْمَوْتَ وَأَنَا أَكْرَهُ مَسَاءَتَهُ

> My servant continues to approach Me through voluntary worship until I love him. And when I love him I will be the ears with which he hears, I will be the eyes with which he sees; I will be the tongue with which he speaks, I will be the hand with which he acts, and I will be the foot with which he walks…[131]

Not only must individuals go through these stages of self-struggle and purification, but the society, the nation and the Ummah must go through them as well. Spirituality is essential for such self-improvement.

One can draw an analogy between the disheveled person mentioned in the earlier hadith, *al-ashʿath aghbar*, and the Muslim Ummah today. That impoverished, yet sincere, person trying to reach the level of perfected character is similar to the Community today. If the Community will engage in the same struggle of self-purification, it will achieve the same level of development. At that time, the Community will be as in the early days of Islam, when its purity and integrity allowed it to develop, expand, improve and build - so much so that it became the center of the world, the fount of civilization and the beacon of knowledge and science.

Then, the Muslim Ummah achieved the ideal of the model city, *al-Madīnat al-fāḍilah,* described by al-Fāʿrābī. This was the implementation of the example of the Madīnat an-Nabī ﷺ on a global scale, establishing the principles of a model state where people lived in the highest level of discipline, responsibility and excellent moral conduct. In such a *Madīnat,* everyone keeps

---

[131] Bukhārī.

respect for the other. No one seeks to dominate the other. Rather, all seek the greater good of the community under inspired leadership. Women have their role, equal as partners, with the role of men, each working in their specializations to the highest level of perfection. People of differing races and beliefs are able live together in harmony, just as in the time of the Prophet ﷺ. In his city, Zoroastrians, Jews and Christians lived in peace and harmony with Muslims and in unity with them. From that unity comes community, and from community comes communion, relationship with the Divine.

STATIONS IN NATION-BUILDING

Before a society will change, the leaders of the community must change, for Allah said:

إِنَّ اللهَ لاَ يُغَيِّرُ مَا بِقَوْمٍ حَتَّى يُغَيِّرُوا مَا بِأَنْفُسِهِمْ

Verily never will Allah change the condition of a people until they change it themselves (with their own souls).[132]

When the leaders, they will spur a societal change in which the society will be able to engage in an internal social, psychological and cultural invigoration and self-examination. Through this, cross-fertilization will occur between different strains and currents in the nation opening the minds and hearts to new ideas and creative thinking while remaining within the broader guidelines of the Shariʿah. This process is not aimed at building castles in the air consisting of speculative theories and postulates, but to implement the knowledge learned in an integrated manner so that it becomes part and parcel of the individual, community, society, nation and finally the Ummah as a whole. This cannot be done purely by study, just as one cannot

[132] Sūratu 'r-Rʿad [Thunder], 13:11

become a doctor, a lawyer, an engineer or an Islamic scholar without training in the real and practical implementation of theory. Rather, this process requires an erudite and qualified teacher who will not only teach the precepts, doctrine and principles of the science of self-purification, but will serve as an exemplar, role model and most importantly provide practical training and guidance in the implementation of the teachings of his discipline.

We are beginning to see such leadership today in the Kingdom of Saudi Arabia, where King Abdullah has increasingly opened society to further debate and provide the opportunity for cross-cultural and cross-school dialogue. Rather than imposing a single monolithic view, King Abdullah has begun laying the groundwork for a long-awaited change in his nation's approach to social, political, ideological and religious thinking that bodes well for its further integration into the world. Such steps as opening up inter-sectarian dialogue between scholars of different schools, increasing freedom of the press and civil debate, instituting the democratic process at the municipal and regional levels of government, opening civic society to women's participation and increasing their participation in local government and social causes, reforming the jihādists through different remanding programs all serve to enhance societal reform in Saudi Arabia.

If a society is focused on fixing internal issues, then that society will be deeply engaged in self-improvement and societal transformation, rather than spending its time seeking to blame external causes for its problems. This allows the transformation of societal energies from externally destructive to internally constructive, and engages the members of society and its leadership in productive debate. By such means, much of the rhetoric which extremist members of the society use to draw the youth into their organizations can be impeded from the outset, for the youth will already be industriously engaged in self-improvement, societal improvement and constructive work whose benefits are rapid and whose progress can be observed.

In contrast, those regimes that turn away from spirituality become morally bankrupt and eventually fail. If we look at the history of the past centuries, we see those regimes that tried to find guidance from material and legalistic principles with no reference to spirituality ultimately found themselves lost. Eventually, they failed and collapsed. This stands in stark contrast to those regimes that have tried to cling, however loosely, to the spiritual, moral and ethical principles behind their founding.

Take, for example, the case of the Soviet Union. At one point, it was a great superpower. It acquired the power to transform itself from a poor nation to one of the greatest military and industrial nations in world. However, because it lacked any spiritual foundation it collapsed, and became as if it had never existed.

However, those regimes which are built on a moral and ethical foundation are successful, prosperous and able to move forward without the dislocating stresses often associated with technological progress.

When leaders emerge in society, either by election or by selection, we see they are successful when their decisions are guided by moral principles, not simply by material concerns. If the latter take precedence, the regime will descend to the lowest degree of morality - to the point it begins to impact the youth. This is particularly true when leaders are corrupt, engaged in underhanded activities such as cheating, lying and bribery. In this way, whole societies are corrupted.

The Prophet ﷺ said:

أَلَا وَإِنَّ فِي الْجَسَدِ مُضْغَةً إِذَا صَلَحَتْ صَلَحَ الْجَسَدُ كُلُّهُ وَإِذَا فَسَدَتْ فَسَدَ الْجَسَدُ كُلُّهُ أَلَا وَهِيَ الْقَلْبُ

> There is in the body a small flesh, if it is clean and pure the whole body will be clean and pure and if it is not, and it is contaminated, then the whole body will be contaminated, and that is the heart.[133]

In this pithy sentence, we find manifold meanings. The heart here can be taken to symbolize society's leadership, for if it is good, the whole society is good, and if it is tainted, the whole nation will be corrupt and degenerate. The Prophet ﷺ's description here is comprehensive, for it encompasses both the individual and society. Morality and good behavior are essential in society, as they empower relationships embodying the highest level of dignity and respect between the citizens and their leader.

In contrast, a society devoid of spirituality is like a body without a soul. It is dead. It is like an engine with no fuel; it becomes nothing but scrap metal. However, with the soul, the body keeps running well, like an engine given high-octane fuel. So, spirituality is for the soul as fuel is for the engine. Just as the body has its nourishment through food, the soul itself has its own source of nourishment, which is good manners. That is why spirituality is very important for leadership and society as a whole.

THE REFORMIST CALLS FOR "JIHAD"

Today the slogan used on lips of every "reformer" or social activist is "jihād." Everyone today speaks of jihād. And while we, as scholars and leaders, know that jihād is a *wājib*, and is even regarded as the sixth pillar by a minority of scholars, few take the care to examine this concept in detail. So, let us first determine the definition of jihād.

One can find countless interpretations of this term which differ from its true spirit and the meaning that Allah intended it in the Holy Qur'ān and in the narrations of the Prophet ﷺ. On the

---

[133] Saḥīḥ Muslim, #4178.

contrary, people use the term Jihād in this time in a way that suits their own whims without realizing the damage that they are causing Islam and Muslims.

What is meant by Jihād? The concept of "holy war" does not occur in the term Jihād, which in Arabic would be *al-ḥarb al-muqaddasah,* in fact this concept cannot be found anywhere throughout the entire Qur'ān. Jihād in the classical sense does not simply mean war. In fact Jihād is a comprehensive term which traditionally has been defined as composed of fourteen different aspects, only one of which involves warfare.

Jihād in its meaning is 'to struggle' as a general description. Jihād derives from the word *juhd,* which means *at-ta'b,* fatigue. The meaning of *Jihād fī sabīlillāh,* struggle in the Way of Allah, is striving to excess in fatiguing the self, to exhaust the self in seeking the Divine Presence and in bringing up Allah's Word, all of which He made the Way to Paradise.

For that reason Allah said:

جَاهِدُوا فِي اللَّهِ حَقَّ جِهَادِهِ

And strive hard (jāhidū) in (the way of) Allah, (such) a striving a is due to Him;[134]

It is essential to understand that under the term jāhidū come many different categories of Jihād, each with its specific context. The common understanding of Jihād to mean only war is refuted by this tradition of the Prophet ﷺ:

---

[134] Sūratu 'l-Ḥajj [The Pilgrimage], 22:78

حدثنا عبد الرحمن بن مهدي عن سفيان عن علقمة بن مرثد عن طارق بن شهاب أن رجلا سأل رسول الله صلى الله عليه وسلم وقد وضع رجله في الغرز أي الجهاد أفضل قال كلمة حق عند سلطان جائر

> A man asked the Prophet ﷺ "Which Jihād is best?" The Prophet ﷺ said, "The most excellent Jihād is to say the word of truth in front of a tyrant."[135]

The fact that the Prophet ﷺ mentioned this Jihād as "most excellent" means that there are many different forms of Jihād.

Ibn Qayyim's Fourteen Categories of Jihad

Islamic scholars, from the time of the Prophet ﷺ until today, have categorized Jihād into fourteen distinct categories. Jihād is not simply the waging of war, as most people today understand. War in fact, or combative Jihād, according to many scholars, is only one of fourteen different categories of Jihād.

In his book *Zād al-Maʿād,* Ibn Qayyim al-Jawzīyyah divided Jihād into fourteen distinct categories:

Jihad Against the Hypocrites

1.1. By heart

1.2. By tongue

1.3. By wealth

1.4. By person.

Jihad Against the Unbelievers

1.5. By heart

[135] *Musnad* of Aḥmad. Similar aḤadīth are narrated in Abū Dāwūd and Tirmidhī.

1.6. By tongue

1.7. By wealth

1.8. By person.

JIHAD AGAINST THE DEVIL

1.9. Fighting him defensively against everything of false desires and slanderous doubts in faith that he throws towards the servant.

1.10. Fighting him defensively from everything he throws towards the servant of corrupt passion and desire.

JIHAD OF THE SELF (*JIHAD AN-NAFS*)

1.11. That he strives to learn guidance and the religion of truth which is there is no felicity or happiness in life or in the hereafter except by it. And when he neglects it, his knowledge is wretched in both words.

1.12. That he strives to act upon it after he has learned it. For the abstract quality of knowledge without action, even if he commits no wrong, is without benefit.

1.13. That he strives to call to Allah and to teach it to someone who does not know it. Otherwise he will be among those who conceal what Allah had revealed of guidance and clarity. His knowledge doesn't benefit him or saves him from Allah's penalty.

1.14. That he strives with patience in seeking to call to Allah. When the creation harms him he bears it all for the sake of Allah.[136]

[136] Ibn Qayyim al-Jawzīyyah, *Zād al-Mʿad.*

IBN RUSHD'S FOUR DIVISIONS OF JIHAD

Ibn Rushd, on the other hand, in his *Muqaddimah,* divides Jihād into four kinds:

1. Jihād of the heart
2. Jihād of the tongue
3. Jihād of the hand
4. Jihād of the sword.[137]

JIHAD OF THE HEART – THE STRUGGLE AGAINST THE SELF

The Jihād of the heart is the struggle of the individual with his or her own desires, whims, erroneous ideas and false understandings. This includes the struggle to purify the heart, to rectify one's actions and to observe the rights and responsibilities of all other human beings.

JIHAD OF THE TONGUE – EDUCATION AND COUNSEL

He defines Jihād of the tongue as:

> To commend good conduct and forbid the wrong, like the type of Jihād Allah ordered us to fulfill against the hypocrites in His Words, *"O Prophet ﷺ! Strive hard against the unbelievers and the hypocrites"*[138].

This is the Jihād the Prophet ﷺ waged in struggling to teach his people. It means to speak about one's cause and one's religion. This is known as the Jihād of Education and Counsel.

Allah first revealed:

اقْرَأْ بِاسْمِ رَبِّكَ

---

[137] *Muqaddimah,* Ibn Rushd (known in the Western world as Averroes), p. 259.

[138] Sūratu 't-Tawbah [Repentance], 9:73

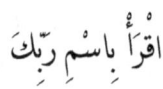

Read in the name of Thy Lord![139]

The first aspect of Jihād of Education is through reading. Reading originates with the tongue.

يَا أَيُّهَا النَّبِيُّ جَاهِدِ الْكُفَّارَ وَالْمُنَافِقِينَ وَاغْلُظْ عَلَيْهِمْ

O Prophet! strive hard [jāhid] against the unbelievers and the Hypocrites, and be firm against them.[140]

JIHAD OF THE HAND – DEVELOPMENT OF CIVIL SOCIETY AND MATERIAL PROGRESS

Jihād of the hand includes the struggle to build the nation through material development and progress, including building up civil society, acquiring and improving every aspect of technology and societal progress in general. This form of Jihād includes scientific discovery, development of medicine, clinics and hospitals, communication, transportation, and all necessary underlying infrastructure for societal progress and advancement, including educational institutions. Building also means to open opportunities to the poor through economic programs and self empowerment.

Another aspect of Jihād by Hand is through writing, for Allah said:

الَّذِي عَلَّمَ بِالْقَلَمِ عَلَّمَ الْإِنسَانَ مَا لَمْ يَعْلَمْ

He taught by means of the pen, taught mankind what he did not know.[141]

The meaning writing includes the use of computers and all other forms of publication.

---

[139] Sūratu 'l-ʿAlaq [The Clot], 96:1

[140] Sūratu 't-Tawbah [Repentance], 9:73

[141] Sūratu 'l-ʿAlaq [The Clot], 96:4,5

JIHAD OF THE SWORD – COMBATIVE WAR

Finally Jihād of the hand includes struggle by the sword (*Jihādun bis-sayf*), as when one fights the aggressor who attacks you in combative war.

REFINEMENT OF *JIHAD AN-NAFS* INTO AN ISLAMIC SCIENCE

Given the above definition of Jihād, we see that of its fourteen aspects, only one involves raising the sword. The remaining thirteen all have to do with either struggle of an individual with his inner state, or the struggle of society as a whole in seeking reform and improvement.

As such, major aspects of Jihād have been generally classified as Jihād an-Nafs, the mortal struggle against the self, and it it this broad topic we will address today as we look at the need of spirituality in creating a society that is capable of not simply existing but in striving to reach a state of perfection, *Iḥsān*.

Devoted and sincere scholars of spirituality performed the great service of calling the Ummah to remembrance of its proper heritage as framed by the Qur'ān and set out in the Prophet's Sunnah. These individuals, in time, came to be known by the name of *ṣafā*, a word derived from the Arabic *ṣafāʿa* which means "to purify," because of the assiduousness with which they applied themselves to holding firmly to the Sunnah and employing it to purify their character from all defects in behavior and morality.

Following the tradition of the Companions of the Prophet ﷺ who used to frequent his company named Āhl aṣ-Ṣuffa ("the People of the Bench"), the practitioners of this regimen lived a communal life. Their dwelling-places were the mosque-schools (*zawāya*), border forts (*ribāṭ*), and guest-houses (*khāniqah*) where they gathered together on specific occasions dedicated to the traditional festivals of the Islamic calendar (*ʿid*), the fast of Ramadan and other occasions of note. They also gathered on a regular basis in associations for the conveying of knowledge (*suḥba*), assemblies to invoke the names of Allah and recite the *adhkār* (plural of dhikr, "remembrance") inherited from the Prophetic Tradition, and circles of study in Islamic law. Yet another reason for their gathering was to hear inspired preaching and moral exhortations (*wiʿaz*).

THE SCHOOLS OF PURIFICATION *(TAZKIYA)*

We know for example, that in the first century after the Hijra, renunciation of the world (*zuhd*) grew as a reaction against worldliness in the society. Derived in principle from the order of Allah to His Righteous Prophet ﷺ to purify people [Qur'ān 2:129, 2:151, 3:164, 9:103, 62:2], the practitioners of this way clove firmly to the Prophetic way of life as it was reflected in the lives of his Companions and their Successors, in the ways they employed to purify their hearts and character from bad manners and to inculcate in their own selves and in those around them the manners and upright moral stature of the Best of Mankind, the Prophet Muhammad ﷺ.

Through slow evolution, this regimen ended up as a school of practical thought and moral action endowed with its own structure of rule and principle. This became the basis used by scholars of the spiritual discipline to direct people on the Right Path. As a result, the world soon witnessed the development of a variety of schools of purification of the ego (*tazkīyat an-nafs*). Such thought, as it spread everywhere, served as a dynamic force behind the growth and fabric of Islamic education. This tremendous advance occurred from the first century after the Hijra to the seventh, in parallel with the following developments:

- Development of the bases of *fiqh* (Law and Jurisprudence), through the Imāms;
- Development of the bases of *ʿaqidah* (System of Belief) through al-Ashʿari and others;

- Development of the science of hadith (Sayings of the Prophet ﷺ), resulting in the six authentic collections and innumerable others;
- Development of the arts of *nahu* and *balāgha* (Speaking and Writing Arabic).

Ṭarīqat or "path" is a term derived from the hadith of the Prophet ﷺ ordering his followers to follow his *sunnah* and the *sunnah* of his successors. The meaning of *sunnah* is "path," "way," which is also the meaning of *ṭarīqat* referred to in the Qur'ānic verse:

وَأَلَّوِ اسْتَقَامُوا عَلَى الطَّرِيقَةِ لَأَسْقَيْنَاهُم مَّاءً غَدَقًا

Had they kept straight on the path (ṭarīqat), We would have made them drink of a most limpid water."[142]

Ṭarīqat thus came to be a term applied to groups of individuals belonging to the school of thought pursued by a particular scholar or "shaykh," as such a person was often called.

Though these shaykhs applied different methods in training their followers, the core of each one's program was identical. The situation was not unlike what we find in faculties of medicine and law today. The approach in different faculties may be different, but the body of law, the state of art in medicine remains essentially the same everywhere. When students graduate from these faculties, each student bears the stamp of its character. Yet, none are considered less a lawyer or doctor because their respective affiliations differ.

In a similar way, the student product of a particular shaykh will bear the stamp of that shaykh's teaching and character. Consequently, the names given to various schools of Sufi thought differ according to the names and the perspectives of their founders. This variation manifests itself in a more concrete fashion, in the different supererogatory devotions, known as

[142] Sūratu'l-Jinn, 72:16

awrād, aḥzāb or *adhkār*, used as the practical methodology of spiritual formation. Such differences, however, have nothing to do with the religious principle. In basic principle, the schools of spiritual purification are essentially the same.

IDENTIFYING THE RUINOUS TRAITS

The regimen under which individuals undertook the path to Allah, was a finely-honed itinerary which charted the course of inward and outward progress in religious faith and practice (*dīn*). Its first step is to set forth in greater jihād, by fighting the seventeen enormities of the self which we will enumerate here in brief.

ANGER (*AL-GHADAB*)

وَالْكَاظِمِينَ الْغَيْظَ وَالْعَافِينَ عَنِ النَّاسِ وَاللَّهُ يُحِبُّ الْمُحْسِنِينَ

Those who control their wrath and are forgiving toward mankind; Allah loveth the good.[143]

A man said to Prophet Muhammad ﷺ, "Advise me." He replied, "Do not become angry."[144]

Anger is the worst of all seventeen of the ruinous traits. It may easily be said that anger is the source from which the others flow. That is why, in the path of spiritual development the levels of attainment are indicated by the reaction of testing with anger.

In the state of anger, one loses the ability to listen to reason, follow good judgment or accept advice. That is why the Prophet Muhammad ﷺ said to his dear companion Abū Bakr aṣ-Ṣiddīq ؓ, "Anger is a form of unbelief."

---

[143] Sūrat Āli ʿImrān [The Family of ʿImrān], 3:134.
[144] Bukhārī.

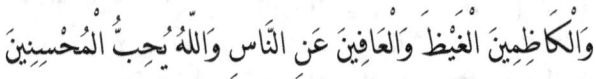

LOVE OF THIS WORLD (*HUBBU 'D-DUNYA*)

Jesus Christ ﷺ said:

The love of this world is the root of every sin.[145]

Those who are in love with this world find it is the cause of troubles and disasters. A poet once wrote, "This world is a carcass, a rotten piece of flesh thrown in the street. Those who pursue it are scavenging dogs." Those who love this world and spend their time seeking more of it, are like scavengers running to devour a carcass. This is the view of a sincere person, who is in full pleasure with his Lord's service and happy with his devotions. For such a person, to glorify and worship Allah sincerely, to give charity and to build a life in the hereafter is preferable. He prefers to spend time remembering Allah and reminding others of Allah, than to be acquiring a portion, however small, of this world's glittering life. In spiritual discipline, holding on to anything that is more than you can eat today—even the sustenance that you keep for tomorrow—is considered evidence of love for this world. Therefore it is better to offer it in the Way of Allah. If you possess more than today's sustenance, such excess is permissible if you give some of it in Allah's Way.

Many illustrious companions of the Prophet ﷺ were quite wealthy, including Sayyidina Abū Bakr ؓ and Sayyidina '`Uthman ؓ. Allah gave them wealth because they did not waste it; they knew the value of wealth and preserved it. Their example was one of discipline. Allah grants wealth to His pious sincere servants because they employ it in useful and productive ways.

To protect yourself from the love of this world, do not look at what others have; it is not your concern. Look at yourself and what you have. You are going to answer to Allah for that, not for others.

---

[145] Īmām Aḥmad.

MALICE (*AL-HIQD*)

ولا تباغضوا

The Messenger of Allah ﷺ said:

> Do not have malice for one another.[146]

And the cure for this negative trait, he related in another Tradition:

> Whoever looks at his brother with love, no malice will exist in his heart.[147]

A community following the Way of Allah—the way of the Prophet Muhammad ﷺ, the Companions and the righteous—never develops destructive intentions, because in such an ideal community, everyone seeks the Straight Path. However, when someone yields to their lower self and lusts after what someone else has, they develop hatred and the intention of harming. Thus malice is something that is cultivated, as opposed to mere feelings of dislike that arise involuntarily at times.

Allah commanded Moses ﷺ to speak a gentle word to Pharaoh. Allah sent Moses ﷺ to show Pharaoh that he was wrong, yet, when Pharaoh rejected the Truth, Moses ﷺ did not raise the Children of Israel against him.

Through these events, Moses ﷺ taught us that we must not harm out of hatred—even hatred for an aggressor. Moses ﷺ challenged Pharaoh by means of knowledge and faith.

---

[146] Ibn Mājah and *Musnad* Aḥmad.

[147] Related by Ibn ʿAbbās.

JEALOUSY (*AL-HASAD*)

حديث أبي هريرة رضي الله عنه قال: قال رسول الله صلى الله عليه وسلم : لا تحاسدوا, ولا تباغضوا, ولا تجسسوا, ولا تحسسوا, ولا تناجشوا, وكونوا عباد الله إخوانا

The Prophet ﷺ said:

Do not envy one another, do not hate each other and do not slander one another. Be servants of Allah, brethren altogether.[148]

Aspiring to have the same good another possesses is envy, while desiring to see it removed from him is jealousy. Because jealousy is the trunk of a great tree among the negative characteristics, human beings need Allah to protect them from it.

An example of this is the cause of the first murder when Cain killed Abel as related in the Holy Qur'ān:

وَاتْلُ عَلَيْهِمْ نَبَأَ ابْنَيْ آدَمَ بِالْحَقِّ إِذْ قَرَّبَا قُرْبَانًا فَتُقُبِّلَ مِن أَحَدِهِمَا وَلَمْ يُتَقَبَّلْ مِنَ الآخَرِ

Recite to them the truth of the story of the two sons of Adam ﷺ. Behold! they each presented a sacrifice (to Allah): It was accepted from one, but not from the other.[149]

The Qur'ān relates:

[148] Bukhārī, Muslim, Ibn Mājah and *Musnad* Aḥmad, with additional wording, "and it is not permitted for a Muslim to cut off his brother over three days..."
[149] Sūratu 'l-Mā'idah [The Spread Table], 5:27.

قَالَ لَأَقْتُلَنَّكَ قَالَ إِنَّمَا يَتَقَبَّلُ اللّهُ مِنَ الْمُتَّقِينَ لَئِن بَسَطتَ إِلَيَّ يَدَكَ لِتَقْتُلَنِي مَا
أَنَاْ بِبَاسِطٍ يَدِيَ إِلَيْكَ لَأَقْتُلَكَ إِنِّي أَخَافُ اللّهَ رَبَّ الْعَالَمِينَ

Said the latter [Cain]: "Be sure I will slay you."

"Surely," said the former [Abel], "(Allah) does accept of the sacrifice of those who are righteous.

If you do stretch your hand against me, to slay me, it is not for me to stretch my hand against you to slay you: for I do fear Allah, the Cherisher of the worlds."[150]

Beyond physical violence, the worst way to destroy humanity is through black magic.

Practitioners of this dark art even tried to perform black magic on Prophet Muhammad ﷺ This was the cause for the revelation of the Chapter of the Daybreak, for although the Prophet ﷺ was divinely protected, Allah wanted us to learn about this dark practice, to be aware of it, to be protected from it and to guard against it for black magic is one of the darkest forms of mischief. Such mischief proceeds from jealousy, the jealousy one person harbors for another.

The Prophet ﷺ said:

الحسد يأكل الحسنات كما تأكل النار الحطب؛

Jealousy consumes good deeds just as fire consumes wood.[151]

---

[150] Sūratu 'l-Mā'idah [The Spread Table], 5:28.

[151] Abū Dāwūd, Ibn Mājah with additional wording "and charity extinguishes sins like water extinguishes flame; prayer is the light of a believer and fasting his protection from the Fire.

According to the pious scholars of the Ummah, the way to eliminate jealousy is to observe the voluntary Prayers of the Night Vigil made before the morning prayer (*Ṣalāt* al-Fajr).

VANITY (*AL-'UJB*)

إِنَّهُ لَا يُحِبُّ الْمُسْتَكْبِرِينَ

He [Allah] loves not the proud.[152]

In a Qudsī hadith Allah says:

قال الله تعالى في حديث قدسي:" الكبر ردائي, و العظمة ازاري, فمن نازعني في واحد منهما, رميته في جهنم و لا ابالي

Pride is My cloak and Greatness is My covering. Whoever competes with Me regarding them, I shall cast them into the Hellfire, and it will not concern Me.[153]

Vanity is a dangerous attribute. Today, children are constantly taught, "Be proud of yourself." Someone who is proud sees himself or herself as the strongest, the prettiest, the smartest, the fastest, the best. They think they can achieve what no one else can. This teaching instills unbridled independence, and encourages the belief that one knows better than everyone else. It also prompts them to reject advice, as they are told that their own thinking is sufficient and superior. This in turn leads to arrogance about which Allah said:

فَلَبِئْسَ مَثْوَى الْمُتَكَبِّرِينَ

Evil indeed shall be the abode of all given to arrogance.[154]

---

[152] Sūratu 'n-Nahl [The Bee], 16:23.
[153] Abū Dāwūd.
[154] Sūratu 'n-Nahl [The Bee], 16:29.

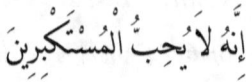

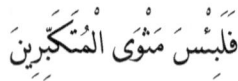

In the time of the Prophet ﷺ, a group of people known as the People of the Bench, *Ahl as-Suffah,* used to sit morning and evening behind the house of Prophet ﷺ reciting Qur'ān, remembering Allah and praising the Prophet ﷺ. ʿAbd Allah ibn Masʿud related:

> A group from among the Quraysh passed by the Messenger of Allah ﷺ while Ṣuhayb, Bilāl, ʿAmmār, Khabāb ؓ and other poor Muslims were with him. They said to the Prophet ﷺ, "O Messenger of Allah ﷺ, have you chosen this class of people from among your entire followers for your closest ones? …Get rid of them and perhaps if you do that we may follow you.

It is then that Allah revealed:

وَلَا تَطْرُدِ الَّذِينَ يَدْعُونَ رَبَّهُم بِالْغَدَاةِ وَالْعَشِيِّ يُرِيدُونَ وَجْهَهُ

Send not away (O Muhammad), those who call on their Lord morning and evening, seeking His face.[155]

Arrogance is to regard oneself higher than others. Allah says, "Come to Me, My servant, with humility. Do not be full of arrogance (*mutakabbir*). I am the One Who gives titles."

Honor, respect and dignity are for believers, but supremacy and superiority are only for Allah. No one else may be al-Mutakabbir, The Imperious.

The Prophet Muhammad ﷺ went on the Night Journey and Ascension into the Presence of Allah, closer than any human being has ever reached in the Divine Presence. When he returned, he never boasted or tried to exalt himself; he only said, "O my Lord, I am Your servant (*ʿabd-Allāh*)!" He was happy to be known as Servant.

---

[155] Sūratu 'l-Anʿam [Cattle], 6:52-53.

سُبْحَانَ الَّذِي أَسْرَى بِعَبْدِهِ

Praise be to Allah who took His servant to His Presence.[156]

The Prophet ﷺ said, "The best moment in all my life, from beginning to end, is when Allah called me Servant!" So we find in this superb example of humility that the Prophet ﷺ is happiest to be a slave of Allah.

Contrast this exemplary manner with Satan's, who replied to Allah when Allah ordered him to bow before Adam ﷺ:

قَالَ أَنَاْ خَيْرٌ مِّنْهُ خَلَقْتَنِي مِن نَّارٍ وَخَلَقْتَهُ مِن طِينٍ

I am better than Adam! You created me from fire and Your created him from mud.[157]

We must know our level as servants. To regard yourself as great is an indication that Satan is entering your veins.

The cure for arrogance is in hunger. When you are hungry, you not only weaken, you lose your arrogance. If you are facing starvation, you eat anything you find. You quickly become humble. For that reason the companions of the Prophet ﷺ came to him and showed him their bellies, tied on them was a stone. The Prophet ﷺ, always the foremost in piety, revealed his stomach and they saw not one stone, but two.

OSTENTATION (*AL-RIYA*)

فَوَيْلٌ لِّلْمُصَلِّينَ الَّذِينَ هُمْ عَن صَلَاتِهِمْ سَاهُونَ الَّذِينَ هُمْ يُرَاؤُونَ

---

156 Sūratu 'l-Isrā [The Night Journey], 17:1.

157 See Sūratu 'l-'Arāf [The Heights], 7, 12 and Sūrah Ṣād, 38:76.

Ah, woe unto worshippers who are heedless of their prayer; those who want but to be seen of men, But refuse even neighbourly needs.[158]

Prophet Muhammad ﷺ said:

Allah does not accept an action if there is any quantity of show in it.[159]

In the time of the Prophet ﷺ, a certain Companion liked to help people, but he also liked everyone to know that he did such good deeds. Concerning this, Allah revealed the last verse of the Chapter of the Cave:

قُلْ إِنَّمَا أَنَا بَشَرٌ مِّثْلُكُمْ يُوحَى إِلَيَّ أَنَّمَا إِلَهُكُمْ إِلَهٌ وَاحِدٌ فَمَن كَانَ يَرْجُو لِقَاء رَبِّهِ فَلْيَعْمَلْ عَمَلًا صَالِحًا وَلَا يُشْرِكْ بِعِبَادَةِ رَبِّهِ أَحَدًا

Say: I am only a mortal like you. My Lord inspires in me that your Allah is only One Allah. And whoever hopes for the meeting with his Lord, let him do righteous work, and make none sharer of the worship due unto his Lord.[160]

Al-Ḥāfiẓ Jalāl al-Dīn as-Suyūṭī interpreted this verse in this manner:

Allah is saying, "If you are requesting to come to Me, to be in My Paradise on Judgment Day, you must do a good work, but that good work must not be accompanied by ostentation. Do not attribute that work to yourself, but to Me, as something which I granted to you personally."

---

[158] Sūratu 'l-Ma'ūn [The Orphan], 107:4-7.

[159] Īmām Ghazālī, *Iḥyā 'Ulūm ud-Dīn* (*Revival of the Religious Sciences*).

[160] Sūratu 'l-Kahf [The Cave], 18:111.

The reason for revelation of this verse was that one of the Companions was in the habit of doing good things and afterwards saying to the Prophet ﷺ, "I did this! I did that!" He sought recognition. Then Allah revealed this verse.[161] By doing so, Allah is saying, "O Muhammad! Tell him that if he wants to do something good, let him do it, but make it purely for Allah, not for recognition for himself. It must be purely for Me."

DEPRESSION (*AL-GHAMM*)

فَرَجَعْنَاكَ إِلَى أُمِّكَ كَيْ تَقَرَّ عَيْنُهَا وَلَا تَحْزَنَ

So We brought thee, (O Moses), back to thy mother, that her eye might be cooled and she should not grieve.[162]

A Prophetic Tradition states:

> Verily Allah, The Glorious and Majestic, by His wisdom and exaltedness created ease and comfort in contentment and certainty; and He created depression and fear in doubt and discontent.

Worrying is external. For the one in whom depression thrives, this negative characteristic penetrates deep into the recesses of the physical body, into the veins and heart. Such a person feels depression in every part of the body and prefers to be alone rather than see anyone.

A depressed person wishes that time would again fly, but, on the contrary, minutes seem like hours, hours like days and days like weeks. Usually, people who lack useful outlets for their energies and feel unfulfilled are subject to these feelings. People who suffer from depression tend to sleep all day and stay awake at night, which allows them to avoid others. At night they engage in frivolous activities that they find entertaining, such as watching

---

[161] Al-Ḥākim in *al-Mustadrak.*

[162] Sūrah ṬāḤā, 20:40.

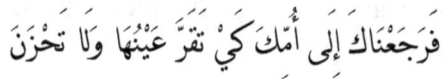

television, playing video games or some other pastime that gives them pleasure.

Depression can only be cured by finding a useful outlet for one's energy, directing it to good works, thereby lifting the cloud of darkness which begin to cover the one who has forgotten to praise Allah and remember Him. The first step in eliminating depression is to find pious sincere believers with whom one can spend time and seek comfort in observing their good character.

THE EIGHT HUNDRED FORBIDDEN ACTS (*AL-MANHIYAT*)

الَّذِينَ يَجْتَنِبُونَ كَبَائِرَ الْإِثْمِ وَالْفَوَاحِشَ إِلَّا اللَّمَمَ إِنَّ رَبَّكَ وَاسِعُ الْمَغْفِرَةِ

Those who avoid great sins and shameful deeds, only (falling into) small faults, - verily thy Lord is ample in forgiveness.[163]

There are 500 acts that the Prophet ﷺ ordered us to do (*mā'murāt*) and 800 acts that the Prophet ﷺ forbade us (*manhīyāt*) from doing.

The Prophet ﷺ said:

> To leave an atom's weight of Allah's prohibitions, is more lovely to Allah than the worshipping of all sentient beings.

To leave one forbidden act for the sake of Allah, is equivalent to performing all 500 of the ordered actions because to leave one forbidden act is extremely difficult for the ego.

A great spiritual teacher, al-Qushayri, noted that, of the 800 forbidden acts mentioned in the Holy Qur'ān, 477 are grave ones (*min al-kabā'ir*). He mentioned further that if a person can eliminate the sixteen reprehensible characteristics that we have explained in the preceding sections, it becomes easy to avoid

---

[163] Sūratu 'n-Najm [The Star], 53:32.

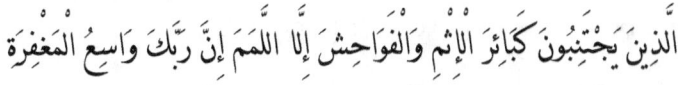

indulging in the the remaining forbidden acts. Thus the 800 forbidden acts are considered one among the seventeen ruinous traits. We intend to describe these in further detail in another volume in the future.

As step three of the next section, in seeking purified character, the servant must address this ruinous trait with the treatment of self-accounting, *muḥāsabah*. This method requires the servant to keep a journal, and note down every bad character trait that he observes in himself. These are traits that only he possesses, for no two individuals are the same. When that journal if finally completed, it will detail a number of the 800 forbidden acts that individual possesses in his or her personality.

THE TEN STEPS OF SPIRITUAL DEVELOPMENT

There are ten steps which make up the discipline of turning away from the seventeen ruinous character traits and setting forth on the path of self-discipline and spiritual attainment. They are:

Standing Up for Truth (*al-Istiqāmah*)
Repenting (*at-Tawbah)*
Auditing (*al-Muḥāsabah*)
Turning Humbly to Your Lord in Surrender (*al-Inābah*)
Contemplating Deeply (*at-Taffakur*)
Remembering Your Subconscious (*at-Tadhakkur*)
Holding Fast (*al-ʿItisām*)
Running to Allah (*al-Firāru il-Allāh*)
Training (*at-Tamrīnu wa 't-Tadbīr*)
Listening (*al-Istimaʿ*)

We will briefly address four out of the ten steps in order to get a feeling for these vital steps in self-development and purification.

STANDING UP FOR TRUTH (*AL-ISTIQAMAH*)

قُلْ إِنَّمَا أَعِظُكُم بِوَاحِدَةٍ أَن تَقُومُوا لِلَّهِ مَثْنَى وَفُرَادَى ثُمَّ تَتَفَكَّرُوا مَا بِصَاحِبِكُم مِّن جِنَّةٍ إِنْ هُوَ إِلَّا نَذِيرٌ لَّكُم بَيْنَ يَدَيْ عَذَابٍ شَدِيدٍ

Say: "I do admonish you on one point: that ye do stand up before Allah,- (It may be) in pairs, or (it may be) singly,- and reflect (within yourselves): your Companion is not possessed: he is no less than a warner to you, in face of a terrible Penalty."[164]

To stand up for Allah means to stand up for Truth against falsehood. Who is standing up for Truth against falsehood today? Before looking at others to judge them, stand for Truth against the wrong within. Fight against the devil in yourself. Stand for Allah against Satan, because Satan is always there, gossiping in your heart. To stand for The Merciful means to keep your eyes open and to be aware of all that is within yourself. This leads to self-realization.

Awareness counters heedlessness. If someone is heedless, he is careless of consequences, unaware of the results of his actions. You should be aware constantly, keeping your defenses up. What is the spiritual weapon of a believer? Ablution.

The Prophet Muhammad ﷺ said:

Ablution is the weapon of the believer.[165]

REPENTING (*AT-TAWBAH*)

We are still beginners, trying to find our way on a long journey. It is a long journey because it is full of obstacles. Something full of difficulties always seems long. Time passes quickly if you entertain

---

[164] Sūrah Ṣabā [Sheba], 34:46.

[165] Arabic: *Al-wuḍū silāḥ ul-mu'min.*

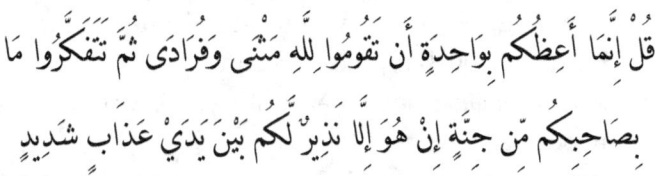

yourself, but someone busy with work sees the time leading up to his vacation as unending. The journey of self-realization is long, but at its end you will reach true happiness, feeling the pleasure of Allah's remembrance, *dhikrullāh*. Know that, until you reach your goal, you will face many obstacles.

When you want to repent, Allah will remove you from the list of oppressors.

وَمَن لَّمْ يَتُبْ فَأُوْلَئِكَ هُمُ الظَّالِمُونَ

And those who turn not in repentance, such are evil-doers.[166]

Do not despair of Allah's mercy. Allah will forgive; Allah is Most Great. Allah says in the Holy Qur'ān:

قُلْ يَا عِبَادِيَ الَّذِينَ أَسْرَفُوا عَلَى أَنفُسِهِمْ لَا تَقْنَطُوا مِن رَّحْمَةِ اللَّهِ إِنَّ اللَّهَ يَغْفِرُ الذُّنُوبَ جَمِيعًا إِنَّهُ هُوَ الْغَفُورُ الرَّحِيمُ

Say: "O my Servants who have transgressed against their souls! Despair not of the Mercy of Allah, for Allah forgives all sins. He is Oft-Forgiving, Most Merciful."[167]

And in another verse:

وَمَا أَرْسَلْنَا مِن رَّسُولٍ إِلاَّ لِيُطَاعَ بِإِذْنِ اللّهِ وَلَوْ أَنَّهُمْ إِذ ظَّلَمُواْ أَنفُسَهُمْ جَآؤُوكَ فَاسْتَغْفَرُواْ اللّهَ وَاسْتَغْفَرَ لَهُمُ الرَّسُولُ لَوَجَدُواْ اللّهَ تَوَّابًا رَّحِيمًا

.... If they had only, when they were unjust to themselves, come unto thee (O Muhammad) and asked

---

[166] Sūratu 'l-Ḥujurāt [The Private Apartments] 49:11.
[167] Sūratu 'l-Zumar [The Groups], 39:53.

Allah's forgiveness, and the Messenger had asked forgiveness for them, they would have found Allah indeed Oft-returning, Most Merciful.[168]

When you realize that you are a sinner with problems, you also realize that you need an intercessor—someone who is more sincere—to take you by the hand. The most sincere, the best intercessor, is the Prophet Muhammad ﷺ.

AUDITING (*AL-MUHASABAH*)

يَا أَيُّهَا الَّذِينَ آمَنُوا اتَّقُوا اللَّهَ وَلْتَنظُرْ نَفْسٌ مَّا قَدَّمَتْ لِغَدٍ وَاتَّقُوا اللَّهَ إِنَّ اللَّهَ

خَبِيرٌ بِمَا تَعْمَلُونَ

O ye who believe! Fear Allah, and let every soul look to what (provision) he has sent forth for the morrow. Yea, fear Allah, for Allah is well acquainted with (all) that ye do.[169]

This verse shows that the soul, not the body, has to prepare provision for the next life. That is why you must begin keeping track of all your negative issues. This can only be done by taking up the weapon of the pen against your enemy, the ego.

How do you audit yourself?

'Umar ibn al-Khaṭṭāb ؓ, the second caliph of the Prophet ﷺ, said:

> Judge yourselves before you are judged; and weigh your actions in the balance before they are weighed; When you are brought to account tomorrow, it will be much easier for you if you have already brought yourself to account today…[170]

---

[168] Sūratu 'n-Nisā [Women], 4:64.
[169] Sūratu 'l-Ḥashr [The Gathering], 59:18.
[170] Aḥmad and Abū Nu'aym.

This step involves auditing yourself by keeping a journal of your deeds, much as the Recording Angels are doing. Once you begin noting down the wrong actions that you do throughout the day, you will end up with a journal full of negative issues. Those who do not take account cannot repent.

People take their beads and make remembrance of Allah, *dhikr*. However, the correct way is not to do *dhikr* first. The correct way is to eliminate your mistakes first. To recite Allah's Name "*Allah, Allah*" 5,000 times may take fifteen minutes. To rcite the holy words, "There is no diety except Allah—*Lā ilāha il-Llāh*" 1,000 times may take seven minutes. Such practices are simple, but what is truly difficult is to prevent yourself from looking at what is forbidden. Grandshaykh ʿAbd Allah ق said that if you see something wrong once, it is not written against you; however, the second look is forbidden. If you see something wrong, look away and say, "O my Lord, that is prohibited." This is far better than doing 500 obligations. Leaving one forbidden thing is more valuable to Allah because it is stepping on your ego and leaving a sin for His sake. It is very difficult to leave something that you desire, that the ego wants, yet this is what we need to do.

Do not leave *dhikr*; but also work every day to eliminate your sins. For each one that you have counted, you have to say, "*Astaghfirullāh*—I repent, and I am not going to repeat that sin."

TURNING HUMBLY TO YOUR LORD IN SURRENDER (*AL-INABAH*)

وَأَنِيبُوا إِلَى رَبِّكُمْ وَأَسْلِمُوا لَهُ مِن قَبْلِ أَن يَأْتِيَكُمُ الْعَذَابُ ثُمَّ لَا تُنصَرُونَ

Turn ye to our Lord (in repentance) and bow to His (Will), before the penalty comes on you: after that ye shall not be helped.[171]

[171] Sūratu 'z-Zumar [The Groups], 39:54.

The seeker who has stepped forth on the way to find truth and reality needs a guide to open that way, to lead him to the presence of the Prophet ﷺ. The second step is to become aware of your shortcomings, and then you must repent and account for your actions. The fourth step is to turn humbly in surrender to your Lord—the essence of Islam.

Surrender is what your Lord wants from you. This step, of turning back to Allah (*al-ināba*), in itself becomes a turning point in your life. This turning point starts with entering into Islam fully without mixing it with sins. Allah says:

يَا أَيُّهَا الَّذِينَ آمَنُواْ ادْخُلُواْ فِي السِّلْمِ كَآفَّةً وَلاَ تَتَّبِعُواْ خُطُوَاتِ الشَّيْطَانِ إِنَّهُ لَكُمْ عَدُوٌّ مُّبِينٌ

O ye who believe! Enter into Islam whole-heartedly; and follow not the footsteps of the evil one; for he is to you an avowed enemy.[172]

Once all ten of the steps of self-discipline and spiritual advancement are accomplished, the servant will begin to approach the Divine Presence, in much as was described in the hadith earlier:

> And when I love him I will be the ears with which he hears, I will be the eyes with which he sees…

CONCLUSION

For certain government posts, you require security clearance. Without such clearance, you may only access unclassified areas. High-level government jobs require high levels of clearance. Applicants must be examined carefully before receiving this high-level clearance. Their family history and criminal records are

[172] Sūratu 'l-Baqarah [The Heifer] 2:208.

examined, along with anything else that might make the candidate a risk. This information affects the level of clearance they are eligible to receive. Depending on the level of clearance, this research might go back as far as the age of five years.

The same is true in spirituality. When the pious servant has achieved these ten levels, he is cleared to access classified materials. At that time, the servant can access the powers of the heart - powers that are found in the heart of every human being without discrimination. Until you access them, these six powers are blocked by the ego.

The tyranny of the self is able to oppress you. All of this power that Allah put in your heart becomes suppressed in a small and narrow place, due to the very high pressure of selfishness and satanic influence. The pressurized place that holds these powers is a black clot in the heart.[173] When you have achieved clearance through progress, that place becomes easy to open. When that pressurized clot is opened, it is like a volcano that erupts, spreading love everywhere.

On the Day of Promises, when Allah asked the assembled souls, "Am I not your Lord?" they answered, "Yes!" You do not remember it now, but Allah took from us a covenant, an oath. What you accepted on that day was recorded.

إِنَّا عَرَضْنَا الْأَمَانَةَ عَلَى السَّمَاوَاتِ وَالْأَرْضِ وَالْجِبَالِ فَأَبَيْنَ أَن يَحْمِلْنَهَا

وَأَشْفَقْنَ مِنْهَا وَحَمَلَهَا الْإِنسَانُ إِنَّهُ كَانَ ظَلُومًا جَهُولًا

[173] "There are jewels in man which have influences on him. The jewel of awe and marvel, the finest of these jewels, is in the center of the human heart. It is where the essence of the being is hidden, a store of energy and power. In that Dārk hidden place many an unknown secret is kept...That spot in the center of the human being, in his heart, is...a black spot." (Ibn ʿArabī, *Divine Governance of the Human Kingdom*, translated by Shaikh Tosun Bayrak, Fons Vitae, 1997, page 180).

"Lo! We offered the trust unto the heavens and the earth and the hills, but they shrank from bearing it and were afraid of it. And man assumed it. Lo! he hath proved a tyrant and a fool."[174]

When you climb up to reach the Reality of Guidance, you can see what kind of oath you took. At that time you will be one of those described by:

مِنَ الْمُؤْمِنِينَ رِجَالٌ صَدَقُوا مَا عَاهَدُوا اللَّهَ عَلَيْهِ

Among the believers are men who have [always] been true to what they have vowed before Allah.[175]

That will be your journey to your reality. Then Allah will dress you with guidance, and grant you permission to assist others. Until then, you are like a toy that speaks, like a parrot, as are today's scholars and lecturers. That is not guidance. Guidance is only for the pious servants (*ṣālihīn*) of Allah.

When you make the migration from bad desires and traits to good character and manners, when you achieve the highest level of moral virtue, you attain the power of spiritual ascension and self-realization. At that point, your ego stands at its limit, not transgressing the bounds of morality and manners. Wonders will be opened for you at that time. However, when you reach that level, do not pretend that such power or vision belongs to you; in reality, it is from Allah.

---

[174] Sūratu 'l-Aḥzāb [The Confederates], 33:72.
[175] Sūratu 'l-Aḥzāb [The Confederates], 33:23

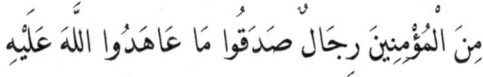

Spiritual Healing in the Islamic Tradition[176]

[176] Harvard Medical School's *Conference on Spirituality and Healing in Medicine II,* Los Angeles 1996.

Renewed interest in spiritual healing methods will only help to further the state of modern medicine as we benefit from the experiences and knowledge of our predecessors in this noble field of healing. Unfortunately, this topic has too often been ignored and dismissed by many contemporary physicians although these remedies have been practiced successfully for thousands of years.

A scientific mind unclouded by preconceived notions is able to discern the validity and utility of a comprehensive approach to health which includes spiritual healing. Professor John Taylor of King's College, London asserted:

> A scientific investigation can only look into that which is physical. The non-physical realm--be it mental, spiritual, ethereal, eternal or any other so far--has defied scientific analysis.
>
> There are certainly ways of obtaining knowledge about the non-physical aspect of experience which provides helpful insights of their nature, but the results so obtained are difficult to describe and relate to the general corpus of knowledge....Indeed, nowadays a scientist must take care to avoid being so biased in the other direction that he becomes over skeptical. He may well refuse to believe what is staring him in the face because it cannot be fitted into his materialistic view of the universe.... Science has so much evolved since a century ago. It should be able to give a satisfactory answer. If not, the scientific method truly will have been found wanting and could well suffer a blow from which it might never recover.

John Taylor, *Superminds,* pp. 55-56

SCIENCE AND SPIRITUAL HEALING

All spiritual healers are true scientists and they have come to the conclusion that behind every creation--be it an atom, cell, or cosmos--a Creating Genius is at work. Therefore, they assert that their patients can be healed by turning to that Creating Genius through devotion, contemplation, and recollection of His Name.

Many modern scientists realized that if a science does not educate, inspire, or lead to the conclusion and realization that the beginning and end, the outward and inward of all, whatever is between the heavens and earth is throbbing with life-giving energy of this Creating Genius, then this science cannot be qualified as normal.

Dr. Robert G. White, a renowned neurosurgeon, is one of many scientists and physicians who, through their research, came to the conclusion that human beings did not just come together, but are the handiwork of an All-Knowing Creative Genius. He writes:

> I am convinced that the brain is the repository of the human spirit, the soul…for me, the practice of medicine and religious faith are inextricably interwoven. I pray a great deal, especially before and after surgery. I find prayer satisfying. I feel there are immense resources behind me, resources I need and want...
>
> Yet the notion that human life is nothing more than a chance confluence of complex molecular biology and electrical activity strikes me as a deviance of logic...I have to believe all this had an intelligent beginning, that Someone made it happen. I cannot accept the proposition that, at random points in time, such substantial entities as intelli-gence, personality, memory, and the human body just sort of fell together.
>
> I also find it unreasonable to suppose that, at brain death, those powerful entities of intelligence, personality, and memory simply cease to exist. Far more reasonable [is] to believe that the essence of us escapes from a container, the

brain, which no longer is capable of supporting us, and finds support in a new dimension.

As to what becomes of the essence of us at brain death, I cannot presume even to speculate. I can only say that logic leads me inescapably to faith--faith that the uniqueness, the individuality, of the human being lives on in this concept we call the soul.

R.G. White, M.D. "Thoughts of a Brain Surgeon", Readers Digest, October, 1978.

THE SCIENCE OF SPIRITUAL HEALING

The science of spiritual healing has traditionally been taught and passed from one healer to another by individualized private instruction. These techniques have been used for centuries by wise philosophers and healers in various regions of the world including Japan, China, North Africa, the Middle East, Central Asia, and the Indian Subcontinent. These were the pioneers of spiritual healing who invented and practiced techniques which many scientists are unaware of even today. In the second half of the 20th century, this spiritual knowledge began to be spread and was taught en masse to those interested in using spiritual healing techniques to alleviate pain and to cure disease.

The spiritual healing process rejuvenates the body's life force and strengthens it through several focal points throughout the body. The spiritual technique produces a neuro-psychological effect which leads the central nervous system to produce a carefully orchestrated endocrine response which relieves pain, heals the disease of the affected areas, and balances the entire body.

HEALTH AS RELATED TO PHYSICAL FITNESS AND ACTIVITY

The human body requires food and drink, however not all such matters are digestible and they do not all become part of the human body. Instead precipitates of unconverted nutrients may settle as sediment and since the body cannot dispose of them naturally, with time, their accumulations can cause various illnesses. Initially, such accumulations may manifest as localized accumulations before they affect the blood and are transported through the blood stream to accessible parts of the body.

Though initially one's condition may manifest in the form of bowel problems, with time, any greater buildup of such sediment becomes more dangerous and manifests as localized illnesses that may spread in the body at later stage. Hence comes the importance of studying the pathology of disease and the history of its development.

Acknowledging physical malaise causing bowel problems, one may accustoms onesself to strong purgative resulting in further complications. In fact, most of such drugs are toxic and can interfere with and eliminate both the good and bad. Addictions to such drugs can further complicate one's condition because they are hot and interactive and they can weaken the immune system, predispose patients to arrythmias, affect the kidney and develop various disorders and deficiencies. Appropriate physical exercise is necessary to refresh the organs, ease the flow of food and nutrients, enhance digestion, and prevent such accumulations.

Furthermore, natural and methodical control of movements and muscular actions lightens the spirit, refreshes the mind, rejuvenates the body organs, improves one's self, strengthens muscular tone, prevents callousness of the joints, strengthens the tendons and ligaments, lessens the possibility of somatic disorders, and abates most illnesses. This also depends on the level of physical exercise, their balance, moderation, or intensity.

In general, routines dedicated to any particular limb strengthen it just like dedicating one's thoughts to a specific subject strengthens one's memory. Hence, each part of the body requires specific routines. The lungs require reading exercise and their levels began from reading silently, and advancing gradually in intensity and loudness. Hearing exercise require careful responsive attention by stimulating the auditory nerves and ears, and it develops to the point where sound either increases in volume or decreases by distance or by intensity of one's wavelength. Speaking exercise increases oral command; and besides helping recognition by physical and mental vision, eye exercises enhance one's vision, strengthens the ocular muscles and in some cases can help correct nearsightedness and farsightedness. Thus, hiking, swimming, normal walking exercise at moderate pace, riding on horseback, archery, and similar sports, are most healthy for the entire body. Adopting such programs of physical exercise even can cure chronic illnesses such as anemia, infectious diseases, ulcers, and colic, among others.

ORIGINS OF ISLAMIC SPIRITUAL HEALING

Spiritual healers inherited the methods that God's messengers were using, and from one generation to another have practiced these methods up to the present time. In the Islamic tradition, healers utilize both medicinal remedies and spiritual means. The spiritual techniques follow scientific principles which utilize the patient's latent energy and the power contained in the devotions and supplications and medi-tations of the prophets, messengers, and "wise men" of God.

Prophet Muhammad (peace be upon him) was once in a session where he was curing people through spiritual methods when he was asked whether or not remedies should be sought from medicines. He said, "Yes, you must seek remedy from medicine, because whatever disease God has created in this world, He has also created its remedy as well. But there is one disease for which He has not created any remedy, which is old age."

Each and every prescribed Qur'ānic verse has its unique healing property which differs from those of other verses. The following are some examples of verses used in spiritual healing.

SIX VERSES OF HEALING: "*AYAT AL-SHIFA*"

وَيَشْفِ صُدُورَ قَوْمٍ مُّؤْمِنِينَ

And [God] shall heal the breast of the believers. [177]

يَا أَيُّهَا النَّاسُ قَدْ جَاءَتْكُم مَّوْعِظَةٌ مِّن رَّبِّكُمْ وَشِفَاءٌ لِّمَا فِي الصُّدُورِ وَهُدًى وَرَحْمَةٌ لِّلْمُؤْمِنِينَ

Mankind there has come to you a guidance from your Lord and a healing for (the diseases) in your hearts, and for those who believe a guidance and a mercy. [178]

يَخْرُجُ مِن بُطُونِهَا شَرَابٌ مُّخْتَلِفٌ أَلْوَانُهُ فِيهِ شِفَاءٌ لِّلنَّاسِ إِنَّ فِي ذَلِكَ لَآيَةً لِّقَوْمٍ يَتَفَكَّرُونَ

There issues from within the bodies of the bee a drink of varying colors wherein is healing for mankind.[179]

وَنُنَزِّلُ مِنَ الْقُرْآنِ مَا هُوَ شِفَاءٌ وَرَحْمَةٌ لِّلْمُؤْمِنِينَ

---

[177] Sūratu 't-Tawbah [Repentance], 9:14.
[178] Sūrah Yūnus [Jonah], 10:57
[179] Sūratu 'n-Nahl [The Bee], 16:69.

And We sent down in the Quran such things that have healing and mercy for the believers.[180]

وَإِذَا مَرِضْتُ فَهُوَ يَشْفِينِ

And when I am ill, it is [God] who cures me.[181]

قُلْ هُوَ لِلَّذِينَ آمَنُوا هُدًى وَشِفَاء

And declare (O Muhammad) that [the Quran] is a guidance and healing for the believers.[182]

ABOUT ENERGY AND HOW SPIRITUAL HEALING WORKS

Spiritual healing is not at all a mysterious process but is in fact very straight forward, albeit oftentimes quite complex. The spiritual healing technique involves the energy field that exists around each of us. Everyone has an energy field or an aura that surrounds and interpenetrates the physical body. This field is intimately associated with the health of the human being.

In different cultures, energy is known by different names. The word "energy" is referred to as:

Ki in Japanese
Chi in Chinese
Prana in Hindi
Qudra in Arabic

Energy is the life breath transmitted to us from the Existing, Everlasting Superpower that overlooks human beings and all creation. Energy regulates our thought patterns and emotions, is

[180] Sūratu 'l-Isrā [The Night Journey], 17:82.
[181] A supplication of Prophet Abraham in Sūratu 'l-Shu'ara [The Poets], 26:80.
[182] Sūrah Fuṣṣilat [Explained in Detail], 41:44.

the source of our life force and is the animating factor in all living beings. It circulates through our bodies and can be harnessed for healing. It is the source of all movement in the universe. When the human body loses its life breath the original energy (or life force) leaves it, allowing the body to decompose. The body goes back to its earthen origins and the spirit returns to its angelic origin of spiritual energy. This energy is never lost and exists without the secret of its nature being understood by science and modern medicine.

This unknown spiritual energy is behind the life of every drop of blood in animate beings, the motion behind every living cell, and the driving force of constellations and galaxies. It carries unlimited perfect and complete powers which are real, active and continuous. The action of this force is genuine because nothing can grow or live in the entire universe without its influence.

This is especially applicable on earth where no trees, grass, vegetation and indeed no life can exist without the intervention of this unknown, unseen energy. It is with this energy that a tiny plant pushes through the middle of a huge desert boulder. This energetic spiritual life force holds the organs, blood vessels, and all body parts in place. When the body's life force diminishes, the anatomic relations of the body's organs are altered and disrupted, which leads to pain, organ dysfunction and an overall deterioration of health.

The spiritual energetic life force creates an energy field around itself like a highly charged magnet or electrode. This force reflects its energy throughout the human body and *becomes the driving life force* behind all of its activities and processes. The life force not only energizes the body but also gives it its identity. As an atom is defined by its constituent electrons, protons, and neutrons--which are also its energy components--so too does the spiritual life force give energy and identity to the physical body.

The healing spiritual energy is analogous to a waterfall. If a waterfall is channeled in the right way, it can be harnessed to produce energy and give light. Similarly, if our blood flow is properly channeled through a balanced, equilibrated system, the driving force of that energy will augment the energy of the weak organs.

In those organs where the life force has been weakened and dissipated, spiritual healing will increase and activate these vital forces. The spiritual healing technique allows the life energies to be exponentially expanded to activate the ill member and heal it.

A similar phenomenon is seen in an atomic reaction, where tremendous power is released from the internal energy of the atom. The energy produced increases geometrically as the activated, energized atom spreads its energy to its neighbors, propagating a chain reaction of energy release.

The same principle of the atomic reaction is used by spiritual healers to harness and activate the life force within the patient. Much in the same way that contemporary physicians direct lasers to heal affected areas of the body, spiritual healers access a similar chain reaction of the body's existing energy, channeling it to the affected areas to heal pain and suffering. When one organ begins to heal, the other organs use the released energy to activate and release their own inherent energy, which in turn promotes physiological equilibrium and relief from pain.

THE THREE PHASES OF SPIRITUAL HEALING

Universal force--or cosmic energy--includes the energies of the planets, stars and galaxies, and whatever is around us of propagating energy fields. This vast, all-pervading force nourishes the soul, the spirit and the energy within each individual and in every living creature. Through the meditative process of spiritual healing, one can access this driving energy which exists in every living cell in the body.

The energy is channeled to the cerebral cortex, which is the processing center of our thoughts. From there it will be intensely focused and channeled in the nuclei of the brain stem, which are activated and stimulated by this focused life force. In turn impulses are sent to the autonomic nervous system, regulating the body's functions, keeping it in equilibrium and free of pain. The concentration of energy in the brain comprises the first phase of spiritual healing.

This process in turn stimulates the vagus nerve to send electrical impulses down the heart's conduction system to the sinoatrial node, through the internodal tracts, through the atrioventricular node, down the Bundles of His, out the Purkinje fibers and into the myocardial wall to begin systole. This migration of energy which fills the heart is the second phase of spiritual healing. Conditions such as angina, congestive heart failure, cardiomyopathy and hypertension, in addition to many other related cardiac diseases, are healed and the patient can then find health and relief from pain.

The energy is then pumped with the blood out of the heart into the vascular system and delivered to the entire body in the third phase of spiritual healing. A major focus of phase three is the aorta, which is the conduit for the healing waves of energy that are carried by the blood.

As the blood flows from the heart, it is first channeled back to the heart via the coronary arteries in a chain reaction that sustains and increases the energy in the heart itself, much in the same way that the sun increases its light through its own nuclear reactions. This cycle produces more and more energy, which pours out into the vascular system with foci in the major arteries, supplying the brain via the carotid arteries. It also travels through the subclavian arteries to the upper extremities, the splanchnic circulation to the abdomen, through the renal arteries to the kidneys, and through the iliac vessels to the lower extremities.

The huge volume of drops of blood are like a waterfall made by a huge river descending over the side of a tall mountain cliff. All vegetation and animals in the water's path are nourished and given life, and every cell in the body is healed when the vital spiritual energy wave reaches it.

A healthy heart will sustain a weak body, but when the heart is weak and diseased--even in a young person--the body will not be healthy or live long. Therefore, maintaining the heart is the first priority for spiritual healers. Furthermore, maintaining the brain is also another important priority to keep the flow of messages functioning properly.

CONTEMPORARY PHYSICIANS AND SPIRITUAL HEALERS

Physicians and scientists are all acquainted with this unquantifiable life force, but are unable to interact with it directly except through its vehicle, the physical body. For that reason, scientists look intently to the outward existing body and invent procedures and techniques to keep the body in homeostasis, striving to keep the vital life force in the body as much as possible and to keep the body free of pain.

The contemporary physician is concerned primarily with the physical body as well as the psychological aspects of human existence. Therapeutics for illness are largely phy-sical, whether in the forms of medication, surgical inter-vention, or otherwise.

Spiritual healers, on the other hand, use an inward approach to healing by applying spiritual techniques and methods to utilize the body's own energy. The difference between the spiritual healers and the physician healers is that the former is healing from inside-to-outside while the latter is healing from outside-to-in. Each are doing good for their patients and both meet on the common ground of curing disease and relieving pain and suffering.

HIGH SENSE PERCEPTION AS A DIAGNOSTIC TOOL

Physicians utilize Magnetic Resonance Imaging (MRI) techniques which use the energy and alignment of the body's atoms to provide images and information about the condition of the body and any potential disease process. The spiritual healer also has advanced diagnostic modalities one of the most important of which is HSP, High Sense Perception.

HSP is a way of perceiving things beyond the normal range of the five senses. With it one can see, hear, smell, taste, and touch things that cannot normally be perceived.

HSP, sometimes referred to as clairvoyance, is not imagination but is a type of seeing in which you perceive a picture in your mind without the use of your normal vision. HSP reveals the dynamic world of the fluid, interacting spiritual energy fields which surround and permeate all living things. This energy supports us, nourishes us, and gives us life. We sense each other with this energy as we are a part of it and it is a part of us.

With HSP, the pathophysiology of pain and disease processes lies right before one's eyes. HSP reveals how most diseases are initiated in the energy field. Distortions in the energy field caused by time and unhealthy living habits are transmitted to the body, becoming a serious illness. Many times the source or initiating cause of this process is asso-ciated with psychological and/or physical trauma.

Since HSP reveals how a disease is initiated, it also reveals how to reverse the disease process. Spiritual energies and auras aid healers in formulating their diagnosis. To develop HSP it is necessary to enter into an expanded state of consciousness. There are many means to achieve this but spiritual meditation is fast becoming the most well known.

THE *NASMA* AND MEDITATION

In the spiritual terminology, the non-physical body is called *nasma*. *Nasma* exists within each physical body as a subtle vapor or energy breeze created by the chemical output of the physical body. The *nasma* is present in human beings just as rose water is present in the rose or as the fire in glowing coals. Being superior with its connection to the divine energy source, it can taste without using the tongue, can see without using the eyes, and can hear without using the ears.

By using the *nasma*, HSP is made available to the spiritual healer. The *nasma* derives its nourishment from the esoteric energy which is released whenever we act, think, or form a belief or intention. The *nasma* in human beings is capable of leaving the physical body at any time through the universal driving force.

When the flow of spiritual energy is disturbed or insufficient, the health of the patient is adversely affected, leading to pain, disease, distress, and so forth. These are signals that we need to rebalance our energy. A positive energy flow nourishes the *nasma* and maintains its structure and foundation, balancing the human system. This balance leads to increased awareness of the body's sensations which in turn leads to good living, following of proper diet, and enjoyment of exercise. The *nasma* then supports and maintains a healthy physical body, in which the chemical and physical systems remain balanced and functioning normally, thus perpetuating physical health.

In the healthy system, the energies in each body not only remain balanced but also support and influence the energy balance in other peoples' bodies. The *nasma* can influence others like a magnet bringing the charges of adjacent metal into its alignment. The energy of a healthy system is thus both self-healing and self-propagating in that it maintains the individual health while strengthening the health of those in one's aura. That is, good health attracts and develops more good health.

The *nasma* can not only influence the physical body, but it can also be affected by a sick body and become weak because of the weakness of the organs. For example, in a weak body a weak *nasma* shows its symptoms in the mental and physical aspects of a person. In the mental sphere, any one of the following will occur: neurosis, depression, hysteria, psychosis, seizures, sleep terror, and insomnia. If this state of affairs is allowed to continue without treatment, the *nasma* becomes so weak that it is rendered incapable of defending itself in the weak body. The patient at this stage suffers either from seizures, psychotic fits, or aggressive behavior. The spiritual healer can strengthen the patient's organs and thereby the *nasma* through the universal driving force, creating a high-energy state in which symptoms of sickness disappear.

MEDITATION AND THE FOCAL POINT OF TREATMENT

In spirituality, good health requires intensive striving by the patient and personal change. Personal change to develop patience, contentment, gratitude, cheerfulness, joy, love, sharing, courage, benefaction, recognition of good deeds, forbearance, and courtesy will improve spirituality and energy flow.

Overactivity even in this field and lack of proper supervision and devotion of a concerned and learned parent, or the dedication of qualified teacher also may lay a heavy burden on the person's intellect. Alternatively, an impasse in spiritual progress may hinder one's spiritual growth, and only a qualified guidance can break through such obstacles. Such training must keep advancing until it develops genuine character, positive traits, and healthy energy flow.

Without personal change in the body's energy flow, one will eventually create other problems which leads back to the source that caused the disease in the first place. Thus, dealing with the source of disease is the focal point of treatment. This search stimulates the deeper part of ourselves that is sometimes called the "higher self" or the "spark of divinity" within us. This divinity within us, the deeper part of ourselves, sends us information about what type of sickness needs to be treated and what type of contact points need to be touched through our meditation. Meditation is a tool which gives deep relaxation and to quiet the mind. This helps to alleviate stress, and therefore enable the internal chemical and hormonal system to regain their equilibrium.

Medical tests have shown that there are definite measurable physiological changes in meditating subjects. The brain itself undergoes changes in the type of electrical waves generated. By using an electroencephalogram (EEG) there is an increase in the generation of alpha waves and sometimes also in the number of theta waves. These indicate a shift of consciousness into a tranquil state of awareness quite different from that of sleep. This state is therapeutic and very restful although the patient is both fully conscious and functional.

The body demonstrates the effects of meditation in various ways. The breathing pattern slows, as does the heart rate, and there is a marked decrease in the level of oxygen consumption and carbon dioxide elimination. However, the physical effects of meditation last longer than the meditation period itself. This is demonstrated by the fact that sufferers of hypertension and many other diseases have, through meditation alone, made such clinically-measurable improvements that they have been able to discontinue their medications. This is very well noted and recorded in spiritual healing books and manuscripts.

How Energy Relates to Disease

Spiritual healers symbolize the flowing of the driving life force in the body and in the universe as vortices of energy made up of a number of smaller spiral cones of energy. These are known in

Islamic terminology as ""*lata'if*", meaning subtle manifestations or layers. The *lata'if* (sing. *lateefa*) are the points of maximum energy intake and are very important focal points of balance within the energy system. Disease and illness occur if a *lateefa* is unbalanced.

Lata'if in adults have a protective screen over them. In a healthy system, these *lata'if* spin in synchronized rhythm with the others, drawing energy from the universal energy field into their center for use by the body. Each one of them is tuned to a specific frequency that helps the body to remain healthy. However, in a diseased system these vortices are not synchronized. The energy of the *lata'if* that make up these vortices may be fast or slow, jerky or lopsided. Sometimes breaks in the entire energy pattern can be observed in which a *lateefa* may be fully or partially collapsed or inverted. These disturbances are related to dysfunction or pathology of the physical body in that area.

HEALING THROUGH MEDITATION AND FOCAL POINTS OF THE *LATA'IF*

The feeling of pain can be completely cured by meditation wherein the dormant energy of a sick body is activated by a spiritual ignition produced by the meditative process. This spiritual process uses seven different focal points in the seven layers, the *lata'if*.

There are seven focal points of the *lata'if*. These are located above and below the heart, above and below the left breast, above and below the right breast, and one on the forehead. Every *lateefa* has a different energy color, and every energy has a different effect on a specific disease. The two focal points above and below the heart are green. The points above and below the left breast are yellow, the ones above and below the right breast are black, and the one on the forehead is white.

Through meditation these seven focal points of the *lata'if* generate energy. Then, like a magnet, these activated focal points attract more energy from the universal cosmic energy source in the shape of tiny floating spheres of light. The size of these spheres depends on which *lateefa* is activated, as there is a different sized sphere for every different color *lateefa*. Depending on the illness, the healer activates the appropriate *lateefa* needed to cure that sickness. In turn, the *lateefa* produces more of its energy color which itself attracts from the universal energy source more of the same light. The result of this positive feedback loop is a tremendous outpouring of shimmering globes of light which descend from the cosmic energy source onto the person of the healer.

Through this flood of colored energy spheres, the healer is energized to the point where he radiates heat from his body through his hands and projects light from his forehead. As a scientist shoots a laser, the spiritual healer emits the light and energy that he receives from the universal force. The healer massages the affected areas and this combination of heat from the hand and light from the forehead immediately begins the healing process.

The healer also prescribes that the patient sit alone for a few hours each day fully relaxed, repeating several thousand times different holy names of God in a special format for the duration of treatment. These holy names are like energy sparks which ignite more flow from the universal energy source. This ignition also activates the focal points of the *lata'if* causing heat to be generated in the body of the patient. This heat is considerably less than the immense power transmitted by the healer, but it is sufficient to cause the patient to break out into a sweat.

At this time, the patient goes to the healer who transmits more energy as before, advancing the patient's treatment. As the moon reflects the light of the sun onto the earth, so too does the healer reflect the universal energy through his body to the patient. This produces a state of immense heat and spiritual interaction between the healer and the patient. This process is repeated for several days or even weeks until the patient recovers.

As he recovers, the patient begins to experience a psychological effect from the dynamic, synergistic interaction between himself and the healer. This psychological effect of recovery and relief from pain induces the endocrine glands to secrete hormones which balance the whole system and begin to cure the ill organs, raising the patient to higher levels of health and spirituality than would be possible in the former painful, diseased condition.

As the surgical patient is anesthetized, so too is the spiritual patient put in a pain-free state in which the spiritual healer can work on him in the way he finds suitable.

CONCLUSION

Disease at any station of the energy field will express itself in that particular level of consciousness. Each expression of disease is manifested as some form of pain, be it physical, emotional, mental, or spiritual. It is essential that we probe the deeper meaning of our illnesses. We need to ask, "What does this illness and pain mean to us? What can we learn from this?"

Pain is the driving belt in the body's own self-defense mechanism that alerts us to correct a situation. Pain is like a warning bell in our system which brings our attention to the fact that something is wrong and forces us do something about it. Pain says, "You are not listening to your whole self." Pain teaches us to ask for help and healing and is, therefore, a key to the education of the soul and to the function of the spirit and the body's energy.

A comprehensive approach to pain relief and health in general which includes spiritual healing will greatly help the progress of modern medicine. While volumes can and have been written on Islamic spiritual healing, it is hoped that this brief introduction will help bring this subject to the attention of the medical community and foster greater appreciation and understanding of this rich tradition and science.

SHARI'AH

WHAT IS A *FATWA*?[183]

[183] Statement by Islāmīc Supreme Council of America, July 5, 2002.

In recent years, the term "*fatwā*" has been widely used throughout the media, usually to indicate that a death sentence has been dealt to someone or some group of people. The limited use of this term has resulted in a limited understanding of its meaning. ISCA therefore offers the following statement to elucidate the true significance of the term "*fatwā*."

Most importantly, a *fatwā* is not by definition a pronouncement of death or a declaration of war. A *fatwā* is an Islamic legal pronouncement, issued by an expert in religious law (*mufti*), pertaining to a specific issue, usually at the request of an individual or judge to resolve an issue where Islamic jurisprudence (*fiqh*), is unclear. Typically, such uncertainty arises as Muslim society works to address new issues – issues that develop as technology and society advance. "Can a Muslim be involved in cloning?" for instance.

We might compare a *fatwā* to the legal ruling of a high court or the Supreme Court, depending on the authority of the mufti behind it. However, a *fatwā* is not binding as is the verdict of the secular courts; while correct and applicable to all members of the Muslim faith, the *fatwā* is optional for the individual to respect or not.

A *qaḍā*, on the other hand, is a legal ruling made by a judge (*qāḍī*) that, issued in a nation where Islamic law is observed, is binding on those to whom it is dealt. Usually issued to resolve a legal dispute, a *qaḍā* may be based on a *fatwā*, yet it applies only to the individuals or groups named in the ruling and no one else. A ruler can impose a *qaḍā* on his entire nation.

Although there is no central Islamic governing authority today – the last having been dismantled with the collapse of the Ottoman Empire, there are generally accepted standards for granting anyone the authority to issue a *fatwā*. This is an extremely rigorous standard requiring many years of training and study. The *fatwā* is not based upon the mufti's own will and ideas, but rendered in accordance with fixed precedents from the sources of Islamic law.

In order to issue an authorized *fatwā* using his individual skills of reasoning, the mufti or scholar must meet the standards of *ijtihād*. This is the highest standard in issuing a juristic ruling. In general, this means he must be able to distinguish between the other scholars' positions and their supporting evidence, and judge one stronger according to the strength or weakness of the evidence.

Imam Shāfiʿī, founder of one of the four great schools of jurisprudence, said:

> It is not allowed for anyone to give a Shariʿah explanation (*fatwā*), except one who knows the Holy Qur'ān completely including what verses are abrogated and by which verses they were abrogated, and which verses resemble each other in the Qur'ān and whether a chapter was revealed in Makkah or Madina. He must know the entire corpus of the Hadith of the Prophet ﷺ, both those which are authentic and those which are false. He must know the Arabic language of the time of the Prophet ﷺ with its grammar and eloquence as well as know the poetry of the Arabs. Additionally, he must know the culture of the various peoples who live in each different nation of the community. If a person has all such attributes combined in himself, he may speak on what is permitted (*ḥalāl*) and what is forbidden (*ḥarām*). Otherwise he has no right to issue a *fatwā*.

While in the distant past there were many scholars with the knowledge required to make independent legal conclusions, there are none of that caliber today. Someone who attained this level of qualification was known as the Imam of a school of law. Today, scholars build their reasoning on that of their predecessors, as in US case law. In practice, this limitation is not as restrictive as it sounds, for the inordinate amount of Islamic case law greatly facilitates such research, except in the most abstruse issues.

While not as rigorous as those required for independent legal reasoning, the qualifications for a scholar to issue a *fatwā* based on legal precedent are nonetheless extremely taxing. He must:

- Know the verses of Qur'ān pertaining to the ruling at hand;
- Know the reason behind the verses of Qur'ān related to the ruling – when each was revealed and why;
- Distinguish the supportive and oppositional verses of the Qur'ān;
- Know all the hadith pertaining to the ruling and the soundness of their chain of transmission;
- Be familiar with the legal precedents of the issue before him, including the arguments or consensus reached by earlier scholars; and
- Be well-versed in the syntax, grammar, pronunciation, idioms, special linguistic uses, customs and culture prevalent at the time of the Prophet ﷺ and succeeding two generations.

It often happens that different Islamic clerics issue contradictory, or competing, *fatwā*s. This divergence of opinion is not considered an issue in Islam; in fact, a well-known saying states that such differences among scholars are God's mercy, for they allow for different conditions and temperaments among people.

In nations that observe Islamic law, *fatwā*s are debated before being issued publicly. They are affirmed only by consensus, which is determined by the supreme religious council of that nation. In such cases, *fatwā*s are rarely contradictory, and carry the power of enforceable law. If two *fatwā*s do contradict one another, the ruling bodies (which often combine civil and religious law) establish a compromise. This differs in the Shiʿa tradition, which demands that each individual Muslim choose one mufti (*marja*ʿ) to follow exclusively in all aspects of religious law.

In nations that do not recognize Islamic law, Muslims confronted with competing *fatwā*s would follow the ruling of the scholar observing their same religious tradition.[184] If two muftis of the same tradition issue conflicting *fatwā*s, a Muslim may choose between them. In practice however, following a particular school is not strictly observed.

These are the requirements for a scholar or religious leader to issue a *fatwā* that is recognized under Islamic law. Having established this, we may now consider whether *fatwā*s issued by militants, including the many we have read in the past five years, have any authority. Again, the worldwide media has repeatedly presented cases in which known Muslim militants use a *fatwā* to either declare war or announce another violent action.

However, unless he who makes the declaration is extremely well-educated and trained in Islamic jurisprudence according to the requirements mentioned above, he has no authority to issue a *fatwā*. The Prophet Muhammad ﷺ said, "Whoever gives *fatwā* without knowledge, the angels of the heaven and the earth curse him."[185] Second, if he is so qualified, the *fatwā* remains non-binding, applying only to those choose to accept and wish to enforce it.

To issue a new *fatwā* as an unqualified and unauthorized individual is impermissible and forbidden in Islam. Of course to relate the rulings of qualified scholars is permitted, provided it is transmitted without changing the context or wording. The *fatwā*s

---

[184] There are four major scholastic traditions or schools of thought among Sunni Muslims.

[185] As reported from the Prophet Muhammad ﷺ by Ibn ʿAsākir in al-Suyūṭī's *Habā'ik*, p. 187, #694.

of unqualified individuals are considered "null and void," according to 'Umar, second caliph of the Prophet ﷺ[186].

[186] 'Umar said, "Such false muftis are the enemies of the religion, misguided and misguiding, and their fatwas are null and void." [no reference]

Viewpoint: Door of '*Ijtihad*' is Open[187]

[187] Published by Common Ground News Service (CGNews), April 12, 2005.

One of the criticisms leveled against Islam is that it is a religion frozen in time, one that has not embraced new paradigms of the modern world. In reality, Islam has always been a living, vibrant faith that adapts to new and changing circumstances.

Though some scholars have attempted to freeze the interpretation of Islam, most accept the view that Islamic Divine Law, or Sharia, is subject to ongoing re-evaluation according to the principles of juristic reasoning, known as *ijtihād*. The purpose of this ongoing process of *ijtihād* is to adapt Sharia to changing societal circumstances. Thus, most Islamic scholars say that "the door of *ijtihād*" remains open.

Ijtihād has a rich and controversial history that is worth examining in order to understand the issues surrounding it today. The concept of *ijtihād* emerged out of necessity in a highly eventful period when the Muslim community was expanding rapidly into new lands and cultures. With expansion, Islam's ability to adapt to new environments was tested, and the community of believers saw the need to develop and formalize methods of adjusting Islamic regulations to various socio-cultural contexts. Brilliant scholars emerged to lead this effort. Each of these luminaries had a direct connection to the Prophet, his companions or their successors - a practice that guaranteed the authenticity of their understanding of this complex process of adaptation.

While the Koran and Hadith (traditions of the Prophet and his companions) were grounded in a fixed time, place and socio-cultural milieu of seventh-century Arabia, Islam's message and the law that it brought was for every time and place. So, scholars sought to penetrate the principles behind the thousands of rulings made in the time of the Prophet and his successors in order to build a system of precedent-based law that would provide a solid foundation for jurists in the future.

These principles include the consensus of scholars, analogy to prior rulings, pursuit of the greater good, the idea that a lesser harm is preferable to a greater harm, and the importance of pre-existing customs and practices. These principles stipulate that law can depend on precedence, not unlike the way that contemporary American laws must conform to the precedent of existing law and court case history, or the way in which Jewish Kashrut law builds on the rulings of earlier scholars, which depend on analogy with situations addressed in the Torah or in the tradition of Moses ﷷ and the Judaic prophets.

Over time, different scholars developed different schools of jurisprudence based on these principles, and after three centuries, there were more than 400 different schools with subtle variations of interpretation. Unfortunately, instead of benefiting from the diversity of opinions, adherents of one school sometimes became adversarial to other schools, insisting that their own interpretation and methodology was the only correct one. This resulted in debate, conflict and finally open bloodshed between adherents of different schools - something their founders never intended.

In order to stop this confusion, fourteenth-century Sunni Islamic scholars banned the creation of new schools. Then the number of "acceptable" schools was whittled down to the four with the largest followings, each named after their founding scholars: Maliki, now found primarily in Africa; Ḥanafī, found in Central Asia, Turkey, the Balkans and the Indian sub-continent; Shāfiʿī, followed in the Middle East and Southeast Asia; and Ḥanbalī, followed mainly in the Arabian Peninsula.

With the establishment of the four schools, the process of *ijtihād* was restricted, in order to prevent the factionalist strife that ensued with a proliferation of methods of interpreting Islamic law, but it was not eliminated. Rather, as time passed these schools refined their founders' principles of deriving law and legal judgments. By the time they emerged as the four Sunni schools, each had established a complete methodology for legal questions in light of changing times, places, circumstances and social milieus.

An oft-cited example is that of Imām Shāfiʿī who, when first formulating the basic rulings of his school in Baghdad, took a relaxed approach to social interaction between men and women in public places. However, after moving to Cairo, he called for stricter rules of separation between genders. When asked why, he cited the cultural differences that he observed between Egyptians and Iraqis that necessitated stricter regulations to prevent adultery.

A more recent example of this sort of reasoning is found in the legal ruling, issued by Sheikh ʿAlī Jumaa, the Grand Mufti of Egypt, which permits Muslims living in non-Muslim lands to buy, sell and serve alcoholic drinks. This ruling came as a shock to many, but was based on solid Islamic juristic reasoning. While it appears to directly contradict the Koran and Hadith, it was based on an earlier ruling by Imām Abū Ḥanīfa, whose school is by far the largest in the world. Imām Abū Ḥanīfa argued that in a place where Sharia is not observed, Muslims may circumvent the law in accordance with vital need. Thus, Sheikh Jumaa derived his ruling not from a newfound openness to alcohol in Islam, but from a principle enunciated early in Islam by Imām Abū Ḥanīfa, founder of one of the four Sunni schools.

These examples demonstrate the living, vibrant nature of Islamic jurisprudence, as well as its ability to respond to new challenges and changing times. However, it must be stressed that this practice of juristic reasoning, or *ijtihād*, is strictly limited to those with the required legal and spiritual training and knowledge.

Jurisprudence requires not just knowledge and understanding of the sacred texts, but a deep comprehension of the circumstances around the issue being addressed and an intuitive spiritual wisdom that guides the jurist toward a decision that fulfils not just the letter of the law, but also the practical realities of a given time and place. The spiritual wisdom needed to derive well-rounded and valued rulings is not something that comes from excessive study or memorization. Rather, it is an inner light that comes from sincere devotion to Allah and a spiritual connection to the source of guidance. That light is developed and maintained by means of rigorous exercises under the guidance of masters of spiritual training and enlightenment.

The history of Islam shows that *ijtihād* and juristic reasoning, conducted by competent and spiritually enlightened scholars, have enabled the social, cultural and intellectual adaptation of Islam to innumerable contexts. This living, vibrant heritage, that is open to change and adaptation, will continue to sustain the faith through many centuries to come.

Democracy According to Traditional Islamic Sources[188]

[188] Presented at *The Conference on The Future of Islam and Democracy*, July 11, 2002, The Ethics and Public Policy Center, Washington, DC.

1. DEMOCRATIC SYSTEMS IN ISLAM

The Qur'ān says:

يَا أَيُّهَا الَّذِينَ آمَنُوا أَطِيعُوا اللَّهَ وَأَطِيعُوا الرَّسُولَ وَأُوْلِي الأَمْرِ مِنكُمْ

Obey Allah, obey the Prophet and obey those in authority among you."[189]

The primary sources of Islamic law are therefore the words and commands of Allah as laid out in the Qur'ān, the sayings and traditions of the Prophet ﷺ (*aḥādīth*), and the rulings of political and religious leaders.

The Holy Qur'ān is the highest standard by which man can order his life. As such, it is a model only the Prophet of Allah could uphold to its fullest. Yet, it is still not possible for the average Muslim to follow the Prophet's example directly. Muslims therefore rely on the authority of their leaders to guide them in upholding the principles of law laid out in the Qur'ān and the traditions. The Prophet ﷺ himself stated, "Whoever is chosen by the people after me will be the caliph, and you must listen to and obey him."[190] Those in authority include the rulers of the nation, its religious scholars and its judges.

1.1 *SHURA*: CONSULTATION AND THE ADAPTABILITY OF ISLAMIC LAW

Rule in Islam is based on the concept of *shūrā,* a term which has two meanings in Islamic governance:

1. *Shūrā* is a referendum on which the majority of people agree, and is the basic method for choosing the ruler in Islam. Similarly, it is the means to approve his decisions. Muhammad Abū Zahrā in

[189] Sūratu 'n-Nisā [Women], 4:59.
[190] *Saḥīḥ Bukhārī.*

The History of Islamic Thought and Leadership in Politics and Belief, writes:
"All the Muslims, including the Shiʿa and all the different schools of thought, [which at one time number over 470] agreed that leadership as defined by the Prophet, in the saying 'If you are three make one your leader' can only be implemented by election. That is done in every district, (*hayy*), at the state level (*wilāyat*) and above that by the federal authority, (*al-idāra al-markazīyya*)."

2. The advisory board (*al-majlis ash-shūrā*), which advises the ruler, is a group of elected experts. The task of such groups is to observe and oversee the ruler (*murāqabat as-sulṭān*). They are in this position to form an opinion of the ruler and his rule, and to control any aspirations he may have to override the rights of the people. They must be aware of the variations in these rights within ethnic, cultural and environmental norms. This system is like that being implemented in America today, where we have the federal system, the state and local governments, and municipalities. The judicial system acts to check the executive and legislative branches, ensuring fair and correct implementation of law. We also have the free press, which acts as a watchdog over the government, issuing warnings at the slightest sign the interests of the people are being betrayed.

Everything that impacts human life accounted for in the law and falls under the jurisdiction of the ruler. Yet the ruler himself has no personal choice in ruling, as do contemporary monarchs. The Prophet ﷺ prohibited the ruler, who has been chosen or appointed, to usurp authority he does not possess. He is tied to the law, which as the ruler is his duty to enforce. The *majlis ash-shūrā* ensures that he does so.

In the Shariʿah there are laws that are immutable or nearly so, similar to the constitutional basis of Western democracy and the US Bill of Rights. However, the remainder of the law is adaptable, changing with:

1. The practical application of the "immutable" law, established in the earlier rulings of judges; ie. case law.
2. Society's evolving needs.

It is the job of the *Dār al-Iftā,* the Center for Legal Rulings, to form the basis for new laws that will address innovations in technology and custom. The Prophet ﷺ did not demand that a particular rule be imposed on new innovations, but allowed the people to develop a law as needed, based on the precedent established in his lifetime and by Islamic scholars in succeeding generations. The evolution of the law was left in the care of the people for laws must take into account geography, environment, ethnic and cultural considerations, and variations in belief and understanding.

Baruch Spinoza said, "Everyone varies in their view of individual life." Each person has a different opinion on every matter, therefore the implementation of *shūrā,* or election by majority, is essential in the formation of a new law that will successfully and effectively govern the people.

1.2 DEMOCRATIC ELECTION OF LEADERS

From the beginning, Islam has mandated democracy through a *shūrā* (elected council of leaders), a process through which people sit together, consult with one another, and select one person to represent them. This process was recently employed in Afghanistan where, according to a fifteen-century old tradition, the people choose representatives who then gathered to choose not only a leader, but a cabinet and national assembly. The recent *loya jirga* that confirmed Hamid Karzai as president of Afghanistan, demonstrated once again that Islamic rule is based on democratic choice.

A clear example of democracy's role in Islam is manifest in the Prophet's (peace be upon him) passing without appointing a successor to rule the Muslim state. He intentionally left it to the Muslims to come together to make this crucial decision based on what he had taught them.

The Azhar scholar Dr. Abū Zahrā said:

> The Prophet ﷺ never gave a single word or sign indicating who his successor would be… and in the meeting which took place to elect the calipha, the Companions were in utter disagreement as to who should succeed the Prophet, but in the end were able to choose Abū Bakr aṣ-Ṣiddīq by the consensus of the majority.[191]

Essentially, there were three groups who differed in who should succeed the Prophet:

The *Anṣār*, the Prophet's supporters in Madinah, who felt the leadership should fall to one among them as they supported the Prophet ﷺ when he immigrated from Mecca.

Another group, led by Abū Bakr ؇ and 'Umar ؇, believed that the immigrants (*Muhājirūn*) who came with the Prophet ﷺ to Madinah should lead, because they were the first to enter Islam.

The third group called on 'Alī ؇ to lead, due to his familial relationship with the Prophet ﷺ.

The disagreement did not last long, as through *shūrā* the three groups quickly reached the consensus that Abū Bakr ؇ had the highest credentials to take the reins of leadership. The majority

---

[191] Al-Azhar in Cairo, Egypt is the oldest Islāmīc university in the world, dating back many centuries, and is considered one of the highest Islāmīc authorities by intellectuals and scholars.

voted for him, and the Islamic precedent for peaceful transition between rulers was introduced. Once the majority had decided, the individual citizens ratified the selection by pledging their allegiance one-by-one to the new head of state.

In electing a candidate from among the three parties vying for succession, the first, most exemplary Muslims imprinted their stamp of religious authenticity on the electoral system. The fact that the Companions *(Sahaba)* did not establish a monarchy or a dictatorship irrevocably demonstrates that leadership in Islam is the choice of the people.

Once a selection is made by the *shūrā* council, each individual Muslim has the option to accept their choice or not. This is known as taking a pledge of allegiance (*baya'*). If a group feels the choice was made unjustly, they may refuse to accept it and form an opposition party. In the end however, a judge accepted by both sides must make a final arbitration and choose between the two parties based on the validity of their claims.

The executive aspect of governance is also conducted through consultation. The ruler, chosen by the *shūrā* and confirmed by the citizen's individual pledge of allegiance, is obliged to consult on executive decisions. He therefore consults with a council, parliament or advisory group whose specific role is to advise.

Whenever the Prophet ﷺ had to make a decision that would affect the Muslim nation in whole or part, he gathered his followers to conduct a *shūrā*. In one instance, before the onset of a battle, one of the companions asked the Prophet ﷺ if the location of the Muslim camp should be chosen through Divine inspiration or consultation. The Prophet ﷺ answered that it should be the product of consultation, and proceeded to follow the group's recommendation to settle beside the nearest water well.

'Umar ؓ, the second caliph, said, "Whoever is chosen by the people after me will be the caliph, and you people must listen to him and obey him."[192] Upon 'Umar's passing, the *shūrā* chose 'Uthmān, and after 'Uthmān's assassination, they chose 'Alī ‎.

With the election of 'Alī there arose a dispute, and Mu'awīya took over the caliphate. Later the rule went to his son, and the system thereby changed from democracy to a monarchy. Thereafter, the selection of the ruler was dynastic and remained so through the time of the Ottoman caliphs

Muawiya separated the political and religious systems. However he regularly consulted with Ibn 'Abbās and Ibn 'Umar, who possessed vastly greater knowledge. The system thus changed into a political leadership advised by religious leaders.

1.3 THE CONSTITUTION OF MADINAH

The democratic election of a leader was the model on which the city of Madinah was founded. The Prophet, while invited by Muslims from that city, became its ruler by the choice of all its citizens, which included Jewish and polytheist tribes. He then developed a binding social contract, a pact signed by all the tribal leaders naming Muhammad as the leader, and establishing laws binding the tribes to cooperation, assistance in defense of the city, and the protection of its inhabitants.

It reads in part:

> The Jews of Banu 'Awf are one nation with the Muslims. The Jews have their religion and the Muslims have theirs, their freedmen and their persons shall be protected except those who behave unjustly or sinfully... Each must help the other against anyone who attacks the people of this document. Their condition must be one of mutual advice, consultation and charity... No man is liable for a crime committed by his ally. Support must be given to him who is wronged... To every small group belongs the share

[192] *Saḥīḥ Bukhārī.*

which is their due, as members of the larger group which is party to this covenant...

This document, The Constitution of Madinah, establishes the importance of consent and cooperation for governance in Islam. According to this pact, Muslims and non-Muslims are equal citizens of the Islamic state, with identical rights and duties. Communities of different religious orientations enjoy religious autonomy, which is essentially wider in scope than the modern idea of religious freedom. The principles of equality, consensual governance and pluralism are beautifully enmeshed in the pact of Madinah.

Since then, this lengthy document has proven an exemplary historical model of a binding social pact in which a multi-religious, multi-cultural society was bound by one law. Note that, in signing the contract, the non-Muslim parties did not accept the Prophet ﷺ as their religious leader, but rather signed with the conviction that he would provide the leadership needed to build an ideal society. In later centuries, the system of governance in Madinah became the basis of the ideal city, a detailed model developed by al-Fāʿrābī and later scholars.

A tradition in Islam states: "Whatever the body of Muslims collectively sees as good is also considered good by Allah, and what they see as bad is also considered bad by Allah." Just as culture, geography and natural circumstances impact our needs, the Prophet ﷺ recognized the importance to develop a system that would be useful for that time or those circumstances. He stated, "Majority opinion is best."[193]

1.4 THE MODEL CITY

Despite the change of the system of succession to a dynastic model, the Islamic system of governance established by Prophet

193 Ibn Mājah.

Muhammad ﷺ evolved rapidly in the fields of law, economics, industry, agriculture and religious understanding. Later, as the Umayyad dynasty was succeeded by the Abbasid, Islamic theology, philosophy and political theory also flourished, culminating in al-Fāʿrābī's *The Model City*, and later in the writing of Naṣr ad-Dīn aṭ-Ṭūsī.

Dr. ʿAbdul-Wāḥid, a scholar of Islamic history at al-Azhar University, writes:

> Al-Fāʿrābī as an Islamic scholar versed in the Qur'ān, hadith and the practice of the Sahaba (companions), and through his extensive study of previous civilizations... composed a formulation of Islamic political theory in a way that had never been done before him.[194]

Al-Fāʿrābī defined fifteen characteristics of the ideal leader:

- Excellent understanding and the ability to quickly observe and grasp what he is told.
- Possesses the power to recollect what he hears, reads, senses; is not forgetful.
- Highly intellectual; can understand the direction of a group from which an idea is generated.
- Eloquence, and ability to express what is in the heart.
- Passion for education and seeks its benefits for all citizens.
- Must not tire easily and be exceedingly patient.
- Not greedy for food and drink.
- Efficient and effective in addressing the physical needs.
- A lover of the truth and its supporters; a hater of falsehood and its supporters.
- Quickly recognizes duplicitous people.
- Extremely generous, above stinginess.

[194] Dr. ʿAlī Abdul Wahid, *Commentary on al-Farabi,* Cairo.

- Worldly wealth must not be a factor; whether it is possessed or not should be of no concern.
- Loves justice and freedom.
- Rejects oppressors and oppression.
- Firmly decides the course that will benefit society, despite intense opposition.

1.5 ISLAM's LEGACY TO THE WEST

The Islamic precedent of developing law and governance according to the will of the majority, as well as adapting legal precedents to address new and evolving needs are Islam's legacy to the Western world. A famous Islamic saying states, "Islam is not simply a religion between the individual and his Lord, but a way of life in which people are taught to live in the world as if they are living forever."

Shaykh ʿAbd al-Ḥalīm Maḥmūd said, "The Islamic culture and civilization as a whole was the source of inspiration and source of information for principles and rules on which the Western civilization built its laws and rules."[195]

Dr. Muhammad Iqbal, in his book *Renewal of Religious Thinking* said, "Europe was extremely slow to grasp Islam, its principles, rules and its scientific perspective."

Briffault, who wrote the book *The Making of Humanity*, said:

"We have to be fair. Roger Bacon studied the Arabic language and sciences in Oxford and they have adopted the Arabic approach about which they wrote. Roger Bacon was like a messenger, bringing principles and rules from the religion of Islam and presenting them to Europe and Christendom."

Dr. Iqbal, quoting *The Making of Humanity* said:

[195] Shaykh ʿAbdul Ḥalīm Maḥmūd, Shaykh al-Azhar, *At-tafkīr al-falsafa fī al-islām* (Philosophy of Thinking in Islam), Chapter, "Islāmīc rules: Between originality and imitation" p. 247.

"What we call today knowledge and its principles, appeared today from the spirit of new research and new ways that have been developed from the examples of what happened before, and the scales of the past and the precedents of the past, and all these principles and rules and scientific curricula, were brought to the European world by the Arabs."

2. INDIVIDUAL FREEDOMS IN ISLAM

2.1 FREEDOM OF SPEECH

The Prophet ﷺ said, "A good believer must listen and obey as long as he is not being ordered to commit a sin."

This hadith delineates the limits between the giver of law and the rule of man. The object of rule in Islam is to implement Allah's Law – that legislated in the Qur'ān and Hadith, known as *Shari'ah* (Islamic law). The ruler who does so is to be followed, and the one who does not is to be corrected. Ensuring the rulers remain on the path of law is the job of the scholars of Islam and their inherent responsibility. It is not the task of the common people, but all citizens are free to express their opinion without fear of retaliation in Islam. Contrary to what is seen in most Muslim nations today, where one word spoken in criticism of the rulers may land a person in prison, Islam allows all to speak, as illustrated so significantly in the case of the lady who corrected the second caliph, 'Umar ؓ.[196]

In contrast to what radical Islamists claim today, *militant* opposition to rulers is not allowed so long as they permit the observance of Islamic worship. Therefore, traditional Muslims understand that a citizen has no right to create confusion, disrupt the peace, upset the leadership, or attempt to eliminate their authority by force as long as the governing authority gives the

[196] See below.

people the freedom to carry out their religious obligations. Under such conditions, a citizen has no right to oppose their nation's system of governance.

2.2 Freedom of Religious Belief

Prophet Muhammad ﷺ freely propagated the message of Islam, yet gave all people the freedom to choose any other religion. Jews, Christians and Zoroastrians were contractual members of the Muslim community. The Qur'ān states:

لاَ إِكْرَاهَ فِي الدِّينِ *"Let there be no compulsion in religion."*[197]

Accordingly, Muslim jurists have concluded that while Islam is the preferred belief and way of life, it cannot be imposed on anyone. In fifteen centuries of Islamic rule throughout the globe, there are no incidents in which Islam was imposed by force according to Islamic law. When non-Muslims became members of a Muslim nation, either through capture of territory or through migration, they were free to practice their beliefs. Furthermore, special consideration was given to believers in heavenly revealed religions: the Jews, Christians (known "People of the Book") Zoroastrians, and later, other faiths. They were afforded not only freedom of religious belief, but were allowed to maintain their own religious law and practices, even when these conflicted with the teachings of Islam.

Islamic civilization is firmly founded on the concept of 'rule of law.' For that reason, the law is published and known, and citizens and courts are expected to uphold it. In addition, Muslim citizens must adhere to Islamic law. If a Muslim citizen commits a religious violation, he is judged according to Islamic law. A non-Muslim citizen is judged in religious issues by the laws of his own faith.

---

[197] Sūratu 'l-Baqarah [The Heifer], 2: 256.

Further, it was deemed unlawful in Islam to desecrate or destroy non-Muslim houses of worship. At first restricted to certain faiths, this category was later extended to include the Hindus of India and other beliefs. A traveler in Muslim lands should not be surprised to see in them churches, synagogues and temples of other faiths, often erected in places of prominence.

Shaykh Aḥmad al-Jurjāwī writes:

> From the beginning of the history of Islam until today, you cannot see that the Muslims come against the Jews or the Christians living among them… Even the Crusades did not originate from Muslims, but came from the Europeans. We see that Ṣalāḥuddīn al-Ayyūbī would even have his physicians treat Christian soldiers and later send them home to England safely.[198]

2.3 Freedom of Commerce

Islam affords the citizens of a Muslim nation the freedom to conduct commerce as they please, as long as their actions are not unlawful. Travel is not restricted. Trade is open and people are free to work in any profession. Islamically, borders and nations exist as subdivisions for administration, not as barriers to migration or material gain.

2.4 Freedom to Petition the Government for Redress

ركب عمر بن الخطاب منبر رسول الله صلى الله عليه وسلم ثم قال: ايها الناس ما اكثاركم في صداق النساء ! ! وقد كان رسول الله صلى الله عليه وسلم واصحابه والصدقات فيما بينهم اربعمائة درهم، فما دون ذلك. ولو كان الأكثار في ذلك تقوى

[198] Shaykh Aḥmad al-Jurjāwī, head of the Science College of the University of al-Azhar, *Ḥikmat at-tashriʿ wa falsafatah*, Cairo.

عند الله او كرامة لم تسبقوهم اليها . فلاعرفن ما زاد رجل في صداق امراة على اربعمائة درهم. قال: ثم نزل. فاعترضتّه امراة من قريش فقالت: يا امير المؤمنين نهيت الناس عن يزيدوا في مهر النساء على اربعمائة درهم؟ قال: نعم. فقالت اما سمعت ما انزل الله في القران؟ قال: واي ذلك؟ فقالت: اما سمعت الله يقول: ﴿ واتيتم احداهن قنطاراً ﴾ الاية. قال: اللهم غفراً، كل الناس افقه من عمر. ثم رجع فركب المنبر فقال: ايها الناس اني كنت نهيتكم ان تزيدوا النساء في صدقاتهن على اربعمائة درهم، فمن شاء ان يعطي من ماله ما احب. قال ابو يعلى: وظنه قال: فمن طابت نفسه فليفعل. اسناده جيد قوي. وفي. رواية: امراة اصابت ورجل اخطا،

'Umar, the second caliph, ascended the pulpit of the Messenger of Allah and said, "O people! Do not go to excess in the matter of women's dowry... And we never knew of a man who gave more than 400 dirhams as dowry." Then he stepped down. A lady of the Quraysh from the congregation challenged 'Umar ؓ saying, "O prince of the believers! Have you told the believers not to exceed 400 dirhams in giving the dowry?" to which 'Umar ؓ replied "yes." She said, "Did you not hear that Allah said, 'If you have given one of them a heap of gold, then take not from it anything; would you take it by slandering (her) and (doing her) manifest wrong?'"[199] ...To this 'Umar ؓ said, "A

---

[199] Sūratu 'n-Nisā [Women], 4:20.

lady hit the target and a man [meaning himself] was wrong."[200]

2.5 TAXATION

The inherence of democratic principles in Islam is made even more clear in examining the application of *zakāt,*[201] a form of taxation applied to Muslim citizens of the state. The system of taxation applied to non-Muslim citizens, who also enjoyed benefits from the state, is known as *jizyā*. Funds collected from *zakāt* and *jizyā* are diligently applied to social welfare and state defense, producing a higher standard of living and suppressing the need to commit crimes. Both systems are extremely similar to the US system of taxation, which benefits everyone.

3. THE HIERARCHY OF LAW

Al-ḥukmu lillāh – Rule belongs to Allah. Traditional Muslims believe that Allah is *al-Ḥākim*, Ruler of Creation. In every moment Allah is the Supreme Judge. Yet, He gave man will. Why? If Allah were to give the rules and demand that we follow them, while knowing we are weak and cannot, it would be oppression. Allah is not an oppressor, but most loving towards His creation. He will not impose on us what we cannot achieve. Through the Qur'ān, Allah told humanity what He prefers for us, His highest standard of behavior.

The Qur'ān was revealed to Prophet Muhammad ﷺ as the exemplar of the highest level morality. Allah said, "This is your capacity as My perfect Servant." Since the rest of humanity are but ordinary human beings, the Prophet ﷺ served as an intermediary, reducing the power of the Divine orders to the capacity of the

---

[200] Abū Ya ʿla.

[201] One of the five pillars of faith, which implements social welfare in affording provision for the needy.

people he addressed. The Prophet ﷺ urged the Muslim community, with the guidance of qualified religious scholars, to use their own minds, judgment and sincerity in seeking out the intent of the law and adjust it according to capacity of the people.

The law is subject to hierarchy. The highest level is obedience to Allah. If you cannot obey all of Allah's commands, then obey the Prophet ﷺ. The level of Divine law – stated in the Qur'ān – is the abstract. It is the ultimate goal and, like the sun in the sky, shines over all but is humanly impossible to reach.

With this understanding in mind, it becomes clear why so many issues are described in only general terms in the Qur'ān. It was the duty of the Prophet ﷺ to explain these issues. Allah said:

مَّنْ يُطِعِ الرَّسُولَ فَقَدْ أَطَاعَ اللّهَ وَمَن تَوَلَّى فَمَا أَرْسَلْنَاكَ عَلَيْهِمْ حَفِيظًا

Whoever obeys the Prophet indeed obeys Allah.[202]

After the Prophet's death, it became the duty of the scholars and rulers to further codify and implement existing laws. Therefore, the next level of the hierarchy is obedience to those in authority, for those unable to maintain obedience to the Prophet ﷺ must at least obey those in authority. People in this position must obey the rulers chosen by election. '

إذا خرج ثلاثة في سفر فليؤمروا أحدهم

The Prophet ﷺ said, "If you are three on a journey, choose one as your leader." [203]

3.1 DIVERGENCE OF OPINION

Imām Ghazālī observed that, in examining the history of all different nations, there are three different approaches to life:

---

[202] Sūratu 'n-Nisā [Women], 4:80.
[203] *Sunan Abū Dāwūd*, 2708, 2709.

Materialistic: The world exists without a creator, and mankind lives only by self-determination.

Intellectual: Issues, known or in the future, can only be solved through reasoning and precedent.

Inspirational: All we need comes through inspiration and revelation, in the relationship between human beings and the subtle realm.[204]

The Qur'ān substantiates the third approach, speaking about all issues and providing a subtle means for understanding every issue of human life.

The first and second approaches to life are manifest in the earliest period of Islamic history, demonstrating that from the earliest point, the polity of the Muslim community was divided in three ways. For this reason, scholars were obligated to substantiate their methodologies through proof and logic. Islam never prohibited or inhibited this dialogue of the intellect; each group was allowed to develop its own vision and approach, not only in political theory, but in philosophy and other areas that, according to Islamists, would be considered heretical.

Both the intellectual and spiritual fields grew tremendously as many different cultures and nationalities entered Islam. This demanded that Muslims apply their intellects to every issue, and not simply rely on the rulings of their ancestors. They were required to start with legal precedents, then refine and adapt them into new laws that accommodate the era and environment in which they lived. This is directly contrary to the approach of the rigid and hard-hearted people, described in the Qur'ān as saying:

إِنَّا وَجَدْنَا آبَاءَنَا عَلَى أُمَّةٍ وَإِنَّا عَلَى آثَارِهِم مُّقْتَدُونَ

[204] *Ibid.*

"Surely we found our fathers on a course, and surely we are followers of their footsteps."[205]

The best program for Islamic rules began slowly, changing slowly, without fanatical imposition of the views of different groups, and began to diverge, from it emerging different streams and methods. The different views and opinions began early in Islam, even in the time of the Prophet ﷺ, as in the example of the order to pray at Banī Quraizah.[206]

A process of examination that leads to majority consensus (*itjihād*) was applied even in the time of Prophet Muhammad ﷺ. This is borne out by the famous hadith of Bani Quraizah, in which the Prophet ﷺ gave a group of Companions the order not to pray that afternoon until they reached the place of Banī Quraizah. Each individual Companion followed his own interpretation of this order; some prayed on the way, believing that what was meant was to try to reach Banī Quraizah but not to miss prayer. Others waited to reach there, but missed the prescribed time for the prayer. The Prophet ﷺ accepted both interpretations, as he intended only that they proceed quickly in order to reach Banī Quraizah sooner.

From this example, jurists derived two fundamental principles of Islamic jurisprudence:

1. Allowance for independent reasoning based on the intent of the law.

2. Allowance for divergence of opinion in interpreting the law.

---

[205] Sūratu z-Zukhruf [The Gold Adornments], 43:23.

[206] Shaykh ʿAbdul Ḥalīm Maḥmūd, Shaykh al-Azhar, *At-tafkīr al-falsafa fī al-islām* (Philosophy of Thinking in Islam), Chapter, "Islāmīc rules: Between originality and imitation"

3.2 THE EVOLUTION OF ISLAMIC LAW

Shaykh Aḥmad al-Jurjāwī, writes:

> What is the wisdom behind obligations in Islam, as rules that do not change? Allah created living creatures and we can see from their actions that the law of the jungle, survival of the fittest. We see the birds have their beaks as weapons. The scorpion and the snakes have poison. Lions and other predators have sharp teeth. Similarly, human beings have a basic primal nature, but have no physical ability for survival. Therefore Allah put fundamental laws and principles, in order to create a decent and stable community in which human beings live in safety and security. By means of these principles and rules, and the different opinions that Allah granted each individual, we see that the ideal community for mankind exists if all meet together and agree on rules by which all will live.

Thus the Qur'ān contains broad, general rules that are immutable, not unlike societal rules of today: the sanctity of life, security and freedom of expression, and the inviolability of these rights. Yet, a democracy is a society governed by the people, for the people. The adaptation of law according to time and circumstance was necessitated by changes in society, and the influx of various cultures and material conditions. Islam first came to one people with one lifestyle. As the religion spread and the borders of Muslim lands expanded, all of the different civilizations, each with their own codes of law, traditions and cultures, had to be incorporated into the Islamic polity. This was not achieved overnight and took great foresight on the part of Muslim jurists. This is most elegantly displayed in the development of the law.

The Qur'ān states:

وَلَوْ شَاءَ اللهُ لَجَعَلَكُمْ أُمَّةً وَاحِدَةً

If Allah so willed, He could make you all one people...[207]

But Allah, in His wisdom, did not. Human society has been allowed to adapt to new circumstances and compete in seeking valid solutions to its many moral and ethical dilemmas.

فَقَالَ رَسُولُ اللَّهِ صلى الله عليه وسلم " مَنْ سَنَّ فِي الإِسْلاَمِ سُنَّةً حَسَنَةً فَعُمِلَ بِهَا بَعْدَهُ كُتِبَ لَهُ مِثْلُ اجْرِ مَنْ عَمِلَ بِهَا وَلاَ يَنْقُصُ مِنْ اجُورِهِمْ شَىْءٌ

> The Prophet ﷺ said, "He who inaugurates a good practice (*sunnatun ḥasana*) in Islam earns the reward of it, and of all who perform it after him, without diminishing their own rewards in the least..."[208]

The Prophet ﷺ comprehended that new situations would arise, and thus gave Muslims the ability to adopt new applications of Islamic law if they were beneficial to the community.

Among numerous other examples of how applications of law have changed is the assembly of the Holy Qur'ān, which during the Prophet's lifetime consisted of loose pages in chronological sequence of divine revelation. The third caliph, 'Uthmān, took the initiative to assemble the revealed verses in the book format we have today. As the Prophet ﷺ had never indicated this should be done, or done so himself, 'Uthmān's act was an innovation. He introduced the notion of change, and thereby established a precedent for what would be considered good or useful innovations in religion.

In the early days of Islam, slavery was permitted as a vestige of the pre-existing social structure. At the same time, Islam introduced many safeguards for the rights of slaves and Muslims

---

[207] Sūratu 'n-Nahl [The Bee], 16:93.

[208] Muslim.

were encouraged to free them to expiate their sins. But it was not until later that scholars voted to abolish slavery altogether.

In Ramadan, the Muslims around the world gather in mosques to pray a nightly congregational prayer known as '*tarāwīḥ.*'[209]This was not practiced in this manner in the lifetime of the Prophet ﷺ, but later implemented as a means to preserve brotherhood among Muslims, and revive their spirits to fast the next day.

Similarly, when Muẓaffar al-Kawkubūrī noticed love for the Prophet ﷺ was diminishing, he introduced the public observance of the Prophet's birthday (mawlid), spending thousands of gold dinars for the event. The scholars of his time defended his act as something good.

Our nation's founding fathers also acknowledged that the people could not follow the law at all times. That is why they established a judicial system to address each breach of law on a case-by-case basis. In other words, application of the law varies based on the individual circumstances at the time.

3.3 The Formation of Different Schools

During the Prophet's time, Islam was spread with great tolerance and openness. The command to pray five times daily came over a period of years. The Arabs, who were fond of alcoholic beverages, were gently weaned from alcohol over a period of twenty years. Those who prayed to idols were not ostracized from their Muslim relatives. Islam was introduced gently, not forcefully.

Initially, law was taught by the Companions of the Prophet ﷺ, who migrated around the Muslim world, forming academic centers wherever they settled. With time, numerous centers of

[209] A special congregational prayer recited only in the month of Ramadan, traditionally in a mosque, in which 1/30 portion of the Holy Qur'ān is recited each night, to complete by the end of Ramadan.

scholarship emerged, with that in Madinah, the city of the Prophet ﷺ being foremost, then Kufa and Damascus. Later such centers of knowledge developed and flourished in Baghdad, Bukhara, Samarqand, Cairo, Cordoba and many other cities. As we see in the spread of all world religions, each school adapted to the temperament and culture of the native people. This precedent was established by the Prophet ﷺ when he sent his deputies to the various tribes of the Arabian Peninsula. He told one emissary to Yemen, Muadh bin Jabal, to deal with the new Muslims lightly and not force Islam on them at once, but to gradually acclimate them to Islamic laws.

The Caliphs ʿUmar ؓ and ʿAlī, Muʿadh ibn Jabal, and the later imāms of the schools all followed different methodologies in examining issues within an Islamic framework. After the Companions came the establishment of hundreds of Islamic schools of thought, each of which were based on the law of Allah, but applied by man.

Dr. Wahba al-Zuhaylī, a scholar of Islamic jurisprudence at the University of Damascus, writes that Sayyidina ʿUmar ؓ cancelled the charity that had been ordered in the time of the Prophet ﷺ for those who converted to Islam (*al-muallafat il-qulūb*). Though present in the law, he ruled that they no longer needed this incentive, as their Islam had become firmly established. ʿUmar ؓ eliminated the rule of cutting the hands for theft in the difficult 'Year of Hunger' despite it being a fundamental rule in the Qur'ān. ʿUmar ؓ was the first to institute the use of prisons to hold people before judgment.[210]

Before the canonization of the four independent schools of thought in the fourth century of Islam,[211] there existed more than

---

[210] Dr. Wahba al-Zuhaylī, *Uṣūl al-fiqh al-Islāmī* (Foundations of Jurisprudence), vol. 2, p. 764.

[211] Known as *"hijri"* date, on which the Islāmīc calenDār is based; from the time the Prophet migrated from Mecca to Madinah.

424 different schools of thought. These had been developed by experts who examined the revelation and precedents as established by the Prophet ﷺ and the early Muslim generations, and formed them into law.

Islamic jurists adopted the application of the law to different peoples and cultures. For instance, Imām Shāfiʿī's school was fully developed and established in Iraq.[212] When he moved to Cairo, he changed many of the rulings. In Iraq, he ruled that two unnecessary movements during prayer would invalidate it. However, in Egypt he changed the limit to three, owing to the more extreme climate and increased irritation of the person in prayer.

Even rules based on the principle of consensus of scholars, *ijmaʿ*, which in itself is difficult to accomplish, can be changed. Dr. Wahba al-Zuhaylī, wrote:

> Consensus of scholars on a certain issue made earlier can be abrogated by the consensus made by a later generation if there were changes in the conditions which are for the common good of the people as time progresses. The followers of the Ḥanbalī school and some of the followers of the Ḥanafī school say that one can reformulate or abrogate a law developed by consensus at one time by a new law that fits the later circumstances.[213]

Islamically, this concept of reformation or rejuvenation of the law is necessitated by change in society over time.

The great philosopher al-Kindī (800-873 CE), whom the renowned Italian philosopher Cardano (1501-1576 CE) described as one of the twelve best philosophers in fundamentals, stated:

---

[212] See *Kitāb al-Umm.*

[213] Dr. Wahba al-Zuhaylī, Professor of Jurisprudence, *Uṣūl al-fiqh al-Islāmī* (Foundations of Jurisprudence), Damascus, Syria, p. 975.

> We must speak the truth: whoever gave us an idea, we must respect his view and opinion, even in the most minor issue. What then do you think of someone who is going to deduce rules and laws that will affect your life in the future?[214]

It is good that we keep looking at what took place in the past, for one cannot come up with a law spontaneously. It is essential to look at the precedents that came before and see in what they were correct and in what they were wrong. Because it is impossible for an event to take place in a moment, for every event might stretch over a period of time, and in later times that issue might be viewed differently. It is better for us to bring all our principles and rules, and all they said before us as well as what they did not say, to put it together in order to derive a useful ruling for our own time.

Ibn Sīnā (Avicenna) said:

> I have decided to collect all that was said and written and compiled by those before, without concern for the differences they had, taking all together, categorizing it and showing the people of my time what the people thought about these issues, in order to clarify and refine the verdicts of the past.

3.4 Levels of Governance

Al-Fāʿrābī (d. 950 CE), a leader in Islamic political thought, expounded these ideas pertaining to the governance of different sizes of community:

- As humanity expanded through the earth and inhabited all its areas, it resulted in the formation of different nations and cultures.
- We can categorize the approach of nations into two: the ideal ones who are able to observe the highest level of principles and rules and those who observe them only partially.

---

[214] Abū Yūsuf Yaʿqūb Ibn Isḥāq al-Kindī, *Rasā'il al-kindī.*

- Those who observe the highest level are divided into three categories:
    - Highest are those in which the whole global society agrees and works together in unity.
    - Second is the localized observance – a region, city or state of the society works together in unity while the rest does not.
    - At the lowest level we find a district or community in which harmony and cooperation are observed.[215] system of government in which all states cooperate together is the goal for success. Yet, as in the federal system in the US, each lower level is semi-autonomous in relation to the level above it. Islam demanded the implementation of a universal political model of governance, not one limited to individual states. Thus, Islam is designed to benefit the entire global community while giving sufficient autonomy to the local regions to develop their own laws subordinate to application of federal law.

Al-Fāʿrābī elaborated that in such a community each individual also has his personal freedom. He is free to choose based on his own desires, good or bad, and he can choose to be a good citizen or a bad one. There is a direction for good and for evil. That is why, in the ideal city divided into three ranks, the society gives the ruler the authority to impose the rule of law and gives the courts the authority to enforce it. The ultimate source of the law is the community. The ideal city is that in which the entire community will unite to decide an issue, and produce principles and rules that will achieve happiness and contentment of the people. Al-Fāʿrābī stated, "For indeed the greatest happiness is that which comes about as a result of the meeting of this city to decide [on its direction]."

---

[215] al-Fāʿrābī, *Al-ārā al-māmūra al-fāḍila* (The Virtuous City).

In explaining the impact of culture, environment and geography versus the impact of revelation on the development of law, Shaykh ʿAbd al-Ḥalīm Maḥmūd, former shaykh of al-Azhar and one of the highest scholars in Islam in recent times, wrote:

> Among these philosophical principles were justice, the existence of good and evil, and the relationship between human beings and the environment and his interactions with it, the most important of these being the freedom of choice. The leadership of Muslim scholars has shown the differences in their views: each was able to deduce different methodologies from which emerged the various schools of thought.[216]

The nation is like a garden with all varieties of flowers, presenting an unending and attractive array of shapes, sizes and colors.

The process of adopting different methodologies began with Wasil bin ʿAtā, a student of Ḥasan al-Baṣrī. He showed the effect of Greek rules and principles on Muslim civilization, and the leaders of the time began to adopt these laws and principles.

4. POLITICAL SYSTEMS IN THE MUSLIM WORLD

Having arisen in the tribal regions of the Arabian Peninsula, the Islamic political structure originally included localized, tribal systems of government. Concurrent with the rule of the caliph, who bore the leadership of Islam as an inheritance from the Prophet ﷺ, each tribe ruled itself within a limited territory, according to tribal loyalties and other factors specific to their community.

With the advent of European colonization, western political values – especially the notion of monarchic rule – were unevenly adopted in various parts of the Muslim polity. Competing with one another, the colonial powers of England, France, Italy, the

---

[216] Shaykh ʿAbdul Ḥalīm Maḥmūd, Shaykh al-Azhar, "*At-tafkīr al-falsafa fī 'l-Islām*", Philosophy of Thinking in Islam, Chapter, "Islāmīc rules: Between originality and imitation" p. 247.

Netherlands, and Portugal each gradually took control of areas of the Muslim nation, as did Russia in the Caucasus and Central Asia. With the influence of these nations came a further appreciation for kingship and dynastic rule.

The colonial influence on the Arab and Muslim world was tremendous. Even after colonial powers ceded, Muslims themselves observed the imported systems of monarchy. Rather than by a revival of Islamic systems of elections and democracy, the vacuum of power was filled by new monarchs. The impact is clearly evident in Saudi Arabia, Jordan, Morocco, Tunisia, Egypt, Malaysia, Iraq, Libya, Oman, and the Persian Gulf states. Furthermore, these nations imbedded the political systems of their patrons for the sake of political benefit. The influence of colonial powers in Muslim nations therefore accounts, in part, for the limited respect for democracy they now exhibit.

Today, Muslim nations are tending toward the democratic ideals embodied in Islam's original political framework, if only for the sake of their relationships with the Western world. Unfortunately, tribal leaders oppose the move towards parliamentary systems, prompting leaders to adopt modern democratic nomenclature for a system that remains autocratic. The titles 'president' or 'prime minister' are common in Muslim countries, and claims are made that elections were held with wide majorities voting for the winning candidate. However, those who remain in power simply usurp terms like 'elections' and 'majority' when in reality they simply do not relinquish their seats. The buds of independent political parties are now beginning to form, but for them to truly flower will require great encouragement from the West.

Shaykh Aḥmad al-Jurjāwī said:

> If we have to give the label of 'Islam' to a group of people, they must in fact be true Muslims. Unfortunately, we must not call today's Muslims true Muslims. That is because

> Islam constitutes rules, discipline, principles and actions based on the rules and principles. Today these have been lost. Islam survives only in lectures and classrooms, for we are not living by Islam today. It has become a name without a body.[217]

> The Azhar scholar, Dr. Abū Zahrā, says:
> We must give rapt attention to disputes regarding political issues and their involvement with the schools of Islamic law. Using the name of Islam, they attempted to give credibility to what were essentially begun as political differences. This is a purely political manipulation of the faith and is not valid.

The democratic model that exists in traditional Islam is for the political elite to govern, while others are entrusted with administration, in consultation with respected members of the community. In fact, many freedoms enshrined in the US Bill of Rights are inherent civil liberties in Islam, including freedom of speech and the equality of men and women. The overriding principles of justice and allegiance to the ruler further reinforce democratic principles.

5. CONCLUSION

American Muslims are in an ideal position to inspire Muslim and Arab countries toward the revival of Islamic democratic systems. A large part of the American political structure constitutes what traditional Muslims have held as the ideal. In America, we are free to practice our faith and way of life and, at the same time, encouraged to participate in the political system.

Here, the system does not prevent anyone from ascending in political rank, but bases political representation on the will of the

---

[217] Shaykh Aḥmad Jurjāwī, paper addressing Conference on Islam and Muslims, Geneva, page 71.

people, which is itself molded by perceptions of success and the candidates' ability to uphold their political responsibilities. Therefore, as American Muslims begin to participate avidly in the political system, they will inevitably become role models for Muslims in the Arab world and elsewhere. This is evident today in Afghanistan and other nations, where second and third-generation American Muslims are returning in large numbers and making their opinions heard.

As eager and suited they may be to support such a change, it would take some time for American Muslims to inspire this shift in Muslim politics. Considering that it took 200 years to establish true democracy in America, we cannot expect that it would be quickly implemented in the Arab world. Although Islam recommends and stands firm on this political system, the fact remains that the people have been raised on a different system that demonstrates little regard for principles of the Islamic faith. Less than fifty years after the Prophet's death, when monarchy became the method of rulership selection, democratic principles began to wear down in the Muslim world. To seek a change in a system so deeply ingrained is to be patient, encouraging democracy to sprout anew from its Islamic roots.

Sadly, to date opposition parties in many countries have been silenced by their lack of funding. Many are struggling against petro-financed Wahhabi regimes, and can succeed only by creating an effective counter-balance. Their campaign would require not only funding, but to be complemented with a comprehensive program of re-education to ensure long-term impact. The US could easily support a successful democratic movement in the Muslim world by utilizing moderate Muslim scholars, protecting them from retaliation, and taking advantage of their full participation in the development of such a plan.

Understanding Islamic Law

INVOKING DIVINE PRINCIPLES AND HUMAN REASON

ISLAM: A COMPLETE PACKAGE

Islamic civilization, since the time of Prophet Muhammad ﷺ until now, is firmly founded on the concept of 'rule of law.' For that reason, the law is published and known, and citizens and courts are expected to uphold it. In addition, Muslim citizens must adhere to Islamic law - Shariʿah. If a Muslim citizen commits a religious violation, he is judged according to Islamic law. A non-Muslim citizen is judged in religious issues by the laws of his own faith.

Islam is a complete package – a complete message and way of life. To fraction it into its component, then examine them individually, will yield little or no understanding of Islam's holistic whole. Inevitably aspects of Islam examined separately, without a wide-ranging grasp of its totality, will be taken in a fragmented context, in which case aspects may take on the appearance of extremism.

However, when viewed from a comprehensive perspective by any fair person, Islam will be found sensible in all its aspects and practices. Could it be otherwise for a faith that powers one of the greatest living civilizations – one whose dynamism and creativity supplied a foundation for countless aspects of modern society?

Shariʿah is the Islamic Law – the disciplines and principles that govern the behavior of a Muslim individual towards his or herself, family, neighbors, community, city, nation and the Muslim polity as a whole, the Ummah. Similarly Shariʿah governs the interactions between communities, groups and social and economic organizations. Shariʿah establishes the criteria by which all social actions are classified, categorized and administered within the overall governance of the state.

Shariʿah first establishes the patterns believers should follow in worshipping Allah: prayers, charity, fasting and pilgrimage.

Islam's law comprises a comprehensive outlook on life. As one looks from a satellite at this planet, the Shariʿah conceives of the earth as a single 'city' with diverse inhabitants—in modern parlance, a 'global village.' Islam looks to the benefit of the society as a whole from a general perspective and presents a theoretical model that if followed provides safety and protection for society.

Shariʿah literally means 'a well-trodden path to water,' the source of all life, representing the Path to Allah, as given by Allah, the Originator of all life.

Islamist Understanding of Shariʿah

Now a great problem today is that a new movement within Islam, the Islamist movement, has innovated a non-traditional approach to Shariʿah which vitiates all of the past approaches and establishes a rigid, hardline and non-pragmatic approach which vitiates all semblance of humaneness, sanity, moderation and decorum which constituted Islamic Law's traditional implementation over the past 14 centuries of history.

Islamist states take the letter of the law – this is 'Black letter law' without regard to precedence. As Christopher Houston asserts:

> Indeed, the logic of the Shariʿah, with its minimal number of clear interdictions, and maximal scope for the interpretative extension of key precepts to particular situations, means that any freezing of the ulama's 'arbitrary' decisions arises not so much from the essential characteristics of the Shariʿah, but from the historic institutionalizing of a particular legal tradition or method of exegesis or from the hegemony of a particular interpretation. Whether this lack of institutional and conceptual closure ironically encourages modern Islamist

> states (Saudi Arabia?) or groups to force such closure is another question. Paradoxically, the provisionality of law-making allows some Islamist groups to interpret the Qur'ān as affirming a radical negation of human autonomy.[218]

Traditional governments in Islam on the other hand, follow precedents established over many centuries – just as is done in the US - they do not follow absolute 'letter of the law.'

Olivier Roy sums up the position of traditional Islam when he writes:

> The Shariʿah is never closed, for it is based not on a core of concepts, but rather on an ensemble of precepts which is at times general, at times precise, and which expands to include the totality of human acts through induction, analogy, extension, commentary, and interpretation.[219]

ISLAM AS A COMPLETE PACKAGE – THREE ASPECTS

Islam is a complete way of life, sent by Allah in the form of revelation by means of Prophet Muhammad ﷺ. As such it covers the three essential needs of human life: physical, intellectual and spiritual. These three aspects of the faith are known individually as:

1 Islam – Divine law

2 *Imān* - Belief

3 *Iḥsān* - Ethics and moral character.

The first aspect, Islam, deals primarily with the physical aspects of the faith, such as its obligations, prohibitions and recommended actions. This is the part of the faith governed by Shariʿah – Islamic law. This aspect cannot however be implemented by itself, but must complement the other two. When

---

[218] Houston, Christopher, "Islāmīsm, Castoriadia and Autonomy", Thesis Eleven, Number 76, February 2004, p. 56.

[219] Roy, Olivier, *The Failure of Political Islam*, Harvard University Press, Cambridge, MA, 1994, p. 10.

the Prophet ﷺ taught Islam to his followers, he taught them all these three aspects at once, in a natural and holistic approach.

SHARI'AH'S PRIMARY OBJECTIVE IS MERCY

Allah says:

وَمَا أَرْسَلْنَاكَ إِلَّا رَحْمَةً لِّلْعَالَمِينَ

And We did not send you (O Muhammad) except as a mercy for all creation.[220]

And the Prophet ﷺ said, "The Most Merciful shows mercy to those who have mercy on others. Show mercy to those on earth, and the One above the heaven will show mercy to you."

From this, and many other source texts, one can summarize the primary objective of the Shari'ah, (*maqsad al-Shari'ah al-asasī*) as Kamali has done:

> The *ulema* [scholars of Islam] have, thus, generally considered *Rahmah* [Mercy] to be the all-pervasive objective of the Shari'ah and have, to all intents and purposes, used it synonymously with *Maslaḥah* [benefit in everyday communal life].[221]

Similarly, Schact observes:

> ...the underlying tendency of the Qur'ānic legislation was to favour the underprivileged; it started with enunciating ethical principles... This feature of Qur'ānic legislation was preserved by Islamic law, and the purely legal attitude, which attaches legal consequences to relevant acts, is often

[220] Sūratu 'l-Anbīyā, 21:107.

[221] Kamali, Muhammad Hashim, "Maqasid al-Shariah: The Objectives of Islāmīc Law", Islāmīc Research Institute, Pakistan, 1999, p. 1.

superseded by the tendency to impose ethical standards on the believer.[222]

Since Mercy is the Shariʿah's primary goal, it is clear that this cannot be achieved if the believers who implement it are not embued with this essential quality.

When society is informed by spiritual values, the purpose of Shariʿah, to bring out mercy to mankind, will be natural manifestation of those values. When an individual's faith is informed by spiritual values his psyche and ethical compass will be balanced and his desire for immoral or criminal acts eliminated or reduced. Without such values, essential in removing the psychological illnesses and the societal ailments which afflict people in difficult physical situations, man becomes nothing more than a political animal and law becomes a means and an end, in-and-of itself.

Followers of Wahhabi movement, created by Muḥammad ibn ʿAbd al-Wahhāb (d. 1787), who make up the majority of implementers seeking 'Islamic' states today, reject the principles of spirituality, rather, they base their view of Islam purely on material aspects. Thus they see that the only approach to handling crime is to punish the perpetrator with a physical punishment.

Despite studying the religious books of his day Muḥammad ibn ʿAbd al-Wahhāb became extremely dogmatic in his understanding of the faith. Imām Abū Zahrā of Al-Azhar University asserts that Muḥammad ibn ʿAbd al-Wahhāb was excessively more extreme in his conceptions than any former scholar. Following his demise "his followers went to even further extremes surpassing all bounds of jurisprudence, declaring countless acceptable matters 'forbidden.' The Wahhabi movement, never content to promulgate its beliefs by tongue or pen, wielded a sword to fight whoever differed from its ideology."[223]

---

[222] Schact, J., *Cambridge Encyclopedia of Islam*, vol. II, pt. VIII/chpt. 4, pg. 539.
[223] Imām Abū Zahra, History of Islāmīc Schools of Thought, Cairo, 1997, p. 208.

BASES OF SHARIʿAH – REVELATION AND REASON

The bases of Shariʿah are four: two are revelatory, coming from Allah, and include the two core sources, the Qur'ān, Islam's holy book, and the Sunnah (the practice and teachings of the Prophet Muhammad ﷺ); and two are based in rational endeavor, consensus (*ijmaʿ*) and analogical juristic reasoning (*qiyās*).

FIQH–APPLICATION OF SHARIʿAH IN REAL LIFE

The Shariʿah, based primarily on texts from Qur'ān and Sunnah, embodies broad, general rules that are immutable, not unlike today's modern societal rules: the sanctity of life, security and freedom of expression, and the inviolability of these rights. The adaptation of law according to time and circumstance is necessitated by changes in society, and the influx of various cultures and material conditions. Islam first came to one people with one lifestyle. As the religion spread and the borders of Muslim lands expanded, all of the different civilizations, each with their own codes of law, traditions and cultures, had to be incorporated into the Islamic polity. This was not achieved overnight and took great foresight on the part of Muslim jurists, being most elegantly brought out in the development of *fiqh*, the jurists' law.

Kamali states:

> The primary sources of Islamic law are twofold: divine revelation (*waḥīy*) and human reason (*ʿaql*). This dual identity of Islamic law is reflected in its two Arabic designations, Shariʿah and *fiqh*. Shariʿah bears a stronger affinity with revelation, whereas *fiqh* is mainly the product of human reason. Shariʿah literally means "the right path" or "guide," whereas *fiqh* refers to human understanding and knowledge. The divine Shariʿah thus indicates the path to righteousness; reason discovers the Shariʿah and

relates its general directives to the quest for finding solutions to particular or unprecedented issues.[224]

Kamali defines *fiqh* as a rational endeavor primarily based on speculative reasoning. Amplifying on this he says:

> *Fiqh* is defined as the knowledge of the practical rules of the Shariʿah, which are derived from the Qur'ān and the Sunnah. The rules of *fiqh* are thus concerned with the manifest aspects of individual conduct. The practicalities of conduct are evaluated on a scale of five values: obligatory, recommended, permissible, reprehensible, and forbidden. The definition of *fiqh* also implies that the deduction of the rules of *fiqh* from the Qur'ān and the Sunnah is through direct contact with the source evidence and necessarily involves …independent reasoning and intellectual exertion (*ijtihād*).[225]

Khalid Muhammad delineates the distinction between Divine Law (Shariʿah) and Jurisprudence (*fiqh*) thus:

> Shariʿah …stands for the normative order that Muslims have developed as an Islamic way of life. Its translation as "Islamic law" is not adequate because Shariʿah covers a wider range of meanings than "law" usually does. Modern Muslim jurists often define Shariʿah as revealed or divine law in order to distinguish it from *fiqh,* the jurists' law, which is jurists' interpretation of Shariʿah, and *qānūn,* which is state law. This distinction aims to stress the divine nature and origin of Shariʿah in order to establish that its norms are binding because they are divine in origin… the Muslim jurists [have made] continuous efforts to keep Islamic law

---

[224] Mohammad Hashim Kamali, *Oxford History of Islam,* "Law and Society: The Interplay of Revelation and Reason in the Shariah", Oxford, 2000.

[225] Mohammad Hashim Kamali, *Oxford History of Islam,* "Law and Society: The Interplay of Revelation and Reason in the Shariah", Oxford, 2000.

acceptable to the people by bringing the legal norms close to social norms [through *fiqh* localized in time and place][226]

SHARI'AH'S FOUNDATIONS

COMMUNAL INTERDEPENDENCE

Islamic law is founded on the principle that individuals rely on other individuals. A single person cannot carry out every aspect of Shari'ah by himself, but needs other individuals that act as well, and from whose combined actions the society benefits as a whole. It is impossible for a person to reach perfection, but Islamic Shari'ah shows that one can reach perfection. How? By bringing all the people together. The society as a whole produces perfection which the individual by himself or herself cannot do. Through individuals striving for perfection and their interactions with each other under the Shari'ah, the entire society is refined.

This principle may be most clearly exemplified in the pilgrimage. A form of worship mandated for each individual, for whoever can afford it at least once in life, it nevertheless engages the entirety of society to accomplish it and it cannot be performed except as a community holding a global perspective. People gather in one place from around the world to fulfill this Divine command at the individual level, and altogether are successful at a single moment in affecting global changes. For that reason, Hajj has often been compared to an international assemblage, in which ideas, images and faith are gathered and shared in a vast revival of the community's dedication to Divine Service, and through service to Allah, service to humankind.

---

[226]Muhammad, Khalid M., Muslim Jurist's Quests for the Normative Basis of Shariah, ISIM Newsletter, Leiden, 2001.

OBJECTIVES OF THE LAW (*MAQASID AL-SHARI'AH*)

The overarching objectives of Shariʿah, where as mentioned above the overarching goal is Mercy, or the benefit of society (*maslaḥah*), are sometimes summarized under the following broad categories:

- Establishment of justice;
- Educating the individual;
- Upholding morality, in public and private;
- Preventing hardship, on individuals and society;
- Preventing oppression.

Shaykh ʿAbd al-Ḥalīm Maḥmūd, a Shaykh of al-Azhar and one of the highest scholars in Islam in recent times, wrote:

> Among these philosophical principles were justice, the existence of good and evil, and the relationship between human beings and the environment and his interactions with it, the most important of these being the freedom of choice. The leadership of Muslim scholars has shown the differences in their views: each was able to deduce different methodologies from which emerged the various schools of thought.[227]

Regarding the Objectives of Shariʿah, Kamali states:

> The precedents of the leading Sahaba (Companions of the Prophet) indicate, on the other hand, that they saw the Shariʿah not only as a set of rules but also as a system of values, where the specific rules were the tangible manifestations of those overriding values....it was not until the time of al-Ghazālī (d. 505H), and then al-Shatibi

[227] Shaykh ʿAbd al-Ḥalīm Maḥmūd, Shaykh al-Azhar, *At-Tafkīr al-falsafa fi 'l-Islām* (Philosophy of Thinking in Islam), Chapter, "Islāmīc rules: Between originality and imitation" p. 247.

(d. 790H), that significant developments were made in the formulation of the theory of *Al-Maqasid*.[228]

LEVELS OF OBSERVANCE

Al-Fāʿrābī (d. 950 CE), a leader in Islamic political thought, expounded these ideas pertaining to the governance of different sizes of community:

As humanity expanded through the earth and inhabited all its areas, it resulted in the formation of different nations and cultures. We can categorize the approach of nations into two: the ideal ones who are able to observe the highest level of principles and rules and those who observe them only partially. Those who observe the highest level are divided into three categories:

- Highest are those in which the whole global society agrees and works together in unity.
- Second is the localized observance – a region, city or state of the society works together in unity while the rest does not.
- At the lowest level we find a district or community in which harmony and cooperation are observed.[229]

Al-Shātibī defined Shariʿah's levels from a different perspective:

> Shariʿah law aimed to protect five basic human interests: religion, life, reproduction, property, and reason. He also found that these basic interests were universally recognized among all other nations. He developed a model of Islamic law consisting of three concentric circles. The innermost circle deals with the essential laws concerning the five basic interests. The second circle covers those laws

---

[228] Kamali, Muhammad Hashim, "Maqasid al-Shariah: The Objectives of Islāmīc Law", Islāmīc Research Institute, Pakistan, 1999, p. 3.

[229] al-Faʿrābī, *Al-ārā al-māmūra al-faḍila* (The Virtuous City).

> and practices that are not directly related to the above-mentioned laws but are assimilated into Shariʿah on account of public convenience... al-Shātibī finds the normative basis of Shariʿah, deeply rooted in human reason and social practices and standards.[230]

Commenting on the role of reason in defining juristic law (*fiqh*), Christopher Houston observes:

> ...the majority of strictures governing the believer's conduct is in both theory and practice debatable and hence revisable.[231]

On this topic, author Messick states, "In the gap between divine plan and human understanding [lies] the perennially fertile space of critique, the locus of an entire politics articulated in the idiom of the Shariʿah."[232]

Mallat Chibli writes:

> The lessons of the classical age, to sum up, are...: the rule of law is established as a principle, so is the concept of the right of man... At the same time, there is a dimension of civil society with its own autonomous regulation which can be found, in first approximation, in the importance of custom [*urf*[and its legal recognition, and in an identifiable sphere of separation of powers with the ruler on the one hand and *ʿulama, muftis* and *qāḍīs,* on the other.[233]

A partially-deficient society is one in which extremes are applied. Such societies take only parts from the whole. Because of

---

[230]Muhammad, Khalid M., "Muslim Jurist's Quests for the Normative Basis of Shariah", ISIM Newsletter, Leiden, 2001, p. 14.

[231] Houston, Christopher, "Islāmīsm, Castoriadia and Autonomy", Thesis Eleven, Number 76, February 2004, p. 56.

[232] Messick, B. *The Calligraphic State*, University of California Press, Berkeley, 1996, p 17.

[233] Mallat, Chibli, Islam and Public Law, "Introduction: On Islam and Democracy", SOAS/Institut du Monde Arabe, June 1990.

this, the society both progresses and suffers at the same time due to the imbalance in its observation of Shariʿah.

Such was often the case in Islamic history, where Islamic Law was implemented at some levels of society and not others. Often the ruler was exempt from provisions of law by royal fiat or explicit decree. Arjomand observes:

> The legal history of medieval Islam is replete with examples of conflict between royal public law and the Shariʿah. The same is true of modern constitutionalism in the Middle East. Clashes between the jurisdiction of the state laws and the Shariʿah surfaced in a basic form in the constitutional debates in Iran in 1907–8, and since then in Pakistan and elsewhere. ...But the civil rights to security of life and property – the first to be introduced in the Muslim world, though at variance with the political culture of the patrimonial and imperial systems of the Middle East – were not contradictory to Islamic law.[234]

SHARIʿAH'S SOURCES

1 REVELATION

Qur'ān

The primary source of Shariʿah are two: Qur'ān and Sunnah. The Qur'ān is held by all Muslims as the ultimate source of law, being revealed from Allah to the Prophet Muhammad ﷺ, and therefore perfect and infallible.

The Qur'ān contains broad, general rules that are immutable, not unlike societal rules of today: the sanctity of life, security and freedom of expression, and the inviolability of these rights. The adaptation of law according to time and circumstance was

---

[234] Arjomand, Saïd Amir, Islam, Political Change and Globalization, Thesis Eleven, Feb 2004.

necessitated by changes in society, and the influx of various cultures and material conditions. Islam first came to one people with one lifestyle. As the religion spread and the borders of Muslim lands expanded, all of the different civilizations, each with their own codes of law, traditions and cultures, had to be incorporated into the Islamic polity. This was not achieved overnight and took great foresight on the part of Muslim jurists. This is most elegantly displayed in the development of the law.

Sunnah

Much of the Qur'ān was revealed through actual events encountered by the Prophet ﷺ, and questions asked and answered by him. The Prophet ﷺ also used the Qur'ān as a basis of his own teaching and adjudication. Nevertheless, the Qur'ān is neither a legal nor a constitutional document, although legal materials occupy a small portion of its text; less than 3 percent of the text deals with legal matters. The legal contents of the Qur'ān were mainly revealed following the Prophet's migration from Mecca to Medina, where he established a government and the need therefore arose for legislation on social and governmental issues.

The second revealed source of Shariʿah is the Sunnah, or practices, injunctions and recommendations of the Prophet ﷺ as well as actions of others he approved or did not rebuff. It is consensus of scholars that the Sunnah is accorded the status of revelation, according to the explicit Qur'ānic text:

وَمَا آتَاكُمُ الرَّسُولُ فَخُذُوهُ وَمَا نَهَاكُمْ عَنْهُ فَانتَهُوا

what the Prophet gives you, take and what he forbids, cease therefrom.[235]

2 REASONING

Hashim Kamali states:

---

[235] Sūratu 'l-Ḥashr [The Gathering], 59:7.

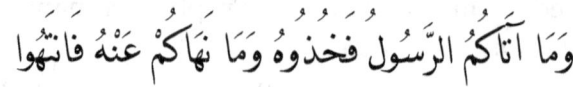

The nonrevealed sources of Shariʿah are generally founded in juristic reasoning (*ijtihād*). This reasoning may take a variety of forms, including analogical reasoning (*qiyās*), juristic preference (*istiḥsān*), considerations of public interest (*istiṣlāḥ*), and even general consensus (*ijmaʿ*) of the learned, which basically originates in *ijtihād* and provides a procedure by which a ruling of juristic reasoning can acquire the binding force of law. Analogy and consensus have been generally recognized by the vast majority of *ʿulama*, but there is disagreement over the validity and scope of many of the rational proofs that originate in *ijtihād*.[236]

Ijtihād, or juristic reasoning through analogy (*qiyās*) is a principle explicitly founded in the authentic Sunnah of the Prophet ﷺ in the famous hadith of Muʿadh.[237] The other principles were originated by the companions after the Prophet ﷺ and "Alī used to formulate his own opinion by means of *Ijithad* based on *qiyās, istishāb, istiḥsān* and *istiṣlāḥ,* always basing his opinion on the broader aims of the Shariʿah."[238]

Before the canonization of the four independent schools of thought, Mālikī, Ḥanafī, Shāfiʿī and Ḥanbalī in the fourth century

---

[236] Mohammad Hashim Kamali, *Oxford History of Islam,* "Law and Society: The Interplay of Revelation and Reason in the Shariah", Oxford, 2000.

[237] Muʿadh ibn Jabal relates that when the Prophet ﷺ sent him to Yemen, he asked, "What will you do if a matter is referred to you for judgment?" Muʿadh said, "I will judge according to the God's Book." The Prophet ﷺ asked, "what if you find no solution in God's Book?" Muʿadh said, "Then I will judge by the Sunnah of the Prophet." The Prophet ﷺ asked, "And what if you do not find it in the Sunnah of the Prophet?" Muʿadh said, "Then I will make *Ijtihad* to formulate my own judgment." The Prophet ﷺ patted Muʿadh's chest and said, "Praise be to Allah who has guided the messenger of His Prophet to that which pleases Him and His Prophet." Narrated by Abū Dāwūd in his *Sunan*

[238] Al-Alwani, Taha Jabir, *Source Methology in Islāmīc Jurisprudence,* International Institute of Islāmīc Thought, Herndon,Virginia, 1990.

of Islam,[239] there existed more than 424 different schools of thought. These had been developed by experts who examined the revelation and precedents as established by the Prophet and the early Muslim generations, and formed them into law.

WHO IS ELIGIBLE TO EXPLAIN THE SHARI'AH?

After the time of the Prophet Muhammad ﷺ, from over 100,000 of his Companions (students who personally met him), fewer than thirty are recorded actually issuing *fatwā*s on new issues in which *Ijtihād*, or juristic reasoning, was required.

Today the authority for *Ijtihād* is with the mufti, or Dar al-Ifta, Center of Rulings, which gives general rulings (*fatwā,* pl. *fatāwā*) about an incident or legal question. As scholars, they are able to look at the entire package of Islam and issue a ruling on the question at hand.

The judge (*qāḍī*) on the other hand issues a judgment (*ray al-qaḍā*) on particular cases or incidents pertaining to an individual or groups, typically in cases involving two adversaries.

These two groups must work together – like two parties in which both seek the best understanding by applying their utmost efforts. The Center of Rulings and the mufti build the information model while the judge applies it to a particular case. Each case studied by the judge (*qāḍī*) is an attempt to comprise a particular verdict based on the legal precedent given by the mufti which can be applied in the specific judgment.

A ruling by a mufti is not given force of law – it is only a response to an issue and it is up to individuals to follow the ruling or not. Law on the other hand, is enforced by individual judgments of the court – typically informed by a *fatwā* but in practical application taking into consideration circumstances and

---

[239] Known as "*hijri*" date, on which the Islāmīc calendar is based; from the time the Prophet ﷺ migrated from Mecca to Madinah.

conditions of plaintiff and defendant. Alternatively, a ruling (*fatwā*) can be made into law by order of the executive office.

It is essential to understand that no one can issue a ruling without qualification, and no one can issue a judgment without qualification. Since rulings have a tremendous impact on the life of society and ruling on the individual, it is essential that those issuing them have excellent moral character, and most importantly that they are qualified.

Allah says,

قُلْ أَرَأَيْتُم مَّا أَنزَلَ اللَّهُ لَكُم مِّن رِّزْقٍ فَجَعَلْتُم مِّنْهُ حَرَامًا وَحَلَالًا قُلْ آللَّهُ أَذِنَ لَكُمْ أَمْ عَلَى اللَّهِ تَفْتَرُونَ

Say: Tell me what Allah has sent down for you of sustenance, then you make (a part) of it unlawful and (a part) lawful. Say: Has Allah commanded you, or do you forge a lie against Allah?"[240]

This verse emphasizes that no one has the right to judge something right or wrong unless he has complete evidence from the pertinent information as found in the source texts, from deep discussion among the people who have a grasp of the issue at hand, and to seek all meaningful evidence. Otherwise one should remain silent for then one would be lying against Allah and against the religion.

Imām Shāfiʿī, founder of one of the four great schools of jurisprudence, said:

> It is not allowed for anyone to give a Shariʿah explanation (*fatwā*), except one who knows the Holy Qur'ān completely including what verses are abrogated and by which verses they were abrogated, and which verses resemble each other

[240] Sūrah Yūnus [Jonah], 10:59.

in the Qur'ān and whether a chapter was revealed in Makkah or Madina. He must know the entire corpus of the Hadith of the Prophet ﷺ, both those which are authentic and those which are false. He must know the Arabic language of the time of the Prophet ﷺ with its grammar and eloquence as well as know the poetry of the Arabs. Additionally he must know the culture of the various peoples who live in each different nation of the community. If a person has all such attributes combined in himself, he may speak on what is permitted (*halal*) and what is forbidden (*haram*). Otherwise he has no right to issue a *fatwā*.

It is related that one of the greatest scholars of Shariʿah, ʿAbd al-Raḥmān ibn Abi Laila said:

> I was able to meet with one hundred and twenty of the Companions of the Prophet ﷺ. Every one of these companions was asked about specific Shariʿah issues, seeking a verdict, but they avoided rendering a decision instead pointing to another companion to issue the answer. They were afraid to give an answer that would be incorrect for which they would be responsible before Allah.

That shows that one can be deeply imbued with Islamic knowledge, as were all the Prophet's Companions, and yet still feel unqualified to give a verdict. All one-hundred and twenty of the Prophet's Companions with whom ibn Abi Laila met were hesitant to issue a *fatwā*.

Imām Nawawī, one of the greatest of Islam's later scholars, related that Imām ash-Shuʿbī and Ḥasan al-Baṣrī and many others of the Successors [generation immediately succeeding the Companions of the Prophet ﷺ] said, "people of today are quick to issue a ruling based on their analysis concerning someone. If an answer had been sought for that same issue at the time of ʿUmar ibn al-Khaṭṭāb ؓ (second caliph of the Prophet ﷺ), he would have gathered all the participants of Badr [i.e. 313 of the foremost Companions of the Prophet] in pursuit of the answer."

Historically, *ijtihād* has been perceived as a concern primarily of the individual scholar and *mujtahid*. But in modern times, *ijtihād* has become a collective endeavor that combines the skills and contributions not only of the scholars of Shariʿah, but of experts in various other disciplines, because acquiring a mastery of all the skills that are important to society is difficult for any one person. Ideally, independent reasoning should be combined with the Qur'ānic principle of consultation (*shūrā*), making it a consultative process, preferably as an integral part of the workings of the modern legislative assembly. *Ijtihād* has also been seen in the past as a juristic concept, a preserve of the jurist to the exclusion of specialists in other disciplines. But as a method by which to find solutions to new issues, *ijtihād* should be exercised by the scholars of Shariʿah as well as by experts in other disciplines, provided that those who attempt this independent reasoning acquire mastery of the relevant data, the Quaran, and the Sunnah. There is thus no reason why experts in Islamic economics and medicine, for example, could not carry out *ijtihād* in their own fields.[241]

DETAILED OBJECTIVES OF THE LAW (*MAQASID ASH-SHARI'AH*)

Schact, in describing the purpose of the Law writes:

In the field of penal law, it is easy to understand that the Qur'ān laid down sanctions for transgressions, but again they are essentially moral and only incidentally penal, so

[241] Mohammad Hashim Kamali, *Oxford History of Islam*, "Law and Society: The Interplay of Revelation and Reason in the Shariah", Oxford, 2000.

> much so that the Qur'ān prohibited wine-drinking but did not enact any penalty, and the penalty was determined only at a later stage of Islamic law. The reasons for Qur'ānic legislation on all these matters were, in the first place, the desire to improve the position of women, of orphans and of the weak in general, to restrict the laxity of sexual morals and to strengthen the marriage tie, to restrict private vengeance and retaliation and to eliminate blood feuds altogether; the prohibition of gambling, of drinking wine and of taking interest are directly aimed at ancient Arabian standards of behaviour.[242]

Shaykh Faraz Rabbani describes the intent behind Divine Law, something which has been strongly highlighted in the current era as people with various agendas, from apologist to extreme Islamist, seek to define Islamic Law within a Western framework of understanding:

> The ultimate worth of actions is based on intention and sincerity, as mentioned by the Prophet ﷺ, who said, "Actions are by intentions, and one shall only get that which one intended." The Shariʿah covers all aspects of human life. Classical Shariʿah manuals are often divided into four parts: ...personal acts of worship;... commercial dealings;...marriage and divorce, and penal laws.
>
> The legal philosophers of Islam, such as Ghazālī, Shāṭibī, and Shāh Walīullāh explain that the aim of Shariʿah is to promote human welfare. This is evident in the Qur'ān, and teachings of the Prophet ﷺ.
>
> The scholars explain that the welfare of humans is based on the fulfillment of necessities, needs, and comforts.
>
> **Necessities**

[242] Schact, J., *Cambridge Encyclopedia of Islam,* vol. II, pt. VIII/chpt. 4, pg. 539.

Necessities are matters that worldly and religious life depend upon. Their omission leads to unbearable hardship in this life, or punishment in the next. There are five necessities: preservation of religion, life, intellect, lineage, and wealth. These ensure individual and social welfare in this life and the hereafter.

The Shariʿah protects these necessities in two ways: firstly by ensuring their establishment and then by preserving them.

Religion: To ensure the establishment of religion, Allah Most High has made belief and worship obligatory. To ensure its preservation, the rulings relating to the obligation of learning and conveying the religion were legislated.

Life: To ensure the preservation of human life, Allah Most high legislated for marriage, healthy eating and living, and forbid the taking of life and laid down punishments for doing so.

Intellect: Allah has permitted that sound intellect and knowledge be promoted, and forbidden that which corrupts or weakens it, such as alcohol and drugs. He has also imposed preventative punishments in order that people stay away from them, because a sound intellect is the basis of the moral responsibility that humans were given.

Lineage: marriage was legislated for the preservation of lineage, and sex outside marriage was forbidden. Punitive laws were put in placed in order to ensure the preservation of lineage and the continuation of human life.

Wealth: Allah has made it obligatory to support oneself and those one is responsible for, and placed laws to regulate the commerce and transactions between people, in order to ensure fair dealing, economic justice, and to prevent oppression and dispute.

Needs and Comforts: Needs and comforts are things people seek in order to ensure a good life, and avoid hardship, even though they are not essential. The spirit of the Shariʿah with regards to needs and comforts is summed up in the Qur'ān,

وَمَا جَعَلَ عَلَيْكُمْ فِي الدِّينِ مِنْ حَرَجٍ

He has not placed any hardship for you in religion,"[243]

And,

مَا يُرِيدُ اللَّهُ لِيَجْعَلَ عَلَيْكُم مِّنْ حَرَجٍ وَلَكِن يُرِيدُ لِيُطَهِّرَكُمْ وَلِيُتِمَّ نِعْمَتَهُ عَلَيْكُمْ لَعَلَّكُمْ تَشْكُرُونَ

Allah does not seek to place a burden on you, but that He purify you and perfect His grace upon you, that you may give thanks.[244]

Therefore, everything that ensures the human happiness, within the spirit of Divine Guidance, is permitted in the Shariʿah.[245]

DEFERRAL OF RULING AND JUDGMENTS

An essential principle for muftis and *qāḍīs* is they must not to be quick in ruling and must examine all the evidences from the Holy Qur'ān, hadith and precedent prior law. The mufti must not think that being quick to respond is due to his own ingenuity, rather he must take painstaking care and be tranquil as he

[243] Sūratu 'l-Ḥajj [The Pilgrimage], 22:78

[244] Sūratu 'l-Mā'idah [The Spread Table], 5:6.

[245] Rabbani, Faraz, Shariah: The Clear Path, BBC Online website URL: http://www.bbc.co.uk/religion/religions/islam/beliefs/sharia/clearpath_intro.shtml.

approaches the problem, in order not to make the slightest error, for the lives of people are in the balance in such decisions. Similarly, he must await changes in circumstances, for conditions and situations might change and evidences might emerge that were not known at the outset of the issue before him. It is thus not uncommon for a mufti to wait many weeks before issuing a *fatwā*. However, where extreme forms of Shariʿah are practiced, *fatwā*s or judgements are often made quickly with insufficient attention to the issues or the Shariatic arguments relating to the judgment.

THE MIDDLE PATH

Islamic Shariʿah calls people to the middle path in all things in belief, worship, ethics, morality, behavior, individual interactions, social interactions and in intellectual understanding. This is the basis of Shariʿah's *ṣirāṭ al-mustaqīm* – the Straight Path.

This essential principle of Shariʿah is known as *"al-wasaṭīyya"*, moderation, as mentioned in the Holy Qur'ān, وَكَذَلِكَ جَعَلْنَاكُمْ أُمَّةً وَسَطًا *"we made you a nation of justice and clemency."*[246] This principle encourages clemency and reasonableness in making judgments.

Allah said:

وَمَا كَانَ الْمُؤْمِنُونَ لِيَنفِرُوا كَآفَّةً فَلَوْلاَ نَفَرَ مِن كُلِّ فِرْقَةٍ مِّنْهُمْ طَآئِفَةٌ لِّيَتَفَقَّهُوا فِي الدِّينِ وَلِيُنذِرُوا قَوْمَهُمْ إِذَا رَجَعُوا إِلَيْهِمْ لَعَلَّهُمْ يَحْذَرُونَ

Nor should the believers all go forth together. If a contingent from each expedition remained behind they could devote themselves to study of religion and admonish the people when they return that thus they may guard themselves from evil.[247]

---

[246] Sūratu 'l-Baqarah [The Heifer], 2:143.
[247] Sūratu 't-Tawbah [Repentance], 9:122.

This Qur'ānic exhortation recommends that a handful of individuals should come forth and study the faith deeply - they become the ones to advise the community in religious issues.

Allah said, فَاسْأَلْ بِهِ خَبِيرًا *"Ask about Allah from one who knowledgable."*[248] and He said: فَاسْأَلُوا أَهْلَ الذِّكْرِ إِن كُنتُمْ لَا تَعْلَمُونَ *"so ask the followers of the Reminder if you do not know,"*[249] indicating the need to ask those possessing knowledge of an issue; not from one's opinion or from someone who is ignorant.

Imām Mālik was once asked about twenty-two different juristic issues. He only responded to two. In answering these he prayed seeking support from Allah and he was not hasty in his responses.

It is said that "the one among you who quickly runs to make *fatwā*, is like one who is running to throw himself into the fire." Such sayings emphasize the importance of deep consideration when making a ruling.

EASE ABOVE ARDOR

Another principle in issuing a *fatwā* the mufti must seek the easiest way that people can apply, which is acceptable in Islam.

Allah said:

يُرِيدُ اللَّهُ بِكُمُ الْيُسْرَ وَلَا يُرِيدُ بِكُمُ الْعُسْرَ

Allah intends every facility for you; he does not want to put you to difficulties[250]

and the Prophet ﷺ said, "make things easy and do not make them difficult."

---

[248] Sūratu 'l-Furqān [The Criterion], 25:59.
[249] Sūratu 'l-Anbīyā [The Prophets], 21:7.
[250] Sūratu 'l-Baqarah [The Heifer], 2:185.

DIFFERENCES AS MERCY

> Prophet Muhammad ﷺ said, "Islam consists in three hundred and thirteen roads (Shariʿah). There is not one upon which one meets Allah, Almighty and Exalted except he enters Paradise through it."[251]

Prophet Muhammad ﷺ said, "It is meritorious for a judge to make an interpretation (*ijtihād*), even if wrong. But for the judge who adjudicates rightly there is twice the merit,"[252] meaning he received the merit of striving to seek a correct judgment and the reward of having done so.

One of the Successors of the Prophet ﷺ, the caliph ʿUmar ibn ʿAbd al-ʿAzīz said, "I don't like to see the Companions of Prophet ﷺ agreeing on the same issue, rather I prefer to see them disagree."

What he meant was that if the Companions, who are the main reference for the Shariʿah, disagree, different valid viewpoints would emerge, and in this way more solutions to the same problem would become available. This kind of dispute never divides the community. In fact there is a saying, "The differences among my Community are a mercy" which the scholars of Islam agree is correct in meaning.

Dr. Muhammad Imara of Al-Azhar in Cairo says:

> It is easy to avoid discussing the differences in the Ummah but it is impossible to remove them and say that all will accept the same ideology and school. Whoever thinks that about the Muslim Ummah can one day be free of schools of thought, is in fact an enemy of freedom and diversity, or believes in an idealistic dream which is, in reality, impossible to expect. For stifling intellectuality and preventing different

[251] A fair narration from Ibn ʿAbbās by al-Ṭabarānī in *al-Kabīr* (12:237).

[252] Bukhārī, Muslim, and several other authentic collections relate this Ḥadīth.

ways of thinking about religion from being expressed, in essence imposes dictatorship on religion…[253]

Muslims are thus presented with competing *fatwās*. In such cases he or she would follow the ruling of the scholar observing the same religious *madhhab*. If two muftis of the same *madhhab* issue conflicting *fatwās*, the common Muslim has his or her choice. In practice however, today holding to a particular tradition is not strictly applied, giving Muslims more flexibility in choosing among alternatives. Extreme Muslims however reject the principle that differences are a mercy and seek to impose one 'brand' of Islam and one set of rulings on everyone. This in practice makes them rigid, unbending and intolerant.

CLEMENCY

In the verses of punishment, one finds that Allah always follows by mentioning forgiveness, as in:

فَمَنْ عُفِيَ لَهُ مِنْ أَخِيهِ شَيْءٌ فَاتِّبَاعٌ بِالْمَعْرُوفِ وَأَدَاءٌ إِلَيْهِ بِإِحْسَانٍ ذَلِكَ
تَخْفِيفٌ مِّن رَّبِّكُمْ وَرَحْمَةٌ فَمَنِ اعْتَدَى بَعْدَ ذَلِكَ فَلَهُ عَذَابٌ أَلِيمٌ

And for him who is forgiven somewhat by his (injured) brother, prosecution according to usage and payment unto him in kindness. This is a concession and a mercy from your Lord. After this whoever exceeds the limits shall be for him a great penalty.[254]

This is made very clear in the Qur'ān wherein each mention of punishment, is followed by the mention of repentance and forgiveness.

---

253 Dr. Muhammad Imāra, "Muslim Unity: an elusive goal", Al-Watan al-ʿArabī.

254 Sūratu 'l-Baqarah [The Heifer], 2:178.

. . .كَتَبْنَا عَلَى بَنِي إِسْرَائِيلَ أَنَّهُ مَن قَتَلَ نَفْسًا بِغَيْرِ نَفْسٍ أَوْ فَسَادٍ فِي الأَرْضِ فَكَأَنَّمَا قَتَلَ النَّاسَ جَمِيعًا وَمَنْ أَحْيَاهَا فَكَأَنَّمَا أَحْيَا النَّاسَ جَمِيعًا وَلَقَدْ جَاءتْهُمْ رُسُلُنَا بِالبَيِّنَاتِ ثُمَّ إِنَّ كَثِيرًا مِّنْهُم بَعْدَ ذَلِكَ فِي الأَرْضِ لَمُسْرِفُونَ

...We decreed for the Children of Israel that whosoever killeth a human being for other than murder or corruption in the earth, it shall be as if he had killed all mankind And if anyone saved a life, it would be as if he had saved all of mankind.[255]

In mentioning the laws of punishment for waging war, the Qur'ān recommends the death penalty. However, even for this most grievous crime it allows a way out

إِلاَّ الَّذِينَ تَابُواْ مِن قَبْلِ أَن تَقْدِرُواْ عَلَيْهِمْ فَاعْلَمُواْ أَنَّ اللّهَ غَفُورٌ رَّحِيمٌ

...except for those who repent before they fall into your power. In that case, know that Allah is Forgiving, Merciful.[256]

Again emphasizing forgiveness, Allah says:

وَلْيَعْفُوا وَلْيَصْفَحُوا أَلَا تُحِبُّونَ أَن يَغْفِرَ اللَّهُ لَكُمْ وَاللَّهُ غَفُورٌ رَّحِيمٌ

...let them forgive and overlook. Do you not wish that Allah should forgive you?[257]

And in respect of cutting the hands of the thief, Allah says:

---

[255] Sūratu 'l-Mā'idah [The Spread Table], 5:32.
[256] Sūratu 'l-Mā'idah [The Spread Table], 5:34.
[257] Sūratu 'n-Nūr [The Light], 24:22.

فَمَن تَابَ مِن بَعْدِ ظُلْمِهِ وَأَصْلَحَ فَإِنَّ اللَّهَ يَتُوبُ عَلَيْهِ إِنَّ اللَّهَ غَفُورٌ رَّحِيمٌ

But if the thief repents after his crime, and amends his conduct, Allah turneth to him in forgiveness; for Allah is Oft-forgiving, Most Merciful.[258]

We see that all these verses which commence as verses of punishment are immediately followed by verses of mercy. That is Islam's way of dealing with criminality to reduce the severity of punishment. That is why a judge must examine each case with great consideration.

> It is reported by 'Āʿishā that the Messenger of Allah ﷺ said: "Ignore the offenses of those seen to possess [good] qualities (*dhawi 'l-ḥayāt*), except in [corporal and capital] penalties."[259]
>
> 'Āʿishā also related that the Prophet ﷺ said: "Stave off the penalties from the Muslims as much as you can, and if any leeway is found then release the detainee. Truly it is preferable for the ruler to pardon mistakenly than to punish mistakenly."[260]

The Companion ʿAbd Allāh ibn Masʿūd said: "Stave off the penalties by way of inconclusive evidence. Avert death from the Muslims as much as you can."[261]

---

[258] Sūratu 'l-Mā'idah [The Spread Table], 5:39.

[259] Narrated by Abū Dāwūd, Aḥmad, and others.

[260] Tirmidhī narrated it from 'Āʿishā without raising it up to the Prophet. It was also narrated from ʿAlī by al-Dāraqutnī; Abū Hurayrah by Ibn Mājah and Abū Yaʿla; ʿAbdullah ibn Amr by Abū Dāwūd and al-Nasā'ī.

[261] Al-Bukhārī. The same was narrated from "Uqba ibn ʿAmir and Muʿadh with *mawqūf* chains and ʿUmar with a *munqatiʿ mawqūf* chain. *Mawqūf* means "Stopped"—a chain arrested at the Companion-narrator without explicit attribution to the Prophet. *Munqatiʿ* means "Cut up"—a chain missing two successive links or missing only the Successor-link.

The caliph 'Umar ؓ said: "To erroneously not apply the penalties because of inconclusive evidence is dearer to me than mistakenly applying them on the basis of inconclusive evidence."²⁶²

Shaykh Yūsuf al-Rifai, commenting on the excessive application of punishments by Salafi extremists, writes:

...you forgot that the Prophet ﷺ said: "The first judgment that shall be passed among the people on the Day of Resurrection shall be over blood [unjustly shed]."²⁶³ Therefore, fear Allah and do not kill a life which Allah made sacred, except in justice!²⁶⁴

MODERATION

إياكم و الغلو في الدين فإنما هلك من كان قبلكم بالغلو في الدين

The Prophet ﷺ said, "Beware of extremism in religion. Those who were before you nothing destroyed them except their extremism in religion."²⁶⁵

The moderate Islamic Shari'ah is described by the verse:

ادْعُ إِلَىٰ سَبِيلِ رَبِّكَ بِالْحِكْمَةِ وَالْمَوْعِظَةِ الْحَسَنَةِ وَجَادِلْهُم بِالَّتِي هِيَ أَحْسَنُ

إِنَّ رَبَّكَ هُوَ أَعْلَمُ بِمَن ضَلَّ عَن سَبِيلِهِ وَهُوَ أَعْلَمُ بِالْمُهْتَدِينَ

---

²⁶² Related by Ibn Abī Shayba and in al-Hārithī's *Musnad Abī Ḥanīfa*, from Miqsam, from Ibn 'Abbās, raised to the Prophet.
²⁶³ Narrated by Aḥmad and the Six except Abū Dāwūd.
²⁶⁴ Al-Sayyid Yūsuf ibn Hashim al-Rifai, *Nasīḥa li ikhwāninā 'ulama najd*, (translated by Dr. Gibril Haddad as Advice to our Brothers the Scholars of Najd), Unpublished mss, Sunnah Foundation, 2000.
²⁶⁵ Imām Aḥmad.

"Invite (all) to the Way of thy Lord with wisdom and beautiful preaching; and argue with them in ways that are best and most gracious...."[266]

This verse shows that even in debates with others, one must use a good form of discussion and dialogue.

Allah prevented Muslims from discussion with non-Muslims except in a moderate way:

وَلَا تُجَادِلُوا أَهْلَ الْكِتَابِ إِلَّا بِالَّتِي هِيَ أَحْسَنُ إِلَّا الَّذِينَ ظَلَمُوا مِنْهُمْ وَقُولُوا آمَنَّا بِالَّذِي أُنزِلَ إِلَيْنَا وَأُنزِلَ إِلَيْكُمْ وَإِلَٰهُنَا وَإِلَٰهُكُمْ وَاحِدٌ وَنَحْنُ لَهُ مُسْلِمُونَ

"and dispute not with the people of the Book except with means better than mere disputation,... and say 'we believe in the revelation that has come down to us and in that which has come down to you. Our God and your God is one and it is to Him that we surrender.'"[267]

And in another place He says:

وَإِن جَادَلُوكَ فَقُلِ اللَّهُ أَعْلَمُ بِمَا تَعْمَلُونَ اللَّهُ يَحْكُمُ بَيْنَكُمْ يَوْمَ الْقِيَامَةِ فِيمَا كُنتُمْ فِيهِ تَخْتَلِفُونَ

If they do wrangle with thee, say, "Allah knows best what it is ye are doing. Allah will judge between you on the Day of Judgment concerning the matters in which ye differ."[268]

GENTLENESS

Islam encourages people to be good hearted:

---

[266] Sūratu 'n-Nahl [The Bee], 16:125.

[267] Sūratu 'l-'Ankabūt [The Spider], 29:46.

[268] Sūratu 'l-Ḥajj [The Pilgrimage], 22:68,69.

فَبِمَا رَحْمَةٍ مِّنَ اللَّهِ لِنتَ لَهُمْ وَلَوْ كُنتَ فَظًّا غَلِيظَ الْقَلْبِ لَانفَضُّوا مِنْ حَوْلِكَ فَاعْفُ عَنْهُمْ وَاسْتَغْفِرْ لَهُمْ

it is part of the mercy of Allah that thou does deal gently with them. Were thou severe or harsh-hearted they would have dispersed from around thee, so pardon them and ask forgiveness for them....[269]

There are many other verses and hadith which will demonstrate the moderation of Shariʿah. The Prophet ﷺ said to his wife 'Āʿishā, "Allah loves gentleness in everything in this life and religion, either in tongue or in deed."

This is evidenced in the following aḥādīth: "Allah loves kindness in all matters and, "Kindness makes things beautiful, violence makes them defective," as well as in the following wisdom of our forebears: "Whoever desires to command the common good, let him do it gently."

PUBLIC INTEREST

The subject of public interest (*maslaḥa*) has been subject of great interest to those studying Shariʿah from the viewpoint of its compability with Western law. On this topic Kamali says:

> Although the leading schools have also recognized considerations of public interest (*istislah*) as a source of law, they have generally tended to impose a variety of conditions on it because of its strong utilitarian leanings. Only the theologian Mālik advocated it as a source of law in its own right, which is why the considerations of public interest are seen as a Maliki contribution to the legal theory of the sources, the *usul al-fiqh*. Whereas analogy

[269] Sūrat Āli-ʿImrān [The Family of ʿImrān], 3:159.

operated within the given terms of the existing law, and juristic preference basically corrected the rigidities of analogy, public interest was not bound by such limitations. Furthermore, it vested the ruler and *mujtahid* with the initiative to take all necessary measures, including new legislation, to secure what he considered to benefit the people.

An example of *istislah*, or public interest is when Imām ibn Ḥanbal issued a verdict permitting compelling the owner of a large house to shelter the homeless.

Imām Aḥmad also endorsed requiring striking workers and craftspeople to continue to provide their services at a fair wage to avoid hardship on society.[270]

Muhammad Khalid, remarking on this topic states:

> [Islamic jurists] frequently invoked the principles of necessity, expediency, preventive measures, state of emergency, and other similar doctrines to reconcile the contradictions between laws and social norms. The contradictions continued because these doctrines were not regularized as "norms" in the legal theory. Nevertheless, some Muslim jurists tried to develop legal theories to regularize the quest for a normative basis of Shariʿah in the social practice and usage of the people.[271]

Haim Gerber discusses the similar concept of *urf,* most commonly observed in Ḥanafī *fiqh*:

> Ibn Abidin's notion that the law was not wholly built on revelation, but that some of the material was collected by the founder *mujtahid* from the customary law of his time.

---

[270] Mohammad Hashim Kamali, *Oxford History of Islam*, "Law and Society: The Interplay of Revelation and Reason in the Shariah", Oxford, 2000.

[271] Muhammad, Khalid M., "Muslim Jurist's Quests for the Normative Basis of Shariah", ISIM Newsletter, Leiden, 2001, p. 13.

He goes on to posit a new legal category within the law—the books of the school, which stand below the texts of revelation (*nass*, Qur'ān and *Sunnah*), and are even eclipsed by the *urf*, laws that derive from local customs.[272]

EXTREMISM

Extremism is described in Islam by two words: *ghuluw* – extremism, extravagance, immoderation, and *tatarraf* – radicalism.

One of the main forms of extremism in religion is complete ignorance of the comprehensive nature of Islam. This is what makes an individual who has knowledge of parts but not the whole think he has entered the circle of scholars when the fact is he knows nothing but bits and pieces that he uses to deduce a verdict. Such a verdict will invariably be fraught with error.

In their ignorance of religion and in their pride, people are lead to hold tight to the literal meanings of the source texts without trying to understand the multiple meanings and the intent and purpose behind the revelation or a relevant action or saying of the Prophet ﷺ. Today extremists are bringing back the school that was known as the school of literality (*al-dhahiri*). That school originally refused to take into consideration *qiyas*, analogy, or reasoning between different rules, or precedence in law.

A simple example: the Prophet ﷺ prohibited individuals from traveling to areas of non-Muslims or areas of unbelievers carrying the Holy Qur'ān.[273] If we look today however, we find that the Holy Qur'ān is on the shelf of the library of any country in the world, Muslim or not.

In the time of the Prophet ﷺ, the concern was that the Holy Qur'ān time was written by hand in fragments of skins and parchment, etc. and there was fear that the words might be

[272] Gerber, Haim. 1999. *Islāmīc Law and Culture 1600–1840*. Leiden: Brill.

[273] In Ḥadīths related by Imām Mālik, Bukhārī and Muslim.

twisted and meanings altered. Today that problem no longer exists, as the Qur'ān has been gathered and formalized, so to travel with the Qur'ān is no longer an issue.

The extremist on the other hand, will declare that the letter of the saying must be obeyed, without taking into consideration the circumstances and reasons for this ruling.

Another example: the Prophet ﷺ said, "a woman must not travel except accompanied by a relative." A mufti, examining this issue in detail, finds that in the past, someone traveling alone, through deserts, mountains and forests might face great ordeals. In emphasizing the respect and honor in which women are held, the Prophet ﷺ asked that she travel with a relative.

Today however, traveling from one place to another is no longer fraught with difficulty. One has complete security and is accompanied by hundreds of fellow passengers in the short time it takes to cover thousands of miles. Therefore there is no longer fear for a woman traveling alone, for she is accompanied by all the people on the plane, whom may be considered as adequate protectors. But the extreme interpretation of the hadith is that a woman cannot travel except with a relative, again emphasizing the literal meaning of the hadith.

If in such minor issues, we see examples of extreme literalism among the non-moderate Muslims, what then when it comes to cutting hands and stoning? These are far more serious issues to consider.

Allah says,

> *but say not for any false thing that your tongues may put forth – this is lawful and this is forbidden, so as to ascribe false things to Allah. For those who ascribe false things to Allah will never prosper.*[274]

[274] Sūratu 'n-Nahl [The Bee], 16:116.

This verse addresses the extremists. Moderate Muslim scholars are extremely surprised to see those who migrated overseas to different countries around the world, seeking study and sustenance, have carried with them this extreme literalist ideology, The result has been the creation of a large number of groups and divisions within the Muslim community, seemingly showing the entire Muslim community as radical in their views and violent in their actions. If the leadership of the immigrant Muslims had shown moderation in the countries to which they moved, and integrated with the culture of the country, they would have greatly changed the stark image of Islam in the eyes of common people.

Khalid Muhammad states:

> Shah Waliullah opens his work [*Ḥujjatullāh al-bāligha*] by refuting those who compared Shariʿah with the commands of a master intending only to test his slavesʿ loyalty and sense of obedience. He rejected this view and argued that Shariʿah laws were not merely forthe sake of obedience; they have human welfare as their goal.[275] Shah distinguished between religion and laws and elaborated his idea that religion is based on the principle of unity, while laws are based on the principles of change and diversity.[276]

Yūsuf Al-Qaradāwī in *Priorities of the Islamic Movement in the Coming Phase* says:

> Third, an individual may impose on himself the hardest conditions if he so wishes, testing his will to the limit, though moderation is the best and most appropriate way as the Prophet ﷺ says, "Allah likes people to take the

[275] Walīullāh, Shāh. N. d. *Ḥujjatullāh al-bāligha*. Lahore: Al-Maktabat al-Salafīyya, 1:86.

[276] Muhammad, Khalid M., "Muslim Jurist's Quests for the Normative Basis of Shariah", ISIM Newsletter, Leiden, 2001, p. 16.

> [facilitation] licences He gave them as He hates their committing of sins [that anger Him]," reported by Aḥmad, Ibn Hibban and Al-Bayhaqi, on the authority of Ibn ʿUmar. It is also in the *Saḥī al-Jāmʿ al-Saghīr*.
>
> However, a *faqih* should not impose hard conditions on Muslims in the matters that concern the wide majority: he has to take into account that among them are the weak, the old and those who have lawful reasons for exception. A hadith says about leading congregational prayers, "He who acts as imām [leader] in prayer should make his prayer short, for among the people [behind the imām] are the old, the ill and those with errands to run." Prayer is a symbol of the various aspects of life Therefore, the *faqihs* of the Islamic Movement just cannot adopt strict opinions that restrict and do not facilitate, and prohibit but do not allow, especially with respect to the issues related to women, family, arts, entertainment and their likes. It also applies to penal codes, where the least punishment should be imposed, including the opinion that the repentance rescinds the *ḥadd*, the opinion that the punishment for drinking wine is a discretionary one, and so on.
>
> I would like our motto in this phase to be the statement of Imām Sufyān Al-Thawri, "Only the trustworthy *faqihs* can give licences, but everybody knows how to pass a restraining pinion."[277]

Khalid Muhammad points out that "at the level of religion, the Sufis, the pietist Muslim mystics, were the first to point out the contradiction between legal norms and Islamic ethical values." He writes:

> The Sufis were critical of the jurists' literal and legalist approach to religious obligation. They suggested an

[277] Yūsuf Al-Qaradāwī, *Priorities of The Islāmīc Movement in the Coming Phase.*

emphasis on Shariʿah the inner meanings of Shariʿah and personal commitment as the motive for obedience to laws, instead of **punishment** and coercion. They criticized jurists' reliance on worldly power. Contrary to the jurists, who lived in the world of text, the Sufis were closer to the masses and their norms. In most Muslim societies, Sufis represented a popular and liberal view of Islam.[278]

ADAPTATION TO SOCIETAL NORMS

Khalid Muhammad writes:

Muslim jurists in the past were quite aware of the constant need to reconcile contradictions between social and legal norms. They continuously adjusted laws to bring them in line with the customs and norms of the people. The normative basis of the institutions and concepts such as family, property, rights, responsibility, criminality, civil obedience, social order, religiosity, international relations, war, peace, and citizenship have changed significantly over the last two centuries.[279]

Iman Shāfiʿī, the founder of one of the four schools of thought, he was living in Bagdhad when he put forth his school of thought as Imām Abū Ḥanīfa and Imām Mālik before him. Imām Shāfiʿī came in the 2nd century of hijri and established his school of thought in Baghdad 1250 years ago Hijri. When he moved from Baghdad to Egypt in the last years of his life, he changed his school of thought. He said, "I saw people more corrupted in Egypt then from Baghdad. So what I wrote previously and explained is insufficient to treat these

[278] Muhammad, Khalid M., Muslim Jurist's Quests for the Normative Basis of Shariah, ISIM Newsletter, Leiden, 2001, p. 13.
[279] Muhammad, Khalid M., Muslim Jurist's Quests for the Normative Basis of Shariah, ISIM Newsletter, Leiden, 2001, p. 11.

corrupted people because I was more lenient. Now I have to be more strict. So I have to change [my rulings]."

Shah Waliullah expounded the theory of evolution of society in four stages and found that social norms played a central role in the evolution of laws.[280]

Ibn Abidin is a well-known Syrian Ḥanafī jurist from the late Ottoman period. He wrote a short treatise on *'urf* [custom] and its position in Islamic law" (Ibn Abidin 1884), explaining the validity of *'urf* as a source of Shari'ah laws. He distinguished between two types of texts: Shari'ah and jurist law (*fiqh*). In case of conflict between a custom or usage and the Shari'ah text, Ibn Abidin rejected only those customs which were absolutely contradictory. In case of conflict with a jurist law text, the custom prevailed as a principle.[281]

One can see this principle employed extensively today. Kamali mentions that "...jurists have gone on record in recent years to issue a verdict (*fatwā*) to declare photography permissible in this light. This is because photography has now become a ubiquitous practice among Muslims everywhere."[282]

In another paper, Kamali writes:

> Mālik is the chief source of the two important doctrines of public interest (*maslaḥa*) and blocking the means (*ṣad aḍ-ḍarā'i*), both of which are eminently rational and rely mainly on personal reasoning. Maliki jurisprudence also attempted to forge a closer link with the practicalities of

---

[280] Cited by Muhammad, Khalid M., Muslim Jurist's Quests for the Normative Basis of Shariah, ISIM Newsletter, Leiden, 2001, p. 16.

[281] Muhammad, Khalid M., Muslim Jurist's Quests for the Normative Basis of Shariah, ISIM Newsletter, Leiden, 2001, p. 17.

[282] Kamali, Mohammed Hashim, Islam, *Iconography and The Taliban*, 2001.

life in Medina and attached greater weight to social customs than other jurists did.[283]

SHARI'AH PERMITS OTHER FAITH COMMUNITIES THEIR OWN LAW

Shaykh Yūsuf al-Qaradāwī writes:

Dhimma means a pact and guarantee. That is to say, the non-Muslims who live in Islamic society and within the Islamic nation, are the responsibility of Allah, His Messenger, and all Muslims, under their guarantee and their protection.

Islam established rules regulating the relations between the Islamic state and non-Muslims …so that these would be natural relations. They are living in Islamic society under the general principle established by the religious legal authorities: 'What is [permitted] to them is [permitted] to us and what is [incumbent] upon them is [incumbent] upon us.' This is the basis for relations with non-Muslims, including the Jews except for that which requires a religious distinction. If their religion commands them to have a day of rest on Saturday, I will not impose upon them to work on Saturday and rest on Friday. No, I must be considerate. I respect what their religion dictates.

Our master 'Umar ibn 'Abd al-'Azīz, whom the religious legal authorities call the fifth Righteous Caliph, sent [a letter] to Imām Ḥasan al-Baṣrī, who was one of the greatest-known religious figures of his time, telling him he was shocked to discover that the Zoroastrians in the land of the Persians, marry their mothers and sisters. How can we allow this? [Ḥasan al-Baṣrī] sent him a letter [of reply]

---

283 Mohammad Hashim Kamali, *Oxford History of Islam*, "Law and Society: The Interplay of Revelation and Reason in the Shariah", Oxford, 2000.

> and said this is permitted by their faith. Don't try to change this. Even if they marry their mothers, their religion allows this.
>
> Respect for the dictations of [other] religions and faiths is one of the most fundamental things for us. We don't get involved in their affairs. Islam is at the top of the tolerance scale; it allows one to do what is forbidden to Muslims, if it is permitted [in one's owns religion], such as eating pork and drinking wine. Wine for the Muslims is the worst evil, it is one of the worst and most severe sins, yet so long as your religion permits it, we won't prevent it [from you]. What is required in this matter is that this [behavior] not be spread among the Muslims.[284]

Schact writes:

> The jurisdiction of the *qāḍī* extended to Muslims only; the non-Muslim subject populations retained their own traditional legal institutions, including the ecclesiastical and rabbinical tribunals, which in the last few centuries before the Arab conquest had to a great extent duplicated the judicial organization of the Byzantine state. This is the basis of the factual legal autonomy of the non-Muslims which was extensive in the Middle Ages, and has survived in part down to the present generation.[285]

'POLITICAL' *FATAWA*

Another cause for extremism in youth their rejection of 'official' muftis whose *fatāwā* mirror their government's policy. Such rubber-stamp scholars issue a *fatwā* on order of the ruler, not based on Islamic reasoning. A nation whose leader is socialist will

[284] Shaykh Yūsuf al-Qaradāwī, Interview on Al-Jazeera: "Our Problem is Not With Judaism".
[285] Schact, J., *Cambridge Encyclopedia of Islam*, vol. II, pt. VIII/chpt. 4, pg. 541.

produce official scholars who endorse socialism. This has become so common in recent times, that such 'official' muftis cause rejection by the youth, and provide a recruitment rationale by which extremists attract them to their fold.

LETTER VERSUS SPIRIT OF THE LAW

The intent of Islamic law is not punitive, as much as corrective and reformative.

Khurram Murad writes:

> It is a significant contribution of Islam that these penalties are called *ḥudūd* (boundaries) and not punishments: they are liabilities incurred as a result of crossing the boundary set by Allah.... Another important function which these punishments serve is educative, and thus preventive and deterrent. The Quʿran alludes to this aspect when it describes them نَكَالًا مِّنَ اللَّهِ *"as exemplary punishment from Allah*[286]." [287]

Therefore before applying the death penalty for a capital offense, the entire case must be investigated by the judge (*qāḍī*). In such case the family pardons the killer, per the Qur'ān's recommendation, the court may reduce the penalty from capital punishment, to prison or exile. The only other grounds for capital punishment are terrorism (*al-ḥirāba, faṣād fi 'l-arḍ*) highway robbery and rape - acts which are critical threats to public security.

Laws were revealed to Prophet Muhammad ﷺ due to real-life situations requiring a judgment. Today the same method is followed in issuing *fatāwā*. Therefore the 'reasons for revelation' (*asbāb an-nuzūl*) are essential to understanding Qur'ānic revealed

---

[286] Sūratu 'l-Mā'idah [The Spread Table], 5:38.

[287] Murad, Khurram, *Shariah: The Way of Justice*,

laws and the objectives (*maqāsiḍ*) behind them. For example, the rules of hijab, the covering of women, were revealed in a time when the hypocrites were ridiculing Muslim women in the streets of Madina.

REDUCTION OF STRINGENCY WITH TIME

One finds that in the early days of Islam some Divine orders were very strict, and were later reduced. For example, Muslims were not allowed sexual relations during the month of fasting due to the initially restrictive rules of the fast. Later revelations to the Prophet permitted intimacy during night hours (fasting occurs between sunrise and sunset).

Initially, the early Muslims were ordered to pray for one third of the night; to build up their spiritual relationship with God. Later this was reduced. Similarly, God initially declared that in a defensive war against an aggressor, unless the ratio of aggressors to Muslims exceeded 10-to-1 the Muslims were obliged to fight. This was later reduced to a ratio of 2-to-1 as the general level of faith decreased with the influx of new converts to the faith.

Thus we see the importance of gauging the capacity of the people to implement any given code of conduct. Today, it cannot be expected that the law be enforced as it was a century ago, as the conditions of life have changed immensely. For that reason, the Prophet ﷺ indicated that in the last days applying the letter of the law would become very difficult, saying that those who would attempt to implement religion in its entirety at that time would be like someone carrying a burning coal.

Another example is the requirement of prayer. The Prophet ﷺ was first told to order his nation to pray fifty times a day. During the Night Journey, this requirement was reduced to five prayers per day.

FLEXIBILITY IN APPLICATION OF SHARI'AH

All the above is found in the theoretical definition of an Islamic state. However, in today's world, such an implementation is nowhere to be found, while those few nations who lay claim to an Islamic system of government are in fact quite far from its true implementation. These 'Islamist' nations tend to interpret Islamic law with the narrowest view, rejecting traditional teachings and scholarship. We find such governments constantly issuing decrees of stoning to death, amputating hands, lashing, and other severe punishments for various crimes.

The current overriding problem is 'Islamic' states follow the letter of the law – 'black letter law' - without regard to precedents. On the other hand, in Islam, traditional governments follow precedents established over many centuries, much as is the case here in the U.S.

In Islam rules are tempered by application. As a simple example, who is allowed to make the judgment to cut the hand of a thief? Let me explain how this is implemented. First of all, you cannot cut the hands of someone who steals in order to eat, as we see today in Argentina. In Islam, the government's first duty is to help the impoverished; you simply cannot cut the hands of people who steal because they are hungry. If a person is in need of medicine and steals it, you cannot cut off his hand. The only time the judgment of cutting the hand applies is when someone steals out of greed, without need, and even then numerous criteria must be met to hand down such a punitive sentence.

Even rules based on the principle of consensus of scholars, *ijma'*, which in itself is difficult to accomplish, can be changed. Dr. Wahba al-Zuhayli, wrote:

> Consensus of scholars on a certain issue made earlier can be abrogated by the consensus made by a later generation if there were changes in the conditions which are for the common good of the people as time progresses. The

> followers of the Ḥanbalī school and some of the followers of the Ḥanafī school say that one can reformulate or abrogate a law developed by consensus at one time by a new law that fits the later circumstances.[288]

Islamically, this concept of reformation or rejuvenation of the law is necessitated by change in society over time.

The Islamists differ from the traditionalists in that the latter call for a reinstitution of *fiqh,* but not necessarily an elimination of existing systems of law.

Islam requires in the case of the thief that the system attempt to rehabilitate him and seek ways to encourage him to repent:

فَمَن تَابَ مِن بَعْدِ ظُلْمِهِ وَأَصْلَحَ فَإِنَّ اللّهَ يَتُوبُ عَلَيْهِ إِنَّ اللّهَ غَفُورٌ رَّحِيمٌ

But if the thief repents after his crime, and amends his conduct, Allah turneth to him in forgiveness; for Allah is Oft-forgiving, Most Merciful.[289]

This means he should be given every chance to reform, such as assisting him to earn a lawful living. It is the state's responsibility to ensure people's life needs are met, such that there is no need to steal. Job opportunities should be provided as a form of social security. Such examples can be found in Brunei, and in a number of other wealthy Muslim countries.

Unfortunately, today we see the reverse being implemented by "Islamic" nations. Someone steals medicine, food, etc. and is punished, while those who amass millions of dollars through dummy corporations, racketeering, money laundering, illicit drug and weapons sales, are never brought to justice. This is the sad condition of some Islamic religious leaders of our time, who follow the letter of the law in contravention of its spirit.

---

[288] Dr. Wahba al-Zuhaylī, Professor of Jurisprudence, *Foundations of Jurisprudence,* Damascus, Syria, p. 975.

[289] Sūratu 'l-Mā'idah [The Spread Table], 5:39.

Followers of Wahhabism, whose teachings many of today's Islamic governments follow, have created a yardstick for Shariʿah that takes it to the harshest extremes when applied to common citizens. Those in power however, typically remain exempt form its application. This is a purely political implementation of the Shariʿah, done for show and thus appears wantonly cruel; utterly lacking wisdom. This is utterly contrary to the Objectives of the Law, Maqasid ash-Shariʿah. The Law was established to better the individual's relationship with his or her Creator and with fellow humans.

Of this rigidity, Schact writes:

> ...the Wahhabis in Arabia in the nineteenth and again in the present century... made it their aim, ... to enforce Islamic law exclusively, to abolish the double system of administration of justice, and to outlaw administrative and customary law.[290]

قال عليه السلام "وايم الله ، لو أن فاطمة بنت محمد سرقت لقطع محمد يدها"

The Prophet ﷺ is reported saying, "By Allah! Even if my daughter Fatimah steals, I would cut off her hand."[291]

His intent was not to show Islam as stern Islam nor to demonstrate a specific parenting style, but rather to demonstrate how abhorrent theft, of any kind, is in the Eyes of God, including: corruption, forgery, bribery, deceit, and larceny. Today however, far from being blind, we see "Shariʿah Law" abused to advance one group against another, while those who manipulate it appear exempt from its impact.

---

[290] Schact, J., *Cambridge Encyclopedia of Islam*, vol. II, pt. VIII/chpt. 4, pg. 539.

[291] Bukhārī.

THE CASE OF ADULTERY

The late Shaykh Abudllah al-Alaili, president of the Council of Muslim Scholars of Lebanon, and a latter-day genius in *fiqh*, writes in *Where is the Mistake?*:

> Let us take another example – that of the punishment of stoning to death for the commission of adultery. In accordance with Islamic Law, the witness must pass his hand or a string between the man and woman, and find it is blocked. According to broad interpretation of the law, there must also be four witnesses, each of whom personally observed the act in detail *"al-mā'il fī 'l-mukhala"* (seeing the act with the eye), otherwise the accusation is dropped, and the witnesses are considered transgressors and defamers. This is what happened to Abī Bakrah, the honorable companion, when he accused Al-Mughīrah bin Shu'ba of adultery; Al-Mughīrah was release with no punishment, while the witness was arrested, when he said: "I only saw this man rising and falling, while on top of the woman, consecutively and taking turns". Although 'Umar ؓ (the second caliph in Islam), was certain that this pious person was telling the truth, he was forced as the leader to consider his testimony insufficient, and thus an act of defamation, so he punished him. On the other hand, Al-Mugīrah, having satisfied his urge retained his innocence.

> Therefore, who can testify, fulfilling all the technical conditions and proofs that the crime was committed? Short of a confession, in practice there is no possibility of fulfilling the stringent evidentiary requirements to guarantee a conviction.

> Another caveat attached to the required evidence to prove the crime of adultery is that without sufficient witnesses, the accuser actually becomes the accused and will be

punished for the very ugly crime of *libel* – for which the accuser will be liable.

This demonstrates the essence of Islamic law, with the intent to raise the highest standard of morality for human beings, while in reality the law is almost impossible to legitimately enforce. Therefore, we see legal and social intent is to prevent an act from occurring by highlighting its enormity and emphasizing the threatened punishment, while not expecting it to be applied.

If it was true, that the penalty for the adultery, of a free wedded woman, is stoning to death, it would have been specifically mentioned, because of its terrible terror; and claiming the abrogation, of the above verses, by the "*hadith*", is reversing the criterion for deduction.

Let us say that we accept their claim, then what will be done with the wedded slave girls, since their penalty, is half of the penalty of the free wedded woman? Should we divide it, into two halves, this claimed stoning? And how should we do so? That is why the interpreters, were forced to say, regarding the slave girls, the penalty is half the number of lashes of the original punishment. Just this concession on their part, refutes the claim of stoning, without their being aware of it.[292]

The concept at issue here "waiving the severest penalties by all available means," is best demonstrated by the following incident. A woman came to the Prophet ﷺ and confessed her adultery. However, the Prophet refused to accept the testimony and turned away from the woman. Time after time he tried to avoid having to implement the letter of the law, but the woman herself came back and insisted.

---

[292] Shaykh ʿAbdullāh al-Alailī, *Where is the Error?*, Beirut.

He urged her to rethink the matter – perhaps she had not committed the act, or she was not in her full senses.

She returned and again confessed her crime. He wanted her to hide the act, but again she insisted. Further, she demanded to be punished. Then she came and said, "I committed that act and I am now pregnant." He instructed her, "Go and deliver the child, then return to me." She insisted on the punishment. So after delivering the child she came back. The Prophet ﷺ then bade her nurse the child for two and a half years. Finally, when all possible excuses had been exhausted, the Prophet had no choice but to implement the law.

However, his compassionate heart overwhelmed him and he told his Companions, "If the forgiveness that lady had received for her atonement was to be spread among all of you, it would suffice."

Thus we see that the message came to correct behavior, not to punish human beings. There is no greater symbol for Allah's dislike of an act than its expression as a form of punishment. Yet, despite this, one fails to find a single verse of Qur'ān ordering the penalty of death by stoning – as if by its absence, Allah were saying this is a punishment only for the most extreme cases of flagrant and wanton sexual activity in public, actions which will eventually destroy the moral fiber of the community.

How does the warping of this application of law take place? This is in fact due to the political reality behind the visage of extremism in every form. In reality ten percent or less of Muslims are fanatic in their ideology, not unlike the communists in recent history. Once they come into power, as in the Nigerian state of Katsina, they must implement their beliefs to prove themselves "righteous."

The first judicial change apparent in an "Islamic" state is stoning adulteresses and cutting the hands of thieves, while the spirit of law is abandoned. In the true Islamic teaching, the absence of the five daily prayers and fasting are greater issues for the community than stealing and adultery, as the abandonment of the daily applications of faith are more apt to quickly erode the social fabric.

Cutting of hands and stoning adulterers was legislated to emphasize the wrong of these particular actions: adultery and stealing. The purpose is not primarily application of the literal punishment, but is rather a means to emphasizing the enormity of these actions and to demonstrate the inhumanity of stealing as a form of injustice, or adultery, as a betrayal of one's spouse.

There are many manifestations in the Shariʿah that must not simply apply the letter of the law when societal issues might induce the crime. Oftentimes the purpose behind a ḥadd ruling is more metaphorical than literal, preventive more than punitive.

As we have elucidated, cutting hands for theft is not the intent of the Shariʿah. Rather the intent is to prevent the commission of crime. This does not differ with the use of the various penalties in the Western modern law, legislated with the intent of eliminating criminal activity.

Al-Shāṭibī writes:

> Throughout Muslim history, those who neglected acquiring mastery over the science of *Al-Maqāsiḍ* did so at their own peril, as it made them liable to error in *ijtihād*. Included amongst these were the *āhl al-bidaʿ* (the proponents of pernicious innovations), who only looked at the apparent text of the Qur'ān without pondering over its ultimate aims and objectives. These innovators [an allusion to the Kharijites] held steadfastly to the literal text of even the *mutashabihah* [the intricate, allegorical segments of the Qur'ān] and premised many conclusions on them.[293]

Keep in mind that when these laws were revealed to the Prophet ﷺ, he was an exceptionally just and merciful leader, as were his successors. For that reason when the lady came

---

[293] Al-Shāṭibī, *Muwafaqāt*,vol. 4, 179.

demanding to be punished for adultery, he made every effort to avoid implementing the prescribed punishment.

For this reason we say that the Islamic Shariʿah as a whole tried to balance all aspects of the community. Moderate scholars found that most problems in a community or society which cause people to violate the law, are found to originate in societal ailments, stemming from the environment and circumstances in which people are found. These make their way of dealing with others wrong, resulting in criminal pathology making them to act in a manner harmful to themselves and to society.

GRADUAL APPLICATION OF SHARIʿAH

Islamic Shariʿah was not revealed piecemeal to the Prophet ﷺ. It was implemented over 23 years, primarily in the last ten, after the establishment of the first Islamic state in Madina. Most of those who seek to re-introduce Shariʿah in their nations, have forgotten the wisdom for the gradual nature of this implementation. This was a necessary interval in the development of Islam, so that the people were not overwhelmed with new regulations and rules of conduct, but rather were able to learn it bit-by-bit, as it was revealed.

A familiar example is the process of revelation which culminated in the prohibition of liquor. The first verse revealed concerning liquor said:

يَا أَيُّهَا الَّذِينَ آمَنُواْ لاَ تَقْرَبُواْ الصَّلاَةَ وَأَنتُمْ سُكَارَى حَتَّىَ تَعْلَمُواْ مَا تَقُولُونَ

O ye who believe! Draw not near unto prayer when ye are drunken, till ye know that which ye utter.[294]

Someone who is drunk neither knows what he is saying and might say something irreverent or even do something immoral,

[294] Sūratu 'n-Nisā [Women], 4:43.

while praying. For that reason the people were not allowed to come prayer while drunk.

Western governments say, "don't drink and drive." Someone caught doing so is liable under the law, even if no crime has been committed. Effectively, drunk-driving becomes a crime. The intent however, is to prevent someone's drunkenness causing an accident. In such a case, the court will even increase the penalty. Thus we see the graduated approach also found in the West, with the 'intent of the law' being the key factor behind legislation.

Revelation of the verse of drunkenness impacted the drinking habits of the Arabs for which they were renowned. Since prayer while drunk was sanctioned, observant Muslims were forced to restrict their drinking to avoid prayer times. Since the five prayers are spread throughout the day, in practice this made drinking something that could only be done at night.

Later it was revealed to the Prophet:

يَسْأَلُونَكَ عَنِ الْخَمْرِ وَالْمَيْسِرِ قُلْ فِيهِمَا إِثْمٌ كَبِيرٌ وَمَنَافِعُ لِلنَّاسِ وَإِثْمُهُمَا أَكْبَرُ مِن نَّفْعِهِمَا

They ask thee concerning wine and gambling. Say: "In them is great sin, and some profit, for men; but the sin is greater than the profit."[295]

This verse, while hinting at the evil of drink, by no means forbade it. It was only some time later when the verse of prohibition was revealed and when news of the revelation spread, the streets of Madina ran red with the flowing of spilled wine.

Thus we see that in the hard-drinking society of pagan Arabia, a graduated approach was essential. It not only provided the

[295] Sūratu 'l-Baqarah [The Heifer], 2:219.

ruling from Allah, but the reasons behind the ruling, which people of intellect always seek.

Now while drinking is prohibited, to drink in private was not culpable before the law. For that reason one can find liquor in private Muslim homes, even in the holy cities. However when the use of drink is obvious and outward, then it is culpable. This is similar to laws for public drunkenness in Western nations.

On this issue, Yūsuf al-Qaradāwī relates:

> There is an example in that respect which is related concerning 'Umar ibn 'Abd al--Aziz, whom the Muslim scholars regard as the fifth rightly-guided caliph and a true follower of his great-grandfather, 'Umar ibn Al-Khaṭṭāb.
>
> 'Umar ibn 'Abd al-'Azīz's son, 'Abd al-Mālik, who was a firm pious young man, said to his father one day, "O father! Why you do not implement the rulings firmly and immediately? By Allah, I would not care if all the world would furiously oppose us so long as we seek to establish the right [that Allah Almighty has enjoined]." These words show how zealous that young man was to destroy all signs of corruption and deterioration immediately and without delay whatever the consequences.
>
> But the wise father said to his son, "Do not deal with matters hastily, son. Allah Almighty [Himself] despised drinking alcohol twice in the Qur'ān and did not declare it forbidden but in the third time. I am afraid that if I enjoined the right on people at one stroke, they would give it up all at once, which might lead to sedition."[296],[297]

---

[296] Cf. Ash-Shātibī's *Al-Muwafaqāt*, vol. 2, p. 94

[297] Shaykh Yūsuf al-Qaradāwī, *Gradualism in Applying the Shari'ah*, website islamonline.net, URL:
http://www.islamonline.net/fatwaapplication/english/display.asp?hFatwaID=104048

EXTREMIST HEGEMONY

The utterly practical aspect of Islamic law is seen to be built into its framework. This aspect is often ignored by non-moderate Muslims, who seek to replace a corrupt society with an ideal one overnight, ignoring the essential inertia of human nature and societal conditioning. Thus, they end up trying to overpower man's resistance by force. This leads to brutal misapplication of the Shariʿah, particularly in the arena of crime and punishment.

Arjomand writes:

> Agitating outside the Constituent Assembly, the fundamentalists, led by Abul-ala Mawdudi, called for the creation of an 'ideological state,' and turned *not* to the constitutional history of the Mughal empire, or any other Muslim state, but rather to the juxtaposition of Western constitutional blueprints to the scriptural sources of Islam. The result was the declaration of God's sovereignty in the 1956 constitution of the Islamic Republic of Pakistan, which the late Fazlur Rahman characterized as a 'comic' transfer of political sovereignty to God, the famous Objectives Resolution of 1949.[298]

The problem today is that extremists are in control of the Muslim mic. Those who went abroad and studied extreme doctrine are being used to perpetuate their ideas and prevent Muslims from living under a reasonable democratic system. They say, "don't talk to us, you don't know our way." They seek to impose a heavy-handed, strict and rigid application of Shariʿah on all the people as soon as they take power, resulting in an "allergic reaction" by the people to Islam and Islamic law, as conveyed by their hardline, fascistic approach.

---

[298] Arjomand, Saïd Amir, "Islam, Political Change and Globalization", Thesis Eleven, Number 76, February 2004, p. 17.

Commenting on this Yūsuf al-Qaradāwī says, "If we want to establish a real Muslim society, we should not imagine that such an end can be achieved by a mere decision issued to that effect by a king or a president or a council of leaders or a parliament."[299]

One wonders how it is acceptable for these same 'Islamists' to allow non-Muslims to train their military, while at the same time outwardly condemning them and considering work with them to be loyalty of the non-Muslims? They accommodated themselves to that by adjusting the law based on precedents in the sources of Shariʿah.

There is a conspiracy here to prevent the spread of democracy because it will remove the hegemony of Islamist oppressors. The mistake is in asking the wrong people for an opinion. Today the most oppressive people claim to speak on behalf of Muslims.

Sohail Hashemi, addressing this problem says:

> ...many Islamic reformers and reform movements shifted their strategy to a "top-down" approach...[conceiving] Islamization as the obligation of the state. The result has been the proliferation of a holistic and authoritarian vision of Islamic life and politics among the most politically active and assertive Islamic intellectuals and groups. In the battle for control of the state being conducted by secular authoritarians on the one hand and religious authoritarians on the other, the gradual and educative path of Islamic reform has been marginalized or repressed altogether.[300]

The result for ideological Islamist regimes has often resulted in a devolution from their stated goals of Islamization through

---

[299] Shaykh Yūsuf al-Qaradāwī, *Gradualism in Applying the Shariʿah*, website islamonline.net, URL: http://www.islamonline.net/fatwaapplication/english/display.asp?hFatwaID=104048

[300] Hashmi, Sohail H., *Cultivating a Liberal Islāmīc Ethos, Building an Islāmīc Civil Society*, Mount Holyoke College, 2004, p. 6.

unification of the judicial and executive roles, sometimes resulting in ironically non-Islamic results. Arjomand states:

> It is interesting to note, however, that with the take-over of the modernized state and its legal framework by the Islamic militants and the declaration of the supremacy of the Shariʿah, the old dualism of public and sacred law reappeared immediately. This dualism enabled the clerical jurists of the Council of Guardians to defend property rights, which were fully consistent with the Shariʿah, against the later encroachments of parliamentary legislation since the early 1980s. But it also introduced fundamental contradictions in the Iranian constitutional law. Furthermore, proclamations notwithstanding, the Islamic law of unilateral divorce was not restored. A court order was required for divorce, and women began to play an increasing role in the family courts as assistant judges. In 1998 the first women judges were appointed, in clear contradiction to the Shariʿah.
>
> The more general result of this new legal dualism was a prolonged constitutional crisis that was partly resolved by Khomeini's assertion of the superiority of state law over the Shariʿah in 1988. This principle was immediately institutionalized by the creation of a Council for the Assessment of the Interest (*maslaḥa*) of the Islamic Regime, which was duly recognized as an organ of the state in the constitutional amendments of 1989.
>
> Various items of legislation previously vetoed by the Council of Guardians for being contrary to the Shariʿah became law, and the Assessment Council showed little hesitation to legislate beyond disputes bills. The result has in general been the strengthening of the authority of the state, but at least in one remarkable case it was a victory

> for women's rights. By a law enacted in November 1992, the Assessment Council instituted alimony as compensation for domestic labor during marriage. This radical departure from Shiite law was justified by the argument that domestic labor was distinct from reproductive duties required by the Shariʿah.[301]

The final result of such divergence from "pure" Islam is too create an autocratic state system which in fact is nothing less than a dictatorship with Islamist "flavor." In such a situation, the enforcers and the same as the adjudicators, making for the typical conflict of interest all fascistic systems embody.

CONCLUSION

Islam aspires to the highest level of behavior at the individual, family and community levels. The Prophet brought different rules in order to accommodate the culture of each nation and tribe. Allah said:

وَلَوْ شَاءَ اللّٰهُ لَجَعَلَكُمْ أُمَّةً وَاحِدَةً

If Allah so willed, He could make you all one people...[302]

Why did He not do so? To allow flexibility in the rules governing mankind and to generate competition. That is why the 'door of *ijtihād'* remains open, allowing new laws to be created as time moves on.

In the time of Prophet Muhammad ﷺ, Islamic Shariʿah was implemented over a span of twenty-three years. However the extremists have reversed this approach. They come to newly revived Muslims, expecting them to adopt every particular of Islam instantly, while exempting themselves. In reality they must

[301] Arjomand, Saïd Amir, "Islam, Political Change and Globalization", Thesis Eleven, Number 76, February 2004, p. 21.
[302] Sūratu 'n-Nahl [The Bee], 16:93.

begin with 'a' and proceed to 'z', but instead they go from 'z' and work backwards.

It is for the same reasons that judges (*quḍāt*) are given the autonomy and authority to administer the application of Shariʿah rules and *fiqh* in a manner which accords with the place and conventions of the time. Christopher Houston notes "much Orientalist commentary on the practice of Islamic law condemns not the slavish legality of the *qāḍī* (judge) but his apparent inordinate discretion. Thus Goldziher criticizes the 'mental gymnastics of [ulema] casuistry' for proving 'detrimental to the inwardness of religion.'"[303]

In a similar vein Schact writes:

> By their decisions, the earliest Islamic *qāḍīs*, did indeed lay the basic foundations of what was to become Islamic law. They gave judgment according to their own discretion or 'sound opinion' (*rāyy*), basing themselves on customary practice which in the nature of things incorporated administrative regulations, and taking the letter and the spirit of the Qur'ānic regulations and other recognized Islamic religious norms into account as much as they thought fit.[304]

In the early time of Islam, these methods were put together as the discussions ensued between the propagators of philosophy (*kalām*) and *ijtihād*. To reduce that contention four schools were formalized as those in authority. That was done by consensus (*ijmaʿ*) of scholars. Whoever references one of these four schools, is considered to have referenced the Qur'ān and Sunnah. Each school while agreeing with the others in the fundaments, differs from the rest in the branches. This provides enormous flexibility to the individual seeking a ruling which fits his needs.

---

303 Houston, Cristopher, "Islāmīsm, Castoriadia and Autonomy", Thesis Eleven, Number 76, February 2004, p. 57.

304 Schact, J., *Cambridge Encyclopedia of Islam,* vol. II, pt. VIII/chpt. 4, pg. 544.

Allah says in the Holy Qur'ān:

إِنَّ سَعْيَكُمْ لَشَتَّىٰ

Verily the ends ye strive for are diverse[305]

and He informed us:

وَلَوْ شَاءَ رَبُّكَ لَجَعَلَ النَّاسَ أُمَّةً وَاحِدَةً وَلَا يَزَالُونَ مُخْتَلِفِينَ

And had thy Sustainer so willed, He could surely have made all mankind one single community: but [He willed it otherwise, and so] they continue to hold divergent views.[306]

In acknowledging such diversity as Allah's own handiwork in creation, Allah sets the precedent for divergence of opinion in thinking. Dr. Imara comments on this saying:

> The appearance of different schools of thought is the fruit of mental and spiritual labor. The result of this struggle is to create opinions and interpretations that move with the time and locale while simultaneously conforming with the intent of the Divine Revealed Law.[307]

In conclusion we will quote Dr. Ausaf ʿAlī where he says:

> Progress never comes without the pain that is caused by new ideas, new interpretations, new constructions, new paradigms, new theories, and new stocktaking of the situation. Of the tens of hundreds and thousands who participate in intellectual discourse, debate, and creative work only a very few turn out to have been right, and they too not entirely. But everyone, including even those who get it all wrong, contributes. What is crucial is that even those who turn out to be wrong in retrospect need

---

[305] Suratu 'l-Layl [Night], 92:4

[306] Sūrah Hūd, 11:118.

[307] Dr. Muhammad Imara, "Muslim Unity: an elusive goal", Al-Watan al-ʿArabī.

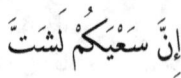

freedom of speech and publication. ...To demand that everyone say only the things said before or look at things in accordance with the established opinions and the decisions of the organized groups or the government of the day is to foreclose all possibilities of any conceptual breakthroughs and thereby the enrichment of the conceptual resources of the community.[308]

[308] Ausaf ʿAlī, Ph.D., "The Politics of Boycotts in the Muslim Community", *The Muslim Magazine*, Vol. 10.

As-Salat
Ritual Prayer: Its Meaning and Manner

PRAYER'S IMPORTANCE IN ISLAM

Prayer is one of the central elements of Islamic practice and worship. Indeed, it is the second of the Five Pillars of Islam and, along with the testimony of faith, the pilgrimage to Mecca, fasting the month of Ramadan and paying the poor tax, forms the essential framework of religious life for Muslims. More than that, the observance of the ritual prayer forms the framework of each Muslim's day, from the pre-dawn morning prayer to the night prayer that precedes sleep.

Prayer, in the ritual sense, is an obligation of the faith, to be performed five times a day by adult Muslims. According to Islamic law, prayers have a variety of obligations and conditions of observance. However, beyond the level of practice, there are spiritual conditions and aspects of prayer which represent its essence.

In the Holy Qur'ān, Allah says:

وَمَا خَلَقْتُ الْجِنَّ وَالْإِنسَ إِلَّا لِيَعْبُدُونِ

I created the jinn and humankind only that they might worship Me. [309]

Thus, prayer first and foremost, is the response to this Divine directive to worship the Creator. Prayer represents the individual's affirmation of servanthood before the Lord of Creation and submission to His Omnipotent Will. It also represents a willing acknowledgment of our weakness and neediness by seeking Divine Grace, Mercy, Abundance and Forgiveness. Prayer, then, is a willful, directed action by the believer, seeking direct, unmediated communication with Allah, for Muslims believe that every human being is of interest to the Divine. It also represents a concrete manifestation of the Islamic conception of freewill, in that the decision to pray is one that must

[309] Sūratu 'dh-Dhāriyāt [The Winnowing Winds], 51:56.

be made by each individual. In this way, prayer is a uniquely "human" form of worship, for all other creatures submit without question to Allah's Will and are engaged in His praise, glorification and remembrance, as the Holy Qur'ān asserts:

تُسَبِّحُ لَهُ السَّمَاوَاتُ السَّبْعُ وَالأَرْضُ وَمَن فِيهِنَّ وَإِن مِّن شَيْءٍ إِلاَّ يُسَبِّحُ بِحَمْدَهِ وَلَكِن لاَّ تَفْقَهُونَ تَسْبِيحَهُمْ إِنَّهُ كَانَ حَلِيمًا غَفُورًا

and there is not a thing but hymneth His praise; but ye understand not their praise.[310]

Prayer, by its very nature, is a form of request or entreaty, and thus requires the full conscious participation of the one praying, with will, intellect, body and soul. The one engaged in prayer is in direct connection with the Creator Who hears everything the supplicant says and responds – though not necessarily in the affirmative – to each request. This is the concrete manifestation of Allah's role as The Hearer, The Aware and The Responsive, which represent three of the ninety-nine Holy Names and Attributes of Allah that form the basis of the Islamic conception of the Divine.[311]

In Islam, there are two forms of prayer. One has ritual, formal requirements and manners, which are essential to its correct observance. This is called *ṣalāt*. The other form is supplicatory prayer, and in its more general sense, represents an open-ended conversation with Allah, which may occur at any time or place, with few restrictions or requirements. It is called *duʿa*.

---

[310] Sūratu 'l-Isrā [The Night Journey], 17:44.

[311] The Hearer - as-Samīʿ, The Aware – al-ʿAlīm, Responsive to those who call on Him - al-Mujīb.

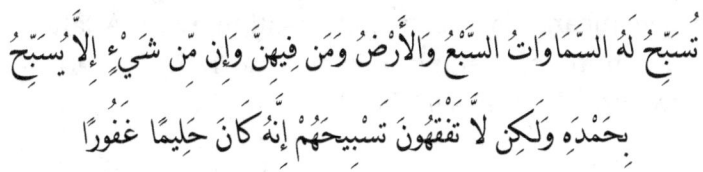

SUPPLICATION

The term *du'a* is derived from the Arabic verb meaning "to supplicate" or "to call upon." Other similar terms for such prayer are *munājah, nidā,* and *aḍ-ḍaru'a.*

Munājah means "a secret conversation with Allah," usually with the intention of seeking delivery and relief. Referring to this form of prayer, Allah says in the Holy Qur'ān:

قُلْ مَن يُنَجِّيكُم مِّن ظُلُمَاتِ الْبَرِّ وَالْبَحْرِ تَدْعُونَهُ تَضَرُّعاً وَخُفْيَةً لَّئِنْ أَنجَانَا مِنْ هَـذِهِ لَنَكُونَنَّ مِنَ الشَّاكِرِينَ

Say: Who delivereth you from the darkness of the land and the sea? Ye call upon Him humbly and in secret, (saying): If we are delivered from this (fear) we truly will be of the thankful.[312]

Nidā means "to call upon Allah while withdrawn from people." The Holy Qur'ān relates the story of the prophet Zachariah who, having no son, beseeched Allah in his old age to give him a successor to inherit his prophetic knowledge and duties:

ذِكْرُ رَحْمَةِ رَبِّكَ عَبْدَهُ زَكَرِيَّا إِذْ نَادَى رَبَّهُ نِدَاء خَفِيًّا قَالَ رَبِّ إِنِّي وَهَنَ الْعَظْمُ مِنِّي وَاشْتَعَلَ الرَّأْسُ شَيْبًا وَلَمْ أَكُن بِدُعَائِكَ رَبِّ شَقِيًّا وَإِنِّي خِفْتُ الْمَوَالِيَ مِن وَرَائِي وَكَانَتِ امْرَأَتِي عَاقِرًا فَهَبْ لِي مِن لَّدُنكَ وَلِيًّا

A mention of the mercy of thy Lord unto His servant Zachariah. When he cried unto his Lord a cry in secret, Saying: My Lord!... give me from Thy Presence a

[312] Sūratu 'l-An'am [Cattle], 6:63.

successor who shall inherit of me and inherit (also) of the house of Jacob... (It was said unto him): O Zachariah! Lo! We bring thee tidings of a son whose name is John; We have given the same name to none before (him).[313]

Aḍ-ḍaruʿa means "a loud entreaty to Allah for safety," as mentioned in the Holy Qur'ān:

وَلَقَدْ أَرْسَلنَآ إِلَى أُمَمٍ مِّن قَبْلِكَ فَأَخَذْنَاهُمْ بِالْبَأْسَاءِ وَالضَّرَّاءِ لَعَلَّهُمْ يَتَضَرَّعُونَ

Before thee We sent (apostles) to many nations, and We afflicted the nations with suffering and adversity, that they might submissively entreat (Him)! [314]

SALAT - RITUAL PRAYER

THE LINGUISTIC ROOT OF PRAYER: *SALAT*

Ritual prayer in Islam, is called *ṣalāt*, a word whose full meaning is best understood by examining its linguistic roots. One of the origins of *ṣalāt* is the root word *ṣilat* which means "connection" or "contact." One of Islam's most renowned philosophers, Ibn Rushd, said:

> It derives from the word "connection" (*ṣilat*) in that it connects the servant with his Creator, meaning that the prayer brings him near His Mercy and connects him to His Generosity and His Heavenly Paradise.[315]

This word is also used in the context of close relations (*ṣilat ar-raḥim*) whose connections with an individual are due to blood ties and are therefore imperishable in the eyes of the Divine. In this

---

[313] Sūrah Maryam, 19:2-7.

[314] Sūratu 'l-Anʿam [Cattle], 6:42.

[315] Ibn Rushd (Averros), *al-Muqaddimah*, the chapter of Prayer, *Dār al-Kutub al-ʿIlmīyyah* Publishing House for Scholarly Texts, 1994, page 50.

sense, prayer is seen as the unseverable bond between the individual and his or her Lord.

Commenting on this, another renowned Qur'ānic exegete, Al-Qurtubī said:

> The word *ṣalāt* derives from the word *ṣilat*, one of the names of fire as when it is said, "The wood is burned by fire."[316]

Al-Qurtubī attributed six different meanings to the word *ṣalāt* in his commentary of the Holy Qur'ān:

> Prayer is the invocation of Allah; it is mercy, as when one says, "O Allah, bestow prayers on Muhammad"; it is worship, as when Allah says, صَلاَتُهُمْ عِندَ الْبَيْتِ *"And their worship at the (holy) House"*;[317] it is a supererogatory prayer, as when Allah says, وَأْمُرْ أَهْلَكَ بِالصَّلَاةِ *"And enjoin upon thy people worship"*;[318] and it is Allah's praise, as when He says, فَلَوْلَا أَنَّهُ كَانَ مِنَ الْمُسَبِّحِينَ *"And had he not been one of those who glorify (Allah)..."*[319] Prayer is also recitation.[320]

SALAT IN SHARI'AH

Ritual prayer is bound by detailed obligations and structure. It encompasses both obligatory (*farḍ*) prayers, which are observed five times daily at specified intervals, as well as voluntary prayers,

---

316 See *Fiqh al-Lughah,* from ath-Thʿalabī. Also in al-Qurṭubī's commentary on the Qur'ān and others.
317 Sūratu 'l-Anfāl [The Spoils], 8:35.
318 Sūrah ṬāḤā 20:132.
319 Sūratu 'ṣ-Ṣāffāt [Those arranged in ranks], 37:143.
320 Cited from al-Qurtubi's *Commentary* by Ibn Rushd (Averros) in *al-Muqaddimah,* chapter on Prayer, *Dār al-Kutub al-ʿIlmīyyah* Publishing House for Scholarly Texts, 1994.

which are performed by the worshipper before or after the obligatory prayers as well as at other times.

THE OBLIGATORY ASPECT OF *SALAT*

Prophet Muhammad ﷺ called prayer "the pillar of religion."[321] No fundamental element of Islam has been stressed as much as prayer in the Holy Qur'ān. Indeed, Allah mentions it in over 700 verses of the holy text. Among those that define its role in the religion of Islam are:

إِنَّ الصَّلاَةَ كَانَتْ عَلَى الْمُؤْمِنِينَ كِتَابًا مَّوْقُوتًا

Worship at fixed hours hath been enjoined on the believers. [322]

حَافِظُوا عَلَى الصَّلَوَاتِ والصَّلاَةِ الْوُسْطَى وَقُومُواْ لِلّهِ قَانِتِينَ

Be guardians of your prayers, and of the midmost prayer. [323]

وَأْمُرْ أَهْلَكَ بِالصَّلَاةِ وَاصْطَبِرْ عَلَيْهَا لَا نَسْأَلُكَ رِزْقًا نَّحْنُ نَرْزُقُكَ وَالْعَاقِبَةُ لِلتَّقْوَى

Enjoin prayer on thy people, and be constant therein. We ask thee not to provide sustenance: We provide it for thee. But the (fruit of) the Hereafter is for righteousness. [324]

[321] Bayhaqī.
[322] Sūratu 'n-Nisā [Women], 4:103.
[323] Sūratu 'l-Baqarah [The Heifer], 2:238.
[324] Sūrah ṬāḤā 20:132.

اتْلُ مَا أُوحِيَ إِلَيْكَ مِنَ الْكِتَابِ وَأَقِمِ الصَّلَاةَ إِنَّ الصَّلَاةَ تَنْهَى عَنِ الْفَحْشَاءِ وَالْمُنكَرِ وَلَذِكْرُ اللَّهِ أَكْبَرُ وَاللَّهُ يَعْلَمُ مَا تَصْنَعُونَ

Recite that which has been revealed to thee of the Book, and observe Prayer. Surely, Prayer restrains one from indecency and manifest evil, and remembrance of Allah indeed is the greatest virtue. And Allah knows what you do. [325]

فِي جَنَّاتٍ يَتَسَاءلُونَ عَنِ الْمُجْرِمِينَ مَا سَلَكَكُمْ فِي سَقَرَ قَالُوا لَمْ نَكُ مِنَ الْمُصَلِّينَ

(They will be) in Gardens (of Delight): they will question each other, and (ask) of the sinners: "What led you into Hell Fire?" They will say: "We were not of those who prayed" [326]

عن بن عمر رضي الله عنهما قال : قال رسول ﷺ : " بني الإسلام على خمس : شهادة أن لا إله إلا الله وأن محمداً رسول الله ، وإقامة الصلاة ، وإيتاء الزكاة ، والحج ، وصوم رمضان

The Messenger of Allah made ritual prayer the second of the five pillars of Islam:

> Islam is built on five: testifying that there is no god except Allah and that Muhammad is the Messenger of Allah,

[325] Sūratu 'l-'Ankabūt [The Spider], 29:45.
[326] Sūratu 'l-Muddathir [The Cloaked One], 74:40-43.

establishing ritual prayer, paying the poor-due, pilgrimage and fasting Ramadan.[327]

Thus, the ritual prayer is an obligation from Allah on every sane, adult Muslim.

قال رسول الله صلى الله عليه وسلم : (أول ما يحاسب به العبد يوم القيامة عن

الصلاة ، فإن صلحت ، صلح سائر عمله ، وإن فسدت ، فسد سائر عمله

The Prophet said:

The first thing about which a person will be questioned on the Day of Judgment is prayer. If it is found to be sound all his other actions will be sound as well. If his prayer is not sound all his remaining actions would be spoiled.[328]

قال رسول بين الرجل والكفر ترك الصلات

The Prophet also said:

Between a man and unbelief is giving up of ritual prayer.[329]

من فاته صلاة العصر فكأنما وتر في أهله وماله

He also said:

The one who missed Ṣalāt al-ʿAṣr, just one of the ritual prayers, is as if he has lost all his family and property.[330]

افضل الاعمال الصلاة لوقتها،

And he said: Ritual prayer in its proper time is the best of deeds.[331]

---

[327] Bukhārī, Muslim and others.

[328] At-Ṭabarānī.

[329] Muslim.

[330] Bukhārī and Mālik in his *Muwaṭṭa*.

وكان آخر وصايا النبي قبل انتقاله إلى الرفيق الأعلى: الصلاة الصلاة وما ملكت أيمانكم

It is reported that the Prophet's last words were:

Prayer! Prayer! And fear Allah regarding those who you are in charge of.[332]

Abū Bakr bin al-Jazā'irī states:

Among the wisdoms in the implementation of prayer is that it purifies and welcomes the worshipper to converse with Allah and His Messenger, and, while he or she remains in the material world, brings him or her into proximity with the Divine in the next life and wards off indecency and manifest evil.[333]

مثل الصلوات الخمس كمثل نهر عذب غمر بباب أحدكم يقتحم فيه كل يوم خمس مرات فما ترون ذلك يبقي من درنه قالوا لاشيء قال صلى الله عليه وسلم فإن الصلوات الخمس تذهب الذنوب كما يذهب الماء الدرن

Allah's Messenger Muhammad ﷺ said:

The simile of the five prayers is like a flowing river of sweet-water in front of the door of one of you, in which he plunges five times a day. What dirt will remain on him? They said, "None." He said, "Surely the five prayers eliminate sins just as water eliminates dirt."[334]

---

331 Al-Khatīb and ibn Najjār.

332 Mawlana Muhammad Yūsuf Khandalvi, *Hayat as-Ṣaḥāba*, IDāra Isha 'at-e-Diniyat Ltd, New Delhi, 1992, p. 101.

333 Abū Bakr bin al-Jazā'irī, *Minhāj al-Muslim*, chapter on Prayer, Dār al-Fikr, Makkah, Saudi Arabia, first edition 1995, page 184.

334 Muslim from Jabir and others from Abū Hurayrah.

عَنْ أَبِي هُرَيْرَةَ، أَنَّ رَسُولَ اللَّهِ صلى الله عليه وسلم كَانَ يَقُولُ " الصَّلَوَاتُ الْخَمْسُ وَالْجُمُعَةُ إِلَى الْجُمُعَةِ وَرَمَضَانُ إِلَى رَمَضَانَ مُكَفِّرَاتٌ مَا بَيْنَهُنَّ إِذَا اجْتَنَبَ الْكَبَائِرَ

Allah's Messenger ﷺ also said:

> The five prayers and from one Friday prayer to the (next) Friday prayer are expiation [for what occurred between them] and Ramadan to Ramadan are expiations for the (sins) committed in between if one abstained from the major sins.[335]

One of the primary aims of prayer is to prevent iniquity and vice.

من لم تنهه صلاته عن الفحشاء والمنكر لم يزدد من الله الا بعدا

The Prophet of Allah ﷺ said:

> The one whose prayer does not prevent him from iniquity and vice, gains nothing from Allah except remoteness.[336]

While the five prayers are an obligation, Muslims are also enjoined to perform other prayers in accordance with the practices of the Prophet Muhammad ﷺ. These include:

- *Witr* (The final prayer to end the day)
- The two festival (ʻ*Eid*) prayers
- The Eclipse Prayer
- The Prayer for Rain

---

[335] Muslim and Tirmidhī. Aḥmad's *Musnad* from Abū Hurayrah relates a similar narration in which the major sins mentioned are *shirk* (association partners with Allah); to turn upon the one whom you have sworn allegiance (the leader of the nation) with one's sword, and to leave the Community of the Holy Prophet.

[336] At-Ṭabarānī reported it from Anas in his *Kabīr*. In another report it reads……"then his prayers are not prayers."

All the above are termed established traditions of the Prophet ﷺ. Other than these are what are classified as voluntary (*at-taṭaww'u*) worship.[337]

In addition, there are a number of supererogatory prayers (*sunan*) which were part of the normative practice of the Prophet Muhammad ﷺ, and which remain part of the everyday worship of many traditionalist Muslims.

HISTORY OF *SALAT*

After the Prophet Muhammad ﷺ was commissioned with prophethood in his fortieth year, the first order he was given by Allah was to pray. It is related that the archangel Jibrīl came to him, and a spring of water gushed out from the rocks in front of them. Jibrīl then showed the Prophet how to perform the ablution that is a prerequisite of the ritual prayer in Islam. Jibrīl then showed the Prophet how to offer the ritual prayer to Allah. The Prophet ﷺ then went home and showed his wife Khadījā ؓ what the archangel Jibrīl had taught him.

After that, the Messenger of Allah began to pray two cycles (*raka'ts*) of ritual prayer twice a day – once in the morning and once in the evening. From that time forward, the Prophet never went through a day without praying. In the ninth year of the Prophet's mission, he was taken by the archangel Jibrīl on a miraculous journey by night to Jerusalem and, from there, ascended to the heavens and the Divine Presence. During this tremendous journey, Allah commanded the Prophet and his followers to observe the ritual-prayer fifty times a day. Returning from the Divine Presence, Prophet Muhammad ﷺ met the prophet Moses who said, "Seek a reduction for your people can not carry it." The Prophet did so and it was granted. After many such dialogues the command was reduced to observe five prayers,

---

[337] *Minhāj al-Muslim*, Abū Bakr bin al-Jazā'irī, the chapter of Prayer, Dār al-Fikr, Makkah, Saudi Arabia, first edition 1995, pages 184-185.

which would be the equivalent of the original command to observe fifty. For this reason, Muslims feel a great debt to the Prophet Moses for this intercession on their behalf.

CONDITIONS OF *SALAT*

In Divine Law (*Shariʿah*), there are a number of requirements for valid ritual prayer:

- Purification
- Time
- Direction
- Covering
- Fundaments of prayer

In addition to these essentials, there are a number of normative practices of the Prophet which are strongly recommended as part of the ritual prayer, known as *sunnah*:

- Congregation/Imāmate
- Humility before the Divine (*Khushuʿ*)
- Place
- Attire

PRAYER IS BASED ON THE SUNNAH

The practice of the Prophet ﷺ is essential to understand the Holy Qur'ān. Allah said:

وَأَقِيمُواْ الصَّلاَةَ وَآتُواْ الزَّكَاةَ

Establish prayers (salat) and pay the poor-due (zakāt).[338]

From this, it is clear both prayer and the poor-due are obligations. However, to find the necessary details to complete the

[338] Sūratu 'l-Baqarah [The Heifer], 2:43, Sūratu 'l-Baqarah, 2:83, Sūratu 'l-Baqarah, 2:110, and others.

prayer, i.e. the manner and timing of the prayer and upon whom it is obligatory, etc., we must turn to the practice of Prophet Muhammad ﷺ. Islamic doctrine states that for every single event in his lifetime Allah revealed to the Prophet's heart what to say and what to do. The Qur'ān and the Prophetic Narrations (*aḥādīth*) both derive from revelation and are thus inseparable sources for understanding and implementing Islam's divine guidance.[339]

The Prophet ﷺ said, "Pray as you see me pray."[340] What is meant here is to follow the method of observing prayer, both in form and in its inward composure and states.

The Prophet ﷺ used to practice the ritual prayer constantly, outside the obligatory times. In doing so he was observing Allah's recommendation:

وَاسْتَعِينُواْ بِالصَّبْرِ وَالصَّلاَةِ وَإِنَّهَا لَكَبِيرَةٌ إِلاَّ عَلَى الْخَاشِعِينَ

Nay, seek (Allah's) help with patient perseverance and prayer: It is indeed hard, except to those who bring a lowly spirit.[341]

---

[339] The Prophet ﷺ said:

> Verily this Qur'ān is difficult and felt as a burden to anyone that hates it, but it is made easy to anyone that follows it. Verily my sayings are difficult and felt as a burden to anyone that hates them, but they are made easy to anyone that follows them. Whoever hears my saying and preserves it, putting it into practice, shall come forth together with the Qur'ān on the Day of Resurrection. Whoever dismisses my sayings dismisses the Qur'ān, and whoever dismisses the Qur'ān has lost this world and the next.

Narrated from al-Hakam ibn 'Umayr al-Thumali by Khatīb in *al-Jami' li Akhlāq al-Rāwī* (1983 ed. 2:189), Qurtubi in his *Tafsīr* (18:17), Abū Nu'aym, Abū al-Shaykh, and Daylamī.

[340] Bukhārī.

[341] Sūratu 'l-Baqarah [The Heifer], 2:45.

According to the scholars of Divine Law recommended acts are divided into three categories: those acts whose demand is confirmed, known as the "confirmed normative practice of the Prophet" (*sunan al-muʿakkadah*). According to Aḥmad Ibn Naqib al-Masri, "Someone who neglects such an act ... deserves censure and blame."[342] Second are those acts that are rewardable in Divine Law, but the one who neglects them deserves no blame. These are called the extra *sunnah* (*sunnah nāfilah*). The third category is the superlatively recommended, "meaning those acts considered part of an individual's perfections."[343] These are called the desirable acts (*mustaḥab*) or decorum (*adab*).

TAHARAH - PURIFICATION

A precondition of ritual prayer in Islam is that the worshipper be in a ritually pure state and perform his or her prayer in a ritually pure location.

There are two levels of ritual impurity, each with its own remedy:

1) Major impurity. This occurs as a result of menstruation, childbirth and sexual intercourse or emission. Its remedy is ritual-bathing, as prescribed in the Holy Qur'ān:

يَا أَيُّهَا الَّذِينَ آمَنُواْ لاَ تَقْرَبُواْ الصَّلاَةَ وَأَنتُمْ سُكَارَى حَتَّىَ تَعْلَمُواْ مَا تَقُولُونَ وَلاَ

جُنُبًا إِلاَّ عَابِرِي سَبِيلٍ حَتَّىَ تَغْتَسِلُواْ

O ye who believe! Approach not prayers with a mind befogged, until ye can understand all that ye say,- nor in a state of ceremonial impurity (Except when travelling on the road), until after washing your whole body. [344]

---

[342] Al-Masri, A., *The Reliance of the Traveller* (N. Keller, Trans.). Dubai, United Arab Emirates: Modern Printing Press, 1991, p. 34.

[343] *Ibid.*, p. 35.

[344] Sūratu 'n-Nisā [Women], 4:43.

2) Minor impurity. This occurs due to answering the call of nature, bleeding, vomiting and sleeping. Its remedy is ritual ablution. This, too, is mentioned in the Holy Qur'ān:

يَا أَيُّهَا الَّذِينَ آمَنُوا إِذَا قُمْتُمْ إِلَى الصَّلَاةِ فَاغْسِلُوا وُجُوهَكُمْ وَأَيْدِيَكُمْ إِلَى الْمَرَافِقِ وَامْسَحُوا بِرُؤُوسِكُمْ وَأَرْجُلَكُمْ إِلَى الْكَعْبَيْنِ

O you who believe! When you get ready for ritual prayer [ṣalāt], wash your faces, and your hands up to the elbows, and lightly rub your heads and (wash) your feet up to the ankles.[345]

عن جابر قال قال رسول الله صلى الله عليه وسلم مفتاح الصلاة الوضوء ومفتاح الجنة الصلاة.

The Holy Prophet said:

Ablution is the key to prayer as prayer is the key to Paradise.[346]

The various schools of Islamic jurisprudence differ slightly in the precise details of ritual ablution and bathing. Emphasized in all, however, is the need to use pure water, free from all contamination, for pure water contains the secret of life and of revivifying what is dead. Allah says in the Holy Qur'ān:

وَجَعَلْنَا مِنَ الْمَاءِ كُلَّ شَيْءٍ حَيٍّ

We made from water every living thing,[347]

And:

---

345 Sūratu 'l-Mā'idah [The Spread Table], 5:6.

346 *Ṭārīkh Iṣfahān.*

347 Sūratu'l-Anbīyā [The Prophets], 21:30.

وَمَا أَنزَلَ اللّهُ مِنَ السَّمَاء مِن مَّاء فَأَحْيَا بِهِ الأرْضَ بَعْدَ مَوْتِهَا

In the rain which Allah Sends down from the skies, and the life which He gives therewith to an earth that is dead...[348]

If water is unavailable, extremely scarce or its use would harm the worshipper, it is permitted to perform substitute ablution using dry earth. The Holy Qur'ān says:

يَا أَيُّهَا الَّذِينَ آمَنُواْ إِذَا قُمْتُمْ إِلَى الصَّلاةِ فاغْسِلُواْ وُجُوهَكُمْ وَأَيْدِيَكُمْ إِلَى الْمَرَافِقِ وَامْسَحُواْ بِرُؤُوسِكُمْ وَأَرْجُلَكُمْ إِلَى الْكَعْبَينِ وَإِن كُنتُمْ جُنُبًا فَاطَّهَّرُواْ وَإِن كُنتُم مَّرْضَى أَوْ عَلَى سَفَرٍ أَوْ جَاء أَحَدٌ مَّنكُم مِّنَ الْغَائِطِ أَوْ لاَمَسْتُمُ النِّسَاء فَلَمْ تَجِدُواْ مَاء فَتَيَمَّمُواْ صَعِيدًا طَيِّبًا فَامْسَحُواْ بِوُجُوهِكُمْ وَأَيْدِيكُم مِّنْهُ مَا يُرِيدُ اللّهُ لِيَجْعَلَ عَلَيْكُم مِّنْ حَرَجٍ وَلَكِن يُرِيدُ لِيُطَهَّرَكُمْ وَلِيُتِمَّ نِعْمَتَهُ عَلَيْكُمْ لَعَلَّكُمْ تَشْكُرُونَ

And if ye are sick or on a journey, or one of you cometh from the closet, or ye have had contact with women, and ye find not water, then go to clean, high ground and rub your faces and your hands with some of it. Allah would not place a burden on you, but He would purify you and would perfect His grace upon you, that ye may give thanks.[349]

Besides cleansing the body, the worshipper must also take care to ensure that his or her clothes are free from impurities that

[348] Sūratu 'l-Baqarah [The Heifer], 2:164.
[349] Sūratu 'l-Mā'idah [The Spread Table], 5:6.

would nullify the prayer. Traditionally, shoes are removed before the prayer because of their tendency to retain impurities.

THE SPIRITUAL SIGNIFICANCE OF *TAHARA*

Ibn Rushd states that the word for ablution, *wuḍū*, derives from the word for light in Arabic, *ḍaw*, signifying the resultant spiritual light that accrues to the one who performs it.[350]

عَنْ نُعَيْمٍ الْمُجْمِرِ، قَالَ رَقِيتُ مَعَ أَبِي هُرَيْرَةَ عَلَى ظَهْرِ الْمَسْجِدِ، فَتَوَضَّأَ فَقَالَ إِنِّي سَمِعْتُ النَّبِيَّ صلى الله عليه وسلم يَقُولُ " إِنَّ أُمَّتِي يُدْعَوْنَ يَوْمَ الْقِيَامَةِ غُرًّا مُحَجَّلِينَ مِنْ آثَارِ الْوُضُوءِ، فَمَنِ اسْتَطَاعَ مِنْكُمْ أَنْ يُطِيلَ غُرَّتَهُ فَلْيَفْعَلْ ".

The Messenger of Allah said:

On the Day of Resurrection, my Community will be called "those with the radiant appendages" because of the traces of ablution. Therefore, whoever can increase the area of his radiance should do so.[351]

عَنْ أَبِي حَازِمٍ، قَالَ كُنْتُ خَلْفَ أَبِي هُرَيْرَةَ وَهُوَ يَتَوَضَّأُ لِلصَّلاَةِ فَكَانَ يَمُدُّ يَدَهُ حَتَّى تَبْلُغَ إِبِطَهُ فَقُلْتُ لَهُ يَا أَبَا هُرَيْرَةَ مَا هَذَا الْوُضُوءُ فَقَالَ يَا بَنِي فَرُّوخَ أَنْتُمْ هَا هُنَا لَوْ عَلِمْتُ أَنَّكُمْ هَا هُنَا مَا تَوَضَّأْتُ هَذَا الْوُضُوءَ سَمِعْتُ خَلِيلِي صلى الله عليه وسلم يَقُولُ " تَبْلُغُ الْحِلْيَةُ مِنَ الْمُؤْمِنِ حَيْثُ يَبْلُغُ الْوُضُوءُ ".

Abū Hurayrah related:

---

[350] Ibn Rushd (Averros), *al-Muqaddimah*, the chapter of Prayer, Dār al-Kutub al-Ilmīyyah Publishing House for Scholarly Texts, 1994.
[351] Bukhārī and Muslim from Abū Hurayrah.

> I heard my intimate friend (the Messenger of Allah) saying, "The radiance of the believer reaches the areas that the water of ablution reaches." [352]

Ablution signifies spiritual purity, which the Prophet was granted when the angels washed his heart, both in his youth and again, later, when angels washed it with the water of the holy well Zamzam on the Night of Ascension.

To gain the full benefit of ablution, the worshipper must perform it with the realization of its inner aspects, washing away the burdens and darkness of worldly life that distract him or her from Divine service. By removing both the physical and mental filth that accumulates through the day, one ignites and seals the latent spiritual energy of one's being by means of the special attributes of water. The extremities washed during ablution are the primary means of interacting with the worldly life, and these must be cleansed of the taint left by that contact.

Ablution begins with washing the hands, signifying that the first level of spiritual energy is in the hands. Human hands contain a Divine Secret, for they are a reflection of the Divine Attribute of Power, which Allah has bestowed in a limited degree on humankind. They provide the means for the outward manifestations of humankind's will to change its circumstances. Thus, hands are a source of change, control and healing. No other creature has been endowed with so great an ability to manipulate its surroundings, and the hands are the main physical instrument of that ability.

The hand can act as a receiver of positive energy. The circle of the body, so clearly illustrated by Leonardo da Vinci, is reflected on a smaller scale in the circle of the hand. Energy can be drawn in through the hands and channeled throughout the body. When one rubs the hands together during ablution, one activates a

---

[352] Muslim from Abū Hurayrah.

spiritual code that Allah has given us within our hands: the power of the ninety-nine Beautiful Names and Attributes that Allah has inscribed on every person's palms.[353] The friction between the two hands creates energy in the form of heat and rubbing them together under water locks in that energy, preventing it from escaping. The water keeps the energy that is generated by rubbing the hands together within the body, where it can be released later.

During the process of ablution the hands are used to convey the water to each other limb and organ, thereby functioning as a dispenser of that divine energy. As the limbs and organs are washed in ablution, each undergoes similar spiritual alterations based on the water, the hands and their energy, and the various movements and recitations that are part of the ablution. For the believer to benefit from the water, it must be pure and clean, otherwise its secret blessings do not reach the body.

On an esoteric level, ablution becomes a metaphor for purifying the heart. Water is always clean in its essence, so the degree of spiritual reception is dependent on keeping the water free from external impurities. If we expand the spiritual metaphor, the water symbolizes the remembrance of Allah. That remembrance is pure, in and of itself, but can be tainted by the darkness of negativity which derives from wrong intent, wrong will and wrong action.

The most powerful energy we carry as human beings is our spiritual energy. Second to that is the physical energy of creativity, which manifests during the act of procreation. In the course of physically expressing this creative energy Allah has placed within us, we enter into a state similar to the spiritual state of annihilation, but not related to the Divine Presence, on the contrary, it is related to the lower self. When this occurs, it is

---

[353] On the right palm one sees the Arabic numerals 1 and 8, signifying 18, and on the left 8 and 1, signifying 81. The sum of these is 99.

essential to wash the body completely, with the intention to restore the spiritual state of purity lost during the act.

Purification of the heart blocks the influence of Satan on the believer. For this reason, the Prophet is reported to have said:

Ablution is the weapon of the believer.[354]

Ablution protects the believer from four enemies of the soul: the lower self or ego (*nafs*), worldly desire (*ḥubb ad-dunyā*), lust (*hawā*) and Satan. However, only through the remembrance of Allah can the believer maintain this defense throughout the day. When the heart begins to beat with Allah's Holy Name, "Allah," Satan is prevented from entering, and the gossips and insinuations of the lower self are gradually reduced until they are no more than a whisper.

At an even higher level of understanding, ablution signifies the state of dissolving the self in the Divine Presence. According to the Sufi master Al-Jīlī:

> … the requirement of using water signifies that purity is not achieved except by the emergence [in the worshipper] of the manifestations of the Divine Attributes, which is the water of life, for water is the secret of life. Dry ablution (*tayammum*) as a substitute [for ablution with water] is the station of purity by necessity, and is thus a symbol of purifying one's self by opposing one's lower-self, combating the tyrannical selfish ego and spiritual exercises. However, even after someone is purified, there is still a chance for him to exist.[355] This is what the Prophet alluded to when he supplicated, "O my Lord give my self its piety and its purity, for You are the best one

[354] Often cited, but not traced to a known Ḥadīth from the Prophet.

[355] Without annihilation. i.e. to see himself as existent before the Ultimate Divine Reality, which at the highest understanding of spirituality, is associating one's self as partner with God.

to purify it."[356] His saying "Give my self its piety," is an indication of [the need for] combating the lower-self by means of spiritual exercises. His saying " ...and its purity, for You are the best one to purify it," is an indication of the heart's attraction to the Divine, for this [attraction] is far more effective than purifying by means of action and opposing the lower-self.[357]

TIMING

The five times of obligatory ritual prayer are:
Fajr: From dawn to sunrise;
Dhuhr: From noon until mid-afternoon;
ʿAṣr: From mid-afternoon to sunset;
Maghrib: From sunset to early evening;
ʿIshā: From early evening to the middle of the night.

These times coincide with the significant temporal changes that are part of each day's cycle on earth as this planet moves through its various stations in relation to the Sun. The Sun, which is the focal point of the solar system, thus becomes a guiding light for the worshiper, indicating the beginning and ending of each prayer's interval. In this way, Muslims are reminded of the story of Abraham, as mentioned in the Holy Qur'ān.

In his yearning and seeking for Allah, Abraham holds a metaphorical debate within himself. His first inclination is to bow before a bright star that shines forth at night, taking it as his Lord. However, when that star sets, his intellect rejects it, seeking something greater as Lord. Seeing the Moon, he determines it to be his Lord until it too sets and he seeks something greater still. Seeing the Sun rise, he supposes it must be his Lord, but despite its blazing glory, it too sets. Finally, Abraham concludes that none

---

356 Muslim, Aḥmad in his *Musnad*, and others from Zayd bin Arqam.
357 al-Jīlī, *al-Insān al-Kāmil* (the Perfect Human), Chapter 'Secrets of Religion and Worship,' section 'The spiritual symbolism of prayer,' pages 260-261.

of these heavenly bodies – and by inference, no created thing – could be his Lord, and thus sets himself firmly on worship of the Unseen Lord:

فَلَمَّا أَفَلَتْ قَالَ يَا قَوْمِ إِنِّي بَرِيءٌ مِّمَّا تُشْرِكُونَ إِنِّي وَجَّهْتُ وَجْهِيَ لِلَّذِي فَطَرَ السَّمَاوَاتِ وَالأَرْضَ حَنِيفًا وَمَا أَنَاْ مِنَ الْمُشْرِكِينَ

...when [the sun] set he exclaimed: O my people! Lo! I am free from all that ye associate (with Him). Lo! I have turned my face toward Him Who created the heavens and the earth, as one by nature upright, and I am not of the idolaters.[358]

Muslims consider the day to begin at sunset, with the evening (*Maghrib*) prayer. This holds tremendous significance on an esoteric, or spiritual, level. The masters of the science of Islamic spirituality, Sufism, see the cycles of prayer as symbolic of the cycles of creation itself. The sunset prayer represents the station of leaving existence. The night prayer, which follows it, represents the station of darkness and death, annihilation and nonexistence.

In some Islamic traditions, funeral prayers for those who have passed away during the preceding day are read immediately after the sunset prayer, indicating this time's correlation with death and the afterlife.

The Holy Qur'ān says:

اللَّهُ يَتَوَفَّى الأَنفُسَ حِينَ مَوْتِهَا وَالَّتِي لَمْ تَمُتْ فِي مَنَامِهَا فَيُمْسِكُ الَّتِي قَضَى عَلَيْهَا الْمَوْتَ وَيُرْسِلُ الأُخْرَى إِلَى أَجَلٍ مُسَمًّى إِنَّ فِي ذَلِكَ لَآيَاتٍ لِّقَوْمٍ يَتَفَكَّرُونَ

---

[358] Sūratu 'l-Anʿam [Cattle], 6:78-79.

It is Allah that takes the souls (of men) at death; and those that die not (He takes) during their sleep: Those on whom He has passed the decree of death, He keeps back (from returning to life), but the rest He sends (to their bodies) for a term appointed.[359]

Awakening to pray just before dawn represents the return to life, the descent through the darkness of the womb to emerge into the light. Metaphorically, the worshipper moves from the station of nonexistence and annihilation back to the station of existence and rebirth. A new day has come, and with it the worshipper is reborn.

The apex of existence is marked by the noon prayer, which begins just as the Sun reaches the peak of brightness. At the zenith, two kingdoms are present and the prayer joins them: the kingdom of heaven, and the kingdom of earth.

The afternoon prayer takes place in a time that signifies the approach of the end, autumn and the last era of worldly life. According to Islamic tradition, the Prophet Muhammad ﷺ and the community of believers he raised appear at the end of humanity's spiritual history, just prior to the Day of Judgment. The coming of the afternoon prayer thus represents the approach of Judgment Day and the Divine Reckoning that it brings. With the setting of the sun, life comes to an end. The worshipper returns to Allah, taking with him an account of his deeds. With the darkness comes annihilation in Allah's Endless Mercy Oceans. It is for this reason that Islam places a strong emphasis on the afternoon prayer.

Thus, each day is a full life cycle, from creation out of nonexistence to Judgment Day and annihilation. Each day has its birth, life and death. In similar fashion the prayer times reflect the five major stages of life: infancy, childhood, youth, maturity and old age.

---

[359] Sūratu 'z-Zumar [The Groups], 39:42.

Facing *Qiblah*

The worshipper faces the Kaʿbah, the holy shrine of Islam, as determined to the best of his or her ability by simple means. This directional focus is called the *qiblah*.

The Kaʿbah is the House of Allah, located in the holy city of Mecca in present-day Arabia. It is the goal of the pilgrimage, which is the fifth pillar of Islam. In Islamic teachings, the Kaʿbah is said to mark the location where the Divine House in the Seventh Heaven, beyond which stands the Supreme Throne, which angels constantly circle in praise and worship of Allah, descended to Earth after the first man and woman, Adam and Eve, were cast out of Paradise for their mistake. In the time of Noah's flood, this heavenly sanctuary was taken up to heaven again. Millennia later, Abraham and Ishmael built the Kaʿbah in the same location, where it stands until today, the first house of worship dedicated to Allah. By facing this location in prayer, each Muslim aims and hopes to reach that holy location at some point in her or his life.

Initially, in the early days of Prophet Muhammad's mission, the believers faced Jerusalem when they prayed, out of respect for the Temple there. This direction represented respect for the previous Divine dispensations brought by Moses and Jesus and the Israelite prophets. Later, Divine legislation altered the direction of prayer to face the Holy House in Mecca:

قَدْ نَرَى تَقَلُّبَ وَجْهِكَ فِي السَّمَاء فَلَنُوَلِّيَنَّكَ قِبْلَةً تَرْضَاهَا فَوَلِّ وَجْهَكَ شَطْرَ
الْمَسْجِدِ الْحَرَامِ وَحَيْثُ مَا كُنتُمْ فَوَلُّواْ وُجُوِهَكُمْ شَطْرَهُ وَإِنَّ الَّذِينَ أُوْتُواْ
الْكِتَابَ لَيَعْلَمُونَ أَنَّهُ الْحَقُّ مِن رَّبِّهِمْ وَمَا اللّهُ بِغَافِلٍ عَمَّا يَعْمَلُونَ

We see thee (O Muhammad) turning of thy face for guidance to the heavens: now shall We turn thee to a prayer-direction that shall please thee. Turn then thy

face in the direction of the Sacred Mosque [Kaʿba]:
Wherever ye are, turn your faces in that direction.[360]

Thus, wherever Muslims live, their prayers have a common focus: the Kaʿbah.

Because of the presence of this blessed shrine, the area surrounding the Kaʿbah is holy. These environs are called the *Ḥarām*, literally "prohibited," meaning a place where sins are prohibited. The Kaʿbah itself is located within the "Prohibited Mosque," *Masjid al-Ḥarām*.[361] The name Prohibited Mosque was given because no one may act on bad desires there. While it is called a mosque, Allah made it more than that. In reality, it is a place where sins are utterly rejected, not only in their outward forms but also in their inner realities. There, even negative thoughts and intentions are considered blameworthy. Only pure, positive desires and good thoughts are accepted. Indeed, within the confines of that holy sanctuary, no hunting is allowed; even the cutting of trees and vegetation is proscribed.

Allah said in the Holy Qur'ān:

سُبْحَانَ الَّذِي أَسْرَى بِعَبْدِهِ لَيْلاً مِّنَ الْمَسْجِدِ الْحَرَامِ إِلَى الْمَسْجِدِ الأَقْصَى
الَّذِي بَارَكْنَا حَوْلَهُ لِنُرِيَهُ مِنْ آيَاتِنَا إِنَّهُ هُوَ السَّمِيعُ البَصِيرُ

Glory to (Allah) Who did take His servant for a Journey
by night from the Sacred Mosque to the farthest Mosque,
whose precincts We did bless, in order that We might
show him some of Our Signs: for He is the One Who
Heareth and Seth (all things).[362]

---

[360] Sūratu 'l-Baqarah[The Heifer], 2:144.
[361] Also translated as the "Sacred Mosque."
[362] Sūratu 'l-Isrā [The Night Journey], 17:1.

This verse describes the important journey that Prophet Muhammad ﷺ made between the Prohibited Mosque in Mecca and the Temple in Jerusalem (referred to as the Farthest Mosque, *Masjid al-Aqsā*[363]), a journey that in one moment bridged three divinely-revealed religions.

SIGNIFICANCE OF THE KAʿBAH

One of the distinctive characteristics of Islamic ritual prayer is that the worshipper is obliged to keep his vision, both external and internal, concentrated upon the *qiblah*. The focus of every worshipper is, and must be, a holy place. People whose understanding is purely external believe facing the Kaʿbah is of intrinsic value.

Those with a mystic understanding know that the Kaʿbah represents the spiritual pole of this world, around which all creation turns. Looking at photographs of the Kaʿbah taken from above, we see the worshippers moving around it in perfectly arranged concentric circles. This assembly gathers in imitation of the heavenly kingdom, for all these circles have one center regardless of their distance from it. At the spiritual level, that

---

[363] ʿAbdullāh Yūsuf ʿAlī's commentary on this verse summarizes traditional commentaries: "The Farthest Mosque," he writes, "must refer to the site of the Temple of Solomon in Jerusalem on the hill of Moriah."
Muslims purposely built a mosque on this hill, according to tradition on the verified site of earlier sanctuaries. It was a strong concern of the early Muslims to restore the site to its earlier function as a place of supplication venerated by all the prophets, including Abraham, David and Solomon. Tradition relates that when the Caliph ʿUmar visited Jerusalem after its conquest, he searched for David's sanctuary or prayer niche (*mihrāb Dāwūd*), which is mentioned in the Qur'ān (38:21), the same site on which his son Solomon later erected the Temple. Satisfied that he had located it, Caliph ʿUmar ordered a prayer-niche (*muṣalla*) to be established there which evolved into a mosque complex later known as the Ḥaram ash-Sharīf, according to Prophetic tradition the third most venerated location in Islam.

center is the Divine Presence. While each worshipper faces the Kaʿbah's walls of stone and mortar, these are not the focus. If we remove the four walls, what do we find? Each person facing someone else. In this is a deep and subtle secret that we leave for the reader to ponder.

When the spiritual seeker realizes his station on the circle of the People of the *Qiblah,* he enters what is known as the Circle of Unconditional Lovers (*dā'irat al-muḥibīn).* That is the circle of Muslims at the first level in the way of Allah: the level of love. Such love is not related to any desire, but is a purely Platonic, spiritual love between the believer and his or her Lord. Allah is the center of the circle, and the believers are each a point on its circumference. Each has his or her own connection to the center. That means each has his own direction, *qiblah,* towards the Divine Presence. As that connection becomes apparent to the believer, that radius becomes like a tunnel into which the seeker begins to step from the circumference of the circle. Upon making his first steps into that tunnel, he begins to discover countless negative characteristics within himself. As he discovers one characteristic after another, he begins to eliminate them, progressing down the tunnel to become a "seeker in the circle of lovers on the spiritual journey," progressing ever nearer to the *qiblah* at the center. In the metaphysics of Ibn ʿArabi, the renowned mystic scholar speaks of a spiritual hierarchy in which the emanations from the Divine are received by a single human receptor who is the leader of all these circles of lovers and through him spreads to the rest of humanity, each according to his or her degree or station. This individual represents the Prophet in his time as the perfect servant of Allah. Thus, under one spiritual leader, all are moving constantly closer to the Divine Presence.

In the Sufi understanding, which delves deeply into the mystic knowledge and symbolism of Islam's outward forms, it is said the Prohibited Mosque represents the heart of the believer. Thus, the inner direction of prayer is towards the sanctified heart. What is the sanctified heart? At the first level of spirituality, the sanctified heart is the heart that is purified of all wrong thoughts, negativity and dark intent. This level is called the Level of the Secret (*sirr*). Once that secret is opened within the sanctified heart, the seeker moves to the heart of the heart, known as Secret of the Secret (*sirr as-sirr*). That is the level of purification from any attachment to worldly desires. Beyond these levels of the heart are "the Hidden" (*khafā*) and "the Innermost" (*akhfā*) levels, representing further stations of purity, in which the heart becomes ever more removed from attachments, turning away from all that is worldly to focus instead on the spiritual realm of the Hereafter. At the highest level, the heart turns away from even that and begins to focus solely on the Divine Presence.

These are levels of achievement. On the spiritual dimension, the believer's focus is to reach a perfected level of character, to learn from it and to be enlightened from it. In order to progress beyond our state of ignorance we must strive to learn and educate ourselves. This can only be accomplished by keeping the company of enlightened individuals who have successfully traversed the Path of Allah, to Allah, and who are granted the ability to guide others. Allah says:

يَا أَيُّهَا الَّذِينَ آمَنُوا اتَّقُوا اللَّهَ وَكُونُوا مَعَ الصَّادِقِينَ

O ye who believe! Fear Allah and be with those who are true (in word and deed).[364]

Allah is aware of every heart. The Holy Qur'ān states:

وَالَّذِينَ جَاهَدُوا فِينَا لَنَهْدِيَنَّهُمْ سُبُلَنَا وَإِنَّ اللَّهَ لَمَعَ الْمُحْسِنِينَ

[364] Sūratu 't-Tawbah [Repentance], 9:119.

Those who struggle for Us, We will guide them in the right ways, the ways that are suitable to them.[365]

The polished heart of the sincere and true believer (*ṣādiq*) is a receptacle for Allah's Heavenly Lights and Divine Blessings. Such a person is like the sun. When the sun rises, the whole world shines from that source of energy and light, the light of mystical gnosis that makes all things visible. For that reason, the Prophet said, "The heart of the [true] believer is the House of the Lord."

COVERING

The Islamic schools of jurisprudence concur that it is essential (*wājib*) for both men and women to cover those parts of their bodies during prayer which should ordinarily be kept covered before strangers. For men, this includes what is between the navel and the knee. For women, it is the entire body, except the face and hands.

As we have said, the purity of what covers the body is essential for the prayer to be acceptable. In one of the first revelations to the Prophet Muhammad ﷺ, Allah says:

وَرَبَّكَ فَكَبِّرْ وَثِيَابَكَ فَطَهِّرْ وَالرُّجْزَ فَاهْجُرْ

And thy Lord do thou magnify! And thy garments keep free from stain! And all abomination shun![366]

The body is not the only thing that must be covered in prayer. During *ṣalāt*, the worshipper is commanded to look only at the location where he or she will prostrate, not to the left or right. In this way, one covers one's gaze and directs oneself to the Vision of Allah, for the Prophet said:

---

[365] Sūratu 'l-ʿAnkabūt [The Spider], 29:69.

[366] Sūratu 'l-Mudaththir [The Cloaked One], 74:3-5.

The perfection of religion (*al-Iḥsān*) is to worship Allah as if you are seeing Him and if you do not see Him, know that He sees you.[367]

Thus, the gaze of the believer must be veiled at the time of worship from everything other than Allah. This derives from a spiritual understanding of the Verse of the Veil in the Holy Qur'ān, in which Allah says:

قُل لِّلْمُؤْمِنِينَ يَغُضُّوا مِنْ أَبْصَارِهِمْ وَيَحْفَظُوا فُرُوجَهُمْ ذَٰلِكَ أَزْكَىٰ لَهُمْ إِنَّ اللَّهَ خَبِيرٌ بِمَا يَصْنَعُونَ وَقُل لِّلْمُؤْمِنَاتِ يَغْضُضْنَ مِنْ أَبْصَارِهِنَّ وَيَحْفَظْنَ فُرُوجَهُنَّ وَلَا يُبْدِينَ زِينَتَهُنَّ إِلَّا مَا ظَهَرَ مِنْهَا وَلْيَضْرِبْنَ بِخُمُرِهِنَّ عَلَىٰ جُيُوبِهِنَّ وَلَا يُبْدِينَ زِينَتَهُنَّ

Say to the believing men that they should lower their gaze and guard their modesty: that will make for greater purity for them: And Allah is well acquainted with all that they do. And say to the believing women that they should lower their gaze and guard their modesty; that they should not display their beauty and ornaments except what (must ordinarily) appear thereof; that they should draw their veils over their bosoms and not display their beauty ... [368]

The emphasis in these verses on lowering the gaze, meaning to guard the eyes from looking at what is forbidden or impure. In the outer sense, this means to refrain from looking with lustful desire at other than one's spouse, for the Prophet said, "The two eyes are two adulterers."[369]

In this regard, a renowned contemporary Sufi saint, and my teacher and guide on the spiritual path, Shaykh Muhammad

---

[367] Bukhārī and Muslim.

[368] Sūratu 'n-Nūr [The Light], 24:30-31.

[369] Bukhārī.

Nazim Adil al-Haqqani, relates the story of a judge (*qāḍī*), called by a woman to annul her husband's marriage to a second wife. The judge asked the plaintiff, whose face was hidden by a face-veil (*burqah*), "Why are you asking me to prevent something permitted in Islamic Divine Law?" The first wife replied, "Your honor, were I to remove my face-veil you would wonder how someone married to so stunning a beauty could seek another woman's companionship?" Upon hearing this the judge swooned. When he came to, his associates asked him what had happened. He replied, "On hearing this woman's reply, I had an epiphany. How is it that our hearts turn to all manner of worldly interests, when Allah Himself is asking us to be with Him alone?"

The next verse says:

> *they should not display their beauty and ornaments except what (must ordinarily) appear thereof; that they should draw their veils over their bosoms and not display their beauty ...* [370]

calling on women to veil their beauty from other than the men in their immediate family, to protect them from men who are all too easily overpowered by desire, and to protect men from their own weaknesses.

Esoteric commentators state that "women" here symbolize attachments to the worldly life. The spiritual meaning of this prohibition then is that, when coming before the Lord of Creation, the seeker must veil himself from all distractions of the worldly life and focus on the One to Whom prayer is directed.

At an even higher level of spiritual understanding, the word "women" refers to the Divine Attributes of Beauty. Thus, the worshipper, is advised to call to mind the Divine Attributes of Majesty, and not become lost in the Attributes of Beauty, which may lead the seeker to lose his or her balance in approaching the Divine Presence.

---

[370] Sūratu 'n-Nūr [The Light], 24:31.

In the Holy Qur'ān, Allah also said:

يَا بَنِي آدَمَ خُذُواْ زِينَتَكُمْ عِندَ كُلِّ مَسْجِدٍ

O Children of Adam! wear your beautiful apparel at every time and place of prayer (masjid).[371]

Here, believers are called upon by Allah to wear their best and most attractive garments when going to pray. The call to manifest "beautiful apparel" at the "place of prayer" can be interpreted as well to be an instruction to adorn the mosques and beautify them, keeping in mind that:

وَأَنَّ الْمَسَاجِدَ لِلَّهِ

The places of worship (masājid) are for Allah (alone). [372]

The three major holy mosques of Islam: the Kaʿbah in Mecca, the Prophet's Mosque in Medina and Masjid al-Aqsa in Jerusalem, are all highly ornamented with gilding, decorative calligraphy, mosaic tiles, inlaid wood, brilliant lamps and other decorations. All other mosques are connected to these for, as we have said, when worshippers stand to pray in any mosque, they must face the Kaʿbah, Allah's Holy House.

ما وسعني سمائي ولا أرضي ولكن وسعني قلب عبدي المؤمن

Allah said, "Neither My heavens contain Me nor My earth. But the heart of My Believing Servant contains Me."[373]

The heart, too, then is a mosque, and for this reason it also must be decorated. The ornamentation of the heart involves

---

[371] Sūratu 'l-ʿArāf [The Heights], 7:31.

[372] Sūratu 'l-Jinn [The Jinn], 72:18.

[373] Al-Ghazālī mentioned it in his Revival of the Religious Sciences. It is similar to an Israelite tradition related by Aḥmad in *al-Zuhd* from Wahb ibn Munabbih.

removing everything that distracts one from the worship of Allah and replacing these impurities with love of the Divine, as we have described earlier. Anything that brings impurity to the heart extinguishes the light that Allah has placed there. This is a form of tyranny, for the Arabic word for tyranny (*ẓulm*) also means darkness. Thus, any darkness which veils the heart from Allah's Holy Light is a form of oppression. This darkness cannot be removed except through repentance and seeking the intercessory prayers of the Prophet. This is why the aforementioned verses about modesty are followed closely by:

اللَّهُ نُورُ السَّمَاوَاتِ وَالْأَرْضِ مَثَلُ نُورِهِ كَمِشْكَاةٍ فِيهَا مِصْبَاحٌ الْمِصْبَاحُ فِي زُجَاجَةٍ
الزُّجَاجَةُ كَأَنَّهَا كَوْكَبٌ دُرِّيٌّ يُوقَدُ مِن شَجَرَةٍ مُّبَارَكَةٍ زَيْتُونِةٍ لَّا شَرْقِيَّةٍ وَلَا غَرْبِيَّةٍ
يَكَادُ زَيْتُهَا يُضِيءُ وَلَوْ لَمْ تَمْسَسْهُ نَارٌ نُّورٌ عَلَى نُورٍ يَهْدِي اللَّهُ لِنُورِهِ مَن يَشَاء
وَيَضْرِبُ اللَّهُ الْأَمْثَالَ لِلنَّاسِ وَاللَّهُ بِكُلِّ شَيْءٍ عَلِيمٌ

Allah is the Light of the heavens and the earth. The parable of His Light is as if there were a niche and within it a lamp: the lamp enclosed in glass: the glass as it were a brilliant star: Lit from a blessed tree, an olive, neither of the east nor of the west, whose oil is well-nigh luminous, though fire scarce touched it: Light upon Light! Allah doth guide whom He will to His Light: Allah doth set forth parables for men: and Allah doth know all things. [374]

"Allah is the Light" does not mean that Allah is light, rather The Light is His while Allah's Essence is unknown. The created cannot know The Creator except by means of His Beautiful Names

---

[374] Sūratu 'n-Nūr [The Light], 24:35.

and Attributes, His Descriptions. Allah's saying He is the Light of the heavens and earth means that whatever is found in the heavens and earth contains that light.[375] Since we are from earth, that light is within each of us, for Allah, being the Just, bestows on all with Divine Fairness. Shaykh Ibrāhīm Hakkī (1703-1780), a renowned Ottoman scholar of Qur'ān, said:

> Without a doubt the complete potential for perfection is found within every human being, because Allah the Most High has placed His own Divine Secrets within the essence of man, in order to manifest from the Unseen His Beautiful Names and Attributes.[376]

قَالَ النَّبِيُّ صلى الله عليه وسلم "كُلُّ مَوْلُودٍ يُولَدُ عَلَى الْفِطْرَةِ، فَأَبَوَاهُ يُهَوِّدَانِهِ أَوْ يُنَصِّرَانِهِ أَوْ يُمَجِّسَانِهِ، كَمَثَلِ الْبَهِيمَةِ تُنْتَجُ الْبَهِيمَةَ، هَلْ تَرَى فِيهَا جَدْعَاءَ"

Therefore, as the Prophet said, "Human beings are born on a natural disposition,"[377] meaning each human being carries that light of primordial faith and predisposition to submission before Allah.

Therefore in Prophet Muhammad ﷺ, being the epitome of humankind and its highest standard bearer, is found the perfect manifestation of the human embodiment of Divine grace and the corporeal manifestation of Divine Attributes. It is due to the Prophet's utter submission, in the state of perfect servanthood, that made him the perfect receptacle for Divine Appearances. That is, the Muhammadan Reality, *(al-ḥaqīqat ul-Muḥammadīyya)* reflects

[375] Kaʿb al-Ahbār makes the entire verse refer to Muhammad, it is a metaphor of the Light of Muhammad. The Messenger of Allah is the niche, the lamp is prophethood, the glass is his heart, the blessed tree is the revelation and the angels who bought it, the oil are the proofs and evidence which contain the revelation.

[376] Ibrāhīm Hakki Erzurumi, *Marifetname*, Cairo, Bulak (Printing House), 1835.

[377] Bukhārī.

the Heart of the Divine Essence, since the Prophet's heart moves without restriction in the orbit of the 99 Divine Names and Attributes. He has been blessed by being adorned by the 99 Names inside of which is a glowing pearl which has yet to appear. Thus many commentators assert that the "Light of the heavens and earth" referred to in the above verse, is the Light of Muhammad ﷺ, whom Allah created from His own Divine Light, and it is this light which shines in the hearts of believers, for the Light of the Prophet is the source of the light of all believers.

Adornment

Allah says in the Holy Qur'ān:

$$\text{يَا بَنِي آدَمَ خُذُواْ زِينَتَكُمْ عِندَ كُلِّ مَسْجِدٍ}$$

O Children of Adam! wear your beautiful apparel at every time and place of prayer...

$$\text{قُلْ مَنْ حَرَّمَ زِينَةَ اللّهِ الَّتِيَ أَخْرَجَ لِعِبَادِهِ وَالْطَّيِّبَاتِ مِنَ الرِّزْقِ}$$

Say (O Muhammad): "Who has forbidden the adoration with clothes given by Allah, which He has produced for His devotees?" [378]

Nafi' related:

'Umar ؓ entered upon me one day as I was praying in a single garment and he said, "Don't you have two garments in your possession?" I said, "Yes." He said, "In your opinion, if I sent you to one of the people of Madina on an errand, would you go in a single garment?" I said, "No." He said, "Then is Allah worthier of our self-beautification or people?"

---

[378] Sūratu 'l-'Arāf [The Heights], 7:31-32.

An adjunct to proper covering is proper physical appearance. The most direct method for establishing one's identity as a traveler upon the path of self-purification is to adopt the correct outward appearance, abandoning the dress of the worldly life and putting on instead the apparel of the hereafter. This is an outward indication of rejecting servitude to the material world (*'abd ad-dunyā*) and asserting one's true identity as a servant of the Divine (*'abd Allah*).

The dress most conducive to spirituality is the garb of Prophet Muhammad ﷺ, the traditional clothing worn by all the prophets and messengers of Allah. For men, this includes wearing the turban, the cloak (*jubbah*) and a ring, and using perfume and a tooth-stick (*miswāk*). For women, it involves wearing loose clothing, covering the hair, arms and legs, with white clothing being the most preferable. Such is the honored dress of the ascetics and lovers of Allah and His Prophet ﷺ, those who reject the illusion of the material world and will settle for nothing less than the perfection and truth of reality.

FUNDAMENTS OF PRAYER

The first and foremost fundamental part of the ritual prayer is intention (*niyyah*).

As in all Islamic worship, the worshipper intends the prayer as a fulfillment of Allah's Order done purely for God's sake. The Prophet Muhammad ﷺ established this as a paramount rule of worship when he said, "Verily all deeds are based on their intention."[379]

The prayer is initiated by the consecratory magnification of Allah (*takbīr*), followed by multiple cycles, each of which follows the same series of postures and recitations: first standing, then bowing, brief standing, prostrating, a brief sitting, a second prostration, and in the even cycles, sitting after the second prostration. Each of these positions also involves specific recitations. While standing, the first

[379] Bukhārī and Muslim.

chapter (Sūratu 'l-Fātiḥa) and other portions of the Holy Qur'ān are recited, either silently or aloud, depending upon the time of prayer. In bowing, the brief standing, prostration and the brief sitting, Allah is glorified and praised in short formulas. While sitting, the testimony of faith (*tashahhud*) is recited, along with greetings to and prayers for Prophet Muhammad ﷺ, Prophet Abraham and their families. In addition, there are a variety of supplemental invocations and recitations that are traditionally part of the practice of most worshippers. The basic essentials of ritual-prayer number about fifteen, depending on the school of jurisprudence followed.[380]

Each obligatory prayer has a prescribed number of cycles to be observed. These are:

Prayer	**# of cycles**
Maghrib (sunset)	3
ʿIsha (night)	4
Fajr (dawn)	2
Ẓuhr (noon)	4
ʿAsr (afternoon)	4

[380] They are:
1. Standing in an upright posture (*qīyām*).
2. The opening affirmation of God's Supreme Greatness (*takbīrat al-iḥrām*).
3. Recitation of the Opening chapter of the Qur'ān (Sūratu 'l-Fatiha).
4. Bowing (*rukuʿ*).
5. Calm composure (*ṭumā'nina*) in the bowing posture.
6. Straightening up from the bowing posture.
7. Calm composure in the erect posture resumed after bowing.
8. Prostration (*sujūd*).
9. Calm composure in the posture of prostration.
10. Sitting between the two acts of prostration.
11. Calm composure in the sitting posture.
12. The final testimony (*tashahhud*).
13. Adopting the sitting posture in order to pronounce the final testimony.
14. The invocation of blessing on the Prophet ﷺ (*ṣalāt al-Ibrāhīmīyya*).
15. The salutation (*taslīm*).

The Stations of *Salat*

The movements of the prayer identify the one praying with all other forms of creation, for the prayer's postures are designed to remind the worshipper of mortality and the traversal through the different stages of life. They also resemble the rising and setting of the celestial bodies, as well as the rotation of the planets upon their axes and the orbits of the moons, planets and suns. These are signs which demonstrate the hierarchical nature of creation and its submission to Divine regulation at every level, for as the Holy Qur'ān states:

وَمِنْ آيَاتِهِ اللَّيْلُ وَالنَّهَارُ وَالشَّمْسُ وَالْقَمَرُ لَا تَسْجُدُوا لِلشَّمْسِ وَلَا لِلْقَمَرِ
وَاسْجُدُوا لِلَّهِ الَّذِي خَلَقَهُنَّ إِن كُنتُمْ إِيَّاهُ تَعْبُدُونَ

Among His Signs are the night and the day, and the sun and the moon. Adore not the sun and the moon, but adore Allah, Who created them, if it is Him ye wish to serve. [381]

Allah further draws our attention to their submissive nature, saying:

أَلَمْ تَرَ أَنَّ اللَّهَ يَسْجُدُ لَهُ مَن فِي السَّمَاوَاتِ وَمَن فِي الْأَرْضِ وَالشَّمْسُ وَالْقَمَرُ
وَالنُّجُومُ وَالْجِبَالُ وَالشَّجَرُ وَالدَّوَابُّ وَكَثِيرٌ مِّنَ النَّاسِ

Hast thou not seen that before Allah prostrate whosoever is in the heavens and whosoever is on the earth, and the sun, and the moon, and the stars, and the hills, and the trees, and the beasts, and many of mankind...? [382]

---

[381] Sūrah Fuṣṣilat [Explained in Detail], 41:37.

[382] Sūratu 'l-Ḥajj [The Pilgrimage], 22:18.

The postures of prayer, then, are symbolic of humanity's relationship to the Divine, moving as they do from standing in assertion of existence and strength, to the bowing of humility and servitude, to prostration in the face of Allah's overwhelming Magnificence and Power and the corresponding realization of one's own utter nonexistence. From this station of utter abasement, the worshipper returns to the intermediate position, between annihilation and independence, to sit between the hands of the Prophet Muhammad ﷺ, greeting the one who is the intermediary between the Divinity and His creation. The Prophet stands at the Station of Perfect Servanthood and is the ultimate exemplar of the condition of servanthood to Allah. Unlike all other creations, Prophet Muhammad ﷺ was divested of all selfhood, dissolved in the Presence of Allah.

وَلِلَّهِ الْمَشْرِقُ وَالْمَغْرِبُ فَأَيْنَمَا تُوَلُّوا فَثَمَّ وَجْهُ اللَّهِ إِنَّ اللَّهَ وَاسِعٌ عَلِيمٌ

Whithersoever ye turn, there is the presence of Allah.
For Allah is all-Pervading, all-Knowing. [383]

THE PEAK OF PRAYER IS *SAJDAH*

ما تقرب العبد إلى الله بأفضل من سجود خفي

The Prophet ﷺ said, "Nothing brings the servant of Allah nearer to the Divine Presence than through his prostrations in secret(*al-khafi*)." [384]

مَا مِنْ مُسْلِمٍ يَسْجُدُ لِلَّهِ سَجْدَةً إِلَّا رَفَعَهُ اللَّهُ بِهَا دَرَجَةً أَوْ حَطَّ عَنْهُ بِهَا خَطِيئَةً.

The Prophet ﷺ said, "There is no Muslim who prostrates himself but he will be raised one degree by Allah or one sin is taken from him."[385]

---

[383] Sūratu 'l-Baqarah [The Heifer], 2:115.

[384] Ibn al-Mubarak *mursalan* via Damrata bin Habib.

As for what that degree consists of, know that it is not something small, for each heaven might consist of one degree. For that, the Prophet ﷺ said about the Last Days:

...حتى تكون السجدة الواحدة خيرا من الدنيا وما فيها

> One prostration will be better than the world and all that is in it.[386]

For these reasons, many among the pious observe extra voluntary prostrations to Allah after completing their obligatory prayers. Whenever they encounter a difficulty, whether spiritual or worldly, they seek refuge in their Lord through prostration to Him.

One must cut down self-pride and make the inner-self prostrate, for one who truly submits to his Lord can no longer submit to his or her self. Once that state is reached, prayer is purely for Allah. That is why the Prophet ﷺ said:

الا اخبركم بما هو اخوف عليكم عندي من المسيح الدجال؟ قال قلنا: بلى، فقال: الشرك الخفي ان يقوم الرجل يصلي فيزين صلاته لما يرى من نظر رجل.

> "Shall I inform you of what I fear for my Community even more than the Anti-Christ?" They said, "Surely!" He said, "Hidden polytheism."[387]

He feared for his community not the outward polytheism of idol-worship, for he was informed by Allah that his community

---

[385] *Musnad* Aḥmad.

[386] Bukhārī. Part of a longer Ḥadīth describing what would occur in the Last Days where ʿIsā ibn Maryam will descend and rule the earth with complete justice and the righteous will prevail over the oppression of wrongdoers.

[387] Ibn Mājah and al-Ḥākim in *al-Mustadrak* (authentic). In a similar vein, the Prophet ﷺ is reported to have said, "Association with God (*shirk*) is stealthier in this community than creeping ants."

was protected from that forever,[388] but the secret polytheism, which is to do something for the sake of showing-off.

حَدَّثَنِي رَبِيعَةُ بْنُ كَعْبٍ الأَسْلَمِيُّ، قَالَ كُنْتُ أَبِيتُ مَعَ رَسُولِ اللَّهِ صلى الله عليه وسلم
فَأَتَيْتُهُ بِوَضُوئِهِ وَحَاجَتِهِ فَقَالَ لِي " سَلْ " . فَقُلْتُ أَسْأَلُكَ مُرَافَقَتَكَ فِي الْجَنَّةِ . قَالَ "
أَوَغَيْرَ ذَلِكَ " . قُلْتُ هُوَ ذَاكَ . قَالَ " فَأَعِنِّي عَلَى نَفْسِكَ بِكَثْرَةِ السُّجُودِ

A man came and asked the Prophet ﷺ, "O Prophet of Allah, pray for me to be under your intercession on Judgment Day and grant me to be in your company in Paradise." The Prophet replied, "I will do so, but assist me in that." The man asked, "How so?" The Prophet said, "By frequent prostration [before God]."[389]

The Prophet ﷺ related that, on the Day of Judgment, as the believers emerge from their graves, angels will come to them to brush the dust from their foreheads. However, despite the best efforts of the angels, some of that dust will remain. Both the resurrected believers and their angelic helpers will be surprised that this dust cannot be removed. Then a voice will call out, "Leave that dust and do not try to remove it, for that is the dust of their prayer-niches, thus will it be known in Paradise that they are My [devout] servants."

This Prophetic Tradition indicates the spiritual value of the prostration of the believers, making as it does even the dust touched by their foreheads hallowed. The power of prayer has a similar effect on the place of prayer itself, as exemplified in the story of the Virgin Mary, as mentioned in the Holy Qur'ān:

---

[388] The Prophet ﷺ said, "I do not fear that you will become polytheists after me, but I fear that, because of worldly interests, you will fight each others, and thus be destroyed like the peoples of old." Bukhārī and Muslim.
[389] *Saḥīḥ Muslim.*

فَتَقَبَّلَهَا رَبُّهَا بِقَبُولٍ حَسَنٍ وَأَنبَتَهَا نَبَاتًا حَسَنًا وَكَفَّلَهَا زَكَرِيَّا كُلَّمَا دَخَلَ عَلَيْهَا زَكَرِيَّا الْمِحْرَابَ وَجَدَ عِندَهَا رِزْقًا قَالَ يَا مَرْيَمُ أَنَّىٰ لَكِ هَٰذَا قَالَتْ هُوَ مِنْ عِندِ اللَّهِ إِنَّ اللَّهَ يَرْزُقُ مَن يَشَاءُ بِغَيْرِ حِسَابٍ

> *Whenever Zachariah went into the prayer-niche where she was, he found that she had food. He said: O Mary! Whence cometh unto thee this (food)? She answered: It is from Allah. Allah giveth without stint to whom He will.*[390]

It was there, in the Virgin Mary's hallowed sanctuary, where she used to find her daily provision in the form of fruits out-of season, that the Prophet Zachariah went to prostrate himself before Allah and beseech Him for a child, and it was there that Allah granted his request.

The places where a Muslim prostrates will bear witness to his or her devotion on the Day of Judgment. It is for this reason that one often sees Muslims changing the location of their prayers, praying the obligatory cycles in one spot and then moving to another area to observe the voluntary cycles (*sunan*).

Ibn 'Abbās ☙, a cousin of the Prophet ﷺ and the greatest early exegete of the Qur'ān, said:

> When Allah commanded Adam to descend to Earth, as soon as he arrived, he went into prostration, asking Allah's forgiveness for the sin he had made. Allah sent the archangel Jibrīl to him after forty years had passed, and Jibrīl found Adam still in prostration.
>
> He had not raised his head for forty years in sincere and heartfelt repentance before Allah.

---

[390] Sūrat Āli-'Imrān [The Family of 'Imrān], 3:37.

The Holy Qur'ān tells us that, after Allah created Adam, He ordered the angels to prostrate before the first man.

وَإِذْ قُلْنَا لِلْمَلَائِكَةِ اسْجُدُوا لِآدَمَ فَسَجَدُوا إِلَّا إِبْلِيسَ أَبَى

When We said to the angels, "prostrate yourselves to Adam", they prostrated themselves, but not Iblis [Satan]: he refused.[391]

Imām al-Qurṭubī, one of the great commentators on the Holy Qur'ān, writes in his exegesis, *at-Tadhkira,* that one of the four Archangels, Isrāfīl (Rafael), had the entire Qur'ān written on his forehead. Allah had given Isrāfīl knowledge of the Holy Qur'ān and wrote all of it between his eyes, and he is the angel who inscribed the destinies of all things in the Preserved Tablets before they were created.[392] Rafael's name in Arabic, which differs from his Assyrianic name Isrāfīl, is ʿAbd al-Raḥmān, servant of The Merciful. This theme of mercy pervades Islamic thought, for it was through Allah's Mercy that the Holy Qur'ān was sent down to the Prophet, about whom The Merciful said:

وَمَا أَرْسَلْنَاكَ إِلَّا رَحْمَةً لِّلْعَالَمِينَ

We sent thee not but as a Mercy for all creatures.[393]

When Allah ordered the angels to make prostration to Adam, Rafael was the first to obey, making prostration and placing his forehead, containing the entire Qur'ān, on the earth, out of respect and honor for Adam, for he perceived the whole of Qur'ān written

---

[391] Sūrah ṬāḤā 20:116.

[392] Hajjah Amina Adil, *Lore of Light*, from Kaʿb al-Ahbār, Arafat Publishing House, Columbo, Sri Lanka, 1989, p. xiii.

[393] Sūratu'l-Anbīyā [The Prophets], 21:107.

on Adam's forehead.[394] Other commentators say the angels fell prostrate before Adam for they perceived the Light of Prophet Muhammad ﷺ shining from his form. There is in reality no discrepancy here, for Allah said in the Holy Qur'ān:

يس وَالْقُرْآنِ الْحَكِيمِ

Yasin, By the Qur'ān, full of Wisdom.[395]

The Prophet Muhammad ﷺ said that YāSīn, the thirty-sixth chapter of the Holy Qur'ān as well as one of his own blessed names, is the heart of the Holy Qur'ān, the very Qur'ān that the Prophet was carrying in his breast. Thus, the light that shone forth from Adam was the Light of the Prophet within him, who in turn was blazing with Allah's Holy Words.

THE HIDDEN -MEANINGS OF THE STATIONS OF *SALAT*

Shāh Walīullāh al-Dehlavī said:

> Know that one is sometimes transported, quick as lightning, to the Holy Precincts (of the Divine Presence), and finds one's self attached, with the greatest possible adherence, to the Threshold of Allah. There descend on this person the Divine transfigurations (*tajallī*) which dominate his soul. He sees and feels things which the human tongue is incapable of describing. Once this state of light passes away, he returns to his previous condition, and finds himself tormented by the loss of such an ecstasy. Thereupon he tries to rejoin that which has escaped him, and adopts the condition of this lowly world which would be nearest to a state of absorption in the knowledge of the

---

[394] Hajjah Amina Adil, *Lore of Light*, from Kaʿb al-Ahbār, Arafat Publishing House, Columbo, Sri Lanka, 1989, p. 9.

[395] Sūrah YāSīn, 36:1-2.

Creator. This is a posture of respect, of devotion, and of an almost direct conversation with Allah, which posture is accompanied by appropriate acts and words... Worship consists essentially of three elements: (1) humility of heart (spirit) consequent on a feeling of the Presence of the Majesty and Grandeur of Allah, (2) recognition of this superiority (of Allah) and humbleness (of man) by means of appropriate words, and (3) adoption by the organs of the body of postures of necessary reverence…

Still greater respect is displayed by laying down the face, which reflects in the highest degree one's ego and self-consciousness, so low that it touches the ground in front of the object of reverence.[396]

Al-Jīlī says:

The secrets and inner-meanings of prayer are uncountable so what is mentioned here is limited for the sake of brevity. Prayer is a symbol of the uniqueness of the Divine Reality (*al-Ḥaqq*), and the [position of] standing in it is a symbol of the establishment of the uniqueness of mankind in possessing something from the Divine Names and Attributes, for as the Prophet said, "Verily Allah created Adam in His Image."[397]

Then the standing towards the *Qiblah* is an indication of the universal direction in the quest of the Divine Reality. The intention therein is an indication of the connection of the heart in this direction. The opening magnification of God's Greatness *(takbīr)* is an indication that the Divine Proximity is larger and more expansive than what may manifest to him because nothing can limit its perspective. Even so, it is vaster still than every perspective or vision that manifests to the servant for it is without end.

---

[396] Shāh Walīullāh al-Dehlavī, *Ḥujjatullāh al-Bālighah*, vol. 1, Secrets of Worship.

[397] Muslim, Aḥmad.

> The recitation of the Opening Chapter, *al-Fatihah,* is an indication of the existence of His Perfection in man because man is the opening of creation, for Allah initiated creation by him when He brought from nothingness the first creation.

What al-Jīlī is referring to here is the Light of Muhammad ﷺ, known also as the First Mind, the Universal Man, and the Microcosm of the Macrocosm.[398] He continues:

> Then there is bowing, which is an indication of acknowledging the nonexistence of all creation under the existence of divine emanations and power. Then standing in the prayer is an indication of the station of subsistence (*al-baqā*). Therefore, one says in his prayer, "Allah hears the one who praises Him," ... an indication of subsistence in that he is the Vicegerent of the Divine Reality. In this way, God relates about Himself by Himself by relating on hearing its truth through the praising of His creation. The prostration is an expression of pulverization of the traits of humanness and their extermination before the unending manifestation of the sanctifying essence. The sitting between the two prostrations is an indication of obtaining the realities of the Divine Names and Attributes. This is because the sitting is being firmly positioned in a place as indicated by the verse where Allah says:
>
> الرَّحْمَٰنُ عَلَى الْعَرْشِ اسْتَوَىٰ
>
> *The Merciful was established on the Throne*[399]
>
> The second prostration is the indication of the station of servanthood and it is the returning from the Divine Reality

[398] What is meant here is that Muhammad is the overall, universal opening of creation due to the fact everything was created from his light.

[399] Sūrah ṬāḤā 20:5.

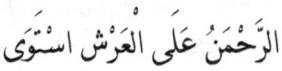

to creation. The salutations [upon the Prophet] are an indication of the attainability of human perfection, for they are an expression of praising Allah, His Messenger and His righteous servants. This is the station of perfection, for the saint is not complete except by his attainment of the Divine realities, by his accord with the Messenger and accord with all of the servants of Allah.

The two sections of the testimony of faith are *Lā ilāha il-Llāh*, "there is no diety except the one God" and *Muḥammadun rasūlullāh*, "and Muhammad is the Prophet of God." Scholars say that *Lā ilāha il-Llāh* represents the Creator and *Muḥammadun rasūlullāh* symbolizes the entirety of creation. The prayer is considered a dual communication: one is between worshipper and Allah, the second is between the worshipper and Allah's perfect servant, Prophet Muhammad ﷺ, the archetype of all the prophets and messengers. Thus one part of the prayer is a communication with the Divine, by means of Allah's Holy Words revealed in the Qur'ān and through bowing and prostration, reciting Allah's glorification, magnification and praise. The other part is the salutation on the Prophet, in which the worshipper addresses the Prophet personally and directly, as leader of the worshippers and the believers, followed by invoking the Lord's blessings on him and on his family.

These realities in fact reflect the doctrine of the Prophet's having attained the zenith of servanthood (*ʿubūdīyyah*) to Allah, and thus the entirety of prayer in itself is built around his person. For the Words of Allah recited are the words revealed to the Prophet and the remainder of the prayer is acknowledging his leadership and spiritual primacy in both this life and the next. Thus scholars assert that even the positions of the prayer are an indication of the Muhammadan Station, for the physical positions reflect the shapes of the letters of the Prophet's heavenly name, Aḥmad, where the first letter *Alif* is represented by the standing position, *Hā* by the bowing stance, *Mīm* in the prostration and *Dāl* in sitting for salutation.

Salat in Daily Life

One may pray individually or communally, in the home, outside, at the mosque or in virtually any clean place. However, observing the prayers at the mosque and in congregation is strongly encouraged. In addition to the regular daily prayers, there is a special Friday noon prayer, called *Jum'ah*. It, too, is obligatory, and must be performed in a mosque, in congregation. It is accompanied by a sermon (*khutbah*) and replaces the normal noon prayer.

Since ritual prayers are performed throughout the waking cycle of the day, they influence the rhythm of the entire day in many Muslim nations. Although it is preferable to worship together in a mosque, a Muslim may pray almost anywhere, such as in fields, offices, factories and universities. Visitors to the Muslim world, where the call to prayer, *adhān*, is made publicly from every mosque at the onset of each prayer time, are often struck by the centrality of prayer in daily life.

Traditionally, the call to prayer is the first thing a newborn baby hears after birth, as the father or a person of piety recites the prayer-call in the infant's right ear and the call to start the prayer (*iqāmah*) in the left.

Mosques

Allah says in the Holy Qur'ān:

قُلْ أَمَرَ رَبِّي بِالْقِسْطِ وَأَقِيمُوا وُجُوهَكُمْ عِندَ كُلِّ مَسْجِدٍ وَادْعُوهُ مُخْلِصِينَ لَهُ
الدِّينَ كَمَا بَدَأَكُمْ تَعُودُونَ

Say: "My Lord hath commanded justice; and that ye set your whole selves (to Him) at every time and mosque, and call upon Him, making your devotion sincere as in

His sight: such as He created you in the beginning, so shall ye return."[400]

When performed in congregation, prayer provides a strong sense of community, equality and brotherhood. All Muslims are welcome in every mosque, regardless of their race, class or nationality. There is no minimum number of congregants required to hold communal prayers. Traditionally, mosques were the centers of their communities, where believers gathered five times daily or, at minimum, once a week. There, the poor found food and assistance; the homeless, shelter; the student of religion, learning. Because of the centrality of prayer in Muslim religious life, mosques are often the dominant structures in Muslim villages, towns and cities. Traditionally, great attention was paid to making these houses of worship more than just halls for prayer. Governments, individuals and communities invested huge sums to make their mosque the visual focus of its neighborhood. In particular, the great mosques, in which the Friday obligatory congregational prayer was held, often became magnificent examples of architecture and art.

The faithful take off their shoes before entering the house of worship out of respect for its sanctity and in keeping with the commandment to the Prophet Moses, when he entered the hallowed ground around the burning bush:

فَلَمَّا أَتَاهَا نُودِيَ يَا مُوسَى إِنِّي أَنَا رَبُّكَ فَاخْلَعْ نَعْلَيْكَ إِنَّكَ بِالْوَادِ الْمُقَدَّسِ طُوًى

When he came to the Fire, a voice was uttered: O Moses! I am thy Lord, therefore put off thy shoes, for thou art in the sacred valley of Ṭūwā.[401]

---

[400] Sūratu 'l-'Araf [The Heights], 7:29.
[401] Sūrah ṬāḤā 20:11-12.

Sincere *Salat*

Ibn ʿAta Allāh, a renowned Egyptian Sufi scholar of the 14th century wrote:[402]

> The ritual prayer is the focal point of heavenly discourse, the source of purity by which the avenues of secrets expand and the gleams of lights radiate. So, if you want to know yourself, it is all by the prayer how you would weigh it. If it causes you to desist from worldly influence, then you know you are one who is given happiness. Other than that, you should be aware of what your feet have dragged along to your prayer, and then you will know that you have not obtained the secrets of prayer. Have you ever seen a lover that does not desire whom he loves?
>
> This is what you take from the prayer of discourse with Allah: when you say:
>
> إِيَّاكَ نَعْبُدُ وإِيَّاكَ نَسْتَعِينُ *"You alone do we worship, and from You alone do we seek assistance"*[403] – and from the discourse with the Messenger, when you say in your prayers, "Peace be upon you, O Prophet, and the Mercy of Allah and His Blessing." You say this in every prayer, whereupon you are cleansed of your sins, only to return to them yet again after receiving the blessings with which the Lord has favored you, which is meeting with your Lord, the highest of blessings.
>
> If one wishes to know his reality and to see his state with his Lord, let him look at his prayer. Either it will produce humility and tranquility or heedlessness and hastiness. So, if

---

[402] Ibn ʿAtā Allāh as-Sakandarī, *at-Tuhfah fī at-Taṣawwuf,* from the Chapter on Prayer, arranged and compiled by Dr. ʿAli Ḥasan al-ʿAridh, The Library of the Superior Achievement, al-Fajalah Egypt, pages 94-98.

[403] Sūratu 'l-Fātiḥa [The Opening], 1:4.

your prayer is not of the first type, then seek to throw dirt on your head out of neglect and sorrow.[404] The one who sits with a perfume maker is given the fragrance of his perfume. The prayer, therefore, is the association with Allah, so when you attend it and you do not obtain from it anything, it indicates a sickness that resides in you, which is either pride or the absence of proper manners. Allah says:

سَأَصْرِفُ عَنْ آيَاتِيَ الَّذِينَ يَتَكَبَّرُونَ فِي الأَرْضِ بِغَيْرِ الْحَقِّ

I shall turn away from My revelations those who magnify themselves wrongfully in the earth.[405]

It is not desired that one rushes from the mosque after his prayer. Rather, he should remember Allah after it and seek His forgiveness from his shortcomings in doing so. For perhaps his prayer is not in a state for it to be accepted. But if you were to seek Allah's forgiveness, thereafter it will be accepted.[406]

Ibn ʿAtā Allāh's warning not leave the mosque too quickly after performing the ritual prayer also has an esoteric meaning. The mosque, in the symbolism of Sufism, signifies the heart, while

---

[404] It is related that Ibn ʿAbbās said, "If you had performed your prayers and you didn't find in your heart humility, when you read the Qur'ān that you don't find a meaning for it and when you remember God by yourself and your tears don't flow, then throw dirt on your head and cry about your loss. Then ask God to provide for you another heart."

[405] Sūratu 'l-ʿArāf [The Heights], 7:146

[406] What it means here that after the pray, one remembers God by magnification, praise and glorification following the obligation prayers. It is related from Abū Hurayrah in *Saḥīḥ Muslim*:

> The one who remembers God at the end of every prayer 33 times (by glorification [*tasbīḥ*], praise [*taḥmīd*] and magnification [*takbīr*]) and ends it with, 'There is not god except God, He has no partners. To Him belongs the Kingdom and all praise and He has power over all things,' his sins will be forgiven even if they were as numerous as the foam of the ocean.

prayers signify the connection between the worshipper and the Divine Presence. Thus, Ibn ʿAta Allah here calls on the faithful to maintain that connection with the Divine Source in the heart and not be too quick to push it aside to return to worldly concerns. This means one should strive to keep that connection with the Divine Presence that has been built up through remembrance and prayer, and not fall into heedlessness.

كان الرسول صلى الله عليه وسلم اذا سلم من الصلاة قال: "استغفر الله ، استغفر الله ، استغفر الله ، اللهم انت السلام و منك السلام تباركت يا ذا الجلال و الأكرام "

After the Messenger of Allah ﷺ used to pray, he would seek Allah's forgiveness three times. This was related by Thawban, who said:

> When he finished from prayer, he would seek Allah's forgiveness three times and say, "O Allah, you are the peace and from you is peace. Blessed you are, O Owner of Greatness and Honor."[407]
>
> Ibn ʿAtā Allāh also wrote:
>
> The simile of some who had performed his prayer without tranquility and humility of heart or presence of contemplation is like the one who presents to the king one hundred empty boxes. Thereafter, he deserves the admonishment of the king because of his lack of intelligence and thought, which the king will utter about him when ever he is mentioned. But the one who prays with tranquility and presence of heart is like the one who presented the king with boxes of precious jewels, for surely the king will delight in that and will return the favor on him and he will always mention to others about the gifts he had received from him.

---

[407] Muslim.

This is because the one who gave has purity of heart, perfection of thought and high aspiration.[408]

I say to you, O servant of Allah, when you enter prayer you are conversing with your Lord and speaking with the Messenger of Allah in the Witnessing, because you are saying, "Peace be upon you, O Prophet, and Allah's mercy and blessings." It is not said, "O you," or, "O so and so," in the language of the Arabs, except to someone who is present in the assembly. So, in your prayers, you should summon in your mind his greatness.[409]

If you wish to know how you will traverse the Bridge on the Day of Judgment, then look at your state in proceeding to prayer in going to the mosque ... for in this world, the prayer is the bridge of uprightness that is not seen by the eyes, but by the enlightened hearts and clear vision. Allah says:

وَأَنَّ هَـٰذَا صِرَاطِي مُسْتَقِيمًا فَاتَّبِعُوهُ وَلَا تَتَّبِعُوا السُّبُلَ فَتَفَرَّقَ بِكُمْ عَن سَبِيلِهِ
ذَٰلِكُمْ وَصَّاكُم بِهِ لَعَلَّكُمْ تَتَّقُونَ

[408] al-Ḥāfiẓ Jalāl al-Dīn as-Suyūṭī recorded in his *Jamʿi* that Abū Hurayrah said: "When any of you are in prayer, he is conversing with his Lord."

[409] To have the image of the Prophet ﷺ in prayer is the highest summoning, even outside the prayer. al-Ḥāfiẓ Jalāl al-Dīn as-Suyūṭī reported from Ibn ʿAbbās that he had a dream in which he saw the Messenger. Thereafter he went to the house of the Mother of Believers in which he was shown a mirror. But he didn't see himself, he saw the image of the Messenger. Khālid al-Baghdādī added it in his *Treatises in Obtaining Connection*, reporting from al-Ḥāfiẓ as-Suyūṭī's, *Tanwīr*. It is noted that this stage is reached after one has obtained constant connection with his spiritual guide (*murshid*) through meditation (*muraqabah*) which guides him into the presence of the Messenger. Thus meditation is an evolution after one has passed the higher stations of *dhikr*; by tongue, by heart, then by the combination of both.

This is my straight way, therefore follow it.[410]

So, the one for whom the path is enlightened follows thereon, but the one for whom his path is darkened does not see where he is stepping and is not able to travel the way; therefore, he will remain in his place standing and bewildered.

يدخل فقراء المسلمين الجنة قبل الأغنياء بنصف يوم، وهو خمسمائة عام

Abū Hurayrah ﷺ related that the Messenger of Allah ﷺ said:

The poor of the Muslims will enter Paradise before the rich by half a day, and each day is five hundred years.[411]

This is because they were foremost in the world in worship and constant in the Friday prayer and the congregation.

NAWAFIL - VOLUNTARY WORSHIP

In addition to the fixed, obligatory ritual prayers (*faraʿid as-ṣalāt*), Muslims consider supererogatory prayers of great importance. Great emphasis is placed on observing the prayers that the Prophet, upon whom be peace and blessings, used to observe in addition to the five prescribed prayers.

In addition to the obligatory prayers, the Prophet observed certain sets of supererogatory ritual-prayers just before and after them. These confirmed *sunnahs* are well-documented.[412] In addition to these, the Prophet would add on additional prayer cycles known *an-nawāfil*. Each of the schools of Islamic jurisprudence classifies these cycles slightly differently, but all

---

410 Sūratu 'l-Anʿam [Cattle], 6:153.

411 At-Tirmidhī related it and it is good.

412 These are two cycles before the dawn prayer, two or four before the noon prayer and two after, either none or two cycles before the afternoon prayer, two after the sunset prayer and two after the night prayer.

agree on the merit of performing these supplemental acts of devotion. Finally, the Prophet would pray additional ritual prayers independent of the obligatory ones. These include:

Prayer just after sunrise (*ishrāq*)
From four to twelve cycles in the forenoon (*duḥā*)
Six cycles after the evening prayer (*awābīn*)
The night vigil (*tahajjud* or *qīyām al-layl*).

أن النبي صلى الله عليه وسلم صلى حتى انتفخت قدماه فقيل له أتكلف هذا وقد

غفر الله لك ما تقدم من ذنبك وما تأخر فقال أفلا أكون عبدا شكورا

When asked why he used to pray so much, to the point that his feet were swollen, the Prophet replied, "Should I not be a thankful servant of Allah?"[413]

In saying this, the Prophet expressed the essence of supererogatory worship, to show gratitude to the Lord and thus to draw nearer to the Divine Presence. The Prophet related regarding the words[414] recited in every prayer from the Opening chapter of the Holy Qur'ān, الْحَمْدُ للهِ رَبِّ الْعَالَمِينَ *"Praise is to Allah, the Lord of the universe,"*[415] that Allah responds by saying, "My servant has praised Me."[416]

QIYAM AL-LAYL - NIGHT VIGIL

One of the most important supererogatory prayers is that of the Night Vigil (*Qīyām al-layl*). The ideal time for voluntary *prayer*, and indeed for spiritual endeavors in general, is at night—preferably after midnight. This is the time when the world is

[413] Bukhārī and Muslim.
[414] Part of the Opening chapter of the Qur'ān (Sūratu 'l-Fātiḥa) whose recitation in prayer is obligatory.
[415] Sūratu 'l-Fātiḥa [The Opening], 1:1.
[416] Muslim, Mālik, at-Tirmidhī, Abū Dāwūd, an-Nasā'ī and Ibn Mājah.

asleep, but the lovers and seekers of God (al-'ibād) are awake and traveling towards reality and their divine destinations. It is under the veil of the night that the plane of consciousness is clear from the chaos of worldly affairs (dunyā), for it is a time when the mind and heart operate most effectively.

Prayer before midnight, whether supplicatory or ritual, is very slow; after midnight, it is very fast.

In one of the first revelations, Allah ordered His Messenger:

قُمِ اللَّيْلَ إِلَّا قَلِيلًا نِصْفَهُ أَوِ انْقُصْ مِنْهُ قَلِيلًا أَوْ زِدْ عَلَيْهِ وَرَتِّلِ الْقُرْآنَ تَرْتِيلًا

Stand (to prayer) by night, but not all night, half of it or a little less. Or a little more; and recite the Qur'ān in slow, measured rhythmic tones.[417]

وقال صلى الله عليه وسلم "ركعتان يركعهما العبد في جوف الليل خير له من الدنيا وما فيها ولولا أن أشق على أمتي لفرضتهما عليهم"

The Messenger of Allah said:

Two cycles of prayer in the late hours of the night are more valuable than all the riches of this world. But for fear of overburdening my followers, I would have made these obligatory.

And:

عليكم بصلاة الليل ولو ركعة واحدة

The Prophet said: Pray the night prayer, if only one rak'ah.[418]

---

[417] Sūratu 'l-Muzzammil [The Enshrouded One], 73:2-4.
[418] Aḥmad recorded in his *Musnad*, and aṭ-Ṭabarānī in his *Kabīr*, from Ibn Anas ؉ which al-Ḥāfiẓ as-Suyūṭī graded it sound

Salman, a renowned Companion of the Prophet, in describing the observance of the night vigil said:

> The man who considered the darkness of night and people's unmindfulness a boon, stood up and said the prayer till the morning, he is a man for whom there is all gain and no loss... adopt those medium-type of supererogatory prayers (*nawāfil*) which you may put up with perpetually.[419]

عَنْ حُذَيْفَةَ، انَّهُ رَاَى رَسُولَ اللَّهِ صلى الله عليه وسلم يُصَلِّي مِنَ اللَّيْلِ . . . " .
فَصَلَّى ارْبَعَ رَكَعَاتٍ فَقَرَاَ فِيهِنَّ الْبَقَرَةَ وَآلَ عِمْرَانَ وَالنِّسَاءَ وَالْمَائِدَةَ اوِ الأَنْعَامَ شَكَّ شُعْبَةُ
.

Hudhayfa related that he saw the Prophet's pray the night vigil and

> I used to stand with Allah's Messenger throughout the night... He prayed four cycles (*raka'ts*) and he would recite Sūrat al-Baqara, Sūrat Āli 'Imrān and Sūrat an-Nisā, Sūrat al-Mā'idat and Sūrat al-Ana'm in them (i.e. the five longest chapters of the Qur'ān). [420]
>
> It is related that the third caliph, 'Uthmān ibn 'Affān, would recite the entire Qu'ran in one prayer during the night.[421]
>
> So much stress did the Prophet put on the importance of the night vigil (*ṣalāt* al-layl) that if he missed it he would make it up.

---

[419] Mawlānā Muḥammad Yūsuf Khandalvī, *Ḥayāt as-Ṣaḥāba,* IDāra Isha 'at-e-Diniyat Ltd, New Delhi, 1992, p. 101.

[420] *Sunan Abī Dāwūd*, Section on Prayer #867.

[421] Abū Nu'aym al-Asfahānī, *Ḥilyat ul-Awlīyā wa ṭabaqāt al-asfiyā,* (The Beauty of the Righteous and Ranks of the Elite, translated by M. Akili), Pearl Press, Philadelphia, 1988, p. 56.

عن سعد بن هشام أن عائشة قالت كان رسول الله -صلى الله عليه وسلم- إذا

صلى صلاة أحب أن يداوم عليها وكان إذا شغله عن قيام الليل نوم أو مرض أو وجع

صلى من النهار اثنتي عشرة ركعة هذا

The Prophet's wife 'Āʿishā said that the Prophet if he initiated any prayer he loved to be constant in it and if his something kept him from the night vigil, sleep or illness or pain, then he used to pray twelve cycles (*rakaʿts*) during the day.[422]

A renowned contemporary Sufi saint, and my teacher and guide on the spiritual path, Shaykh Muhammad Nazim Adil al-Haqqani, says:

> The last third of the night is the best of times to pray at night because Allah the Most High is looking therein at His servant. Our master ʿAbd-Allāh ad-Dāghestānī, may Allah always elevate his stations, used to invite me to his association during the last third of the night because it is the time of heavenly manifestation. He would say that, in this time, there is no veil between Allah and His servant. So, each of you should awake in the third part of the night to pray and be present in the hour of heavenly manifestations. O Allah, make us among those who stand in prayer at night, seeking the vision of Your Face.
>
> There is no possibility to receive sainthood without the night vigil. The night vigil is ordained for the Prophet, also for the Friends of Allah it is considered obligatory and, as related to the community, it is a strong practice (*sunnah*). Without a doubt, the servant will not receive the station of sainthood if he is not connected to Allah. And a token of

[422] *Saḥīḥ ibn Khuzaymah,* Section "making up the night vigil if missing it due to illness, or work or sleep," #1170.

the one who is connected with the Lord Almighty is the night vigil. This is the greatest means of sainthood, by which Allah adorns His servant with the secret of sainthood during the last third of the night. Therefore, be awake at this time of the night, whether engaged in your prayer or in something else, so that nothing will obstruct you from being present in this time for which you will obtain this special mercy. [423]

The renowned Egyptian Sufi Ibn ʿAtā Allāh as-Sakandarī said:

Two cycles of ritual prayer before Allah during the night is better than thousands of cycles of prayer during the day.

عن أبي أمامة الباهلية عن رسول الله –صلى الله عليه وسلم– قال عليكم بقيام الليل

فإنه دأب الصالحين قبلكم وهو قربة لكم إلى ربكم ومكفرة للسيئات ومنهاة عن الإثم

The Messenger of Allah ﷺ says:

Keep to observing the night prayer for it is the devotion of the righteous before you, it brings you closer to your Lord and it wipes away offenses, replaces sins and removes sin.[424]

Without a doubt you do not pray two cycles in the night except that you will find its rewards on your scales on the Day of Requital. Is a servant purchased for any reason other than to serve? Do you see a servant who is purchased merely to eat and sleep, who does not perform

[423] *al-Irshād ash-Sharīf,* Mawlana Shaykh Muhammad Naẓim al-Haqqani, private manuscript.

[424] Ibn Asākir reported it from Abū ad-Dārdā and Ibn as-Sīna from Jābir. Ad-Daylamī recorded something similar from Ibn ʿUmar with the notable addition, "...it extinguishes the anger of God and wards off the heat of hellfire from his family on the Day of Judgment." Aḥmad recorded in his *Musnad*, and at-Ṭabarānī in his *Kabīr,* from Ibn Anas, "You should pray the night prayer, even if it's only one cycle." al-Ḥāfiẓ as-Suyūṭī graded it as sound.

his duties? You are nothing more than a servant that Allah has brought into existence for His worship. He created you for His obedience; your purchase is for His service:

إِنَّ اللّهَ اشْتَرَى مِنَ الْمُؤْمِنِينَ أَنفُسَهُمْ وَأَمْوَالَهُم بِأَنَّ لَهُمُ الجَنَّةَ

Lo! Allah hath bought from the believers their lives and their wealth because for them is Paradise.[425]

We conclude this section with the words of Shaykh ʿAbd Allāh al-Fāʿiz ad-Dāghestānī, may God preserve his sanctity, who said about the night vigil:

> Even if a servant rises in the time of heavenly manifestations and he is a non-Muslim in faith, and he does something in that hour, because of that he too would obtain the level of belief before passing from this life. He will be guided and safe because he was awake during the hours of heavenly manifestations, and he would consequently receive that special mercy. It is not possible for anyone who receives even a drop from that mercy, to remain wretched or to remain in unbelief. He is safe even if a tyrant; in time he will turn back to Allah, and if he is a sinner, he will repent. There is no ambiguity that this mercy will change his state.

The Perfection of *Salat*

In reality, *ṣalāt* is a state of heedfulness that must be kept constantly and perpetually throughout the day. Those committed to this path seek to maintain a state of mindfulness in each breath, not forgetting their Lord for even a single moment.

[425] Sūratu ’t-Tawbah [Repentance], 9:111.

The perfection of prayer means to be aware of Allah's Presence, "as if you see Him," and to demonstrate one's devotion and servitude to Him. Allah said:

وَمَا خَلَقْتُ الْجِنَّ وَالْإِنسَ إِلَّا لِيَعْبُدُونِ مَا أُرِيدُ مِنْهُم مِّن رِّزْقٍ وَمَا أُرِيدُ أَن يُطْعِمُونِ

I created the jinn and humankind only that they might worship Me. No Sustenance do I require of them, nor do I require that they should feed Me. [426]

Allah initially commanded Prophet Muhammad's follower to observe fifty prayers a day, but with His mercy this obligation was reduced to five. In the Divine Balance, the five prayers are thus considered as fifty. Calculating the time required to observe fifty prayers, it would require all of a worshipper's waking hours, less time to eat and make ablution. Thus those who observe the five prayers perfectly, with complete submission to Allah and complete presence before Allah will be in fulfillment of the above verse. For those, Allah provide sustenance without their needing to work, for they are fulfilling the Divine Directive properly.

THE PINNACLE OF WORSHIP

Ritual prayer is known as the "pinnacle of worship," for it contains the essential aspects of all five pillars of Islamic worship: the testification of faith, prayer itself, charity, fasting and pilgrimage.

The first pillar, the testification of faith is observed in each ritual prayer, when one bears witness to the Oneness of God and the Prophethood of Muhammad ﷺ during the sitting phase (*at-tashahhud*).

---

[426] Sūratu 'dh-Dhāriyāt [The Winnowing Winds], 51:56.

Charity (*zakāt*), the third pillar consists of giving $2^{1/2}$ percent of one's wealth to the needy for the sake of Allah. Ritual prayer encompasses this pillar in the sense that the most important thing that one possesses is the body and spirit. In ritual prayer one give one's whole person and time to Allah.

The fourth pillar, fasting (*ṣawm*) is accomplished immediately on entering the prayer, for one must withhold from all worldly actions, including eating, drinking, relations with others, and, even more stringent than the ritual fast, one may not converse except with the Lord.

The last pillar of Islam pilgrimage (hajj) is encompassed when the worshipper directs himself or herself to the Kaʿaba the focal point of the pilgrimage.

PRAYER IS ASCENSION TO THE DIVINE

الصلاة معراج المؤمن

It is said: "Ritual prayer is the ascension (*miʿrāj*) of the believer."[427]

The Prophet therefore had, according to Islam's Gnostic scholars, not just one, but 24,000 ascensions during his life.

When the worshipper begins a sincere prayer, saying "Allah is Greatest," the ascension begins. If one is truly observant of the rights and duties of the prayers with their perfection, this will be apparent for as soon as you enter the prayer inspiration of Divine knowledge will begin to enter you heart along with increased yearning for the Divine Presence. If these secrets are not coming to you, it signifies your prayers are not ascending to the Divine Presence, and that that you are falling into Satan's traps.

Sayyid Ḥaydar ʿAmūlī writes:

[427] Renowned as a Ḥadīth but no valid chain found.

> His [the Prophet's] words, "I have been given coolness of the eye in prayer," refer to nothing else but the contemplation of the Beloved by the eye of the lover, who draws near in the stillness of the prayer... On seeing the Beloved, the eye too becomes stilled and it ceases to look at anything other than Him in all things.[428]

Thus the worshipper attains the state, related in the Holy Tradition:

عَنْ ابي هُرَيْرَةَ، قَالَ قَالَ رَسُولُ اللَّهِ صلى الله عليه وسلم " إِنَّ اللَّهَ قَالَ مَنْ عَادَى لِي وَلِيًّا فَقَدْ اذَنْتُهُ بِالْحَرْبِ، وَمَا تَقَرَّبَ إِلَيَّ عَبْدِي بِشَىْءٍ احَبَّ إِلَيَّ مِمَّا افْتَرَضْتُ عَلَيْهِ، وَمَا يَزَالُ عَبْدِي يَتَقَرَّبُ إِلَيَّ بِالنَّوَافِلِ حَتَّى احِبَّهُ، فَإِذَا احْبَبْتُهُ كُنْتُ سَمْعَهُ الَّذِي يَسْمَعُ بِهِ، وَبَصَرَهُ الَّذِي يُبْصِرُ بِهِ، وَيَدَهُ الَّتِي يَبْطُشُ بِهَا وَرِجْلَهُ الَّتِي يَمْشِي بِهَا، وَإِنْ سَأَلَنِي لأُعْطِيَنَّهُ، وَلَئِنِ اسْتَعَاذَنِي لأُعِيذَنَّهُ، وَمَا تَرَدَّدْتُ عَنْ شَىْءٍ انَا فَاعِلُهُ تَرَدُّدِي عَنْ نَفْسِ الْمُؤْمِنِ، يَكْرَهُ الْمَوْتَ وَانَا اكْرَهُ مَسَاءَتَهُ "

> ...My servant shall continue to draw nearer to Me by performing the supererogatory acts of virtue until I love him; when I love him, I become his ears with which he hears, his eyes with which he sees, his hands with which he grasps, and his feet with which he walks; if he were to ask of Me, I will grant his request, if he were to seek refuge in Me, I will protect him...[429]

As to the Messenger's state during prayer, his wife 'Ā'ishā reported:

---

[428] Sayyid Haydar Amulī, *Inner Secrets of the Path*, Element Books, London, 1983, p. 233.

[429] Bukhārī.

He would weep continuously until his lap became wet. He would be sitting and keep weeping until his auspicious beard became drenched. Then he would weep so much the ground became wet.[430]

Abū Bakr aṣ-Ṣiddīq, the first caliph of the Prophet, would stand in prayer as if he were a pillar. Commenting on this, one of the early transmitter of traditions, Mujahid, said, "this is the fearfulness (*khushu*ʿ) in prayer."

صلوا كما رأيتموني أصلي

The Prophet said, "Pray as you see me pray."[431]

He did not say, "Pray as you have heard I prayed," nor "Pray as I taught my companions." This hints at something very profound. The vision of the Prophet ﷺ is something that is true, and this is witnessed by countless Friends of Allah.

قال رسول الله صلى الله عليه وسلم "من رآني فقد رأى الحق"

Thus, the Prophet's saying, "Who saw me in a vision, in truth saw me,"[432] to the Sufi commentators carries the meaning, "Whoever saw me in a vision will see me in reality." For Sufis, the first level of witnessing *(mushāhadah)* is to sense the Prophet present before them. The final stage of witnessing, which is "to worship God as if you see Him,"[433] was achieved by the Prophet during the Ascension when he was brought to the station of nearness (*qurb*), *"two bow's lengths or*

---

[430] Mawlānā Muḥammad Yūsuf Khandalvī, *Ḥayāt as-Ṣaḥāba*, IDāra Isha 'at-e-Diniyat Ltd, New Delhi, 1992, p. 101.

[431] Bukhārī.

[432] Muslim, n. 2267.

[433] Part of the long "Jibrīl Ḥadīth" in which the Prophet ﷺ describes the three levels of religion: submission, faith and perfection of character. The latter he described as "to worship God as if you see Him, and if you don't see Him, know that He sees you." Narrated by Bukhārī and Muslim.

nearer,"[434] to the Divine Presence. The Sufis affirm that true prayer brings the worshipper to the state of witnessing Allah and His Prophet, thereby attaining true unity with the Beloved. For this reason, prayer is compared to the union of marriage, *wisal*. Indeed, they explain the two salutations of peace, made to end the prayer, as a return from extinction, to greet the world as a new person.

It is said of the Prophet's fourth successor, his cousin ʿAlī ibn Abī Ṭālib ﷺ, that when he prayed, he was utterly oblivious to his surroundings. Once he was injured by an enemy arrow, which penetrated his foot. It could not be removed without causing immense pain. He said, "I will pray, at which time remove it." They did as he directed. Upon completing the prayer he asked his companions, "When are you going to remove the arrow?" ʿAlī ibn Abī Ṭālib ﷺ used to say, "Even if the Veil were lifted, it would not increase my certainty," referring to his state of Witnessing the Divine Presence.[435]

We conclude with a story, related about the great Sufi master Shaykh Abū 'l-Ḥasan ash-Shādhilī.

> The scholars of Alexandria came to him to test him and he read what was in their hearts before they spoke and said, "O pious scholars, have you ever prayed?"
>
> They said, "Far be it from any of us to leave prayer."
>
> He then recited the verse:

إِنَّ الْإِنسَانَ خُلِقَ هَلُوعًا إِذَا مَسَّهُ الشَّرُّ جَزُوعًا وَإِذَا مَسَّهُ الْخَيْرُ مَنُوعًا إِلَّا الْمُصَلِّينَ

[434] Sūratu 'n-Najm [The Star], 53:9.

[435] Sayyid Haydar Amuli, *Inner Secrets of the Path,* Element Books, London, 1983, p. 233.

Lo! man was created anxious, Fretful when evil befalleth him, And, when good befalleth him, grudging, except those who (really) prays.[436]

"So," he asked, "do any of you all pray like this?" They were silent. Then the shaykh said to them, "Then, none of you has ever prayed!"

The real prayer is performed purely for the pleasure of Allah, conversing with Him in variations of delight, humbleness and awe which is void of hypocrisy and repute. No doubt it brings about the remembrance of Allah and the heart inherits awe of Him.[437]

Conclusion

Salat as Divine Service

While the ritual prayer we have just examined in detail is one of the five pillars of Islam, in reality all of Islam is essentially a form of prayer. For the meaning of prayer is worship and the essence of all worship is to seek Allah. Seeking the Face of Allah is the goal and the means are the Divinely-prescribed forms of action as well as voluntary forms of bringing the worshipper closer to the Divine Presence.

Allah says:

وَلِلّهِ يَسْجُدُ مَن فِي السَّمَاوَاتِ وَالأَرْضِ طَوْعًا وَكَرْهًا وَظِلالُهُم بِالْغُدُوِّ وَالآصَالِ

[436] Sūratu 'l-Ma'arij [The Ascensions], 70:19-22.

[437] Ibn 'Atā Allāh as-Sakandarī, *at-Tuhfah fī at-Taṣawwuf,* from the chapter of Prayer, pages 94-98, arranged and compiled by Dr. 'Alī Ḥasan al-'Ariḍ, Maktabah al-Jihādi al-Kubra- The Library of the Superior Achievement, al-Fajalah Egypt.

And to Him prostrate all that is in the heavens and on earth; willingly or by compulsion.[438]

وَلِلّٰهِ يَسْجُدُ مَا فِي السَّمَاوَاتِ وَمَا فِي الأَرْضِ مِن دَآبَّةٍ وَالْمَلآئِكَةُ وَهُمْ لاَ يَسْتَكْبِرُونَ

And He says: *and to Allah prostrate all that is in the heavens and the earth.* [439]

And He says: *and there is not one thing except that it glorifies with Allah with His praise.*[440]

These verses indicate that all of creation, regardless of form or substance, are in fact in a state of prayer, for prostration and glorification are the essence of prayer. They cannot be in other than that—even those who disobey, in their disobedience—are in fact submitting to the ultimate Holy Will of Allah and the Destiny prescribed for them.

However the key to the Lord's Bounty is to seek Him and submit willingly with one's entire being. To become a Muslim means to accept saying, "O Allah! I admit that You are the Creator and I am your slave." This is the first level of submission, slavery, but it is not servanthood. Servanthood is higher.

True servanthood of Allah means to become obedient. The servant has no will of his or her own, but is subject to the will of the master at all times. Islam does not ask human beings to serve a cruel and whimsical master, but rather the Creator of all things, Who is the Aware, the Subtle, in His all-encompassing knowledge of both the needs and desires of His servants.

---

[438] Sūratu 'r-Ra'd [Thunder], 13:15.
[439] Sūratu 'n-Nahl [The Bee], 16:49.
[440] Sūratu 'l-Isrā [The Night Journey], 17:44.

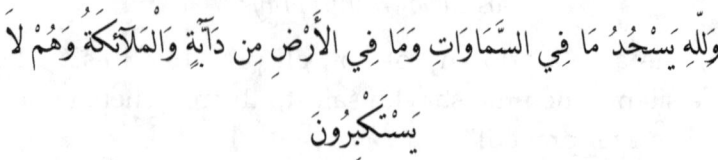

One who attains this level of submission in Islam becomes *ʿabd*, servant to the Lord. In Islam this is considered the highest achievement—the state of servanthood, known as *ʿubudīyyah*. For that reason the Prophet said:

عَنْ خَيْثَمَةَ بْنِ عَبْدِ الرَّحْمَنِ، عَنْ أَبِيهِ، أَنَّ رَسُولَ اللَّهِ صَلَّى اللَّهُ عَلَيْهِ وَسَلَّمَ قَالَ إِنَّ مِنْ خَيْرِ أَسْمَائِكُمْ عَبْدَ اللَّهِ وَعَبْدَ الرَّحْمَنِ.

The names dearest to God are ʿAbd Allāh (servant of God) and ʿAbd al-Raḥmān (servant of the Most Merciful).[441]

Allah says:

سُبْحَانَ الَّذِي أَسْرَى بِعَبْدِهِ لَيْلاً مِّنَ الْمَسْجِدِ الْحَرَامِ إِلَى الْمَسْجِدِ الأَقْصَى الَّذِي بَارَكْنَا حَوْلَهُ لِنُرِيَهُ مِنْ آيَاتِنَا إِنَّهُ هُوَ السَّمِيعُ البَصِيرُ

Glory to (Allah) Who did take His Servant for a Journey by night from the Sacred Mosque to the farthest Mosque, whose precincts We did bless, in order that We might show him some of Our Signs.[442]

Allah specified Prophet Muhammad ﷺ in this verse with the title "servant," *ʿabd*, and again, relating to Prophet Muhammad's ascension to the Divine Presence, when He says:

فَأَوْحَى إِلَى عَبْدِهِ مَا أَوْحَى

So did (Allah) convey the inspiration to His Servant-(conveyed) what He (meant) to convey.[443]

---

[441] Abū Dāwūd.

[442] Sūratu 'l-Isrā [The Night Journey], 17:1.

[443] Sūratu 'n-Najm [The Star], 53:10.

لَقَدْ رَأَى مِنْ آيَاتِ رَبِّهِ الْكُبْرَى

... For truly did he see, of the Signs of his Lord, the Greatest!" [444]

Of the station Prophet Muhammad ﷺ attained in that rapture, Imām Nawawī, one of the great scholars of Islam, says, "Most of the scholars say that the Prophet saw his Lord with the eyes of his head."

The unique greatness of Allah's Messenger, Muhammad ﷺ, is that he saw the Lord of Creation, thus making him the perfected monotheist (*muwaḥḥid*). Prophet Muhammad's grasp of Divine Unity, *tawḥīd,* was perfected by ascension to the Divine Presence. Everyone else's understanding of Divine Unity falls short of the Messenger's. Despite this, the Prophet maintained absolute humility, never seeing himself as important, but rather as a servant, honored by the Master of masters.

It is related that when the Prophet reached the highest levels and most distinguished stations Allah revealed to him, "With what shall I honor you?" The Prophet said, "By relating me to You through servanthood (*'ubūdīyya*)."[445]

Thus true prayer is nothing less than Ascension to the Station of true Servanthood, which is the Station of Submission. In that station, Divine Unity becomes manifest, and there, the servant reaches the state where he hears what no ears have heard, sees what no eyes have seen and tastes the reality of Divine Oneness. In this state of witnessing, the servant perceives only the Lord. He sees all existence through His Existence and the realization that all proceeds from the One. That is known as the station of annihilation, in which the servant no longer sees herself or himself, no longer sees anything, but only sees, feels and is

[444] Sūratu 'n-Najm [The Star], 53:18.
[445] Related by Abū Qāsim Sulaymān al-Anṣārī.

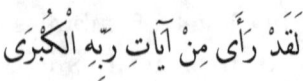

immersed in the Presence of the Lord without any partner and with no likeness.

Principles of Leadership in War and Peace[446]

[446] Presented at the *WORDE International Conference of Islamic Scholars Islam & Civil Society in the 21st Century:A Path to Transformation*, Jakarta, December 21, 2003

Discussing the rules of military engagement in modern times, the illegitimacy of terrorism and the prohibition of suicide as a means of combat.

In this presentation we would like to shed light on the meaning of Jihād, a term that has become universally known today. One can find countless interpretations of this term which differ from its true spirit and the meaning that Allah intended it in the Holy Qur'ān and in the narrations of the Prophet ﷺ. On the contrary people are use the term Jihād in this time in a way that suits their own whims without realizing the damage that they are causing Islam and Muslims.

What is meant by Jihād? The concept of "holy war" does not occur in the term Jihād, which in Arabic would be *al-ḥarb al-muqaddasah*. Throughout the entire Qur'ān, one cannot find a term that expresses the meaning "holy war." Rather the meaning of combative Jihād expressed in Qur'ān or hadith is simply war.

That said, we will show in this presentation, that Jihād in the classical sense does not simply mean war. In fact Jihād is a comprehensive term which traditionally has been defined as composed of fourteen different aspects, only one of which involves warfare.

In this presentation we will explain unambiguously the different aspects of Jihād defined by the Prophet ﷺ together with what renowned mainstream Muslims scholars have written about this subject citing them at length in order to arrive at an accurate understanding of this term.

Islamic thought includes all educational endeavors and scholarly opinions made in distinguishing Islam's core principles, its simplicity and its tenderness and compassion in its approach to all aspects of human relations.

Today there are many individuals who study Islam from a superficial point of view and emerge with their own ideas and imaginary interpretations which often diverge greatly from the established legislation in the area of study. Because of such studies lacking a true basis in Islamic jurisprudence, many non-Muslims are given a bad understanding about Islam.

So in this presentation we will return to the original source texts bringing up the issue of Jihād in order to explain its various different facets and clarify its understanding once and for all.

THE MEANING OF JIHAD

Jihād in its meaning is 'to struggle' as a general description. Jihād derives from the word *juhd,* which means *at-ta'b,* fatigue. The meaning of *Jihād fī sabīlillāh,* struggle in the Way of Allah, is striving to excess in fatiguing the self, to exhaust the self in seeking the Divine Presence and in bringing up Allah's Word, all of which He made the Way to Paradise.

For that reason Allah said:

جَاهِدُوا فِي اللَّهِ حَقَّ جِهَادِهِ

And strive hard (jāhidū) in (the way of) Allah, (such) a striving a is due to Him;[447]

It is essential to understand that under the term *jāhidū* come many different categories of Jihād, each with its specific context. The common understanding of Jihād to mean only war is refuted by this tradition of the Prophet's:

حدثنا عبد الرحمن بن مهدي عن سفيان عن علقمة بن مرثد عن طارق بن شهاب أن رجلا سأل رسول الله صلى الله عليه وسلم وقد وضع رجله في الغرز أي الجهاد أفضل قال كلمة حق عند سلطان جائر

[447] Sūratu 'l-Ḥajj [The Pilgrimage], 22: 78

A man asked the Prophet ﷺ "Which Jihād is best?" The Prophet ﷺ said, "The most excellent Jihād is to say the word of truth in front of a tyrant."[448]

The fact that the Prophet ﷺ mentioned this Jihād as "most excellent" means that there are many different forms of Jihād.

IBN QAYYIM'S FOURTEEN CATEGORIES OF JIHAD

Islamic scholars, from the time of the Prophet ﷺ until today, have categorized Jihād into more than fourteen distinct categories. Jihād is not simply the waging of war, as most people today understand. War in fact, or combative Jihād, according to many scholars, is only one of fourteen different categories of Jihād.

In his book *Zād al-Ma'ad,* Ibn Qayyim al-Jawzīyyah divided Jihād into fourteen distinct categories:

JIHAD AGAINST THE HYPOCRITES

1.15. By heart
1.16. By tongue
1.17. By wealth
1.18. By person.

JIHAD AGAINST THE UNBELIEVERS

1.19. By heart,
1.20. By tongue
1.21. By wealth
1.22. By person.

---

[448] *Musnad* of Aḥmad. Similar aḥadīth are narrated in Abū Dāwūd and Tirmidhī.

JIHAD AGAINST THE DEVIL

1.23. Fighting him defensively against everything of false desires and slanderous doubts in faith that he throws towards the servant.

1.24. Fighting him defensively from everything he throws towards the servant of corrupt passion and desire.

JIHAD OF THE SELF

1.25. That he strives to learn guidance and the religion of truth which is there is no felicity or happiness in life or in the hereafter except by it. And when he neglects it, his knowledge is wretched in both words.

1.26. That he strives to act upon it after he has learned it. For the abstract quality of knowledge without action, even if he commits no wrong, is without benefit.

1.27. That he strives to call to Allah and to teach it to someone who does not know it. Otherwise he will be among those who conceal what Allah had revealed of guidance and clarity. His knowledge doesn't benefit him or saves him from Allah's penalty.

1.28. That he strives with patience in seeking to call to Allah. When the creation harms him he bears it all for the sake of Allah.[449]

IBN RUSHD'S CATEGORIZATION OF JIHAD

Ibn Rushd, in his *Muqaddimah,* divides Jihād into four kinds:

1. Jihād of the heart
2. Jihād of the tongue
3. Jihād of the hand
4. Jihād of the sword.[450]

---

[449] Ibn Qayyim al-Jawzīyyah, *Zād al-Ma'ād.*

JIHAD OF THE HEART – THE STRUGGLE AGAINST THE SELF

The Jihād of the heart is the struggle of the individual with his or her own desires, whims, erroneous ideas and false understandings. This includes the struggle to purify the heart, to rectify one's actions and to observe the rights and responsibilities of all other human beings.

JIHAD OF THE TONGUE – EDUCATION AND COUNSEL

He defines Jihād of the tongue as:

> To commend good conduct and forbid the wrong, like the type of Jihād Allah ordered us to fulfill against the hypocrites in His Words, *"O Prophet! Strive hard against the unbelievers and the hypocrites"*[451].

This is the Jihād the Prophet ﷺ waged in struggling to teach his people. It means to speak about one's cause and one's religion. This is known as the Jihād of Education and Counsel.
Allah first revealed:

اقْرَأْ بِاسْمِ رَبِّكَ

Read in the name of Thy Lord![452]

The first aspect of Jihād of Education is through reading. Reading originates with the tongue.

يَا أَيُّهَا النَّبِيُّ جَاهِدِ الْكُفَّارَ وَالْمُنَافِقِينَ وَاغْلُظْ عَلَيْهِمْ

O Prophet! strive hard [jāhid] against the unbelievers and the Hypocrites, and be firm against them.[453]

---

[450] *Muqaddimah*, Ibn Rushd (known in the Western world as Averroes), p. 259.
[451] Sūratu 't-Tawbah [Repentance], 9:73.
[452] Sūratu 'l-'Alaq [The Clot], 96:*1*
[453] Sūratu 't-Tawbah [Repentance], 9:73

JIHAD OF THE HAND – DEVELOPMENT OF CIVIL SOCIETY AND MATERIAL PROGRESS

Jihād of the hand includes the struggle to build the nation through material development and progress, including building up civil society, acquiring and improving every aspect of technology and societal progress in general. This form of Jihād includes scientific discovery, development of medicine, clinics and hospitals, communication, transportation, and all necessary underlying infrastructure for societal progress and advancement, including educational institutions. Building also means to open opportunities to the poor through economic programs and self empowerment.

Another aspect of Jihād by Hand is through writing, for Allah said:

الَّذِي عَلَّمَ بِالْقَلَمِ عَلَّمَ الْإِنسَانَ مَا لَمْ يَعْلَمْ

He taught by means of the pen, taught mankind what he did not know[454

The meaning writing includes the use of computers and all other forms of publication.

JIHAD OF THE SWORD – COMBATIVE WAR

Finally Jihād of the hand includes struggle by the sword (*Jihādun bis-sayf*), as when one fights the aggressor who attack you in combative war.

JIHAD IN HISTORY AND LAW

Following this brief summary, let us now consider the nature of Jihād more fully as it appears in the history and law of Islam.

---

[454] Sūratu 'l-'Alaq [The Clot], 96:4,5.

Saʿīd Ramaḍān Būṭi, a contemporary Orthodox scholar from Syria states, in his seminal work on the subject *Jihād in Islam*[455]:

> The Prophet ﷺ invited the unbelievers peacefully, lodged protests against their beliefs and strove to remove their misgivings about Islam. When they refused any other solution, but rather declared a war against him and his message and initiated the fight, there was no alternative except to fight back.[456]

The most fundamental form of Jihād, usually overlooked in today's pursuit of newsworthy headlines, is the Jihād of presenting the message of Islam—*daʿwah*. Thirteen years of the Prophet's ﷺ 23-year mission consisted purely of this type of Jihād. Contrary to popular belief, the word Jihād and related forms of its root word *jāhada* are mentioned in many Makkan verses in a purely non-combative context.

Combative Jihād in the technical usage of Islamic law means "the declaration of war against belligerent aggressors." It is not a haphazard decision taken by anybody but only by the leader of the nation. The principles of Islamic jurisprudence state that the actions of the leader must be guided by the interests of the people.

THE JIHAD OF EDUCATION

Thus we see that the building blocks of today's democracy present in the Prophet's ﷺ message from its very outset when the Jihād of Education took on the aspects of struggle in the Messenger's first years of preaching, as the chiefs of the Makkan tribes sought to suppress the freedom of expression, speech and debate that were sought by the Prophet ﷺ in teaching the new faith. Allah states in the Qur'ān:

---

[455] Muḥammad Saʿīd R. Al-Būṭī, *Jihad fil-islām*, Dār al-Fikr, Beirut, 1995.
[456] *Ibid*. p. 44.

ادْعُ إِلَى سَبِيلِ رَبِّكَ بِالْحِكْمَةِ وَالْمَوْعِظَةِ الْحَسَنَةِ وَجَادِلْهُم بِالَّتِي هِيَ أَحْسَنُ إِنَّ رَبَّكَ هُوَ أَعْلَمُ بِمَن ضَلَّ عَن سَبِيلِهِ وَهُوَ أَعْلَمُ بِالْمُهْتَدِينَ

Invite (all) to the Way of thy Lord with wisdom and beautiful preaching; and argue with them in ways that are best and most gracious: for thy Lord knoweth best, who have strayed from His Path, and who receive guidance.[457]

Calling people to Islam and making them acquainted with it in all its aspects through dialogue and kind persuasion is the first type of Jihād in Islam, in contrast to the imagined belief that Jihād is only of the combative form. This is referred to in the Qur'ān where Allah says:

فَلَا تُطِعِ الْكَافِرِينَ وَجَاهِدْهُم بِهِ جِهَادًا كَبِيرًا

So obey not the disbelievers, but strive against them (by preaching) with the utmost endeavor with it (the Qur'ān)[458]

Here the word "strive," *jāhidū,* is used to mean struggle by means of the tongue—preaching and exhortation—and to persevere despite the obstinate resistance of some unbelievers to the beliefs and ideals of Islam.

Ibn ʿAbbās

Ibn ʿAbbās, and others said that Allah's words *"strive with the utmost endeavor"* denote the duty of preaching and exhortation as the greatest of all kinds of Jihād. Ibn ʿAbbās said that "with it" refers to the Holy Qur'ān.[459] Thus Jihād here considered as most essential by Ibn ʿAbbās, cousin and associate of the Prophet ﷺ and

457 Sūratu 'n-Nahl [The Bee], 16:125

458 Sūratu 'l-Furqān [The Criterion], 25:52

459 Muḥammad Saʿīd R. Al-Būṭī, *Jihād fil-islām,* Dār al-Fikr., Beirut, 1995, p. 16.

foremost exegete of the Qur'ān, is the call to the Word of Allah; the Jihād of Education.

Imām Mālik bin Anas

Imām Mālik bin Anas stated in *al-Mudawwanat al-kubrā*:[460]

> The first of what Allah has sent His Messenger ﷺ is to call people to Islam without fighting. He didn't give him permission to fight nor to take money from people. The Prophet ﷺ stayed like that for thirteen years in Makkah, bearing all kinds of persecutions, until he left for Madīnah.

Ibn Qayyim al-Jawzīyyah

Ibn Qayyim al-Jawzīyyah says in *Zād al-ma'ād*:

> Allah commanded the Jihād of Education when He revealed:
>
> وَلَوْ شِئْنَا لَبَعَثْنَا فِي كُلِّ قَرْيَةٍ نَذِيرًا فَلَا تُطِعِ الْكَافِرِينَ وَجَاهِدْهُمْ بِهِ جِهَادًا كَبِيرًا
>
> *If We willed, We could raise up a warner in every village. Therefore listen not to the Unbelievers, but strive against them with the utmost strenuousness, with the (Qur'ān).*[461]

This is a Makkan Chapter, therefore He command therein the Jihād of the non-Muslims by argumentation, elocution and conveying the Qur'ān.[462]

Imām Nawawī

Imām Nawawī in his book *al-Minhāj*, when defining Jihād and its different categories, said:

> ...one of the collective duties of the community as a whole (*farḍ kifāyah*) is to lodge a valid protest, to solve problems

---

[460] Imām Mālik bin Anas, *al-Mudawwanat al-kubrā*, p.180.

[461] Sūratu 'l-Furqān [The Criterion], 25:51,52

[462] Ibn Qayyim al-Jawzīyyah, *Zād al-Ma'ād.*

of religion, to have knowledge of Divine Law, to command what is right and forbid wrong conduct.[463]

Imām ad-Dardīr

The explanation of Jihād in Imām al-Dardir's book *Aqrab al-Masālik* is that it is propagating the knowledge of the Divine Law commending right and forbidding wrong. He emphasized that it is not permitted to skip this category of Jihād and implement the combative form, saying, "the first [Islamic] duty is to call people to enter Islam, even if they had been preached to by the Prophet ﷺ beforehand."[464]

Imām Bahūtī

Similarly, Imām Bahūtī commences the chapter on Jihād in his book *Kashf al-qinā'a* by showing the injunctions of collective religious duties (*kifāyah)* that the Muslim Nation must achieve before embarking on combative Jihād, including preaching and education about the religion of Islam, dismissing all the uncertainties about this religion and making available all the skills and qualifications which people might need in their religious, secular, physical and financial interests because these constitute the regulations of both this life and the life to come. Hence, *daʿwah*—performing the activities of propagating Islam and its related fields of knowledge—is the cornerstone of the 'building' of Jihād and its rules; and any attempt to build without this 'stone' would damage the meaning and reality of Jihād.[465]

Dr. Saʿīd Ramāḍān al-Būṭī

Al-Būṭī says in his book *al-Jihād fil-islām* states:

---

[463] al-Nawawī, *al-Minhāj,* p. 210.

[464] Imām al-Dārdīr, *Al-Sharḥ al-saghīr.*

[465] Manṣūr bin Yunus al-Baḥūtī, *Kashf al-qinā'a*, p. 33.

The most significant category of Jihād was the one established simultaneously with the dawn of the Islamic *da'wah* (calling for Islam) at Makkah. This was the basis for the other resulting kinds accorded with the situations and circumstances.[466]

Removing all misconceptions and stereotypes in clarifying the image of Islam held by non-Muslims, building a trusting relationship and working with them in ways that accord with their way of thinking, are all primary forms of Educational Jihād. Similarly, establishing a strong community and nation which can fulfill all physical needs of its people, thereby creating for them conditions in which the message will be heard, rather than being lost in the strife and struggle of everyday life, are requirements and form a basic building block of the Jihādic concept. These foundations fulfill the Qur'ānic injunction:

وَلْتَكُن مِّنكُمْ أُمَّةٌ يَدْعُونَ إِلَى الْخَيْرِ وَيَأْمُرُونَ بِالْمَعْرُوفِ وَيَنْهَوْنَ عَنِ الْمُنكَرِ
وَأُوْلَئِكَ هُمُ الْمُفْلِحُونَ

Let there arise out of you a band of people inviting to all that is good, enjoining what is right, and forbidding what is wrong: and these it is that shall be successful.[467]

Until this is accomplished the conditions of combative Jihād remain unfulfilled.[468]

Sayyid Sābiq

Sayyid Sābiq, in his renowned work *Fiqh as-Sunnah* says:

---

466 *Jihād fil-islām*, Muḥammad Sa'īd R. Al-Būṭī, Dār al-Fikr, Beirut, 1995, p. 16.
467 Sūrat Āli-'Imrān [The Family of 'Imrān], 3:104.
468 *Musnad* Aḥmad. Similar aḥādith are narrated in Abū Dāwūd and Tirmidhī.

Allah sent His Messenger ﷺ to all of mankind and ordered him to call to guidance and the religion of truth. While he dwelled in Makkah, he called to Allah by using wisdom and the best exhortation. It was inevitable for him to face opposition from his people who saw the new message as a danger to their way of life. It was through the guidance of Allah that he faced the opposition with patience, tolerance and forbearance. Allah says:

وَاصْبِرْ لِحُكْمِ رَبِّكَ فَإِنَّكَ بِأَعْيُنِنَا

So wait patiently (O Muhammad) for thy Lord's decree, for surely thou art in Our sight[469]

فَاصْفَحْ عَنْهُمْ وَقُلْ سَلَامٌ فَسَوْفَ يَعْلَمُونَ

Then bear with them (O Muhammad) and say: Peace. But they will come to know [[470]

فَاصْفَحِ الصَّفْحَ الْجَمِيلَ

So forgive, O Muhammad, with a gracious forgiveness[471]

Here we see that Allah does not permit the fighting of evil with evil, or to wage war on those who fight opposed the message of Islam nor to kill those who cause discord to the Muslims. And He said:

ادْفَعْ بِالَّتِي هِيَ أَحْسَنُ فَإِذَا الَّذِي بَيْنَكَ وَبَيْنَهُ عَدَاوَةٌ كَأَنَّهُ وَلِيٌّ حَمِيمٌ

[469] Sūratu 't-Tūr [Mt. Sinai], 52:48.
[470] Sūrat Āli-'Imrān [The Family of 'Imrān], 3:89.
[471] Sūratu 'l-Ḥijr [The Stony Tracts], 15:85.

Nor can goodness and Evil be equal. Repel (Evil) with what is better: Then will he between whom and thee was hatred become as it were thy friend and intimate![472]

As the persecution continued, it became harder and harder to bear, reaching its peak when the Quraysh conspired against the life of the Noble Messenger ﷺ. At this time, it became imperative that he migrate from Makkah to Madīnah, both for his personal safety, for the very survival of the new faith, and in an effort to avoid war. Thus thirteen years after the commencement of Qur'ān's revelation, the Prophet ﷺ ordered his companions to emigrate to Madīnah.

Here we see that the Prophet ﷺ did not engage in repulsing the aggressive attacks against the Muslims by his tribesmen, but sought to avoid conflict and avoid their persecution by means of migration.

ESTABLISHMENT OF THE ISLAMIC NATION/STATE

Sayyid Sābiq continues:

وَإِذْ يَمْكُرُ بِكَ الَّذِينَ كَفَرُوا لِيُثْبِتُوكَ أَوْ يَقْتُلُوكَ أَوْ يُخْرِجُوكَ وَيَمْكُرُونَ وَيَمْكُرُ اللَّهُ وَاللَّهُ خَيْرُ الْمَاكِرِينَ

And when those who disbelieve plot against thee (O Muhammad) to wound thee fatally, or to kill thee or to drive thee forth; they plot, but Allah (also) plotteth; and Allah is the best of plotters [473]

Madīnah thus became the new capital of Islām. As a nation-state for the Muslims, and their new home, an entirely new

---

[472] Sūrah Fuṣṣilat [Explained in Detail], 41:34.
[473] Sūratu 'l-Anfāl [The Spoils], 8:30.

political situation had evolved. Whereas before the Muslims had been a persecuted minority with no land or political base, upon establishing Madīnah as a nation ruled by the legislation of Islam, and a sanctuary to which new Muslims under persecution could flee, it was imperative to protect this homeland from the aggressive designs of the enemy, who sought nothing less than the complete extirpation of the Muslim faith and killing of its adherents. Thus when the enemies opened war against them the situation of the Muslims became gravely dangerous, taking them to the brink of destruction at the hands of the enemy, in which case the very message was in danger of being lost.[474]

So Jihād in its combative sense did not come about until after the Prophet ﷺ and his Companions were forced to leave their country and hometown of Makkah, fleeing for safety to in Madīnah after thirteen years of propagating the call to the faith and calling for freedom of belief. Allah said:

ثُمَّ إِنَّ رَبَّكَ لِلَّذِينَ هَاجَرُواْ مِن بَعْدِ مَا فُتِنُواْ ثُمَّ جَاهَدُواْ وَصَبَرُواْ إِنَّ رَبَّكَ مِن بَعْدِهَا لَغَفُورٌ رَّحِيمٌ

But verily thy Lord,- to those who leave their homes after trials and persecutions, - and who thereafter strive and struggle [for the faith] and patiently persevere, - Thy Lord, after all this is oft-forgiving, Most Merciful.[475]

So we see that after the migration to Madīnah, Allah described Jihād as a struggle which was suffered patiently through persecution and trial.

[474] Sayyid Sabiq, *Fiqh as-Sunnah*, 2nd ed., vol. 3, (Beirut: Dār al-Fikr, 1980).
[475] Sūratu 'n-Nahl [The Bee], 16:110.

FIRST LEGISLATION OF COMBATIVE JIHAD

Even then the legislation to fight was not made until the Makkans set out to eliminate the newly established Islamic nation, by building an army and setting forth with the intention of assaulting and destroying the community in Madīnah.

Sayyid Sābiq continues:

The first verse revealed regarding fighting was:

أُذِنَ لِلَّذِينَ يُقَاتَلُونَ بِأَنَّهُمْ ظُلِمُوا وَإِنَّ اللَّهَ عَلَى نَصْرِهِمْ لَقَدِيرٌ الَّذِينَ أُخْرِجُوا مِن
دِيَارِهِمْ بِغَيْرِ حَقٍّ إِلَّا أَن يَقُولُوا رَبُّنَا اللَّهُ وَلَوْلَا دَفْعُ اللَّهِ النَّاسَ بَعْضَهُم بِبَعْضٍ لَّهُدِّمَتْ
صَوَامِعُ وَبِيَعٌ وَصَلَوَاتٌ وَمَسَاجِدُ يُذْكَرُ فِيهَا اسْمُ اللَّهِ كَثِيرًا وَلَيَنصُرَنَّ اللَّهُ مَن يَنصُرُهُ
إِنَّ اللَّهَ لَقَوِيٌّ عَزِيزٌ الَّذِينَ إِن مَّكَّنَّاهُمْ فِي الْأَرْضِ أَقَامُوا الصَّلَاةَ وَآتَوُا الزَّكَاةَ وَأَمَرُوا
بِالْمَعْرُوفِ وَنَهَوْا عَنِ الْمُنكَرِ وَلِلَّهِ عَاقِبَةُ الْأُمُورِ

Sanction is given unto those who fight because they have been wronged; and Allah is indeed Able to give them victory; Those who have been driven from their homes unjustly only because they said: Our Lord is Allah. For had it not been for Allah's repelling some men by means of others, cloisters and churches and oratories and mosques, wherein the name of Allah is oft mentioned, would assuredly have been pulled down. Verily Allah helpeth one who helpeth Him. Lo! Allah is Strong, Almighty. Those who, if We give them power in the land, establish worship and pay the poor due and enjoin kindness and forbid iniquity. And Allah's is the sequel of events.[476]]

This verse shows that permission for fighting is granted for three reasons:

---

[476] Sūratu 'n-Nabā [The Tidings], 78: 39-40.

1) They were oppressed by their enemies and expelled by them from their homes unjustly for no reason except that they practice the religion of Allah and say, "Our Lord is Allah." They then came under the obligation to take back the country from which they had been expelled.

2) Where not for Allah's permission for this type of defense, all places of worship, [including churches, synagogues and mosques] would have been destroyed in which the name of Allah is remembered [see page 387] for a more detailed explanation of this aspect] because of the oppression of those who aggressively oppose belief.

3) The goal of victory is to establish the freedom of religion, establish the prayer, to give charity and to command the good and forbid what is disliked.

This last justification also means that as long as preaching and practice are not circumscribed, the Muslims cannot fight a Jihād against a country in which Muslims freely practice their religion and teach Islam.

In the second year after the Migration, Allah ordered the Muslims to fight by saying:

كُتِبَ عَلَيْكُمُ الْقِتَالُ وَهُوَ كُرْهٌ لَّكُمْ وَعَسَى أَن تَكْرَهُوا شَيْئًا وَهُوَ خَيْرٌ لَّكُمْ

وَعَسَى أَن تُحِبُّوا شَيْئًا وَهُوَ شَرٌّ لَّكُمْ وَاللَّهُ يَعْلَمُ وَأَنتُمْ لَا تَعْلَمُونَ

Warfare is ordained for you, though it is hateful unto you; but it may happen that ye hate a thing which is good for you, and it may happen that ye love a thing which is bad for you. Allah knoweth, ye know not.[477]

This verse shows that in general warfare was disliked, not something sought after, but despite this, it was called for at times when the security of the nation was threatened by external belligerency.

Thus, with a simple studious examination of the relevant verses, we discover then that there were two different kinds of Jihād: that of Makkah and that of Madīnah. The one in Makkah was primarily by education. In Madīnah Jihād was by two methods:

1) education and

2) fighting after the enemies attacked the Prophet ﷺ within his own city-state. Additionally, the Muslims who had been expelled invoked the right to return to their homeland, and if opposed to use force.

As we explained earlier there are fourteen different categories of Jihād, only one of which entails fighting. Since it is this, the combative Jihād, which is now so much the focus of this paper we will now speak on the principles of such combat, who can declare combative Jihād and the reasons Muslims fight.

Combative Jihād was authorized only after the Prophet ﷺ migrated along with his followers from Makkah to Madīnah, having been persecuted and finally expelled from their country running from persecution and torture. This is not unlike what we see today: people running from persecution in their home countries, becoming refugees in foreign nations. And the supporters, al-Anṣār, of Madīnah, welcomed the refugees al-Muhājirūn, and shared with them all they possessed of their wealth and their homes.

[477] Sūratu 'l-Baqarah [The Heifer], 2:216.

The struggle in the way of Allah, *Jihādun fī sabīlillāh,* when the Prophet ﷺ began by teaching the Qur'ān in his country, Makkah, was primarily one of enlightenment and education while in Madīnah his message became the basis for a model constitution for civic society and social life. This is borne out by the emphasis the Prophet ﷺ made on caring for the poor, the emancipation of slaves, giving rights to women and building a civic society by levying taxes on the rich to benefit the poor, establishing community centers and community homes in which people could meet. These teachings were brought to a society in Makkah in which anarchy ruled and for this reason the Prophet ﷺ was persecuted and fled to Madīnah. There he was able to establish a nation-state based on freedom of speech, and freedom of religion where all religions flourished together without conflict.

In establishing this society in Madīnah, the Prophet ﷺ sought to keep his new nation safe, just as today every country has security as a dominant concern. Therefore he built up an army of his followers to keep his borders safe from any enemy attack. In particular they were under great threat due to the Prophet's ﷺ teaching opposing the hegemony of tyrants.

Thus Madīnah became the first city for the believers in which the new message, Islam, was established and they sought to keep it safe. Just as all nations do today, they built up an army and weaponry. And, just as done in the modern world, if anyone attacks a nation, they are obliged to respond and repel those who attacked them.

So the majority of Muslims scholars including Imām Abū Ḥanifa, Imām Mālik and Imām Aḥmad ibn Ḥanbal say that combative Jihād is to defend oneself and to attack the aggressors.

RELIGIOUS FREEDOM OF NON-MUSLIMS

It is a right for the people of the Book to practice the laws of their religion, judges and courts, enforcing the rules of their own religion among themselves. Their churches or temples are not to be demolished nor are their crosses [religious symbols] to be broken.

اتركوهم وما يدينونه

The Messenger of Allah ﷺ said, "Leave them to what they worship."

Additionally, it is the right of a Christian or Jewish spouse of a Muslim is that she is taken to the church or to the temple. And it is not the right of her husband to prevent her from going.

Islām permits them the foods that their religion allows for food or otherwise. Swine are not killed because of them nor is their wine destroyed as long as it is permitted to them. Therefore they have more latitude than the Muslims, who are prohibited from wine and eating pork.

They have the freedom in the laws of marriage, divorce and charity and to conduct these affairs as they wish without any conditions or limits.

Their honor and rights are under the protection of Islām and they are given freedom to the right of deliberation and discussions within the limits of reason and decorum, while adhering to respect, good conduct and avoiding rudeness and harshness. Allah says:

وَلَا تُجَادِلُوا أَهْلَ الْكِتَابِ إِلَّا بِالَّتِي هِيَ أَحْسَنُ إِلَّا الَّذِينَ ظَلَمُوا مِنْهُمْ وَقُولُوا آمَنَّا
بِالَّذِي أُنزِلَ إِلَيْنَا وَأُنزِلَ إِلَيْكُمْ وَإِلَٰهُنَا وَإِلَٰهُكُمْ وَاحِدٌ وَنَحْنُ لَهُ مُسْلِمُونَ

And dispute ye not with the People of the Book, except with means better (than mere disputation), unless it be with those of them who inflict wrong (and injury): but say, "We believe in the revelation which has come down to us and in that which came down to you; Our God and your God is one; and it is to Him we bow (in Islam)."[478]

وَإِنْ أَحَدٌ مِّنَ الْمُشْرِكِينَ اسْتَجَارَكَ فَأَجِرْهُ حَتَّى يَسْمَعَ كَلَامَ اللَّهِ ثُمَّ أَبْلِغْهُ مَأْمَنَهُ ذَلِكَ بِأَنَّهُمْ قَوْمٌ لَّا يَعْلَمُونَ

If one amongst the Pagans ask thee for asylum, grant it to him, so that he may hear the word of Allah; and then escort him to where he can be secure. That is because they are men without knowledge. [479]

This also shows that even if unbelievers come to the Muslims, seeking to live and work in their nation for any reason, it is ordered to grant them safety and security to demonstrate the great care and compassion Islam takes in the care of others. Then such are free to move where they like. This clarifies the understanding that combative Jihād is only against transgressors.

In the view of some schools, Islam equates the punishments for Muslims and non-Muslims except for those things permitted in their faith such as drinking wine or eating pork.

Islām makes lawful eating what the People of the Book slaughter and Muslim men are permitted to marry their women where Allah says:

الْيَوْمَ أُحِلَّ لَكُمُ الطَّيِّبَاتُ وَطَعَامُ الَّذِينَ أُوتُوا الْكِتَابَ حِلٌّ لَّكُمْ وَطَعَامُكُمْ حِلٌّ لَّهُمْ وَالْمُحْصَنَاتُ مِنَ الْمُؤْمِنَاتِ وَالْمُحْصَنَاتُ مِنَ الَّذِينَ أُوتُوا الْكِتَابَ مِن

[478] Sūratu 'l-ʿAnkabūt [The Spider], 29:46.

[479] Sūratu 't-Tawbah [Repentance], 9:6.

$$\text{قِبَلِكُمْ إِذَا آتَيْتُمُوهُنَّ أُجُورَهُنَّ مُحْصِنِينَ غَيْرَ مُسَافِحِينَ وَلَا مُتَّخِذِي أَخْدَانٍ}$$

...

This day are (all) things good and pure made lawful unto you. The food of the People of the Book is lawful unto you and yours is lawful unto them. (Lawful unto you in marriage) are (not only) chaste women who are believers, but chaste women among the People of the Book, revealed before your time,- when ye give them their due dowers, and desire chastity, not lewdness, nor secret intrigues...[480]

Islām sanctions visiting and counseling their sick, offering them guidance and dealing with them in business. It is established that when the Messenger of Allah ﷺ passed to his Lord, his armor was given as credit for a debt from a Jewish person.

In another case, when some of the Companions sacrificed a sheep the Prophet ﷺ said to his servant, "Give this to our Jewish neighbor."

It is obligatory for the leader of the Muslims (caliph) to protect those of them who are in Muslim lands just as he would Muslims and to seek the release of those of them who are captured by the enemy.

$$\text{مَنْ قَتَلَ مُعَاهِداً، لَمْ يَرِحْ رَائِحَةَ الجَنَّةِ}$$

The Messenger of Allah ﷺ forbade killing a convenanter when he said:

The one who kills a convenanter will not smell the fragrance of paradise.[481]

And it can be truly said that in Arab and Muslim nations, the Christians, the Jews and all other non-Muslims are in fact

---

[480] Sūratu 'l-Mā'idah [The Spread Table], 5:5.
[481] Ibn Mājah reported it in his *Sunan*, from 'Abd-Allāh bin 'Amr ☼.

covenanters, for they pay their taxes supporting the nation's standing army, so it is the duty of the ruler to protect the safety of the covenanter. The concept of a covenant of protection, while not explicitly spelled out today, is fulfilled through government taxation.

The popular, yet controversial, Islamic scholar Shaykh Yūsuf al-Qaradāwī said:

> Jihād is an obligation on everyone but not killing and fighting.

Citing Ibn Qayyim's division of Jihād into thirteen different levels including struggle against the ego, shaytan, the establishment of education, etc., only one of them being combat against an aggressor, Shaykh al-Qaradāwī states:

> Whoever looks into the sources as to the understanding of Jihād, will see that one can be a mujāhid [of the 13 categories] but it is not necessary to be a combatant; that is only when combat is forced on you by the invasion of your country.

FORCED CONVERSION?

We have seen above that the foundation of Jihād is Islamic propagation (*daʿwah*). The question often asked is whether Islam condones and teaches the forced and armed conversion of non-Muslims. This is the image sometimes projected by Western scholars and as any Muslim scholar will tell you, is seriously flawed. The Qur'ān clearly states:

لَا إِكْرَاهَ فِي الدِّينِ قَد تَّبَيَّنَ الرُّشْدُ مِنَ الْغَيِّ

There is no compulsion in religion, the path of guidance stands out clear from error [482]

---

[482] Sūratu 'l-Baqarah [The Heifer], 2:256 and 60:8.

In this verse, the word *rushd* or *"path of guidance"* refers to the entire domain of human life, not just to the rites and theology of Islam.

> There is no debate about the fact that pre-Islamic Arabia was a misguided society dominated by tribalism and a blind obedience to custom. In contrast, the clarity of Islam and its emphasis on reason and rational proofs excluded any need to impose it by force. This verse is a clear indication that the Qur'ān is strictly opposed to the use of compulsion in religious faith. Similarly, Allah addressed the Prophet ﷺ saying:

فَذَكِّرْ إِنَّمَا أَنتَ مُذَكِّرٌ

Remind them, for you are only one who reminds.[483]

Allah addresses the believers, urging them to obey the injunctions of Islam:

وَأَطِيعُواْ اللّهَ وَأَطِيعُواْ الرَّسُولَ وَاحْذَرُواْ فَإِن تَوَلَّيْتُمْ فَاعْلَمُواْ أَنَّمَا عَلَى رَسُولِنَا الْبَلاَغُ الْمُبِينُ

Obey Allah, and obey the Messenger, and beware (of evil): if you do turn back, then know that it is Our Messenger's duty to proclaim (the message) in the clearest manner. [484]

However, this verse makes it clear that the Messenger's ﷺ duty is only to proclaim and preach the message; it remains to each individual to accept and to follow.

As for forced conversion, no reliable evidence exists that Muslims ever intended or attempted to impose the specific rites

[483] Sūratu 'l-Ghāshīyah[The Overwhelming] 88:21.
[484] Sūratu 'l-Mā'idah [The Spread Table], 5:92.

and beliefs of Islam. The histories of Central Asia, Spain, India, the Balkans and all of Southeast Asia are concrete proof of this.

ISLAM'S HISTORY OF GOOD-TREATMENT OF NON-MUSLIMS

It is thus well-established in history, that when persecution took place in non-Muslim lands against the People of the Book, they would seek refuge with the leader of the Muslims (caliph), and this refuge was not refused. A well-known example of this is the plight of the Jews in Andalusia after it was conquered by the Spanish and taken from the hands of the Muslim Moors. With the imposition of the infamously cruel Inquisition in 1492, Jews and Muslims had no choice but to flee their homes, convert to Catholicism or die. The Jews sought the protection of Sultan Suleyman of the Ottoman Empire and caliph of the Muslims and asylum was granted. For this reason, one finds a sizable population of Jews in Istanbul, which was seat of the Ottoman Empire at that time.

CONDITIONS FOR COMBATIVE JIHAD

The ruler, the Imām, is completely answerable to the people and their legal apparatus, the most important representatives of whom are the scholars. The position of the law is that only at such a time when it can be reasonably proven that;

- there are aggressive designs against Islam; and,
- there are concerted efforts to eject Muslims from their legally acquired property; and,
- that military campaigns are being launched to eradicate them.

At such a time the ruler can declare and execute the provisions of combative Jihād.

PRE-CONDITION: LEADERSHIP

Saʿīd Ramāḍān al-Būṭī *Jihād in Islam* in says:

It is known that Islamic Shari'ah rules can be divided into two groups: first the Communicative Rules (*Aḥkām at-Tablīgh*) – that inform you of how to behave in your life, including all matters of worship and daily life and second the Rules of Leadership (*Aḥkām al-Imāmah*) which are related to the judicial system, the Imām or leader.

> The Rules of Leadership are those rules that have been directed from the leader to the citizens. In the time of the Prophet ﷺ he was leader, so this applied to anything directed from himself to the Muslims. After the Prophet ﷺ, such directives became the responsibility of the caliph, his successor. This means the Imām of the Muslims is the leader of every Muslim nation. He is the person responsible for the application of the rules as he sees fit. These rules are flexible within the geographical, societal and cultural norms of the nation, which the leader can exercise by Allah's grace, to apply them for the benefit of all the people.

Declaring combative Jihād is the topmost responsibility of the Imām (leader, president or king of a nation). He is the only responsible body that can declare the time and place of Jihād, lead it or terminate its mission. It is in no way the responsibility of individual Muslims to declare Jihād without the order of the leader. Note in this regard the *ʿulama* are not in the position to issue a call for combative Jihād.

There are two kinds of combative Jihād. One is the combative Jihād to fight a nation which aggresses against a Muslim nation, under the orders of the Imām, or leader. The second category of combative Jihād, which is called *aṣ-ṣa'il,* means the fight against an assailant, attacker or violater. We will not go into this aspect as it falls under the Communicative Rules, not the Rules of Imāmate.

This is based on the hadith related by ʿAbd Allāh ibn ʿUmar, in which the Prophet ﷺ said, "He who is killed in defense of his belongings or in self-defense or in defense of his religion is a martyr."[485]

The category *aṣ-ṣa'il* refers to someone defending his private possessions as when someone attacks him at home or his business in order to steal, to harm, or out of hatred due to differences of religion. This does not come under the aspect of Imāmah, where nations are involved.[486]

Ibn Qudāma

It is an essential pre-condition that there be a leader of the Muslims, an Imām, to declare combative Jihād. In *al-Mughni,* Ibn Qudāma, a respected scholar of the Ḥanbalī school, states:

> Declaring Jihād is the responsibility of the Ruler and is his independent legal judgment. And it is the duty of the citizens to obey whatever he regards appropriate.[487]

Al-Dardīr

Al-Dardīr says: "proclaiming Jihād comes through the Ruler's assignment of a commander."[488]

Al-Jazā'irī

Abū Bakr Al-Jazā'irī states that the pillars of combative Jihād are:

> A pure intention and that it is performed behind a Muslim Ruler and beneath his flag and with his permission.... And

[485] Narrated by Abū Dāwūd, ibn Mājah, Tirmidhī, and Aḥmad.
[486] Muḥammad Saʿīd R. Al-Būṭī, *Jihād fīl-islām,* Dār al-Fikr, Beirut, 1995, pp. 108-109.
[487] Ibn Qudāma, *Al-Mughnī,* Vol. 9, p. 184.
[488] al-Dārdīr, *Al-Sharḥ al-Saghīr,* Vol. 2, p. 274.

it is not allowed for them to fight without a Ruler because Allāḥ says:

يَا أَيُّهَا الَّذِينَ آمَنُواْ أَطِيعُواْ اللّهَ وَأَطِيعُواْ الرَّسُولَ وَأُوْلِي الأَمْرِ مِنكُمْ

O ye who believe! Obey Allah, and obey the Messenger, and those charged with authority among you.[489] [490]

al-Tahanūī

According to *Kashf al-qinā'a* by al-Tahanūī:

Ordering combative Jihād is the responsibility of the Imām and his legal judgment (*ijtihād*) because he is the most knowledgeable about the enemy's status and their nearness or farness, their intention and conspiracy.[491]

Al-Qirafī

Al-Qirafī said:

The leader [president or king] is the one who has been elected for the foreign policy of his county, and he has entrusted by the propel to conduct the common affairs of the state, sign treaties, forbid wrong deeds, suppress criminals, fight aggressors, and settle people down in their homes and the like.[492]

Mawardī

Mawardī, a Shafiʿite authority, while enumerating the obligations of a Muslim ruler says:

---

[489] Sūratu 'n-Nisā [Women], 4:59.

[490] Abū Bakrʿs al-Jazā'irī, *Minhāj al-Muslim*, Chapter of Jihād.

[491] al-Tahanūī, *Kashf al-qinā'a*, vol. 3, p. 41.

[492] Al-Qirafī, *al-Aḥkām fī tamiyyiz al-fatawā*, p. 24.

His sixth obligation is to conduct [combative] Jihād against those who show hostility against Islam…[493]

Al-Sarkhasī

Al-Sarkhasī in *al-Mabsūṭ* said:

The Ruler of the Muslims must almost always exert all efforts to lead an army himself or dispatch a military detachment of Muslims; and trust in Allah to aid him in achieving victory.[494]

Ash-Sharbīnī

Ash-Sharbīnī said:

Collective-duty Jihād becomes applicable when the Imām fortifies the frontiers (to gain equal military parity with the enemy), reinforces the fortresses and ditches, and arms his military leaders. It also becomes relevant by the Imām or his deputy's leading the army... [495]

The Pakistani monthly *Renaissance,* in discussing the authorization for declaring combative Jihād says:

Both the Qur'ān and the established practice of the prophets of Allah explicitly say that Jihād can only be waged by a state. No group of people have been given the authority to take up arms, because individual groups if given this license will create great disorder and destruction by fighting among themselves once they overcome the enemy. A study of the Qur'ān reveals that the Makkan Surahs do not contain any directive of combative Jihād for the fundamental reason that in Makkah the Muslims did not have their own state.

---

[493] Abū 'l-Ḥasan ʿAlī Mawardī, *al-Aḥkām al-sulṭānīyyah*, 1st ed., (Beirut: Dār al-Kitāb al-ʿArabī, 1990), p. 52.

[494] Al-Sarkhasī, *al-Mabsūṭ*, vol. 10, p. 3.

[495] Al-Sharbīnī, *Mughnī al-muhtāj*, vol. 4, p. 210.

Islam does not advocate "the law of the jungle." It is a religion in which both human life and the way it is taken hold utter sanctity. Thus Islam does not give Muslims any right to take life unless certain conditions are fulfilled. So, it was not until an Islamic state was established in Madīnah that the Qur'ān gave the Muslims permission to take up arms against the onslaught mounted by the Quraysh:

أُذِنَ لِلَّذِينَ يُقَاتَلُونَ بِأَنَّهُمْ ظُلِمُوا وَإِنَّ اللَّهَ عَلَى نَصْرِهِمْ لَقَدِيرٌ الَّذِينَ أُخْرِجُوا مِن دِيَارِهِمْ بِغَيْرِ حَقٍّ إِلَّا أَن يَقُولُوا رَبُّنَا اللَّهُ وَلَوْلَا دَفْعُ اللَّهِ النَّاسَ بَعْضَهُم بِبَعْضٍ لَّهُدِّمَتْ صَوَامِعُ وَبِيَعٌ وَصَلَوَاتٌ وَمَسَاجِدُ يُذْكَرُ فِيهَا اسْمُ اللَّهِ كَثِيرًا وَلَيَنصُرَنَّ اللَّهُ مَن يَنصُرُهُ إِنَّ اللَّهَ لَقَوِيٌّ عَزِيزٌ

To those against whom war is made, permission is given [to fight] because they have been oppressed and verily Allah is Most Powerful to help them. [They] are those who have been expelled from their homes without any basis, only because they said: 'Our Lord is Allah.'[496]

Consequently, the Prophet ﷺ never retaliated in Makkah to the inhuman treatment which was given to him as well as to some of his Companions. He preferred to suffer and be persecuted than to counter attack his enemies, since Muslims at that stage had not fulfilled this all important pre-requisite of combative Jihād: establishment of a state.

Similarly, the earlier prophets were not allowed by the Almighty to wage war unless they had established their political authority in an independent piece of land. For instance, the

496 Sūratu 'l-Ḥajj [The Pilgrimage], 22:39-40.

Prophet ﷺ Moses, as is evident from the Qur'ān, was directed to wage war only after he had fulfilled this condition. Since the Prophet ﷺ Jesus and his Companions were not able to gain political authority in a piece of land, they never launched an armed struggle to defend themselves, despite intense persecution.

> Consequently, there is a consensus among all authorities of Islam that only an Islamic State has the authority to wage Jihād. [And where is the Islamic state today, with its fundamental principles? Therefore one easily concludes that today there is no valid state under which to wage combative Jihād.] Groups parties and organization have no authority to raise the call to arms. Whoever undertakes war without the authorization of the ruler in fact disobey the religion.[497]
>
> Referring to the pre-requisite of state authority, the Prophet ﷺ said:
>
> A Muslim ruler is the shield (of his people). A war can only be waged under him and people should seek his shelter (in war).[498]

Sayyid Sābiq

This condition is so explicit and categorical that all the scholars of this Ummah unanimously uphold it. Sayyid Sābiq, while referring to this consensus, writes:

> Among *kifāyah* obligations, there is a category for which the existence of a ruler is necessary e.g., [combative] Jihād and administration of punishments.[499]

---

[497] Shehzad Saleem in "No Jihad without a State," Renaissance Monthly, December 1999.

[498] Bukhārī.

Zafar Aḥmad ʿUthmānī

Zafar Aḥmad ʿUthmānī, a Ḥanafite jurist writes:

It is obvious from the Hadith narrated by Makḥūl [500] that Jihād becomes obligatory with the ruler who is a Muslim and whose political authority has been established either through nomination by the previous ruler similar to how Abū Bakr transferred the reins [of his Khilāfah to 'Umar] or through pledging of allegiance by the ʿ*ulama* or a group of the elite …in my opinion, if the oath of allegiance is pledged by ʿ*ulama* or by a group of the elite to a person who is not able to guard the frontiers and defend honour [of the people] organize armies or implement his directives by political force neither is he able to provide justice to the oppressed by exercising force and power, then such a person cannot be called 'Amir' (leader) or 'Imām' (ruler). He, at best, is an arbitrator and the oath of allegiance is at best of the nature of arbitration and it is not at all proper to call him 'Amir' (leader) or an 'Imām' (ruler) in any [official] documents nor should the people address him by these designations. ...It is not imperative for the citizens to

---

499 Sayyid Sābiq, *Fiqh as-Sunnah*, 2nd ed., vol. 3, (Beirut: Dār al-Fikr, 1980), p. 30. cited by Shehzad Saleem in "No Jihad without a State," Renaissance Monthly, December 1999.

500 The complete text of the Ḥadīth is:

حدثنا أحمد بن صالح حدثنا ابن وهب حدثني معاوية بن صالح عن العلاء بن الحارث عن مكحول عن أبي هريرة قال

قال رسول الله صلى الله عليه وسلم الجهاد واجب عليكم مع كل أمير برا كان أو فاجرا والصلاة واجبة عليكم خلف كل مسلم برا كان أو فاجرا وإن عمل الكبائر والصلاة واجبة على كل مسلم برا كان أو فاجرا وإن عمل الكبائر

Makḥūl narrates from Abū Hurayrah who narrates from the Prophet ﷺ: "*Jihad* is obligatory upon you with a Muslim ruler whether he is pious or impious, and the prayer is obligatory upon you behind every Muslim whether he is pious or impious even if he is guilty of the major sins." (*Sunan Abū Dāwūd*, No. 2171)

> pledge allegiance to him or obey his directives and no [combative] Jihād can be waged alongside him.[501]

Imām Farāhī

In the words of Imām Farāhī:

> In one's own country, without migrating to an independent piece of land, [combative] Jihād is not allowed. The tale of Abraham and other verses pertaining to migration testify to this. The Prophet's ﷺ life also supports this view. The reason for this is that if [combative] Jihād is not waged by a person who holds political authority, it amounts to anarchy and disorder.[502]

Al-Albānī

The Salafi scholar Al-Albānī, stressing the necessity of Jihād being established by the ruler of the Muslims said:

> In the present time there is no Jihād in the Islamic land, while undoubtedly there is combat taking place in numerous places but there is no Jihād, established under a solely Islamic banner that abides by Islamic legislation.

From this we can understand that it is not permitted for a soldier to act according to his own wishes, but he is obliged to follow the rules of the commander and his commands and that commander who was delegated with proper authority by the Caliphate of Muslims. So we can ask ourselves today, "Where is the Caliphate of Muslims in the present time?" Since there is no caliphate the fundamental principle of leadership is no longer

---

[501] Zafar Aḥmad 'Uthmānī, *'Ila 'l-Sunan*, 3rd ed., vol. 12, (Karachi: Idāratu 'l-Qur'ān wa 'Ulūmi'l-Islāmīyyah, 1415 AH), pp. 15-16. Cited by Shehzad Saleem in "No Jihad without a State," Renaissance Monthly, December 1999.

[502] Farāhī, *Majmuʿah tafasir-i-farāhī*, 1st ed., (Lahore: Faran Foundation, 1991), p. 56. Cited by Shehzad Saleem in "No Jihad without a State," Renaissance Monthly, December 1999.

present. So while there still remains combat between one nation and another it is no longer considered as fulfilling the religious obligation that Jihād entails.

These represent only a sampling of many quotes from scholars regarding the combative Jihād demonstrate the responsibility of the Imāmate in ordering it. The Imām [Ruler] in fact, is the only one responsible in repelling aggressors and to see what actions are fitting for the country. The actual title whether he be called Imām, caliph, king or president, is not important – his position as ruler is what counts. The leader is the one who has been elected to administer the foreign policy of his nation, and he has been entrusted by the people to conduct the common affairs of the state, sign treaties, forbid wrong deeds, suppress criminals, fight aggressors, and settle people down in their homes and the like.

This specific duty can never devolve to a group of people living in a country who come against a government by terrifying innocent citizens. It is not acceptable in Islam by any means for someone to declare combative war if he is not in the position of leadership.

The many aforementioned rulings of scholars and the many verses of Qur'ān and hadith citation expose the methods of the so-called "Islamic parties"[1] who establish states within the state and act as if they are the rightful rulers of Muslims.

Their methodology is to initiate war by attacking non-Muslims in their country or other countries, and they do this without the permission of the Muslim rulers or the Muslim nation and without the consensus of its scholars. What happens then? The result is that everyone suffers from the disastrous consequences of their actions. This subject is discussed in detail on page 426.

SELF-DEFENSE

Naturally every community has the right to self-defense and in the case of Islam, where religion is the primary dimension of human existence, war in defense of the nation becomes a religious act. A lack of understanding of this quality of Islam, its non-secularism; has also contributed considerably to the fear that when Islam talks about war it means going to war to convert. This might be true in other cultures, but Islam must be allowed to speak for itself.

Al-Dardīr says of this:

Jihād becomes a duty when the enemy takes [Muslims] by surprise.[503]

Saʿīd Ramaḍān al-Būṭī shows that fighting in this case is an obligation of the community as a whole.

عن سعيدِ بنِ زيدٍ قال: سمعتُ رسُولَ اللّهِ صلّى اللّهُ عليهِ وسَلّم يقول: "من قُتِلَ دونَ مالِهِ فهو شهيدٌ. ومن قُتِلَ دونَ دمِهِ فهو شهيدٌ. ومن قُتِلَ دونَ دينِهِ فهو شهيدٌ".

This is based on the Prophet's ﷺ saying, "He who is killed in defense of his belongings, or in self-defense, or for his religion, is a martyr."[504]

Allah said:

لَا يَنْهَاكُمُ اللَّهُ عَنِ الَّذِينَ لَمْ يُقَاتِلُوكُمْ فِي الدِّينِ وَلَمْ يُخْرِجُوكُم مِّن دِيَارِكُمْ أَن تَبَرُّوهُمْ وَتُقْسِطُوا إِلَيْهِمْ إِنَّ اللَّهَ يُحِبُّ الْمُقْسِطِينَ

Allah does not forbid you from those who do not remove you from your homes (by force) and who do not fight you because of your religion, that you act kindly and justly towards them... [505]

This verse mentions a fundamental principle of Islam regarding Muslim/Non-Muslim relationships. Muslims are

---

[503] al-Dārdīr, *Al-Sharḥ al-Saghīr*, Vol. 2, p. 274..

[504] Abū Dāwūd and Tirmidhī.

[505] Sūratu 'l-Mumtahina [She that is to be examined], 60:8.

enjoined to act kindly and justly towards members of other faiths except in two circumstances; firstly, if they dispossess Muslims of their legitimate land-rights, and; secondly, if they engage in hostilities towards Muslims by killing or attacking them, or show clear intent to do so (*al-ḥirābah*) because of their religion. In the second eventuality, it is the duty of the Muslim ruler to declare combative Jihād as a defensive action to repel such attacks.

It is evident from the Qur'ān and other sources that the armed struggle against the polytheists was legislated in the context of specific circumstances after the Prophet ﷺ had migrated from Makkah to Madīnah. There he secured a pact with the Jewish and Arab tribes of the city, who accepted him as the leader of their community. In the milieu of this newly-founded base of operations, under the governance of Divine legislation and the leadership of the Prophet ﷺ, Islam attained the status of a nation with its corequisite territory and the accompanying need to protect its self-interests. At that time the divine command was revealed permitting Jihād, but this occurred only after:

- Persistent refusal of the Makkan leadership (the Prophet ﷺ being in Madīnah at the time) to allow the practice of Islam's religious obligations, specifically to perform the Ḥajj at Makkah. Note that despite this belligerency, the Prophet ﷺ agreed to a truce.

- Continuous unabated persecution of Muslims remaining at Makkah after the Prophet's emigration to Madīnah triggered an armed insurrection against Qurayshite interests in the Hijāz.

- Makkans themselves starting off military campaigns against the Muslims at Madīnah with the sole objective of eradicating Islam.

- Key security pledges being abrogated unilaterally by a number of tribes allied to the Prophet ﷺ, forcing him into a dangerously vulnerable position.

These conditions for defensive Jihād involving armed struggle were then clearly specified in the Qur'ān:

وَقَاتِلُوا۟ فِي سَبِيلِ اللّهِ الَّذِينَ يُقَاتِلُونَكُمْ وَلاَ تَعْتَدُوا۟

And fight in the way of Allah those who fight against you, and do not transgress [limits] for Allah likes not the transgressors.[506]

Explaining this verse, Sayyid Sābiq states:

This verse also consists of prohibiting aggression due the fact that Allah does not love aggression. This prohibition is not abrogated by any verse and is a warning that aggression is devoid of Allah's love. Verses that consist of such warnings are not abrogated because aggression is tyranny and Allah never loves tyranny. Therefore a legal war is justified only when it is to prevent discord and harm to the Muslims and for them to have the freedom to practice and live according to their religion.[507]

Allah says:

أَلاَ تُقَاتِلُونَ قَوْمًا نَّكَثُوا۟ أَيْمَانَهُمْ وَهَمُّوا۟ بِإِخْرَاجِ الرَّسُولِ وَهُم بَدَؤُوكُمْ أَوَّلَ مَرَّةٍ

Will you not fight a people who have violated their oaths and intended to expel the Messenger while they did attack you first?[508]

---

[506] Sūratu 'l-Baqarah [The Heifer], 2:190.
[507] Sayyid Sābiq, *Fiqh as-Sunnah.*
[508] Sūratu 't-Tawbah [Repentance], 9:13.

The clear picture that emerges here is that the command to fight was given in relation to specific conditions. Thus the declaration of war is not an arbitrary act at all.

أُذِنَ لِلَّذِينَ يُقَاتَلُونَ بِأَنَّهُمْ ظُلِمُوا وَإِنَّ اللَّهَ عَلَى نَصْرِهِمْ

To those against whom war is made, permission is given (to fight), because they are wronged;- and verily, Allah is most powerful for their aid;[509]

EXPULSION

The Qur'ān then goes on to describe the conditions of those who are permitted to fight:

وَمَا لَنَا أَلاَّ نُقَاتِلَ فِي سَبِيلِ اللّهِ وَقَدْ أُخْرِجْنَا مِن دِيَارِنَا وَأَبْنَآئِنَا

They said: "How could we refuse to fight in the cause of Allah, seeing that we were turned out of our homes and our families?"[510]

الَّذِينَ أُخْرِجُوا مِن دِيَارِهِمْ بِغَيْرِ حَقٍّ إِلَّا أَن يَقُولُوا رَبُّنَا اللَّهُ وَلَوْلَا دَفْعُ اللَّهِ
النَّاسَ بَعْضَهُم بِبَعْضٍ لَّهُدِّمَتْ صَوَامِعُ وَبِيَعٌ وَصَلَوَاتٌ وَمَسَاجِدُ يُذْكَرُ فِيهَا
اسْمُ اللَّهِ كَثِيراً وَلَيَنصُرَنَّ اللَّهُ مَن يَنصُرُهُ إِنَّ اللَّهَ لَقَوِيٌّ عَزِيزٌ

(They are) those who have been expelled from their homes in defiance of right,- (for no cause) except that they say, "our Lord is Allah". Did not Allah check one set of people by means of another, there would surely have been pulled down monasteries, churches, synagogues, and mosques, in which the

[509] Sūratu 'l-Ḥajj [The Pilgrimage], 22:39.
[510] Sūratu 'l-Baqarah [The Heifer], 2: 246.

name of Allah is commemorated in abundant measure. Allah will certainly aid those who aid his (cause);- for verily Allah is full of Strength, Exalted in Might, (able to enforce His Will).[511]

Explaining this verse, Imām Abū Ja'far ibn Jarīr aṭ-Ṭabarī explained that were Allah not to check one set of people by means of another then "monasteries belonging to Christians, synagogues belonging to Jews and mosques belonging to Muslims, where Allah's Name is often mentioned, will all be destroyed." Thus Islam here makes the upholding of religious freedom, not for Muslims alone, but as is stressed by the order of the religions mentioned in the verse in which the rights of non-Muslims are upheld first, and lastly those of Muslims.

The Qur'ān then goes on to describe the attributes those whom He ordains for defense of the faith, and protecting the right of religious freedom, saying:

الَّذِينَ إِن مَّكَّنَّاهُمْ فِي الْأَرْضِ أَقَامُوا الصَّلَاةَ وَآتَوُا الزَّكَاةَ وَأَمَرُوا بِالْمَعْرُوفِ وَنَهَوْا عَنِ الْمُنكَرِ وَلِلَّهِ عَاقِبَةُ الْأُمُورِ

(They are) those who, if We establish them in the land, establish regular prayer and give regular charity, enjoin the right and forbid wrong: with Allah rests the end (and decision) of (all) affairs.[512]

Here Allah describes them as those who are sincere and pious, for they establish prayer and give charity, prevent wrongdoing and enjoin good conduct.

---

[511] Sūratu 'l-Ḥajj [The Pilgrimage], 22:40.
[512] Sūratu 'l-Ḥajj [The Pilgrimage], 22:41.

DENIAL OF RELIGIOUS FREEDOM

In later times, the Muslims engaged in warfare to establish the "Pax Islamica" or Islamic Order. The legal and political order must flow from the divine imperative (Qur'ān, Sunnah, etc.). It alone guarantees the rights of every individual by keeping in check all the dark psychic tendencies of man and so preventing him from indulging in anti-social behaviors, from political aggression, right down to the commonest criminal act. It is for this that the Qur'ān calls on the believers to go forth in defense of those whose rights and liberty have been trampled by the unbridled tyranny of oppressors and conquering armies, or who are prevented from freely hearing the word of Allah espoused to them by preachers and educators. Allah says:

وَمَا لَكُمْ لاَ تُقَاتِلُونَ فِي سَبِيلِ اللّهِ وَالْمُسْتَضْعَفِينَ مِنَ الرِّجَالِ وَالنِّسَاء وَالْوِلْدَانِ الَّذِينَ يَقُولُونَ رَبَّنَا أَخْرِجْنَا مِنْ هَـذِهِ الْقَرْيَةِ الظَّالِمِ أَهْلُهَا وَاجْعَل لَّنَا مِن لَّدُنكَ وَلِيًّا وَاجْعَل لَّنَا مِن لَّدُنكَ نَصِيرًا

How should ye not fight for the cause of Allah and of the feeble among men and of the women and the children who are crying: "Our Lord! Bring us forth from out this town of which the people are oppressors! Oh, give us from Thy presence some protecting friend! Oh, give us from Thy presence some defender!"[513]

This verse gives two explanations, among other reasons for fighting:

1. Fighting in the cause of Allah, which is the intent the religion calls for until discord has vanished and the religion is practiced freely for Allah alone. This means

[513] Sūratu 'n-Nisā [Women], 4:75.

one cannot fight a Jihād against a country in which Muslims can freely practice their religion and teach Islam to others.

2. The second one is fighting for the sake of the weak, such as those who converted to Islām in Makkah, but were unable to undertake the migration to Madīnah. The Quraysh tortured them until they prayed to Allah for liberation. They had no means of protection from the persecution of the oppressors.

Allah permitted armed Jihād against an aggressor, where He said:

إِنَّ اللَّهَ اشْتَرَى مِنَ الْمُؤْمِنِينَ أَنفُسَهُمْ وَأَمْوَالَهُم بِأَنَّ لَهُمُ الْجَنَّةَ يُقَاتِلُونَ فِي سَبِيلِ اللَّهِ فَيَقْتُلُونَ وَيُقْتَلُونَ وَعْدًا عَلَيْهِ حَقًّا فِي التَّوْرَاةِ وَالإِنجِيلِ وَالْقُرْآنِ وَمَنْ أَوْفَى بِعَهْدِهِ مِنَ اللَّهِ فَاسْتَبْشِرُوا بِبَيْعِكُمُ الَّذِي بَايَعْتُم بِهِ وَذَلِكَ هُوَ الْفَوْزُ الْعَظِيمُ

Lo! Allah hath bought from the believers their lives and their wealth because the Garden will be theirs: they shall fight in the way of Allah and shall slay and be slain. It is a promise which is binding on Him in the Torah and the Gospel and the Qur'ān.[514]

So the rule of repelling aggression is not specifically for Muslims, but is the role of anyone following the Torah and the Gospel—the right to fight those who attack them. Giving one's self in Allah's Way, means repelling the aggressor. "*A promise binding on Him in truth*" means Allah took it on Himself as a right, not only in the Qur'ān but in the Torah and the Gospel, giving the believers the Garden of Paradise in exchange for their selves and their lives.

[514] Sūratu 't-Tawbah [Repentance], 9:111.

He said, *"Allah bought from the believers their lives and their wealth."* This also means to give one's wealth for building up society, for the welfare of others, for establishing hospitals, school and civic society.

CAN MUSLIMS FIGHT IF RELIGIOUS PRACTICE IS NOT PROSCRIBED?

Allah said:

لَا يَنْهَاكُمُ اللَّهُ عَنِ الَّذِينَ لَمْ يُقَاتِلُوكُمْ فِي الدِّينِ وَلَمْ يُخْرِجُوكُم مِّن دِيَارِكُمْ أَن
تَبَرُّوهُمْ وَتُقْسِطُوا إِلَيْهِمْ إِنَّ اللَّهَ يُحِبُّ الْمُقْسِطِينَ إِنَّمَا يَنْهَاكُمُ اللَّهُ عَنِ الَّذِينَ
قَاتَلُوكُمْ فِي الدِّينِ وَأَخْرَجُوكُم مِّن دِيَارِكُمْ وَظَاهَرُوا عَلَى إِخْرَاجِكُمْ أَن
تَوَلَّوْهُمْ وَمَن يَتَوَلَّهُمْ فَأُوْلَئِكَ هُمُ الظَّالِمُونَ

Allah forbids you not, with regard to those who fight you not for (your) Faith nor drive you out of your homes, from dealing kindly and justly with them: for Allah loveth those who are just.

Allah only forbids you, with regard to those who fight you for (your) Faith, and drive you out of your homes, and support (others) in driving you out, from turning to them (for friendship and protection). It is such as turn to them (in these circumstances), that do wrong.[515]

One sees here that Allah does not hinder the Muslims from dealing justly and kindly with those who do not fight them for their religion. Thus we see that Muslims today live in many non-Muslim nations, and they are living in peace, observing all their religious obligations and are free to practice their faith.

---

[515] Sūratu 'l-Mumtahina [She that is to be examined], 60:8,9.

Today one cannot find any nation in which mosques are forced to close, or the authorities are removing the Qur'ān or other religious books, or Muslims are prevented from praying, paying their poor-due, fasting or attending the pilgrimage. Instead we find that all Muslims today are free to practice their faith in every nation, around the globe.

On the contrary, we find that in non-Muslim universities Islamic texts are kept and preserved, including large troves of ancient manuscripts.

فَاحْكُم بَيْنَهُمْ بِالْقِسْطِ إِنَّ اللّهَ يُحِبُّ الْمُقْسِطِينَ

Judge between them with justice. Surely Allah loves those who are just.[516]

This shows that Islam urges the believers to practice goodness with those who are doing good to them, and thus they are not permitted to attack them.

وَإِنْ أَحَدٌ مِّنَ الْمُشْرِكِينَ اسْتَجَارَكَ فَأَجِرْهُ حَتَّى يَسْمَعَ كَلاَمَ اللّهِ ثُمَّ أَبْلِغْهُ مَأْمَنَهُ ذَلِكَ بِأَنَّهُمْ قَوْمٌ لاَّ يَعْلَمُونَ

If one amongst the Pagans ask thee for asylum, grant it to him, so that he may hear the word of Allah; and then escort him to where he can be secure. That is because they are men without knowledge.[517]

This also shows that even if unbelievers come to the Muslims, seeking to live and work in their nation for any reason, it is ordered to grant them safety and security to demonstrate the great care and compassion Islam takes in the care of others. Then such

---

[516] Sūratu 'l-Mā'idah [The Spread Table], 5:42.

[517] Sūratu 't-Tawbah [Repentance], 9:6.

are free to move where they like. This clarifies the understanding that combative Jihād is only against transgressors.

POSSIBILITY OF SUCCESS

Jihād against countries who are guilty of oppression and persecution only becomes compulsory after all political negotiations have failed, if the enemy is set on aggression. Additionally, the Muslims may fight when there is a likelihood of success. The state must make preparation of whatever is necessary from weapons, materials and men with the utmost possible scope as Allah says:

وَأَعِدُّواْ لَهُم مَّا اسْتَطَعْتُم مِّن قُوَّةٍ

Make ready for them all thou canst of (armed) force[518]

This means the leader must prepare and establish what is necessary of weapons, material and men with the utmost possible scope, as well as spending to the utmost from the nation's capability and expending every effort, for it is Allah's rule that without strength you cannot fight, or to do so would result in killing one's self and killing one's people and the creation of mayhem (*fitnah*), which in fact is worse than killing, where Allah says:

وَالْفِتْنَةُ أَشَدُّ مِنَ الْقَتْلِ

for tumult and oppression (fitnah) are worse than slaughter;[519]

Creating mayhem (*fitnah*) might grow to become a war or become a hate crime against innocent people. That is why Allah said it is worse than killing. *Fitnah* is the work of *munāfiqīn*, hypocrites. This is in fact conspiracy, the result of which may be a

---

[518] Sūratu 'l-Anfāl [The Spoils], 8:40.

[519] Sūratu 'l-Baqarah [The Heifer], 2:191.

great war instigated between one or more nations, which may end up in the death of thousand or millions of innocents.

الآنَ خَفَّفَ اللّهُ عَنكُمْ وَعَلِمَ أَنَّ فِيكُمْ ضَعْفًا فَإِن يَكُن مِّنكُم مِّئَةٌ صَابِرَةٌ يَغْلِبُواْ مِئَتَيْنِ

وَإِن يَكُن مِّنكُمْ أَلْفٌ يَغْلِبُواْ أَلْفَيْنِ بِإِذْنِ اللّهِ وَاللّهُ مَعَ الصَّابِرِينَ

Now Allah has lightened your [task] for He knows that there is weakness among you. So if there are of you a hundred steadfast person, they shall overcome two hundred, if there are a thousand of you, they shall overcome two thousand with the leave of Allah and Allah is with the patient.[520]

Thus Allah declared that if the ratio of Muslim warrior to their opponents is half (1:2) they may fight and they will be given Divine Support in an open fight facing the enemy directly, warrior-to- warrior. This was a reduction from the original ratio, in which the believers were obligated to fight even if the ratio of Muslims to their opponents was one to ten.

WITHOUT ADEQUATE FIGHTING CAPACITY SHOULD WAR BE INSTIGATED?

The above verse also means if there the enemy is twice the Muslim force, then there is no possibility of success and therefore at that time you must not set forth. To do so will create nothing but *fitnah*—a state of hostility and confusion.

Here the question arises: how can a group declare combative Jihād against an entire nation, when the group possesses no more than a few dozen or a few hundred dedicated warriors? If it is not permitted for 19 people to fight a group in excess of 38, what then about instigating war against a massively fortified and armed nation of over 250 million? This is in reality nothing more than

[520] Sūratu 'l-Anfāl [The Spoils], 8:66.

mayhem, and the result is endangerment of the entire Muslim Ummah. This is nothing but *fitnah*: confusion, sedition, disorder and mayhem, and the Prophet ﷺ declared those who create turmoil to be under Allah's curse:

The Prophet ﷺ said:

> Confusion/sedition/mayhem (*fitnah*) is dormant. Allah curses the one who rouses it.

Today's radicals justify combative Jihād without state authority by citing the skirmishes carried out by one of the Muslim converts against the Makkans. Renaissance's Shehzad Saleem explains:

> We know from history that after the treaty of Hudaybiyyah, Abū Basīr defected to Madīnah. According to the terms of the treaty he was duly returned back to the Quraysh by the Prophet ﷺ. He was sent back in the custody of two people of the Quraysh. He killed one of his two custodians and again defected to Madīnah. When he arrived in Madīnah, the Prophet ﷺ was angry with what he had done. Sensing that the Prophet ﷺ would once again return him to the Quraysh, he left Madīnah and settled at a place near Dhu'l-Marwah, where later on other people joined home. From this place, they would attack the caravans of the Quraysh.

If these guerrilla attacks are analyzed in the light of the Qur'ān, the basic thing which comes to light is that whatever Abū Basīr and his companions were doing was not sanctioned at all by Islam. The Qur'ān says that the actions and deeds of a person who has not migrated to Madīnah are not the responsibility of an Islamic state:

وَالَّذِينَ آمَنُوا وَلَمْ يُهَاجِرُوا مَا لَكُمْ مِنْ وَلَايَتِهِمْ مِنْ شَيْءٍ حَتَّى يُهَاجِرُوا

And as to those who believed but did not migrate [to Madīnah], you owe no duty of protection until they migrate. [521]

Not only did the Qur'ān acquit the newly founded Islamic state of Madīnah from the actions of these people, we even find the following harsh remarks of the Prophet ﷺ about Abū Basīr when he returned to Madīnah after killing one of his two custodians:

وَيْلُ أُمِّهِ مِسْعَرَ حَرْبٍ لَوْ كَانَ لَهُ

His mother is unfortunate! Though he has the right, he is going to ignite the flames of war.[522]

Is Islam by Nature Hostile to non-Muslims?

The idea, often postulated in the media, that Islam is hostile to non-Muslims simply because they are non-Muslims, is a major a misconception. According to the majority of scholars, beyond the conditions described above, there exists no valid reason to hold any hostility towards them. Sayyid Sābiq says:

The relationship of Muslims with non-Muslims is one of acquaintance, cooperation, righteousness and justice for Allah says:

يَا أَيُّهَا النَّاسُ إِنَّا خَلَقْنَاكُم مِّن ذَكَرٍ وَأُنثَى وَجَعَلْنَاكُمْ شُعُوباً وَقَبَائِلَ لِتَعَارَفُوا إِنَّ أَكْرَمَكُمْ عِندَ اللَّهِ أَتْقَاكُمْ إِنَّ اللَّهَ عَلِيمٌ خَبِيرٌ

O mankind! We created you from a single (pair) of a male and a female, and made you into nations and tribes, that ye may know each other (not that ye may despise (each other). Verily

---

[521] Sūratu 'l-Anfāl [The Spoils], 8:72.

[522] Bukhārī.

the most honoured of you in the sight of Allah is (he who is) the most righteous of you. And Allah has full knowledge and is well acquainted (with all things).[523]

And in advising righteousness and justice He says:

لَا يَنْهَاكُمُ اللَّهُ عَنِ الَّذِينَ لَمْ يُقَاتِلُوكُمْ فِي الدِّينِ وَلَمْ يُخْرِجُوكُم مِّن دِيَارِكُمْ أَن تَبَرُّوهُمْ

Allah does not forbid you from those who do not remove you from your homes (by force) and who do not fight you because of your religion, that you act kindly and justly towards them...[524]

Among the basics of this relationship is mutual, general well-being (or welfare) of a society and strengthening human relations.[525]

The reference in this verse is to the non-Muslims in general.

LOYALTY AND ENMITY (*AL-WALA WAL-BARA'A*)

Many of today's self-appointed Islamic leaders and scholars state:

> Enmity for the sake of God (*al-barā'a*) means to declare opposition in deed, to take up arms against His enemies...[526]

Sayyid Sābiq says:

> This meaning doesn't permit prevention of friendship with the non-Muslims. The prohibition exists when friendship with the non-Muslims is meant in aggression against the

[523] Sūratu 'l-Ḥujurāt [The Private Apartments], 49:13.
[524] Sūratu 'l-Mumtahina [She that is to be examined], 60:8.
[525] Sayyid as-Sābiq, *Fiqh as-Sunnah*.
[526] Muhammad Sā'īd al-Qahtānī , *Al-Walā wal-Barā'*, Translated by Omar Johnstone.

Muslims. Serious dangers to the existence of Islam come from assisting the non-Muslims who are [actively] working against the Muslims, weakening the power [and security] of the believing society.

As far as the relationship between the Muslims and non-Muslim subjects (*dhimmis*) living in Muslim nations, harmony, peace, with good manners and courtesy, friendly social intercourse, mutual welfare and cooperation for the sake of righteousness and good conscience are all that Islām calls for.

Even with regard to those who fought against the Muslims, despite their enmity, Allah says:

عَسَى اللَّهُ أَن يَجْعَلَ بَيْنَكُمْ وَبَيْنَ الَّذِينَ عَادَيْتُم مِّنْهُم مَّوَدَّةً وَاللَّهُ قَدِيرٌ وَاللَّهُ غَفُورٌ رَّحِيمٌ

It may be that Allah will grant love (and friendship) between you and those whom ye (now) hold as enemies. For Allah has power (over all things); And Allah is Oft-Forgiving, Most Merciful.[527]

Does Islam Call for Ongoing War against Non-Muslims?

Some Orientalists as well as some radical interpreters of Islam, assert that Islām condones an ongoing combative Jihād, that it means a continual war upon the non-Muslims until they repent and accept Islam or else pay the polltax. However the majority of Muslims scholars reject this view, citing as evidence:

وَإِنْ أَحَدٌ مِّنَ الْمُشْرِكِينَ اسْتَجَارَكَ فَأَجِرْهُ حَتَّى يَسْمَعَ كَلَامَ اللَّهِ ثُمَّ أَبْلِغْهُ مَأْمَنَهُ ذَلِكَ بِأَنَّهُمْ قَوْمٌ لَّا يَعْلَمُونَ

[527] Sūratu 'l-Mumtahina [She that is to be examined], 60:7.

...and if anyone of the polytheists seeks your protection then grant him protection, so that he may hear the Word of Allah, and then escort him to where he can be secure, that is because they are men who know not.[528][529]

The Imāms argued from this that as long as the condition that they are submissive and willing to live peacefully among the believers our divine obligation is to treat them peacefully, despite their denial of Islam. The succeeding verse:

فَمَا اسْتَقَامُواْ لَكُمْ فَاسْتَقِيمُواْ لَهُمْ إِنَّ اللّهَ يُحِبُّ الْمُتَّقِينَ

So long as they are true to you, stand you true to them. Verily! Allah loved those who fear Allah.[530]

This verse instructs the Muslims to observe treaty obligations with meticulous care, and not to break them unless the other side breaks them first.

Based on the clear arguments of the scholars from Qur'ān and hadith, the majority concluded that physical fighting is not a permanent condition against unbelievers, but only when treaties are broken or aggression has been made against Muslim territory (*dār al-Islām*) by unbelievers.

On the other hand, Educating non-Muslims about Islam is a continuous Jihād, per the agreed-upon, mass-transmitted hadith:

عن ابي هريرة، عن رسول الله صلى الله عليه وسلم قال: "امرت ان اقاتل الناس حتى يشهدوا ان لا اله الا الله. . .

The Messenger of Allah ﷺ said, "I have been ordered to fight the people until they declare that there is no god but

---

[528] Sūratu 't-Tawbah [Repentance], 9:6.
[529] The singular exception to this consensus being the opinion of Imām Shāfi'ī.
[530] Sūratu 't-Tawbah [Repentance], 9:7.

> Allah and that Muhammad is His Messenger, establish prayers, and pay poor-due..."[531]

In his book *al-Jihād fīl-Islām*, Dr. Saʿīd Ramaḍān Būṭi explains this hadith in detail based on the understanding of the majority of jurists, showing that linguistically the word "fight" here and in many other places does not refer to combat, rather to struggle, including in its scope *daʿwah*, preaching, exhortation and establishment of the state apparatus whereby Islamic preaching is protected. It does not mean forcing anyone to become Muslim at the point of a sword, and numerous examples can be cited from the life history of the Prophet ﷺ showing he never forced conversion, nor did his Successors.

Dr. Būṭi explains that the linguistic scholars of hadith showed that the word *uqātil* أقاتل used by the Prophet ﷺ in fact means "fight" and not *aqtul* أقتل "kill". In Arabic, this word is used in terms of defending against an attacker or an oppressor, it is not used to mean attack or assail.

In light of this, Dr. Būṭī shows that this hadith connotes:

> I have been ordered by Allah to fulfill the task of calling people [peacefully] to believe that God is One and to defend any aggression against this divine task, even though this defense requires fighting aggressors or enemies.[532]

Dr. Būṭī explains that this hadith is reminiscent of a saying by the Prophet ﷺ on the occasion of the Treaty of Hudaybiyyah:

وإن هم أبوا فوالذي نفسي بيده لأقاتلنهم على أمري هذا حتى تنفرد سالفتي ولينفذن الله أمره

[531] A mass-transmitted Ḥadīth narrated by Bukhārī, Muslim, Abū Dāwūd, Tirmidhī, an-Nasā'ī, Ibn Mājah from Abū Hurayrah.

[532] Muḥammad Saʿīd R. Al-Būṭī, *Jihād fīl-islām*, Dār al-Fikr, Beirut, 1995, p. 58.

> where he told his mediator, Badil ibn Warqa, "But if they do not accept this truce, by Allah in whose Hands my life is, I will fight with them, defending my Cause till I get killed."[533]

By these words, Badil ibn Warqa was tasked with inviting the Quraysh to peace, and simultaneously, warning of the ongoing war which had already exhausted them. Dr. Būṭī remarks:

> The Prophet's ﷺ words "I will fight with them defending my Cause," in this context certainly means that he, while inclining to peace with the enemy, would react to their combative aggression in the same way, if they had insisted on their aggression.[534]

Note also that in the years after the Treaty was signed, it was the Quraysh who violated the treaty. Near the end of the seventh year after migration, the Quraysh along with the allied Banī Bakr tribe, attacked the Banī Khuzaʿah tribe, who were allies of the Muslims. The Banī Khuzaʿah appealed to the Prophet ﷺ for help and protection.

The Banī Khuzaʿah sent a delegation to the Prophet ﷺ requesting his support. Despite this provocation and clear violation of the treaty, the Prophet ﷺ avoided acting in haste to renew hostilities. Instead he sent a letter to the Quraysh demanding payment of blood money for those killed, and a disbandment of their alliance with the Banī Bakr. Otherwise, the Prophet ﷺ said, the treaty would be declared null and void.

Quraysh then sent an envoy to Medina to announce that they considered the Treaty of Hudaybīyyah null and void. However they immediately regretted this step—and therefore the leader of Quraysh Abū Sufyān, himself traveled to Madīnah to renew the contract. Despite having been the greatest enemy of the Muslims,

---

[533] Bukhārī.

[534] Al-Būṭī, *Op. cit.*

and despite the Quraysh already being in violation of the pact they had solemnly entered into, no hand was laid on this Qurayshi chief—someone who infamous for his persecution and harm to Muslims in Makkah. He was even permitted to enter the Prophet's ﷺ mosque and announce his desire to reinstate the treaty.

From this, one can argue that if the state of unbelief were sufficient pretext for war, then the Prophet ﷺ would have been warranted in seizing Abū Sufyān and initiating hostilities against the Quraysh then and there. However, on the contrary, Abū Sufyān came and went from Madīnah freely and only after some time were the hostilities renewed based on the Makkans aggressive violation of the pact.

Allah says:

. . .وَقَاتِلُوا الْمُشْرِكِينَ كَافَّةً كَمَا يُقَاتِلُونَكُمْ كَافَّةً وَاعْلَمُوا أَنَّ اللَّهَ مَعَ الْمُتَّقِينَ

...and fight the mushrikūn, [polytheists Pagans] all together as they fight you all together. But know that Allah is with those who restrain themselves.[535]

Here we understand "*fight the unbelievers collectively as they fight you collectively*" means "treat them in the same way as they treat you." Commenting on this, Dr. Būṭī says, "You should deal with the unbelievers kindly and equitably, unless they are rampant and out to destroy us and our faith. Hence the motive for [combative] Jihād becomes self-defense."[536]

Finally Allah says:

فَإِنِ اعْتَزَلُوكُمْ فَلَمْ يُقَاتِلُوكُمْ وَأَلْقَوْا إِلَيْكُمُ السَّلَمَ فَمَا جَعَلَ اللَّهُ لَكُمْ عَلَيْهِمْ سَبِيلاً

[535] Sūratu 't-Tawbah [Repentance], 9:36.

[536] Muḥammad Saʿīd R. Al-Būṭī, *Jihād fīl-islām*, Dār al-Fikr, Beirut, 1995, p. 92.

So, if they hold aloof from you and wage not war against you and offer you peace, Allah alloweth you no way against them.[537]

This verse is referring to the people who were not among those people involved in fighting the Muslims and they stayed away from the battle between the two groups and this is what Islām calls for. We see here an explicit statement from Allah, that it is not permitted to fight with those who are not engaged in belligerency, despite their being non-believers in Islam.

WHO IS INVOLVED IN COMBAT?

COMMUNAL OBLIGATION

Let us begin with the most prevailing common understanding held by both Muslims and non-Muslims who are not Islamic scholars, that Jihād means war against unbelievers.

Combative Jihād is not an obligation on every individual among the Muslims, rather it's an communal obligation (*farḍ kifāyah*) fulfilled when some take on the duty to repel the enemy. Allah says:

وَمَا كَانَ الْمُؤْمِنُونَ لِيَنفِرُوا كَافَّةً فَلَوْلَا نَفَرَ مِن كُلِّ فِرْقَةٍ مِّنْهُمْ طَائِفَةٌ لِّيَتَفَقَّهُوا فِي
الدِّينِ وَلِيُنذِرُوا قَوْمَهُمْ إِذَا رَجَعُوا إِلَيْهِمْ لَعَلَّهُمْ يَحْذَرُونَ

And the believers should not all go out to fight. Of every troop of them, a party only should go forth, that they (who are left behind) may gain sound knowledge in religion, and that they may warn their folk when they return to them, so that they may beware[538]

---

[537] Sūratu 'n-Nisā [Women], 4:90.
[538] Sūratu 't-Tawbah [Repentance], 9: 122]

We see from this verse that Allah is showing that combative Jihād is not for everyone. If a group of people have been assigned to go for combative Jihād by their leader, the rest must not go. Rather their duty is to stay behind and study, in order to educate themselves and to educate others.

So from this verse, Allah split the people who participate in Jihād into two categories: One group goes to battle and the other stays behind to develop understanding of the religion in order to teach others. So even when combative Jihād has been called for, both those who go forth to combat and those who stay behind to develop understanding of religion are participants in Jihād. This verse makes those who stay behind and study the religion equal to those who go forth to battle, by saying: "their duty is to stay behind and study, in order to educate themselves and to educate others."

In this verse Allah emphasized that not all the believers should go out to fight. This indicates that there is a decision to be made: who will go to fight and who will not? This implies existence of leadership who must first decide if it is necessary to go for fighting or not. It is not the case that people from here and there may issue a call to go for fighting, which will result in nothing but anarchy.

Mu'adh ibn Jabal related:

Acquire knowledge because doing so is goodness, seeking it is worship, reviewing it is glorifying Allah and researching it is Jihād...[539]

From this we can see that to learn the religion becomes more important than participation in battle, for it will elaborate for you all the beliefs and the rulings of all that Muslims must do in this life. To understand the rulings of the religion, including those related to Jihād, is essential and can only be accomplished by

---

[539] Imām Ibn Rajab al-Ḥanbalī, *Warathatu'l-Anbiyā'*. Chapter 8, pgs. 37-38.

study and education. If someone has not studied comprehensively the rulings of Jihād, he will easily come to the conclusion that every issue that is raised entails combative Jihād, whereas this indeed is not the case.

CONSCRIPTION

Participation in combative Jihād becomes assigned to an individual when he is ordered by the leader to be present in the line of fire:

لاَ هِجْرَةَ، وَلَكِنْ جِهَادٌ وَنِيَّةٌ، وَإِذَا اسْتُنْفِرْتُمْ فَانْفِرُوا

> Hence the Messenger of Allah ﷺ said: "There is no migration (after the opening of Makkah), but Jihād and good intention. So when you are called to go forth in stopping aggression, then do so."[540]

This means when you are called out by your leader, and we have explained before who has the right to issue a declaration of war, the Imāmate leader, you must obey, as that is part of obedience to Allah, the Prophet ﷺ and those in authority. And the condition for such a declaration of war is when the enemy suddenly attacks a land. In that case combative Jihād is appointed on its inhabitants and they must go forth to defend their nation from aggression.

Along with this it is incumbent on any group who seek to fight as soldiers in the way of Allah against aggression by unbelievers, to firstly pledge themselves to their leader—someone who fits the profile of Imāmate from knowledge, piety and effectiveness—who organizes the army. Thereafter they organize their ranks, and prepare them to fight.

Setting forth when called is mandatory on the Muslim when: male; possesses sound reason; attained the age of maturity; is

[540] Bukhārī reported it from Ibn 'Abbās.

healthy and whose family possesses sufficient funds for what they need until he completes the duty assigned him by the leader.

Allah said, setting the rules for Jihād, *"and the believers should not all go out to fight"*[541]

The verse begins with that statement to emphasize that not every person goes forth to battle, and it goes on to explain that *"from every troop of them, a party only should go forth, that those who are left behind may gain some knowledge in religion and that they may warn their folk when they return tot hem that they may beware."*

Allah is showing that from every group, only a party of them goes forth. That means the army is to be taken from different citizens from various parts of the country, *"from every group of them,"* and today means volunteers or recruits who have been assigned and trained go forth to fight, while the rest of the citizens remain behind to train and educate themselves.

لَّيْسَ عَلَى الضُّعَفَاء وَلاَ عَلَى الْمَرْضَى وَلاَ عَلَى الَّذِينَ لاَ يَجِدُونَ مَا يُنفِقُونَ
حَرَجٌ إِذَا نَصَحُواْ لِلّهِ وَرَسُولِهِ

Not unto the weak nor unto the sick nor unto those who can find naught to spend is any fault (to be imputed though they stay at home) if they are true to Allah and His messenger.[542]

This verse means there is no obligation on those who have a weak personality, or a radical mentality, nor on those who have no talent, to go forth, for war will not be good for them. This indicates only those persons selected by the Ruler or his appointed leaders should go forth; not those who might commit rash actions because of excessive emotional zeal nor those who are

[541] Sūratu 't-Tawbah [Repentance], 9:122]
[542] Sūratu 't-Tawbah [Repentance], 9:91]

mentally ill and might commit crimes like the throwing of bombs, suicide attacks and so forth.

As Ibn Qayyim al-Jawzīyyah said in *Zād al-ma'ād*:

The Prophet ﷺ said:

المجاهد من جاهد نفسه في طاعة الله والمهاجر من هجر الخطايا والذنوب

The fighter is the one who fights himself in obedience to Allah and the one who emigrates is the one who emigrates from iniquities.[543]

The Jihād of the self is a prerequisite over the Jihād of the enemy in the open and initial basis for it.

Without a doubt, the one who didn't fight his self (or someone who does not do what he is commanded and does not leave what has been forbidden goes to battle in the way of Allah) it is not possible for him to make combative Jihād against the external enemy. How is this it possible for him to fight his [external] enemy, when his own enemy which is right beside him, dominates over him and commands him? So as he did not wage war on the [internal] enemy of Allah, it is even more impossible for him to set out against the enemy until he fights himself in order for departure.[544]

لَيْسَ عَلَى الْأَعْمَى حَرَجٌ وَلَا عَلَى الْأَعْرَجِ حَرَجٌ

There is no blame for the blind, nor is there blame for the lame, nor is there blame for the sick (that they go not forth to war).[545]

SURPRISE ATTACK

When the enemy suddenly arrives in a place which the Muslims reside, it is obligated for the inhabitants to go out

---

[543] Aḥmad recorded it in his *Musnad*, from Faḍālah bin Ubayd.

[544] Ibn Qayyim al-Jawzīyyah, *Zād al-Ma'ād.*

[545] Sūratu 'l-'Ankabūt [The Spider], 29:17.

and fight them and it is not allowed for anyone to be exempt from this obligation.

AGE REQUIREMENT

Ibn ʿUmar said, "I was presented to the Messenger of Allah ﷺ at the time of the battle of Uḥud when I was fourteen years of age, and he didn't give me permission to fight."

This is because Jihād is not obligated except on the one who has reached the appropriate age.

JIHAD OF WOMEN

ʿĀʾishā asked, "O Messenger of Allah ﷺ, is Jihād obligated for women?" He said, "Jihād without fighting. Ḥajj and ʿUmrah [are their Jihād]."[546]

Allah says:

وَلَا تَتَمَنَّوْا مَا فَضَّلَ اللَّهُ بِهِ بَعْضَكُمْ عَلَى بَعْضٍ لِلرِّجَالِ نَصِيبٌ مِمَّا اكْتَسَبُوا وَلِلنِّسَاءِ نَصِيبٌ مِمَّا اكْتَسَبْنَ وَاسْأَلُوا اللَّهَ مِنْ فَضْلِهِ إِنَّ اللَّهَ كَانَ بِكُلِّ شَيْءٍ عَلِيمًا

And covet not the thing in which Allah hath made some of you excel others. Unto men a fortune from that which they have earned, and unto women a fortune from that which they have earned. (Envy not one another) but ask Allah of His bounty. Lo! Allah is ever Knower of all things[547]

It is reported by ʿIkrimah ؓ that some women inquired about Jihād and other women said, "We wish that Allah grant us a

[546] Related by Muslim and Bukhārī.

[547] Sūratu 'n-Nisā [Women], 4:32.

portion of the reward the military expeditions receive from the reward of what the men share."

This does not prevent women from going out to treat the wounded.

It is reported that the Prophet ﷺ was out on a military expedition and Umm Salīm was with him and other women from the al-Anṣār. They were giving water to the fighters and treating the wounded.[548]

Parents' Permission

In the case of a major, obligatory combative Jihād, the parents' permission is not required, but as far as the voluntary combative Jihād, their permission is a must but from just one if the other has passed away.

Ibn Mas'ūd related:

I asked the Messenger of Allah ﷺ which action is most loved to Allah and he said, "Prayer in its time. Then I said, "then what," and he said, "Being good to your parents." Then I said, "what after that?" He said, "Jihād in the way of Allah."[549]

Ibn ʿUmar said:

A man came to the Prophet ﷺ and asked permission for combative Jihād and he said, "Are not your parents alive?" He said, "Yes." Then he said, "Then ask them first, then fight."[550]

One does not go out in Jihād except if he has completed providing for the needs of his family and the service of his parents. For this is the prerequisite of Jihād; even more it is the best Jihād.

---

[548] Muslim, Abū Dāwūd and at-Tirmidhī.
[549] Muslim and Bukhārī recorded it.
[550] Bukhārī, Abū Dāwūd, and an-Nisā'ī. at-Tirmidhī graded it sound.

JIHAD BETWEEN MUSLIMS

Properly speaking Jihād, in the case of internal dissension, only occurs when two conditions are met and the Muslims fight in support of the *Imām* against the offending parties:

1) a just leader (*Imām*)

2) fighting unjustifiable insurrection. In Islam allegiance and obedience to a just authority is obligatory.

It must be noted also that rebellions against authority and especially political authority simply for the sake of rebellion have no place in the concept of Jihād. In this age of relativism, the spirit of rebellion seems to have penetrated every layer of society. However, Islam and its principles cannot be made subservient to these cultural trends.

In some of the contemporary "Islamic" groups, Jihād has been adapted to a virtually Marxist or Socialist concept of class revolt aimed at overthrowing the authority of the state. In the often fervently materialistic milieu of contemporary political and revolutionary ideologies, Islam is inevitably reduced to nothing more than a social philosophy. This reductionism simply amounts to an abysmal misunderstanding of the essential function of Islam, which is to turn the "face" of the human receptacle away from the world of disharmony and illusion to the tranquility and silence of Divine awareness and vision. Inward Jihād, as we alluded to at the beginning of this presentation, has a key role to play in this respect.

SEEKING PEACE

The ruler, the political leader of the whole country, has the power to ratify peace treaties consistent with the interests of the Muslims.

Allah said:

يَا أَيُّهَا الَّذِينَ آمَنُواْ ادْخُلُواْ فِي السِّلْمِ كَآفَّةً وَلاَ تَتَّبِعُواْ خُطُوَاتِ الشَّيْطَانِ

Enter into peace completely and do not follow the steps of Satan. [551]

And:

وَإِن جَنَحُواْ لِلسَّلْمِ فَاجْنَحْ لَهَا وَتَوَكَّلْ عَلَى اللّهِ إِنَّهُ هُوَ السَّمِيعُ الْعَلِيمُ

And if they incline to peace, incline thou also to it, and trust in Allah.[552]

Sayyid Sābiq states:

This verse is the command to accept peace when the enemy accepts it, even if their acceptance is known to be beforehand to be deception and deceit.[553]

Allah says:

وَقَاتِلُوهُمْ حَتَّى لاَ تَكُونَ فِتْنَةٌ وَيَكُونَ الدِّينُ لِلّهِ فَإِنِ انتَهَواْ فَلاَ عُدْوَانَ إِلاَّ عَلَى الظَّالِمِينَ

And fight them on until there is no more tumult or oppression, and there prevail justice and faith in Allah; but if they cease, Let there be no hostility except to those who practice oppression.[554]

From this verse we see that fighting is exhorted until oppression is ended. Thus with the words, *"but if they cease,"* Allah legislates that once justice prevails and no one is prevented from observing their belief in Allah, then fighting should end. Allah grants that arms be set aside, *"except to those who practice oppression."*

---

[551] Sūratu 'l-Baqarah [The Heifer], 2:208.

[552] Sūratu 'l-Anfāl [The Spoils], 8: 60.

[553] Sayyid Sābiq, *Fiqh as-Sunnah*.

[554] Sūratu 'l-Baqarah [The Heifer], 2:193.

وَقَاتِلُوهُمْ حَتَّى لَا تَكُونَ فِتْنَةٌ وَيَكُونَ الدِّينُ كُلُّهُ لِلّه فَإِنِ انتَهَوْاْ فَإِنَّ اللّهَ بِمَا يَعْمَلُونَ بَصِيرٌ

And fight them on until there is no more tumult or oppression, and there prevail justice and faith in Allah altogether and everywhere; but if they cease, verily Allah doth see all that they do. [555]

Thus peace is not only permitted but called for, after the adversary, even if still inimical, ceases its aggression. However precaution and watchfulness is not to be abandoned in this situation, for here Allah reminds the Muslims of His Own Attribute, *"verily Allah doth see all that they do."*

The Prophet ﷺ said, after establishing the Islamic state in Madīnah, that the way of the Muslims is one. No single group can autonomously declare war or fight, nor can any one group make peace by itself, but the entire country must make peace. A peace treaty can be made by the country's leader and all subjects of the country are bound by that decision, regardless of whether the leader was appointed or elected. The final decision is up to the ruler after his consultation with others.

If a state has no leader then it must select one, or all the neighboring states and nations must come together and agree on a treaty with any foreign country. This applies today in the case of the Middle East Crisis. This applies as much to peace as it does to war. No individual or group may come forth and declare a Jihād: such will be a false Jihād. All Muslim nations and their leaders must come together for a decision of war or peace and that is the only accepted process.

It is imperative to keep in mind that all such verses were revealed a specific times pertaining to specific historical events.

[555] Sūratu 'l-Anfāl [The Spoils], 8:39.

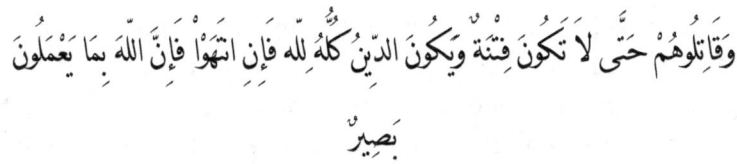

Our concern today is that radical extremists employ these verses outside their proper historical and revelatory context, merely cutting and pasting together what suits their evil inclinations, without accurate or sufficient knowledge of the applicability or otherwise of such verses.

TAXATION

Ibn Qudāma said that a treaty of peace involves agreeing with combatant non-Muslims for an end to hostility for a period of time, whether it involves paying a tax or not. He asserted that Muslims are allowed to make peace treaties that do not require non-Muslims to pay a tax, because the Prophet ﷺ of Allah did so on the occasion of the Hudaybīyya Treaty. Ibn Qudāma says that Imām Aḥmad gave this opinion as did Imām Abū Ḥanīfa.[556]

CONDUCT OF COMBAT

PROHIBITION OF KILLING NON-COMBATANTS

Islam prohibits utterly the killing of those who are not actual military personnel.

حدثنا عثمان بن أبي شيبة حدثنا يحيى بن آدم وعبيد الله بن موسى عن حسن بن صالح عن خالد بن الفزر حدثني أنس بن مالك أن رسول الله صلى الله عليه وسلم قال انطلقوا باسم الله وبالله وعلى ملة رسول الله ولا تقتلوا شيخا فانيا ولا طفلا ولا صغيرا ولا امرأة ولا تغلوا وضموا غنائمكم وأصلحوا وأحسنوا إن الله يحب المحسنين ﴿وَأَحْسِنُوا إِنَّ اللَّهَ يُحِبُّ الْمُحْسِنِينَ﴾

[556] Ibn Qudāma, *al-Mughnī*, vol. 12, pp. 691-693.

The Prophet ﷺ sent the following message to his military leaders who were setting forth in the way of Jihād to stop hostile advances and defend Muslim territories:

Advance in the name of Allah, with Allah, on the pattern of the Messenger of Allah ﷺ. That means do not to kill the elderly, infants or children and women. Do not exceed the proper bounds. Gather your spoils and make peace وَأَحْسِنُوا إِنَّ اللَّهَ يُحِبُّ الْمُحْسِنِينَ *"and do good. Lo! Allah loveth those who do good."*[557] [558]

حدثنا أبو الوليد الطيالسي حدثنا عمر بن المرقع بن صيفي بن رباح قال رباح بن ربيع قال كنا مع رسول الله صلى الله عليه وسلم في غزوة فرأى الناس مجتمعين على شيء فبعث رجلا فقال انظر علام اجتمع هؤلاء فجاء فقال على امرأة قتيل فقال ما كانت هذه لتقاتل قال وعلى المقدمة خالد بن الوليد فبعث رجلا فقال قل لخالد لا يقتلن امرأة ولا عسيفا

The Prophet ﷺ passed by a woman who was killed and said, "She was not engaged in fighting." The Prophet ﷺ then sent to the Muslim leader Khālid ibn al-Walīd the following message, "The Prophet ﷺ orders you not to kill women or servants."[559]

---

[557] Sūratu 'l-Baqarah [The Heifer], 2:195.

[558] Abū Dāwūd narrated it in his *Sunan* from Anas bin Mālik ؓ.

[559] Narrated in the *Sunan* of Abū Dāwūd *from Rābiḥ ibn Rabiʿ*, and Aṭ-Ṭabārī narrated a similar tradition in his *al-Awsaṭ* from Ibn ʿUmar ؓ. Similar narrations are related in Ibn Mājah, and Aḥmad from Hanzalah.

This was to show the reason in the prohibition of killing her was due to the fact she was not with the fighters. The inference here is "the reason we fight them, is because they fight us, not on the simple principle that they are disbelievers." This is clear evidence the woman was not a fighter and the Prophet ﷺ prohibited her killing. From the strong expression the Prophet ﷺ made, going so far as to send a letter to his topmost military commander, we see how concerned he was to prevent any such incidents, and to insure that every single Muslim warrior was aware of the rules of combat.

The question arises here: when someone explodes a bomb or commits a suicide attack in a public place, how many innocent women, children and elderly people are killed? If for one woman's death, the Prophet ﷺ scolded his top general, Khālid ibn al-Walīd, what then about killing twenty, thirty or even hundreds of non-combatants, some of whom may even be Muslim?

Just as the Messenger of Allah ﷺ forbade the killing of women and the young he forbade killing priests.

> The first caliph Sayyidina Abū Bakr aṣ-Ṣiddīq's commandment to the leader of the first Islamic military expedition after the Prophet ﷺ was:
>
> ...No hermit should be molested...Only those should be killed who take up arms against you.[560]
>
> So we see from these various narrations of the Prophet ﷺ—and there are many more like them—that the Prophet ﷺ prohibited the Muslims to fight anyone, Muslim or non-Muslim, even if they are unbelievers, if they are not transgressors against the security of the nation.

This shows that terrorist acts, in particular suicide attacks which kill indiscriminately, are utterly unacceptable forms of

[560] Cited in *Tārīkh aṭ-Ṭabarī*, vol. 3, pp. 226-227.

combat, even during valid combat authorized for defense of the nation.

PROHIBITION OF BURNING THE ENEMY

أن رسول الله صلى الله عليه وسلم أمره على سرية قال فخرجت فيها وقال إن وجدتم فلانا فأحرقوه بالنار فوليت فناداني فرجعت إليه فقال إن وجدتم فلانا فاقتلوه ولا تحرقوه فإنه لا يعذب بالنار إلا رب النار

It is prohibited to burn the enemy with fire because the Messenger ﷺ said, "Kill [the enemy] but do not burn him. For no one punishes with fire except the Lord of the Fire."[561]

This hadith illustrates the Prophet's emphasis on mercy and avoidance of harm when he established such laws of conduct on the battlefield. In modern times only were such rules of warfare established, as the Geneva Convention, in which it is impermissible to kill or torture prisoners of war. Similarly, we see that 1400 years ago, the Prophet ﷺ established details rules of warfare in which even using fire in combat was prohibited, something which modern legislators of warfare have been loathe to adopt.

According to this hadith, weapons of fire are not approved by Allah. Allah prohibited burning, yet the majority of attacks by Islamic groups today involve bombs and explosions, such as the attacks on the World Trade Center on 9/11, where 3,000 people were incinerated.

---

[561] Abū Dāwūd narrated it in his *Sunan,* from Muḥammad bin Ḥamzah al-Aslamī ؓ from his father ؓ.

PROHIBITION OF MUTILATING THE DEAD

كان نبي الله صلى الله عليه وسلم يحثنا على الصدقة وينهانا عن المثلة فأتيت
عمران بن حصين فسألته فقال كان رسول الله صلى الله عليه وسلم يحثنا على
الصدقة وينهانا عن المثلة .

Imrān bin Ḥuṣayn said the Messenger of Allah ﷺ encouraged us to give charity and forbade us from mutilation.[562]

PROHIBITION OF DESPOILING

Abū Bakr aṣ-Ṣiddīq commanded the leader of the first Islamic military expedition after the Prophet ﷺ saying:

...No fruit-bearing trees are to be cut down and no crops should be set on fire. No animal should be killed except those slaughtered for eating...Only those should be killed who take up arms against you.[563]

SUICIDE ATTACKS

One of Islam's fundamental principles is the sanctity of life. Islam prohibits killing those who are not combatants, except those involved in a direct battle face-to-face between warriors. There is simply no room for maneuver in Islam to justify the killing of innocents, even as a form of mass retribution, which many radicals today use as justification for their large-scale attacks on civilians. For Islam prohibits blood feud and specifies retribution only towards the one who committed a crime.

Allah says:

---

[562] Narrated in Bukhārī.

[563] Cited in *Tārīkh aṭ-Ṭabarī*, vol. 3, pp. 226-227.

وَلَا تَقْتُلُوا النَّفْسَ الَّتِي حَرَّمَ اللّهُ إِلاَّ بِالْحَقِّ

Slay not the life which Allah has made sacrosanct unless it be in a just cause.[564]

وَمَن يَقْتُلْ مُؤْمِنًا مُّتَعَمِّدًا فَجَزَآؤُهُ جَهَنَّمُ خَالِدًا فِيهَا وَغَضِبَ اللّهُ عَلَيْهِ وَلَعَنَهُ

وَأَعَدَّ لَهُ عَذَابًا عَظِيمًا

And whoever kills a believer intentionally, his recompense is Hell to abide therein, and the Wrath and the Curse of Allah are upon him, and a great punishment is prepared for him, [565]

Since no one can say for sure "this person is not a believer" it becomes forbidden to kill any human being without just cause.

Suicide itself is specifically prohibited in:

وَلَا تَقْتُلُوا أَنفُسَكُمْ إِنَّ اللّهَ كَانَ بِكُمْ رَحِيمًا

Kill yourselves not, for Allah is truly merciful to you.[566]

and:

وَلَا تُلْقُوا بِأَيْدِيكُمْ إِلَى التَّهْلُكَةِ وَأَحْسِنُوَا

Throw not yourselves into the mouth of danger.[567]

Thus we see the general principle enunciated here that killing oneself is forbidden. The Qur'ān did not leave anything without an explanation. This is a general principle that no one is permitted to kill another or to kill himself.

---

[564] Sūratu 'l-An'am [Cattle], 6:151.

[565] Sūratu 'n-Nisā [Women], 4:93.

[566] Sūratu 'n-Nisā [Women], 4:29.]

[567] Sūratu 'l-Baqarah [The Heifer], 2:195.

KILLING NON-COMBATANTS

The one who attacks the enemy in repelling his aggression, fighting under the authorized leader of the Muslims, and fights and is killed becomes a martyr (*shahīd*). But to attack a public location where the ones killed are killed randomly without knowing if they are combatants or not, is forbidden.

Today's militant radical Islamists cite a ruling by the Shafi'ī scholar al-Mawardī in which he stated that when involved in combative Jihād, if the enemy has mixed non-combatants among warriors either by chance or intentionally as "human shields" then Muslim archers are allowed to fire on the enemy, despite the fact that due to the randomness of shooting, non-combatants might die. Spinning off this, they argue that this ruling justifies bomb attacks against civilian areas.

This is nothing but a twisting of the law to suit their purposes. This ruling is very specific in that it allows such attacks on the assumption that it is the combatants that are targeted by the archers, not the civilians, who only happen to be present or, in the worst case, have been placed as "human shields." The assumption of the jurist is also that the Muslims and the enemy are engaged in face-to-face fighting, between combatants. However, the attacks carried out by such militants in fact do not target combatants: rather they are typically placed in public locations more frequented by civilians, including innocent women, children and non-military persons.

In Islamic law, one cannot build a case on doubtful assumptions, such as "those people are likely all engaged in fighting Muslims." Such an argument is false and the result is the killing of innocent without justification.

PROHIBITION OF SUICIDE

Islam utterly forbids suicide.

عن عمران بن حصين قال: قال رسول الله صلى الله عليه وسلم:"من قتل نفسه بشيء في الدنيا عذب به في الآخرة".

On this the Prophet ﷺ said:
Whoever killed himself in the world with anything, then Allah will punish him by that same thing on the Day of Judgment.[568]

... جندب بن عبد الله في هذا المسجد ... قال قال رسول الله صلى الله عليه وسلم كان فيمن كان قبلكم رجل به جرح فجزع فأخذ سكينا فحز بها يده فما رقأ الدم حتى مات قال الله تعالى بادرني عبدي بنفسه حرمت عليه الجنة

The Prophet ﷺ said:
Among those who were before you, there was a man who was inflicted with wounds. He felt despair, so he took a knife and with it he cut his hand; blood kept flowing until the man died. Allah the Exalted said, "My slave has caused death on himself hurriedly; I forbid Paradise to him."[569]

حدثنا حبَّان بن موسى: أخبرنا عبد الله: أخبرنا معمر، عن الزُهري، عن سعيد بن المسيَّب، عن أبي هريرة رضي الله عنه قال: شهدنا مع رسول الله صلى الله عليه وسلم خيبر، فقال رسول الله صلى الله عليه وسلم لرجل ممن معه يدَّعي الإسلام: (هذا من أهل النار). فلما حضر القتال قاتل الرجل من أشد القتال، وكثرت به الجراح فأثبته، فجاء رجل

---

568 Reported by Abū Awānah in his *Mustakhraj* from the Ḥadīth of Thābit bin ad-Daḥāk. A similar Ḥadīth is reported by Abū 'Umrān by al-Bazzār but its chain contains Isḥāq ibn Idrīs who is "discarded."

569 Bukhārī.

من أصحاب النبي صلى الله عليه وسلم فقال: يا رسول الله، أرأيت الذي تحدثت أنه من أهل النار، قد قاتل في سبيل الله من أشد القتال، فكثرت به الجراح، فقال النبي صلى الله عليه وسلم: (أما إنه من أهل النار) . فكاد بعض المسلمين يرتاب، فبينما هو على ذلك إذ وجد الرجل ألم الجراح، فأهوى بيده إلى كنانته فانتزع منها سهما فانتحر بها، فاشتد رجال من المسلمين إلى رسول الله صلى الله عليه وسلم فقالوا: يا رسول الله صدَّق الله حديثك، قد انتحر فلان فقتل نفسه، فقال رسول الله صلى الله عليه وسلم: (يا بلال، قم فأذِّن: لا يدخل الجنة إلا مؤمن، وإن الله ليؤيِّد هذا الدين بالرجل الفاجر

Narrated Abū Hurayra:
We were in the company of Allah's Messenger ﷺ on an expedition, and he remarked about a man who claimed to be a Muslim, saying, "This (man) is from the people of the (Hell) Fire." When the battle started, the man fought violently till he got wounded. Somebody said, "O Allah's Apostle! The man whom you described as being from the people of the (Hell) Fire fought violently today and died." The Prophet ﷺ said, "He will go to the (Hell) Fire." Some people were on the point of doubting (the truth of what the Prophet ﷺ had said) while they were in this state, suddenly someone said that he was still alive but severely wounded. When night fell, he lost patience and committed suicide. The Prophet ﷺ was informed of that, and he said, "Allah is Greater! I testify that I am Allah's Slave and His Apostle." Then he ordered Bilāl to announce amongst the people: 'None will enter Paradise but a Muslim, and Allah may support this religion (i.e. Islam) even with a disobedient man.'

عن أبي هريرة . . .أن رسول الله صلى الله عليه وسلم قال من قتل نفسه بحديدة فحديدته في يده يتوجأ بها في بطنه في نار جهنم خالدا مخلدا فيها أبدا ومن قتل نفسه بسم فسمه في يده يتحساه في نار جهنم خالدا مخلدا فيها أبدا ومن تردى من جبل فقتل نفسه فهو يتردى في نار جهنم خالدا

The Prophet ﷺ said:
Whoever throws himself down from a high mountain and kills himself will be throwing himself down from a mountain in the Fire of Hell for all eternity. Whoever takes poison and kills himself will be taking poison in the Fire of Hell for all eternity. Whoever kills himself with a weapon (literally, iron) will be holding it in his hand and stabbing himself in the stomach in the Fire of Hell for all eternity).[570]

The Prophet ﷺ said:
Indeed, whoever (intentionally) kills himself, then certainly he will be punished in the Fire of Hell, wherein he shall dwell forever.[571]

أخبرنا اسحق بن منصور قال أنبأنا أبو الوليد قال حدثنا أبو خيثمة زهير قال حدثنا سماك عن أبي سمرة:–أن رجلا قتل نفسه بمشاقص فقال رسول الله صلى الله عليه وسلم أما أنا فلا أصلي عليه

A person [engaged in battle] killed himself with a broad-headed arrow. The Messenger of Allah ﷺ said, "As for me, I will not pray over him."

---

[570] Reported by al-Bukhārī, 5778.
[571] Bukhārī (5778) and Muslim (109 and 110).

Even the mufti of the most fundamentalist school of law in Islam, the "Wahhabi/Salafi" school of thought, declared that suicide bombings have never been an accepted method of fighting in Islam. The Mufti of Saudi Arabia, Shaykh ʿAbd Al-ʿAzīz Āl-Shaikh declared, "To my knowledge so-called 'suicide missions' do not have any legal basis in Islam and do not constitute a form of Jihād. I fear that they are nothing but a form of suicide, and suicide is also prohibited in Islam." This echoes an earlier *fatwā* by his predecessor, the late Saudi mufti Shaykh ʿAbd Al-ʿAzīz bin Bāz.

Like the suicide attackers of September 11th, those who commit such atrocities in the name of religion are wrong. They can find no support for their actions in our creed. Nor can those who explode themselves and others indiscriminately in shopping centers, theaters or houses of worship find any justification in the faith's pristine teachings.

One justification the terrorists make is the following account from the life of the Prophet ﷺ in which the Prophet's paternal cousin az-Zubayr ibn al-ʿAwwām, was participating in a battle against the Byzantine Army. Az-Zubayr said to a group of Muslim soldiers, "Who will promise to go with me and fight our way through the enemy lines until we reach the end of their lines, then go around their camp back to our current position?" A group of fighters said, "we promise." Az-Zubayr lead a group of fighters and fought their way through many enemy lines until they reached the end of the Roman camp. They then went around the Roman camp and returned to the Muslim army.

The logic the terrorists use is that they were certain to die and thus committed suicide while fighting the enemy. In fact az-Zubayr did not tell his companions "let us kill ourselves," especially before going on this challenging task. He only exposed himself and them to what is commonly expected in any form of warfare—the probability of being killed by the enemy. He did not intend to die, but to fight, and with Allah's support to win, else to die by the enemy's hand. This is not suicide, rather it is bravery and heroism. Thus the terrorists' "logic" is shown for what it is, illogical.

Islam has always required perfect chivalry and discipline. For that reason, soldiers are ordered to endure and fight even in the face of tremendous odds. The Islamic rules of military conduct never permit using civilians as targets or as hostages. In Islam, even so-called "collateral damage" is unacceptable. Therefore, if a Muslim kills himself, along with innocents, it is a doubly forbidden act.

Shaykh Yūsuf al-Qaradāwī issued a *fatwā* condemning the tragic suicide attacks of 9-11, stating:

> Even in times of war, Muslims are not allowed to kill anybody save the one who is indulged in face-to-face confrontation with them." He added that they are not allowed to kill women, old persons, or children, and that haphazard killing is totally forbidden in Islam. Shaykh Qaradāwī on another occasion defined terrorism as "the killing of innocent people...with no differentiation between the innocent and the foe.

Another widely followed religious scholar, As-Sayyid Tantāwī, Grand Shaykh of Islam's highest institution of learning, the University of Al-Azhar, has said that attacks against women and children are "not accepted by Islamic law." Al-Azhar's Research Academy, shortly after September 11, declared that a "Muslim should only fight those who fight him; children, women and the elderly must be spared." Therefore terrorism and its crime against civilians is impermissible under any interpretation of Islamic law. This ruling does not change based on geographical locality.

The Prophet ﷺ said:

> ...Whoever fights under the banner of a people whose cause is not clear, who gets flared up with family pride, calls people to fight in the cause of their family honor or fights to support his kith and kin, and is killed, then he dies in a state of *jāhilīyyah*.
>
> Whoever indiscriminately attacks my Ummah, killing the righteous and wicked among them, sparing not even those firm in faith, and fulfilling not a pledge made with whoever was given a promise of security, has nothing to do with me and I have nothing to do with him.[572]

This shows us very clearly, that those who indiscriminately attack both Muslims and non-Muslims by suicide bombings, killing innocent people, and without focusing on anyone in particular, are rejected completely by the Prophet ﷺ. Such is the case in many Muslim countries today, including the land of Hijaz, Pakistan, Darfur, Egypt, Algeria, Iraq and so forth. What is taking place in these nations today is clearly are described in this hadith, "Whoever indiscriminately attacks my Ummah, killing the righteous and wicked among them, sparing not even those firm in faith."

Emphasis in this hadith on "fulfilling not the pledge made with whoever was given a promise of security" is reference to those citizens who keep their civic obligations by paying taxes and pledging their allegiance to the government. Thus both Muslim and non-Muslim citizens are encompassed in the scope of meaning of this hadith, and as for those who aggress against them, "he has nothing to do with" the Prophet ﷺ and the Prophet ﷺ has "nothing to do with him."

If someone asks, "What about suicide bombings against non-Muslims?"

We say: "This is utterly wrong."

---

[572] Muslim.

FALSE RULINGS SUPPORTING SUICIDE ATTACKS

Often those who justify suicide attacks cite as evidence the story of the Companion al-Baraʿ ibn Mālik at the Battle of Yamāma, in which the Muslims fought Musaylima the Liar, who had begun the war by attacking the Muslims.

> The Muslims gained ground against the idolaters the day of Yamāma until they cornered them in a garden in which Musaylima was staying. Al-Baraʿ ibn Mālik said: "O Muslims, throw me to them!" He was carried aloft until when he was above the wall, he penetrated [the enclosure]. Then he fought them inside the garden until he opened it for the Muslims and the Muslims entered. Then Allah killed Musaylima.
>
> Al- Baraʿ threw himself onto them and fought them until he opened the gate after having received more than eighty cuts. Then he was carried away and tended. Khālid [ibn al-Walīd] visited him for a month.[573]

The Companion threw himself into the ranks of the enemy, in order to throw open the fortress' door, knowing full well that he would likely be killed in the process.

Studying this analogy, one finds that it is not relevant, for in the incident cited the two combatant armies were fighting face-to-face. In the process he did not kill innocent people. He threw himself with the intention of either opening the door or dying in the attempt. In fact his death was expected at the hands of the enemy, not by his own action. And this, like the earlier example of az-Zubayr ibn al-ʿAwwām, is exemplary of chivalry and bravery, not of intent to commit suicide.

[573] The first narration is by Bāqi ibn Makhlad in his *Musnad* narrated from Ibn Isḥāq. The second is from Thumama, from Anas. Both are cited by Hāfiẓ Ibn Ḥajar in *al-Iṣāba fī tamyiz al-ṣaḥāba,* Vol. 1 p. 279-280.

Suicide bombings are something in which innocent people are killed, some might even be supporters of one's cause, while others are innocent. Thus this example does not apply. Such an act on the contrary is not suicidal; it is an act of bravery which is accepted in every nation and culture.

This means that whoever goes on his own and declares his own rulings, independent of the ruler of the Muslim Nation, falls under the label of *Jāhilīyyah* – pre-Islamic ignorance and unbelief. Such a person establishes his own group and his own false rulings on fighting, causing all the people to fall into tribulations due to his aggression.

This hadith demonstrates the Prophet's emphatic opposition to those who would declare a false combative Jihād. This 1400 year-old hadith is also a very clear prediction by the Prophet ﷺ, that a people will arise who will create havoc and confusion, who are arrogant and proud of themselves, and who despite appearances, are in fact fighting for the sake of their families and tribes. And this is not Jihād by any means but in fact falsifies the concept of Jihād totally.

Here we see the Prophet ﷺ extended shelter to a combatant pagan who was promised shelter by a Muslim woman. How then are we allowing today's beheadings of those people who are working to help stability and bringing provision and supporting human rights in Iraq. They take innocent people and behead them, people who have been given shelter by the existing government and they are non-combatants.

"Whoever indiscriminately attacks my Nation killing the righteous and the wicked among them, and fulfilling not a pledge made with whoever was given a promise of security, has nothing to do with me and I have nothing to do with him."

This portion of the hadith makes it abundantly clear that if someone attacks a person whose safety has been pledged by the nation's government to uphold, the Prophet ﷺ is abandoning the attacker and dissociating himself from him. For the believer, nothing could be more distressing than for the Prophet ﷺ to abandon him.

PRISONERS OF WAR

In regard to prisoners of war, Allah says:

حَتَّى إِذَا أَثْخَنتُمُوهُمْ فَشُدُّوا الْوَثَاقَ فَإِمَّا مَنًّا بَعْدُ وَإِمَّا فِدَاءً حَتَّى تَضَعَ الْحَرْبُ أَوْزَارَهَا

At length, when ye have thoroughly subdued them, bind a bond firmly (on them): thereafter (is the time for) either generosity or ransom: Until the war lays down its burdens.[574]

قال الرسول : يا ام هاني اجرنا من اجرتي

It was related from Umm Hānī bint Abī Ṭālib ﵃, who said to the Prophet ﷺ, "My brother ʿAlī said he will kill a person to whom I gave shelter, so-and-so son of Hubayra," who was a combatant pagan at that time. The Prophet ﷺ said, "We shelter the person whom you have sheltered."[575]

In a similar vein, the hadith where the Prophet ﷺ said:

He who gives a promise of safety to a man in regards to his life, then kills him, I am innocent of the actions of the killer, even if the one killed was a disbeliever.

It is established that the Prophet ﷺ captured prisoners yet never did he compel or force anyone to embrace Islām. The same holds true for his Companions.

---

[574] Sūrah Muḥammad, 47:4.

[575] Bukhārī and Muslim.

The Companions of the Messenger of Allah ﷺ used to ransom captives and rejected killing them saying, "What would we gain from killing them?"

REBELLION AGAINST RULERS

The scholar Ibn Nujaym said, "it is not permitted for there to be more than one state leader (*Imām*) in a time period. There may be many judges, even in one state, but the leader is one."[576] Al-Bahjūri said, "It is an obligation to obey the leader, even if he is not fair or trustworthy or even if he committed sins or mistakes."[577] Abū Ḥanifa's school says that the head of the state, the Imām, cannot be expelled for being a corrupt person (*fāsiq*).[578]

Al-Bahjūrī

Al-Bahjūrī said, "... you have to obey the Ruler even if he is oppressive."

This means that a group or individual are not permitted to declare war against the ruler of a nation, especially by means of terrorizing the people through planting bombs, and suicide attacks which kill innocents and incite mayhem.

And in his explanation of *Saḥīḥ Muslim* al-Bahjūrī said, "...it is forbidden to come against the ruler,"[579]

Amin Ahsan Islahi

While commenting on the underlying reasons which form the basis of state authority for combative Jihād, Amīn Aḥsān Iṣlāḥī writes:

> The first reason [for this condition] is that Allah Almighty does not like the dissolution and disintegration of even an

---

[576] Ibn al-Nujūm *Al-Ashbāh wal-nadhā'ir*, p. 205

[577] Al-Baḥjūrī, *Sharḥ Saḥīḥ Muslim*, vol. 2, p. 259.

[578] Imām Abū Ḥanīfa, *Sharḥ al-aqā'id an-nasafiyya*, p.180-181.

[579] Al-Baḥjūrī, *Hashiyyat al-Baḥjūrī 'ala sharḥ al-ghizzī*, vol. 259.

evil system until a strong probability exists that those who are out to disintegrate the system will provide people with an alternative and a righteous system. Anarchy and disorder are unnatural conditions. In fact, they are so contrary to human nature that even an unjust system is preferable to them....this confidence [that a group will be able to harmonize a disintegrated system and integrate it into a united whole] can be reposed in such a group only as has actually formed a political government and has such control and discipline within the confines of its authority that the group can be termed as *al-Jama'ah* [the State]. Until a group attains this position, it may strive [by religiously allowable means] to become *al-Jama'ah* – and that endeavor would be its Jihād for that time – but it does not have the right to wage an 'armed' Jihād.

The second reason is that the import of power which a group engaged in war acquires over the life and property of human beings is so great that the sanction to wield this power cannot be given to a group the control of whose leader over his followers is based merely on his spiritual and religious influence on them [rather than being based on legal authority]. When the control of a leader is based merely on his spiritual and religious influence, there is not sufficient guarantee that the leader will be able to stop his followers from *fasād fi'l-arḍ* (creating disorder in the society). Therefore, a religious leader does not have the right to allow his followers to take out their swords (that is to wage an armed struggle) merely on the basis of his spiritual influence over them, for once the sword is unsheathed there is great danger that it will not care for right and wrong and that those who drew it will end up doing all [the wrong which] they had sought to end. Such radical groups as desire revolution and the object of whom is nothing more than disruption of the existing system and deposition of the ruling party to seize power for themselves play such games – and they can, for in their eyes disruption of a system is no calamity, nor is it cruelty or any kind an evil. Everything is right to them [as long as it serves their purpose].[580]

يَكُونُ بَعْدِي أَئِمَّةٌ لا يَهْتَدُونَ بِهُدَايَ، وَلاَ يَسْتَنُّونَ بِسُنَّتِي، وَسَيَقُومُ فِيهِمْ رِجَالٌ قُلُوبُهُمْ قُلُوبُ الشَّيَاطِينِ فِي جُثْمَانِ إِنْسٍ" .

قَالَ: قُلْتُ: كَيْفَ أَصْنَعُ؟ يَا رَسُولَ اللهِ إِنْ أَدْرَكْتُ ذَلِكَ؟ قَالَ: "تَسْمَعُ وَتُطِيعُ لِلأَمِيرِ، وَإِنْ ضُرِبَ ظَهْرُكَ، وَأُخِذَ مَالُكَ، فَاسْمَعْ وَأَطِعْ

Hudhayfa bin al-Yaman narrated a hadith in which he said: The Prophet ﷺ said, "there will be after me leaders who do not follow my guidance and do not follow my *Sunnah*, and there will be among them men whose hearts are like those of Satan in the body of a human being." And I asked the Prophet ﷺ, "What I should do at that time if I reach it?" He said, "listen and obey the ruler, even if he lashed your back and took your money, listen and obey."[581]

أفلا نقاتلهم؟ قال: لا، ما صلوا " ومن حديث عوف بن مالك رفعه في حديث في هذا المعنى " قلنا يا رسول الله أفلا ننابذهم عند ذلك؟ قال: لا، ما أقاموا الصلاة " وفي رواية له " بالسيف " وزاد " وإذا رأيتم من ولاتكم شيئا تكرهونه فاكرهوا عمله ولا تنزعوا يدا من طاعة

[580] Islāḥī, Amīn Aḥsān, *Da'wat-i-Dīn awr us ka ṭarīqah-i-kar* (Urdu; ch. 14, pp. 241-2).
[581] *Saḥīḥ Muslim.*

In another narration, Awf bin Mālik ﷺ said, "O Prophet of Allah, do you recommend that we fight them?" He said, "No, don't fight them as long as they do not prevent you from your prayers. And if you see from them something that you dislike, dislike their acts, do not dislike them. And do not take your hand out from obedience to them." [582]

مَنْ كَرِهَ مِنْ أَمِيرِهِ شَيْئاً فَلْيَصْبِرْ عَلَيْهِ، فَإِنَّهُ لَيْسَ أَحَدٌ مِنَ النَّاسِ خَرَجَ مِنَ السُّلْطَانِ شِبْراً، فَمَاتَ عَلَيْهِ، إِلاَّ مَاتَ مِيتَةً جَاهِلِيَّةً

It is narrated from ʿAbdullāh ibn al-ʿAbbās ﷺ, that the Prophet ﷺ said:

If someone dislikes his ruler, he must be patient, because if he comes against the ruler in a rebellious or destructive manner by only a handspan and dies, he dies in a state of pre-Islamic ignorance (*jāhilīyyah*) and sin.[583]

Other hadiths with similar purport are:

سَتَكُونُ عَلَيْكُمْ أَئِمَّةٌ تَعْرِفُونَ مِنْهُمْ وَتُنْكِرُونَ، فَمَنْ أَنْكَرَ قال أبو دَاوُدَ قال هِشَامٌ بِلِسَانِهِ فَقَدْ بَرِيءَ، وَمَنْ كَرِهَ بِقَلْبِهِ فقدْ سَلِمَ وَلَكِنْ مَنْ رَضِيَ وَتَابَعَ، يَا رَسُول الله أَفَلاَ نَقْتُلُهُمْ؟ قال أبو دَاوُدَ: أَفَلاَ نُقَاتِلُهُمْ؟ قال: لاَ مَا صَلَّوْا"

The Prophet ﷺ said, "There will be upon you leaders who you will recognize and disapprove of; whoever rejects them is free, whoever hates them is safe as opposed to those who are pleased and obey them," they said, "should we not fight them." He said, "No, as long as they pray."

---

[582] *Saḥīḥ Muslim.*

[583] Bukhārī and Muslim.

وعن عوف بن مالك رَضِيَ اللَّهُ عَنهُ قال سمعت رَسُول اللَّهِ صَلَّى اللَّهُ عَلَيهِ وَسَلَّم يقول: <خيار أئمتكم الذين تحبونهم ويحبونكم، وتصلون عليهم ويصلون عليكم. وشرار أئمتكم الذين تبغضونهم ويبغضونكم، وتلعنونهم ويلعنونكم!> قال: قلنا يا رَسُول اللَّهِ أفلا ننابذهم؟ قال: <لا ما أقاموا فيكم الصلاة، لا، ما أقاموا فيكم الصلاة. . .

> The Prophet ﷺ said, "The best of your leaders are those you love and they love you, you pray for them and they pray for you. The worst of your leaders are those who anger you and you anger them and you curse them and they curse you." We replied, "O Messenger of Allah should we not remove them at that," He said, "No, as long as they establish the prayer amongst you..."[584]

These source texts are clear evidence that whoever lives under a particular government must obey the ruler and live peacefully. They are prohibited from taking up arms against him. Uprising or violence by any group against the ruler is completely rejected in Islam, and was prohibited by the Prophet ﷺ and will be a cause of death on the way of ignorance (*jāhilīyyah*). Thus Islam considers rebellion against the ruler a great iniquity. These hadith affirm that one must be patient with one's ruler, even if he commits oppression. These hadith refer to the leader of a nation, not the leader of a small group. Therefore groups that take up violent struggle against their regimes are prohibited in Islam and are by default illegal and blameworthy.

In fact the true path to correction of the mistakes of a ruler is according to the hadith "a most excellent Jihād is when one speaks

---

584 Narrated in Ad-Dārimī's *Sunan* and a similar Ḥadīth is related in *Musnad* Aḥmad.

a word of truth in the presence of a tyrannical ruler."[585] Note here the hadith does not mention fighting the ruler, but rather praises the one who corrects the ruler by speech. Armed and violent opposition to a state regime can never be recognized as Jihād in the way of Allah, despite the claims of many groups. Unfortunately we see today countless individuals and groups who label their rulers and their governments apostates or unbelievers, thereby giving themselves the excuse to declare "Jihād" against them, asserting that this is because they do not rule by what was revealed to the Prophet ﷺ. Even worse, they go further by terrorizing and killing government officers, members of the armed forces and public servants, simply because they are easy targets. These groups use a "militant Islamic" ideology to justify such felonious action, declaring the ruler, the government, and its officers to be criminals standing in the way of "true Islam", who must be eliminated. Thus, those who are innocent of any crime, but who are earning a living and raising their families, such as officers and officials of ministries and departments, county and city officials and police, become targets of these extremist ideologues. Such groups do not hesitate to kill them in surprise attacks, terrorizing the entire nation by blasting here and there and harming the innocent.

If the ruler commits wrong, it is not permitted to label him an apostate, nor to indoctrinate people to use militancy to oppose him. In the time of the Prophet ﷺ after the conquest of Makkah, a Companion named Ḥātib ibn Abī Balta, assisted some of the enemy by supporting them extensively and passing them secret information. It may be that no one today supports a tyrannical ruler as Ḥātib supported the unbelievers at that time.

---

[585] Narrated by Abū Saʿīd al-Khuḍrī in Abū Dāwūd and Tirmidhī.

قال: يا رسول الله لا تعجل علي، إني كنت أمرأ ملصقا في قريش، ولم أكن من أنفسها، وكان من معك من المهاجرين لهم قرابات بمكة، يحمون بها أهليهم وأموالهم، فأحببت إذ فاتني ذلك من النسب فيهم، أن أتخذ عندهم يدا يحمون بها قرابتي، وما فعلت كفرا ولا ارتدادا، ولا رضا بالكفر بعد الإسلام، فقال رسول الله صلى الله عليه وسلم: (لقد صدقكم)

When questioned as to his motives, Ḥātib replied:

O Prophet of Allah! Don't hasten to give your judgment about me. I was a man closely connected with the Quraish, but I did not belong to this tribe, while the other emigrants with you, had their relatives in Mecca who would protect their dependents and property. So, I wanted to compensate for my lacking blood relation to them by doing them a favor so that they might protect my dependents. I did this neither because of disbelief nor apostasy nor out of preferring disbelief (*kufr*) to Islam.

The Prophet of Allah ﷺ said, "Ḥātib has told you the truth."[586]

We see here that the Prophet ﷺ though fully aware of Ḥātib's actions, never considered him to be outside the fold of Islam, nor did he inflict any punishment on him. Regarding Ḥātib and his support of the unbelievers Allah revealed the following verse:

يَا أَيُّهَا الَّذِينَ آمَنُوا لَا تَتَّخِذُوا عَدُوِّي وَعَدُوَّكُمْ أَوْلِيَاء تُلْقُونَ إِلَيْهِم بِالْمَوَدَّةِ وَقَدْ كَفَرُوا بِمَا جَاءَكُم مِّنَ الْحَقِّ يُخْرِجُونَ الرَّسُولَ وَإِيَّاكُمْ أَن تُؤْمِنُوا بِاللَّهِ رَبِّكُمْ

[586] *Ṣaḥīḥ Bukhārī.*

O you who believe! Do not take My enemy and your enemy for friends: would you offer them love while they deny what has come to you of the truth, driving out the Messenger and yourselves because you believe in Allah, your Lord?[587]

Though the verse reprimands Ḥātib showing him in the wrong, nonetheless Allah did not take him out of the state of faith yet continued to address him with the honorable title "*O you who believe,*" despite his assisting the enemies of Islam.

This constitutes proof that even if someone assists a regime that does not support Islam, one cannot harm that person as the Prophet ﷺ did not inflict any punishment on Ḥātib. One wonders then how today so many groups freely label those working for the government as renegades and apostates, and issue fierce edicts to kill them? Their work with the government might be for their livelihood, or for building a bridge of trust for the Islamic community to ensure a better future relationship or a better understanding of Islam. Such actions are baseless in Islam and are founded on an extremist ideology, far removed from the middle path which always constitutes this blessed religion of Allah.

THE INNER JIHAD

Islam is not a rhetorical religion, it is based on unity, love and rational action. Soon after the Prophet's death, Islam radiated outwardly from its earthly center, the *Ka'aba,* implacable symbol of the faith. Jihād was the dynamic of this expansion. Outwardly it embodied the power of Islam against error and falsehood, while inwardly it represented the means of spiritual awakening and of transcending the self. Referring to this, the Prophet ﷺ said while returning from battle:

قدمتم خير مقدم، وقدمتم من الجهاد الأصغر إلى الجهاد الأكبر: مجاهدة العبد هواه

[587] Sūratu 'l-Mumtahina [She that is to be examined], 60:1.

We are now returning from the lesser Jihād to the greater Jihād, the Jihād against the self.[588]

The Prophet ﷺ is reported to have said during the Farewell Pilgrimage:

المجاهد من جاهد نفسه في الله

... The Fighter in the Way of Allah is he who makes Jihād against himself (*jāhada nafsah*) for the sake of obeying Allah.[589]

Allah says in the Holy Qur'ān,

وَالَّذِينَ جَاهَدُوا فِينَا لَنَهْدِيَنَّهُمْ سُبُلَنَا

Those who have striven for Our sake, We guide them to Our ways. [590]

In this verse, Allah uses a derivative of the linguistic root of the word "Jihād" to describe those who are deserving of guidance, and has made guidance dependent on Jihād against the false desires of the soul. Therefore, the most perfect of people are those who struggle the most against the selfish promptings of the ego for Allah's sake. The most obligatory Jihād is that against the base side of the ego, desires, the devil, and the lower world.

The great Sufi Al-Junayd said:

Those who have striven against their desires and repented for Allah's sake, shall be guided to the ways of sincerity. One cannot struggle against his enemy outwardly (i.e. with the sword) except he who struggles against these enemies inwardly. Then whoever is given victory over

---

[588] Ghazālī, in the *Iḥyā'*, al-'Irāqī said that Bayhaqī related it on the authority of Jābir and said: There is weakness in its chain of transmission. According to Nisā'ī in *al-Kunā* is a saying by Ibrāhīm ibn Ablah.

[589] Tirmidhī, Aḥmad, Ṭabarānī, Ibn Mājah, and al-Ḥākim.

[590] Sūratu 'l-'Ankabūt [The Spider], 29:69.

them will be victorious over his enemy, and whoever is defeated by them, his enemy defeats him.

DHIKR: THE REMEMBRANCE OF ALLAH

عَنْ أَبِي الدَّرْدَاءِ؛ أَنَّ النَّبِيَّ صلى الله عليه وسلم قَالَ (أَلاَ أُنَبِّئُكُمْ بِخَيْرِ أَعْمَالِكُمْ، وَأَرْضَاهَا عِنْدَ مَلِيكِكُمْ، وَأَرْفَعِهَا فِي دَرَجَاتِكُمْ، وَخَيْرٍ لَكُمْ مِنْ إِعْطَاءِ الذَّهَبِ وَالْوَرِقِ، وَمِنْ أَنْ تَلْقَوْا عَدُوَّكُمْ فَتَضْرِبُوا أَعْنَاقَهُمْ، وَيَضْرِبُوا أَعْنَاقَكُمْ؟) قَالُوا: وَمَا ذَاكَ؟ يَا رَسُولَ اللهِ !قَالَ ذِكْرُ اللهِ

The Prophet ﷺ said:
Shall I tell you something that is the best of all deeds, constitutes the best act of piety in the eyes of your Lord, elevates your rank in the hereafter, and carries more virtue than the spending of gold and silver in the service of Allah, or taking part in Jihād and slaying or being slain in the path of Allah?" They said: "Yes!" He said: "Remembrance of Allah."[591]

Thus one finds the principles of the spiritual Jihād are based on eliminating the ugly, selfish and ferocious characteristics of the ego through spiritual training and mastery of *dhikr*, the Remembrance of Allah. This remembrance takes many forms: each school of Sufism focuses on a different form of ritual *dhikr* to enable the seeker to approach the Divine Presence, varying from individual silent recitation and chanting to vocal group sessions. It is this spiritual struggle that raises humankind and instills in him

---

591 Related on the authority of Abū al-Dārdā by Aḥmad, Tirmidhī, Ibn Mājah, Ibn Abī al-Dunyā, al-Ḥākim, Bayhaqī, and Aḥmad also related it from Muʿadh ibn Jabal.

the sense of relationship with His Creator, and the proper perspective in relating to all creation, always calling for love between humanity and striving in Allah's Way for better understanding between various communities of all faiths. Through this spiritual Jihād the effect of the selfish ego on the soul of the seeker will be removed, uplifting his state from depression, anxiety and loneliness to one of joy, satisfaction and companionship with the Most High.

CONCLUSION AND POLICY RECOMMENDATIONS

It is apparent that the understanding of Jihād as a concept is dismally blurred by the ongoing rhetoric employed by financially-empowered Islamist activists and extremist scholars. Disregarding centuries of classical scholarship, using a simplistic, literal approach to the Qur'ān and holy traditions of the Prophet, they have built a convincing picture of Jihād as militant, continuing warfare between the Muslims and non-Muslims; a situation they contend will maintain until the end of time.

The only way to dispel the false notions of Jihād put forth by the extremists, who are massively funded by external sources, is an equally strong effort put forth by Muslim governments in re-education of their populations, in particular the youth, with a correct understanding of this term. Such efforts must be sustained and ongoing and must have the support of modern, moderate Muslim scholars in each nation.

We propose the following recommendations for each nation engaging in these re-education efforts:

1) follow-on discussions to create a response to the current abuse of the term Jihād;

2) development and staging of public presentations to educate the public based on the information and discussions in (1);

3) publish literature detailing the accurate definition of Jihād and distributing this literature in large quantities;
4) encourage modern, moderate scholars to stand up and speak up in opposition to the extremists;
5) Create a national podium for modern, moderate scholars;
6) Publish in public media the proceedings of the above-mentioned debates and discussions by modern, moderate scholars.

THE QUESTION OF WIFE-BEATING IN ISLAM

> Islam upholds the values of mercy, compassion and love in the conduct of family affairs. There is nothing cruel or arbitrary about Islam's rulings relating to matters of marriage, children and family life. For this reason, the arbitrary *fatwās* by some contemporary scholars of a literalist bent that claim wife-beating is acceptable simply do not stand up in the face of true Islamic scholarship. These rulings are based on a narrow interpretation of a particular Qur'ānic verse, but there are numerous valid and acceptable interpretations of the verse.
>
> Instead of blindly following in the footsteps of previous literalists interpretations, it is time Muslim scholars try harder to find novel, yet still valid, interpretations based on classical methods of *ijtihād*. This does not require "thinking outside the box," but simply extending the boundaries of the box in which they think.

In my travels around the world, one question I am constantly asked is "Are Muslim men allowed to beat their wives?" While this is a hot topic today in the West, as Islam is explored from every angle by people of every faith and background, what is most surprising is how often it is Muslims who are posing it. In asking this question, I feel that many Muslims feel they have been betrayed by those intellectuals and scholars who continue to insist on imposing simplistic, singular edicts on complex and pluralistic issues. An Islamic ruling on this subject today must fit with classical understandings while addressing the normative values of today's global civilization.

Today, when someone sneezes in the East, it can be heard in the West. Therefore, it behooves Muslims – particularly Muslim scholars – to be judicious in their responses to questions of law and the guidance they provide to the common people, for it is a principle of the faith that if one feels embarrassed about a word or an action, that is a sign of Allah's displeasure with it.

Rulings about wife-beating revolve around a single verse of the Holy Qur'ān. For Muslims, the Holy Qur'ān continues to retain immense authority in their lives. Revealed to the Prophet Muhammad ﷺ, over a period of 23 years by the Archangel Jibrīl, Muslims consider the Holy Qur'ān the literal Word of God, unaltered and unedited. It is, therefore, not only a book of inspirational value, but a book of practical guidance in many affairs – many of which are not generally considered to be part of the purview of religion in the West. These include marital relations.

The verse in question is typically translated:

الرِّجَالُ قَوَّامُونَ عَلَى النِّسَاء بِمَا فَضَّلَ اللّهُ بَعْضَهُمْ عَلَى بَعْضٍ وَبِمَا أَنفَقُواْ مِنْ أَمْوَالِهِمْ فَالصَّالِحَاتُ قَانِتَاتٌ حَافِظَاتٌ لِّلْغَيْبِ بِمَا حَفِظَ اللّهُ وَاللاَّتِي تَخَافُونَ نُشُوزَهُنَّ فَعِظُوهُنَّ وَاهْجُرُوهُنَّ فِي الْمَضَاجِعِ وَاضْرِبُوهُنَّ فَإِنْ أَطَعْنَكُمْ فَلاَ تَبْغُواْ عَلَيْهِنَّ سَبِيلاً إِنَّ اللّهَ كَانَ عَلِيًّا كَبِيرًا

Men are the protectors and maintainers of women, because God has given the one more (strength) than the other, and because they support them from their means. Therefore, the righteous women are devoutly obedient, and guard in (the husband's) absence what God would have them guard. As to those women on whose part ye fear disloyalty and ill-conduct, admonish them (first), (next), separate from them in bed, (and last) beat them (lightly); but if they return to obedience, seek not against them means (of annoyance): For God is Most High, great (above you all).[592]

[592] Sūratu 'n-Nisā [Women], 4:34

Within this verse, one word invokes controversy: *w'aḍribūhunn,* from the Arabic verb *"ḍaraba."*

From this one word, many of today's scholars assert that a man may beat his wife. For example, Professor Shahul Hameed, of India, writes on IslalmOnline.net:

> Some scholars argue that the word in this context does not mean "beat" or "hit". It means just "leave [them]". But it is obvious – and Allah knows best – that the word stands here for punishment …[593]

Usually, such scholars qualify the verb "beat," as in the above translation by Yūsuf ʿAlī, by the adverb "lightly," but the idea that wife-beating in any sense has sanction in religion flies in the face of ethics and morality for most people.

In any case, from such scholarly discussions, it is apparent that all are striving, based on their intellectual capacity and knowledge of Qur'ānic interpretation, to reduce the harshness of the punishment they see outlined in this verse.

QUR'AN'S UNIVERSAL HUMAN VALUES

Before we explain these Qur'ānic verses in the light of today's universal human values, we must examine the importance of family in Islam, both as it relates to the individual and society as a whole.

Islam is very intent on protecting "family values." Allah speaks of the essential family unit, the couple, repeatedly in the Holy Qur'ān, saying:

وَمِن كُلِّ شَيْءٍ خَلَقْنَا زَوْجَيْنِ لَعَلَّكُمْ تَذَكَّرُونَ

593 http://www.islamonline.net/servlet/Satellite?cid=1123996220182&pagename=IslamOnline-English-AAbout_Islam%2FAAboutIslamCounselorE%2FAAboutIslamCounselorE.

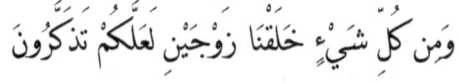

And of every thing We have created pairs.[594]

The Holy Qur'ān describes humankind as originating from a single soul, from which Allah created everyone, both male and female:

خَلَقَكُم مِّن نَّفْسٍ وَاحِدَةٍ ثُمَّ جَعَلَ مِنْهَا زَوْجَهَا

He created you from one being, then from that (being) He made its mate;[595]

And:

يَا أَيُّهَا النَّاسُ اتَّقُواْ رَبَّكُمُ الَّذِي خَلَقَكُم مِّن نَّفْسٍ وَاحِدَةٍ وَخَلَقَ مِنْهَا زَوْجَهَا وَبَثَّ مِنْهُمَا رِجَالاً كَثِيرًا وَنِسَاء وَاتَّقُواْ اللّهَ الَّذِي تَسَاءلُونَ بِهِ وَالأَرْحَامَ إِنَّ اللّهَ كَانَ عَلَيْكُمْ رَقِيبًا

O mankind! reverence your Guardian-Lord, who created you from a single person, and created, of like nature, his mate, and from them twain scattered (like seeds) countless men and women;- reverence Allah, through Whom ye demand your mutual (rights), and (reverence) the wombs (that bore you): for Allah ever watches over you.[596]

Since Allah created both male and female from a single, primordial soul, the married couple must share what is quintessential in all humankind: qualities of compassion, mercy, tenderness, dignity and honor as described in another verse:

---

[594] Sūratu 'dh-Dhāriyāt [The Winnowing Winds], 51:49

[595] Sūratu 'z-Zumar [The Groups], 39:6

[596] Sūratu 'n-Nisā [Women], 4:1

وَمِنْ آيَاتِهِ أَنْ خَلَقَ لَكُم مِّنْ أَنفُسِكُمْ أَزْوَاجًا لِّتَسْكُنُوا إِلَيْهَا وَجَعَلَ بَيْنَكُم مَّوَدَّةً وَرَحْمَةً إِنَّ فِي ذَلِكَ لَآيَاتٍ لِّقَوْمٍ يَتَفَكَّرُونَ

And among His Signs is this, that He created for you mates from among yourselves, that ye may dwell in tranquility with them, and He has put love and mercy between your (hearts): verily in that are Signs for those who reflect.[597]

Here God describes husband and wife as "dwelling" with one another. The Arabic term used is *taskunū*. It is derived from the word for tranquility, meaning the husband is a home and place of tranquility for the wife, as the wife is for the husband. Thus, God shows that both husband and wife share and hold the same rights and the same beliefs, and the same behavior is expected from one to the other. In other words, a just and fair balance must be set in order to maintain a tranquil, happy home.

It is worth noting that, in this verse, God mentioned women first, thereby asserting their primacy in the home setting and, in the balanced wording of the verse, demonstrating their rights as equal with men. In this way, Islam builds up the structure of the marital relationship between two people by putting them on an equal footing. As they share that same original soul, it only follows that they must dwell together in tranquility, love and mercy. A true family institution can only exist when each side complements and completes the other, just as a lamp without electricity will not give light any more than will electricity without a lamp. The two halves, male and female, need each other. Thus, God describes spouses as garments for one another:

هُنَّ لِبَاسٌ لَّكُمْ وَأَنتُمْ لِبَاسٌ لَّهُنَّ

[597] Sūrah Rūm [Rome], 30:21

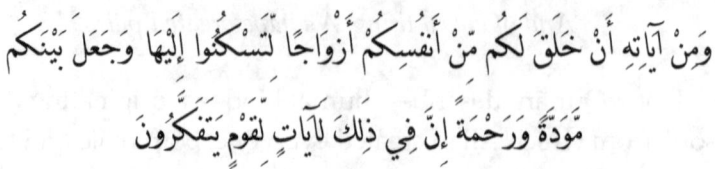

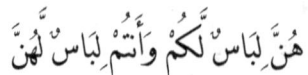

They are raiment for you and ye are raiment for them.[598]

A garment provides protection, hides faults, maintains dignity and beautifies the wearer. This is what husband and wife do for each other in Islam's concept of the ideal family.

God gave each member of the couple different characteristics. God gave a tremendous responsibility to women when He created them to bear children, to breastfeed and to nurture the coming generation. God also gave them many noble attributes, including compassion, tenderness and innocence. It is impossible to imagine that God would give women such excellent characteristics only to bear the hardship of their husbands' cruelty.

Here we cite Syed Qutb, who said:

> Let us go over what we have clarified earlier in terms of the honor which Allah bestowed on both aspects (male and female) of the human being; and in term of women's rights which stems from her human character; and in terms of the Muslim woman retaining her civic personality along with all the rights which come with it…the right to choose her partner in life, the right to manage her own affairs and the right to manage her own money …
>
> It is in no way a battle between men and women. These methods are not meant to crush the head of a woman who starts to deviate, in order to put her back in chains like you would do with a wild dog.
>
> This is absolutely not Islam. These are cultural practices which pertain to certain regions and which took place during certain ages when not just one aspect of the human

[598] Sūratu 'l-Baqara [The Heifer], 2:187.

being was degraded, but the whole human being became morally degraded … [under the control of lust]."[599]

As we further examine the Qur'ānic verse which some of today's more literalist commentators cite as sanctioning wife-beating, we must keep this viewpoint in mind. Consider what the Prophet ﷺ said about the purpose of Islam:

قال النبي صلى الله عليه وسلم" انما بعثت لأتمم مكارم الأخلاق"

"(It is) to perfect the moral character of people."[600]

For this reason, Allah said:

وَلَا تَنسَوُا الْفَضْلَ بَيْنَكُمْ

"And forget not kindness among yourselves."[601]

And also:

وَلَا تَنسَوُا الْفَضْلَ بَيْنَكُمْ

"They (women) have rights similar to those (of men) over them in kindness."[602]

Where then, in such a family and community structure is there place for the sanctioned cruelty, violence and anger which wife-beating entails?

---

[599] Qutb, Syed, *Fī Dhilāl al-Qur'ān (In the Shades of the Qur'ān)*, Volume 2, p. 650-653, Cairo: Dār ash-shurūq, 2005.

[600] Related by al-Bazzāz, as mentioned by Imām Ibn Ḥajar (?) in *Fatḥ al-Bārī fi Sharḥ al-Bukhārī*, and Imām Aḥmad's *Musnad* with slightly different wording.)Aḥmad Ibn Ḥanbal (d. 241/855), *al-Musnad*, 6 vols., Cairo, AH 1313.(

[601] Sūratu 'l-Baqara [The Heifer], 2:237.

[602] Sūratu 'l-Baqara [The Heifer], 2:228.

THE SOCIETY IN WHICH THE HOLY QUR'AN WAS REVEALED

Sayyid Qutb also stated:

> These words and directions and all the issues surrounding them paint a picture of the conflict between the dregs of the Age of the Ignorance and the direction that Islam gave to that society.

The Holy Qur'ān was revealed before the establishment of Islamic society, in a barbaric social environment in which spousal abuse, murder and even infanticide were commonplace. Islam came to tame this uncivilized tribal society and set up the rule of law. Understanding this historic reality will help us to understand Islam's ability to adjust to every time and situation. Moreover, it will help us appreciate how the Prophet implemented Islam in a way that transformed this cutthroat clannish society into a highly civilized community in which the rights of both men and women were respected at all levels of individual and societal conduct.

If we examine the broader history of human civilization we see that, in most cases, societies tend to evolve over time. Europe's transition from the Middle Ages to the Renaissance is a case in point. Recognizing this, Islam was able to restrict the wild behavior that prevailed at the time of its revelation while, at the same time, leaving the door open for future scholars to adapt the faith to new and different social conditions. Islam has always upheld the highest standard of morality and ethics. Therefore, when human society ascended in its moral and ethical character, Islam was already there and thus the standards of Islamic morality moved even higher.

An example of this is the way in which Islamic societies responded to the issue of slavery. When slavery was the norm, Islam was primarily concerned with ensuring that the conditions of slavery were humane. However, when human societies evolved beyond slavery, the entire concept of slavery was abandoned in Islam and effectively prohibited.

Today, only Islamic extremists still accept slavery as something permissible in Islam, seeking to revert to anachronistic behavior despite the fact that the world's yardstick of behavior has become elevated above that. While the Prophet did not abolish slavery, he did everything within his power to eliminate this vice by making the emancipation of slaves a rewarded action and the penance for many mistakes. He also established rules for slavery that made it easy for slaves to attain freedom themselves through a variety of different means. Inspired by this, his Companions were diligent in finding every means to free slaves, regardless of their race or creed. It is only within the last two centuries that other civilizations reached the high bar set by Islam more than 1,400 years ago.

While Islam has always been in the vanguard of moral evolution, it has never retreated when broader social norms have degenerated or degraded. Thus, Islam stands at the zenith of perfection, always moving one step ahead of the rest of society and never sliding back. The Prophet remains the exemplar of righteous conduct for all Muslims, in every time and place.

A LINGUISTIC NOTE

Let us now examine in depth at the verse in question in light of these understandings. In it the word *ḍaraba,* as conjugated *"w 'aḍribūhunna,"* and this is the cause of much confusion today. This word is typically translated as "beat," but it also has many different meanings. For example, the same verb can also be translated as "to tap," "to mix," "to mingle," "to separate," "to oscillate," "to fly," "to incline towards," "to throb," "to multiply," "to play music," "to move," "to go for a walk," "to migrate," "to settle down," "to dwell," and "to quote a wise a saying" among others. In fact, the root word *ḍaraba* has over 54 meanings in even the most abridged dictionary (Hans-Wehr).

In many cases, the verb *ḍaraba* is modified by another word, usually a noun or preposition, relating to the object of the verb. This has a great impact on the meaning. *Ḍaraba* must apply on, to or with something, as in these dictionary meanings: "To range about," "to strike one's notice," "to take an active part," "to impart wisdom," "to pitch a tent," etc. However, in the case of the verse in question, there is no modifier in the original Arabic. In only one other instance in Qur'ān is *ḍaraba* used without such a modifier. In such unusual cases, the modifier is often inferred. Thus, the door is left open to a multitude of jurisprudentially legitimate and linguistically valid meanings.

As is this case with many Arabic words, the context is important in determining which meaning is meant. In light of the Qur'ān, and also in the light of the Prophet's own personal actions, sayings and behavior, it could not possibly mean striking to hurt with violence. To determine the correct meaning here, one must consider the term in the broader context of the Prophet's teachings of kindness to women, including the many statements (hadith) in which he specifically prohibited wife-beating.

PROPHET MUHAMMAD'S HIGH REGARD FOR WOMEN

Indeed, just after the revelation of this verse, when some of his companions took the word *"w 'aḍribūhunna"* literally, and struck their wives, the Prophet ﷺ objected to their behavior, saying:

فقال النبي صلى اللّه عليه وسلم: "لقد طاف بآل محمد نساءٌ كثيرٌ يشكون أزواجهنّ،

ليس أولئك بخياركم

Indeed, a large group of women gathered here, in my house, complaining about their husbands. You will not find those men the best of you.[603]

Rather, the Prophet ﷺ instructed his Companions:

قال: "أطعموهنَّ مما تأكلون، واكسوهنَّ مما تكتسون، ولا تضربوهن، ولا تقبِّحُوهُنَّ" .

Do not beat them, and do not revile them.[604]

قال (النبي)" ألاَ واَستَوْصُوا بالنساء خيراً فإنهن عَوَانٍ عندكم. . . ألا إنّ لكم على نسائكم حقاً ولنسائكم عليكم حقّاً فأما . . ."

"I remind you concerning women to do good! They are your commited helpers and companions ,.... Indeed you have on your women rights and your women have rights on you..."

This is in concert with the ethos of Islam as a faith, where the Prophet ﷺ said,

قَالَ رَسُولُ اللَّهِ صلى الله عليه وسلم "لاَ ضَرَرَ وَلاَ ضِرَارَ"

"there is no harm and no retribution [in religion]."[605]

---

[603] reported by Aḥmad Ibn Ḥanbal (d. 241/855), *al-Musnad*, 6 vols., Cairo, AH 1313., Sulaymān ibn Ashʿath Abū Dāwūd as-Sijistānī al-Azdī, *Sunan Abū Dāwūd,* (authenticated by Muḥammad Muḥyīddīn bin ʿAbdul Ḥamīd), #2144, Beirut: Dār al-Fikr, and Aḥmad ibn Shuʿayb Abū Abdur-Raḥmān an-Nisāʾī, *Sunan al-Nisāʾī,* (authenticated by ʿAbdul Fattāḥ Abū Ghuddah), Aleppo: Maktab al-Matbuʿat al-Islāmīyya,1986. Muḥammad Ibn Ḥibbān, *Saḥīḥ Ibn Hibban bi tartīb ibn Balban,* Beirut: Muassasah ar-Risālah, 1993, and al-Nisabūrī, al-Ḥākim. *Al-Mustadrak ʿala al-saḥīḥayn.* Ed. Musṭafā ʿAbd al-Qādir ʿAtā'. Beirut: Dār al-Kutub al-ʿIlmiyyah,1411 AH. The Arabic text:
قال رسول الله صلى الله عليه وسلم: "لاتضربوا إماء الله" فجاء عمر إلى رسول الله صلى الله عليه وسلم فقال: ذئرن النساء على أزواجهن، فرخّص في ضربهنَّ، فأطاف بآل رسول الله صلى الله عليه وسلم نساءٌ كثير يشكون أزواجهن، فقال النبي صلى الله عليه وسلم: "لقد طاف بآل محمد نساءٌ كثيرٌ يشكون أزواجهنَّ، ليس أولئك بخياركم"

[604] Sulaymān ibn Ashʿath Abū Dāwūd as-Sijistānī al-Azdī, *Sunan Abū Dāwūd,* (authenticated by Muḥammad Muḥyīddīn bin ʿAbdul Ḥamīd), #2144, Beirut: Dār al-Fikr.

واستوصوا بالنساء خيرا، فانما هن عوان عندكم، ليس تملكون منهن شيئا غير ذلك الا أن يأتين بفاحشة مبينة، فان فعلن فاهجروهن في المضاجع واضربوهن ضربا غير مبرح، فان أطعنكم فلا بتغوا عليهن سبيلا. ألا وان لكم على نسائكم حقا، ولنسائكم عليكم حقا، فأما حقكم على نسائكم فلا يوطئن فرشكم من تكرهون، ولا يأذن في بيوتهم لمن تكرهون. ألا وان حقهن عليكم أن تحسنوا اليهن في كسوتهن وطعامهن".

And it is related that the Messenger of Allah ﷺ said:
"I remind you concerning women to do good! Verily they are your committed helpers....And their rights upon you are that you should have excellent disposition towards them in clothing them and feeding them." [606]

فَاتَّقُوا اللَّهَ عَزَّ وَجَلَ فِي النِّسَاءِ فَإِنَّهُنَّ عِنْدَكُمْ عَوَانٌ لَا يَمْلِكْنَ لِأَنْفُسِهِنَّ شَيْئًا وَإِنَّ لَهُنَّ عَلَيْكُمْ وَلَكُمْ عَلَيْهِنَّ حَقًّا ...

And in another version Allah's Messenger ﷺ said:
Fear Allah, the Exalted, in respect to your women! For verily they are your committed partners and helpers, they hold nothing for themselves, and indeed they have rights on you and you have rights on them ..."

---

[605] Ibn Mājah al-Qazwīnī. *Sunan Ibn Mājah.* Ed. Maḥmūd Fu'ād ʿAbd al-Bāqī. Beirut: Dār al-Fikr, Kitāb al-Aḥkām, 2430, 2431. Mālik ibn Anas Abū Abdullāh al-Asbāhī, *Muwaṭṭa Imām Mālik,* Bāb al-Makatib, Damascus: Dār al-Qalam, 1991.

[606] Imām Tirmidhī (209-279 AH), *Sunan at-Tirmidhī.* Beirut: Dār Iḥyā' al-Turath al-ʿArabī, n.d.

فاتقوا الله في النساء . فإنكم أخذتموهن بأمان الله. واستحللتم فروجهن بكلمة الله. ولكم
عليهن أن لا يوطئن فرشكم أحدا تكرهونه. فإن فعلن ذلك فاضربوهن ضربا غير مبرح.
ولهن عليكم رزقهن وكسوتهن بالمعروف.

And in another version Allah's Messenger ﷺ said:

Fear Allah, the Exalted, in respect to your women! Verily you have taken them [as life partners] as a Trust from Allah and marital relations with them have been permitted you by Allah's Word. It is true that you have certain rights regarding your women,...They have the right to be fed and clothed in kindness.[607]

Finally, the Prophet ﷺ said:

عن عائشة، قالت: قال رسول الله صلى الله عليه وسلم:- "خيركم خيركم لأهله،
وأنا خيركم لأهلي، وإذا مات صاحبكم فدعوه".

"The best of you is the best to his family and I am the best among you to my family."[608]

THE IMPORTANCE OF INTERPRETING THE HOLY QUR'AN

The correct approach to understanding such "problematic" verses requires deep scholarship, seeking not only the reason a verse was revealed and what events transpired in connection with its revelation, but also a genuine understanding of the intent behind that revelation, a comprehensive grasp of the classical Arabic language of Qur'ān and often a knowledge of the various

---

[607] Muslim b. al-Ḥusayn al-Qushayrī. *Saḥīḥ Muslim.* Second Edition. Ed. Muḥammad Fu'ād ʿAbd al-Bāqī, Beirut: Dār Iḥyā' al-Turāth al-ʿArabī, 1978.

[608] Imām Tirmidhī (209-279 AH), *Sunan at-Tirmidhī.* Beirut: Dār Iḥyā' al-Turāth al-ʿArabī, n.d., 3985, *hasan saḥīḥ.*

dialects used by the tribes in the different places in which the Holy Qur'ān was revealed – for each tribe's usage of a word might differ from the others. To one it may have meant one thing, and to another something else. It truly takes an expert in linguistics to understand all the meanings in a verse, both explicit and inferred. As Muslims, we must know that many times the Prophet and his Companions explained a verse of the Holy Qur'ān in a manner quite different than the apparent meaning of the text.

Moreover, the Holy Qur'ān often uses allegories suited to all readers: young and old, male and female. In using allusive rather than direct language, the Holy Qur'ān is purposefully moderate and vague when discussing issues that are not suitable for all ages and levels of understanding. It is for just this reason that classical scholars insist that accessing the true meanings of the Holy Qur'ān can only be done by means of a knowledgeable scholar, well-versed in such subtleties.

Classical commentators believe the best understanding of Qur'ānic terms comes from the Holy Qur'ān itself, by seeking the meaning of a word in one verse by studying its use in other verses. In the case of the root word *ḍaraba,* one finds this verb used 58 times in the Holy Qur'ān, each with its own meaning and context.

To fully understand and correctly interpret the verse in question, one must consider what God says elsewhere in the Holy Qur'ān about the relationship between husbands and wives. In doing so, it is obvious that wife-beating has no place in this context, for God says to men:

وَعَاشِرُوهُنَّ بِالْمَعْرُوفِ

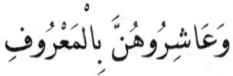

Live with your wives on a footing of kindness and equity.[609]

Allah also calls on Muslims to "revere the wombs (that bore you)"[610] in the first verse of the chapter titled "The Women"—an abstract of Islam's teachings regarding the treatment of women.

Treating women harmfully is forbidden in the Holy Qur'ān:

وَلَا تُمْسِكُوهُنَّ ضِرَارًا لِّتَعْتَدُوا

Do not retain your wives to harm them ...[611]

Rather love, mercy and reverence are the measure of a marriage, for the Holy Qur'ān says:

وَجَعَلَ بَيْنَكُم مَّوَدَّةً وَرَحْمَةً

And He has put love and mercy between your (hearts)[612]

Even when married life has become unbearable, the Holy Qur'ān states the spouses must go their separate ways peacefully:

وَإِنِ امْرَأَةٌ خَافَتْ مِن بَعْلِهَا نُشُوزًا أَوْ إِعْرَاضًا فَلَا جُنَاحَ عَلَيْهِمَا أَن يُصْلِحَا بَيْنَهُمَا صُلْحًا وَالصُّلْحُ خَيْرٌ وَأُحْضِرَتِ الْأَنفُسُ الشُّحَّ وَإِن تُحْسِنُوا وَتَتَّقُوا فَإِنَّ اللَّهَ كَانَ بِمَا تَعْمَلُونَ خَبِيرًا

---

609 Sūratu 'n-Nisā [Women], 4:19.

610 وَالأَرْحَامَ

611 Sūratu 'l-Baqara [The Heifer], 2:231.

612 Sūrah Rūm [Rome], 30:21.

If a wife fears cruelty or desertion on her husband's part, there is no blame on them if they arrange an amicable settlement between themselves; and such settlement is best.[613]

Note here the reference to "cruelty ... on her husband's part." In this verse, God makes cruelty grounds for a wife to seek divorce with no qualifications. Given this, how can beating then be considered permissible?

THE CAUSE FOR REVEALING THIS VERSE

To reach a complete understanding of the true meaning of this verse, we must also examine the context of its revelation. It was revealed in a time when the pagan Arabs were emerging from a period of extreme wildness, a period in which women were treated like chattel and consequently were highly promiscuous in their own behavior. Adultery and sexual dalliances by men and women were commonplace. Islam sought to restrict the expression of sexuality within the bounds of marriage and prevent adultery. Therefore, where the verse says "As to those women on whose part ye fear disloyalty and ill-conduct," classical scholars have explained the meaning of "disloyalty and ill-conduct" (*nushūz*) as referring to sexual infidelity.[614]

Similarly, the Prophet said:

فخطب الناس وقال: . . .ولكم عليهن أن لا يوطئن فرشكم أحدا تكرهونه.

---

[613] Sūratu 'n-Nisā [Women], 4:128.

[614] The term *nushūz* (lit., "rebellion," but here rendered as "ill-will") comprises every kind of deliberate bad behavior of a wife towards her husband or of a husband towards his wife, including what is nowadays described as "mental cruelty;" with reference to the husband, it also denotes "ill-treatment," in the physical sense, of his wife (cf. verse 128 of this surah). (Asad' s commentary)

> It is your right that they do not make friends with anyone whom you do not approve, and never commit adultery.[615]

It is in this context that the verse applies. As in all teachings of the Prophet, a process is followed in correcting wrong behavior. In revealing the rules and practices of Islam to the Prophet, God never expected new behavior to be adopted instantly, but always took a staged approach. This is seen in the way that relations between men and women were gradually modified over the period of time during which Qur'ān was being revealed. At first, this subject was not addressed and men and women were not prevented from committing illicit sexual behavior, something rampant in the wild society preceding Islam. Then, as the Holy Qur'ān came down in stages, it encouraged marriage, and simultaneously proscribed adultery and fornication. This was followed gradually by restricting behavior that might lead to sexual impropriety.

The Prophet ﷺ said:

> عن عمرو بن الأَحْوَص أنه شهد حجة الودَاع مع رسول الله صلى الله عليه وسلم، فحمِد الله وأثنى عليه وذكّر ووعظ فقال: " ألاَ وآستَوْصُوا بالنساء خيراً فإنهن عَوَانٍ عندكم ليس تملكون منهن شيئاً غير ذلك إلا أن يأتين بفاحشة مُبَيِّنة فإن فعلن فاهجروهن في المضاجعِ وآضربوهن ضرباً غيرَ مُبَرِّحٍ..

> I remind you concerning women to do good! Verily, they are your helpers and you do not hold on them anything except that, <u>except where they have been guilty of open</u>

615 Muslim b. al-Ḥusayn al-Qushayrī. *Saḥīḥ Muslim.* Second Edition. Ed. Muḥammad Fu'ād 'Abd al-Bāqī, Beirut: Dār Iḥyā' al-Turāth al-'Arābī, 1978..

> lewdness. If they do that, you can chastise them, but only symbolically.[616]

"Only symbolically" is the interpretation of the word *ghayra mubarriḥ* in the Prophet's wording, by one of the transmitters of the hadith, al-Ḥasan, the grandson of the Prophet and one of the great commentators of Qur'ān.

From this example, we can see that the intent of the verse is to prevent behavior on the woman's part which would destroy the foundation of the marriage, bring about societal corruption, and as the Holy Qur'ān foresaw, prevent the spread of dangerous diseases. An equivalent verse addressing the man's behavior is 4:128 (see below).

QUR'AN-TO-QUR'AN INTERPRETATION

Let us examine some of the possible meanings of the word *ḍaraba* from the Qur'ān itself.

There are 58 different uses of the verb *ḍaraba* in the Holy Qur'ān with different meanings or shades of meaning. The verses using this verb are: 14:24, 16:75, 16:76, 16:112, 30:28, 36:78, 39:29, 43:17, 66:10,66:11, 4:94, 4:101, 5:106, 14:45, 18:11, 25:39, 30:58, 39:27, 3:156, 17:48, 25:9, 43:58, 16:74, 43:5, 29:43, 59:21, 2:26, 13:17, 13:17, 14:25, 24:35, 47:3, 24:31, 24:31, [repeated twice in a verse], 8:50, 47:27, 73:20, 2:60, 7:160, 18:32, 18:45, 20:77, 26:63, 36:13, 38:44, 8:12, 8:12, 2:73, 4:34, 22:73, 43:57, 57:13, 2:61, 3:112, 3:112, 47:4, 2:273, 37:93.617

All of these uses of *ḍaraba* can be interpolated into verse 4:34, and each yields a meaning different from "beat them."

---

[616] Imām Tirmidhī (209-279 AH), *Sunan at-Tirmidhī.* Beirut: Dār Iḥyā' al-Turāth al-ʿArābī , n.d.

[617] Al-Baʿalbakī, Rūḥī, *Al-Mawrid al-mufahris fī li-alfādh al-Qur'ān al-karīm* (An Indexed Dictionary of the Noble Qur'ān), Beirut: Dār al-ʿIlm lil-Malāyīn, 1999. p.1418, 1419.

The interpolation of words and meanings into verses of the Holy Qur'ān is a common practice in Qur'ānic interpretation, one followed by the classical commentators of the first generation until today. In fact, nearly all scholars commonly interpolate words into this verse: As to those women … admonish them (first), (next), separate from them in bed, (and last) beat them (lightly).

Here, each of the words in parentheses is inferred. They do not exist in the Arabic text. In doing this, scholars invoke the need for linguistic and semantic correctness, as well as reasonableness. All of this is due to the extremely concise wording of the Holy Qur'ān. That is why the Qur'ān must not always be taken literally, but must be interpreted from a linguistic, juristic and cultural standpoint. If this is not done, the verse reads: "admonish them, separate from them in bed, and beat them (lightly)," eliminating the stages of rectification, rather applying them all at once, something which flies in the face of the Holy Qur'ān's ethos of moderation in all affairs. No scholar has ever supported this meaning.

TWELVE QUR'ANIC MEANINGS OF *DARABA*

The most common use of this word in the Holy Qur'ān is not as the verb "to beat," but as verb phrases of the form:

1) *"To quote an example"* as in وَلَمَّا ضُرِبَ ٱبْنُ مَرْيَمَ مَثَلًا- *"Wa lamma duriba ibnu maryama mathalan "- "And when the son of Mary is quoted as an example,"*[618]

2) *"To use the parable"* as in أَن يَضْرِبَ مَثَلاً مَّا بَعُوضَةً *"an yadriba mathalan" – "Allah disdains not to use the parable"*[619]

[618] Sūratu z-Zukhruf [The Gold Adornments], 43:57.
[619] Sūratu 'l-Baqara [The Heifer], 2:26.

Similarly, in variant linguistic forms:

3) *"To set forth the parable"* as in as in يَضْرِبُ اللَّهُ الْحَقَّ وَالْبَاطِلَ

-*"yadribu Allāhu al-ḥaqqa wa al-bāṭila"* - *"thus does Allah set forth the parable of Truth and falsehood.*[620]

Therefore, if we reexamine the verse in question in light of these interpolations, it should yield a meaning closer to: "separate from them in bed, (and) cite an example to them," which could mean "make a comparison of their behavior to those who were chastised in the Holy Qur'ān," as in:

ضَرَبَ اللَّهُ مَثَلًا لِّلَّذِينَ كَفَرُوا امْرَأَةَ نُوحٍ وَامْرَأَةَ لُوطٍ كَانَتَا تَحْتَ عَبْدَيْنِ مِنْ عِبَادِنَا صَالِحَيْنِ فَخَانَتَاهُمَا فَلَمْ يُغْنِيَا عَنْهُمَا مِنَ اللَّهِ شَيْئًا وَقِيلَ ادْخُلَا النَّارَ مَعَ الدَّاخِلِينَ

Allah sets forth, for an example to the Unbelievers, the wife of Noah and the wife of Lut: they were (respectively) under two of our righteous servants, but they were false to their (husbands), and they profited nothing before Allah on their account.[621]

Another variation on this usage is:

4) *"To make a comparison"* as in وَضَرَبَ لَنَا مَثَلًا- *"wa daraba lana mathalan"* – *"and he makes comparisons for Us"*[622]

In this sense the verse would read: "separate from them in bed, (and) make comparisons for them," as in "compare your behavior to such-and-such."

---

[620] Sūratu 'r-Rʿad [Thunder], 13:17.
[621] Sūratu't-Taḥrīm [The Banning], 66:10.
[622] Sūrah YāSīn, 36:78.

Other uses of *ḍaraba* in the Holy Qur'ān other than "to strike" or "to beat" are:

5) *"To be covered with"* as in وَضُرِبَتْ عَلَيْهِمُ الذِّلَّةُ وَالْمَسْكَنَةُ - *"wa duribat 'alayhim adh-dhillatu wal-maskana" – "and they were covered with humiliation and misery,"*[623]

In this sense the verse would read: "separate from them in bed, (and) humiliate them,"

6) *"To brand with"* as in ضُرِبَتْ عَلَيْهِمُ الذِّلَّةُ- *"duribat 'alayhim adh-dhillat" - "they were branded with humiliation."*[624]

In this sense the verse would read: "separate from them in bed, (and) brand them with their wrongdoing" in the sense of "make it known widely that they are misbehaving," or: "separate from them in bed, (and) brand them with humiliation, meaning "make known their ill-conduct so they will be shamed into abstaining from it."

7) *"To strike a path"* as in فَاضْرِبْ لَهُمْ طَرِيقًا فِي الْبَحْرِ *"fadrib lahum tarīqan fī al-baḥr" –" We sent an inspiration to Moses: "Travel by night with My servants, and strike a dry path for them through the sea."*[625]

In this sense the verse would read: "separate from them in bed, (And) strike a path for them," meaning "show them a path to self-examination and self-correction," or "show them a path to leave, a way out," meaning the relationship has come to an end.

---

[623] Sūratu 'l-Baqara [The Heifer], 2:61.
[624] Sūrat Āli-'Imrān [The Family of 'Imrān], 3:112
[625] Sūrah ṬāḤā 20:77.

8) *"To go about"* as in: إِذَا ضَرَبُواْ فِي الأَرْضِ- *"idhā darabū fī al-arḍi"* - *"when they are going about in the Earth."*[626]

In this sense the verse would read: "separate from them in bed, (and) leave them." This meaning has recently been given much press after Dr. Laleh Bakhtiar used it in her translation of the Holy Qur'ān.

9) *"To set forth"* as in: مَا ضَرَبُوهُ لَكَ إِلَّا جَدَلًا - *"mā darabūhu laka"* - *"This they set forth to thee ..."*[627]

In this sense, the verse would read: "separate from them in bed, (and) set forth to them," meaning "expound to them their wrongdoing."

10) *"To set up"* as in: فَضُرِبَ بَيْنَهُم بِسُورٍ لَّهُ بَابٌ- *"faḍuriba baynahum bi-sūrin"* -*"So a wall will be set up between them"*[628]

In this sense the verse would read: "separate from them in bed, (and) set up a barrier (between you and them)."

11) *"To utterly ignore"* as in أَفَنَضْرِبُ عَنكُمُ الذِّكْرَ صَفْحًا- *"Shall We utterly ignore you"* – *"Afanaḍribu ʿankumu adh-dhikra ṣafḥan"*[629]

In this sense the verse would read: "separate from them in bed, (and) ignore them."

---

[626] Sūrat Āli-ʿImrān [The Family of ʿImrān], 3:156.
[627] Sūratu z-Zukhruf [The Gold Adornments], 43:58.
[628] Sūratu 'l-Ḥadīd [Iron], 57:13.
[629] Sūratu z-Zukhruf [The Gold Adornments], 43:5.

12) *"To draw over"* as in وَلْيَضْرِبْنَ بِخُمُرِهِنَّ عَلَى جُيُوبِهِنَّ - *"wal-yadribna bi-khumūrihinna 'ala juyūbihinna" – "let them draw their veils over their bosoms"*[630]

In this sense, the verse would read: "separate from them in bed, (and) then lovingly draw them towards you," meaning that after the pressure of separation, the warmth of affection will restart the relationship afresh.

The last verse compared is particularly important, because it applies specifically to women. Given the absence of debate over how *ḍaraba* is interpreted here, why should it carry such a different meaning in the verse in question?

VALID DICTIONARY INTERPRETATIONS

There are other meanings of the word *ḍaraba* besides those used in the Holy Qur'ān. The Arabic-English Dictionary, *al-Mawrid*[631] gives 31 different meanings for *ḍaraba*. The *Hans-Wehr Arabic-English Dictionary*[632] lists 58 meanings. Let us examine how some of these different translations may apply to the verse in question.

For example, some commentators on them Holy Qur'ān have suggested the meaning *"separate from them in bed, and prevent them (from going out)."* This particular meaning is apropos when studying the verse as a whole, for the entire sequence can then be translated as:

> If you find your wives committing adultery or dallying with other men,
> then admonish them.

---

[630] Sūratu 'n-Nūr [The Light], 24:31.

[631] Al-Ba'albakī, Rūḥī, *Al-Mawrid: A Modern Arabic-English Dictionary*. Dār al-'Ilm lil-Malāyīn, 15th Edition, 2001.

[632] *Hans-Wehr Arabic-English Dictionary of Modern Written Arabic*, Edited by J.M. Cowan, Spoken Language Services, Ithaca, 1976.

(If they continue), then separate from them in bed. (Finally, if they still persist), and prevent them from going out.

This meaning is certainly consistent with another verse in the Holy Qur'ān:

وَإِنِ امْرَأَةٌ خَافَتْ مِن بَعْلِهَا نُشُوزًا أَوْ إِعْرَاضًا فَلَا جُنَاحَ عَلَيْهِمَا أَن يُصْلِحَا بَيْنَهُمَا صُلْحًا وَالصُّلْحُ خَيْرٌ

If a wife fears cruelty or desertion on her husband's part, there is no blame on them if they arrange an amicable settlement between themselves; and such settlement is best.[633]

How could the Holy Qur'ān on one hand endorse the beating of the wife and only a little later allow her to seek a divorce based on that very cruelty?

Another pertinent dictionary meaning of the verb *ḍaraba* is "to have sexual intercourse." In other languages as well, the verb 'to strike' is also used to mean sexual intercourse — for example, it means this in Somali, a derivate language of Arabic, and even the old Germanic verb *focken,* "to strike" became a well-known vulgarism for sexual intercourse in English.

وقيل: معناه أكرهوهن على الجماع واربطوهن، من هجر البعير إذا شدّه بالهجار.

وهذا من تفسير الثقلاء< تفسير الكشاف/ الزمخشري>

One of the great early classical commentators on the Qur'ān Al-Zamakhsharī, said:

It is said that it (*ḍaraba*) means 'have intercourse with them and then hold them firmly…' and this is the meaning

[633] Sūratu 'n-Nisā [Women], 4:128.

> given by the greatest commentators [of the Holy Qur'ān].[634]

Raghib in his classical commentary on the Holy Qur'ān *al-Mufradāt fi gharīb al-Qur'ān* gives the meanings of these words with special reference to this verse saying that *ḍaraba* metaphorically means "to have sexual relations." This is cited as well in the foremost Arabic dictionary, al-Ifrīqī's *Lisān al-ʿArab*.[635] In this one case, the verb *ḍaraba* stands alone with no object, as Raghib cites: ' وضَرَبَ الفحلُ الناقة *ḍaraba al-fahl an-nāqah'* – "the stallion camel covered the mare camel,"[636] which appears in the same linguistic form as the verse under consideration.

The great Sufi scholar al-Qushayrī said in his commentary on the verse in his *The Alluded Subtleties*:

أي ارتقوا في تهذيبهن بالتدريج والرفق، وإنْ صَلُحَ الأمر بالوعظ فلا تستعمل العصا بالضرب، فالآية تتضمن آداب العِشْرة.

> What is meant here is to encourage them to correct themselves in stages and with kindness. But if the matter is not settled by admonishing then it is not to beat her (with a stick or the hand) because the verse implies the conduct of engaging in sexual relations.[637]

This interpretation fits the context of the verse exceedingly well. The *ḍaraba* stage in the process follows temporary

---

[634] al-Zamakhsharī, Abū al-Qāsim Maḥmūd ibn ʿUmar , Al-Kashshāf ʿan Haqā'iq at-Tanzil, "The Discoverer of Revealed Truths", Egypt: Dār al-Kutub al-ʿIlmīyyah, 2003.

[635] Al-Ifrīqī, Ibn Mundhir. *Lisān al-ʿArab,* Egypt: Muassat al-ʿIlmīyyah lil-matbuʿat,2005.

[636] Al-Asfahānī, Rāghib, *al-Mufradāt fi gharīb al-Qur'ān*, Beirut: Dār al-Maʿrifah, 1999.

[637] Qushayrī, Abū 'l-Qāsim ʿAbdu 'l-Karīm al-, *Latā'if al-isharat bi tafsīr al-Qur'ān* [The Subtleties and Allusions in the Commentary of the Qur'ān]. Egypt: Dār al-Kutub al-ʿIlmīyyah, 2000.

suspension of relations between the spouses. Note also that among the many meanings of this term two opposite meanings are used here: "to separate" and "to mingle." The sense of separation meant here relates back to the verb *uḥjur*, which means "to separate from them in bed," immediately preceding, while the senses of "inclining towards," "mingling," and "settling down," and "having sexual intercourse" are looking ahead to the marital reconciliation (*tawfîq*) in the next phrase (*w 'aḍribūhunna*). This is a good example of the extremely subtle, intricate intertwining of meanings in the Arabic of the Holy Qur'ān, which are usually lost in translation.

We know from other statements of the Prophet that Allah showers a couple with spiritual blessings when they engage in licit sexual relations. Using this meaning the verse can be translated:

> As for women on whose part ye fear disloyalty and ill-
> conduct,
> admonish them (first),
> (Next), separate from them in bed,
> (And last) go to bed with them (when they are willing).

Another linguistic meaning we find is "to turn away," "to disregard" and "to avoid speaking" - in each case with the qualifier that one should look to intermediaries to solve the issue. This coincides with the verse which follows saying:

. . . فَإِنْ أَطَعْنَكُمْ فَلاَ تَبْغُواْ عَلَيْهِنَّ سَبِيلاً إِنَّ اللّهَ كَانَ عَلِيّاً كَبِيراً وَإِنْ خِفْتُمْ

شِقَاقَ

بَيْنِهِمَا فَابْعَثُواْ حَكَماً مِّنْ أَهْلِهِ وَحَكَماً مِّنْ أَهْلِهَا . . .

And if ye fear a breach between them twain (the man and wife), appoint an arbiter from his folk and an arbiter from her folk. If they desire amendment Allah will make them of one mind. Lo! Allah is ever Knower, Aware.[638]

The renowned commentator of The Holy Qur'ān, Imām as-Sūyūṭi says in his *Durar*:

> If strife ensues between a man and wife, he should seek counsel from the righteous men and someone who is his peer in righteousness among the women so they can determine which one of the two is in the wrong [and help them correct it].[639]

In the context given, beating would not be used, rather softness, good conduct and the intervention of outside parties.

THE CORRECT UNDERSTANDING OF "BEATING"

Finally, in evaluating the common meaning used by most translators, "to beat," we must also understand its meaning in the light of the statements by the Prophet himself and in the light of the statements of the commentators on the Holy Qur'ān.

Prophet Muhammad ﷺ explicitly forbade the beating of any woman, saying:

خرج عبد الرزاق وابن سعد وابن المنذر والحاكم والبيهقي عن إياس بن عبد الله ابن
أبي ذئاب قال: قال رسول الله صلى الله عليه وسلم: "لا تضربوا إماء الله"

Never beat the handmaidens of God.[640]

[638] Sūratu 'n-Nisā [Women], 4:35.
[639] al-Ḥāfiẓ as-Suyūṭī, as-. *Durar*. 2nd ed. Beirut: Dār al-Fikr, 1403.
[640] *Sunan Abū Dāwūd*, (authenticated by Muḥammad Muḥyīddīn bin ʿAbdul Ḥamīd), #2144, Beirut: Dār al-Fikr, Aḥmad ibn Shuʿayb Abū Abdur-Raḥmān an-Nisā'ī, *Sunan al-Nisā'ī*, (authenticated by ʿAbdul Fattāḥ Abū Ghuddah), Aleppo: Maktab al-Matbuʿat al-Islāmīyya,1986., Ibn Mājah al-Qazwīnī. *Sunan Ibn Mājah*. Ed. Maḥmūd Fu'ād ʿAbd al-Bāqī. Beirut: Dār al-Fikr, Kitāb al-Aḥkām, Aḥmad

Divine Law forbids harmful beating of any kind and mandates retribution for those who perpetrate it.

In the *Ḥāshīyya* of al-Dusūqī to Ibn al-ʿArafa al-Mālikī he says:

أما الضرب المبرح، فقد نهى عنه الشارع حتى وإن كان فيه صلاح الزوجة واستقامتهاوجاء في حاشية الدسوقي لابن عرفه المالكي (ولا يجوز الضرب المبرح ولو علم الزوج أنها لا تترك النشوز إلا به، فإن وقع فلها التطليق عليه والقصاص) .

And beating other than symbolically is forbidden, even if the husband knows that the wife will not stop her wrongdoing except by means of it. And if it happened the wife is permitted to seek divorce because of it and retribution.[641]

The Prophet Muhammad ﷺ also said:

إذا استنشقت فبالغ إلا أن تكون صائما ولا تضرب ظعينتك كما تضرب أمتك

Do not beat your noble wife like a slave.[642]

The Prophet ﷺ also said:

قال رسول الله صلى الله عليه وسلم: "لاتضربوا إماء الله"

Do not beat God's maidservants.[643]

---

ibn Ḥanbal. *Al-Musnad*. 20 vols. Ed. Aḥmad Shākir and Ḥamza Aḥmad al-Zayn. Cairo: Dār al-Ḥadīth, 1995, Ḥākim, al-. *Mustadrak*. 524, Kitāb al-Imān, Beirut: Dār al-Kutub al-ʿArabī, n.d., al-Bayhaqī, Aḥmad ibn al-Ḥusayn ʿAlī ibn Mūsā Abū Bakr, *Sunan al-Bayhaqī al-Kubra*, Mecca: Maktaba Dār al-Bāz,1994., Ibn Mundhir, Abū Bakr ʿAbd ar-Razzāq ibn Himām as-Sanaʿanī, *Mūsānnaf Abd ar-Razzāq*, Al-Maktab al-Islāmī, 1403, and Ibn Saʿad.

641 Muḥammad ibn ʿArafa al-Dasūqī (d. 1815), *Ḥāshīyya ad-Dasūqī*, Beirut: Dār al-kutub al-ʿIlmīyya.

642 Ḥākim, al-. *Mustadrak*. 524, Kitāb al-Imān, Beirut: Dār al-Kutub al-ʿArabī, n.d. Abū Dāwūd.

Also:

وأخرج عبد الرزاق عن عائشة عن النبي صلى الله عليه وسلم قال: "أما يستحي أحدكم أن يضرب امرأته كما يضرب العبد، يضربها أول النهار ثnم يضاجعها آخره".

The Prophet ﷺ said, "Are you not ashamed to beat your wives as one beats a slave, you beat her in the daytime and have intercourse with her in the night?"[644]

Speaking more generally, the Prophet ﷺ said:

أخبرنا أبو نصر بن قتادة أنا أبو علي الرفاء القروي أنا علي بن عبد العزيز ثنا أبو غسان مالك بن إسماعيل ثنا اسرائيل عن الأعمش عن شقيق عن عبد الله قال قال رسول الله صلى الله عليه وسلم اجيبوا الداعي ولا تردوا الهدية ولا تضربوا الناس أو المسلمين

Respond when someone calls you, do not refuse a gift and beat not the people nor the Muslims.[645]

The following hadith are also related:

وعن أبي أمامة أن رسول الله صلى الله عليه وسلم وهب لعلي غلاما فقال لا تضربه فإني نهيت عن ضرب أهل الصلاة وقد رأيته يصلي . هذا لفظ المصابيح .

---

643 Abū Bakr ʿAbd ar-Razzāq ibn Himām as-Sanaʿanī, *Mūsānnaf ʿAbd ar-Razzāq*, Al-Maktab al-Islāmī, 1403,

644 Abū Bakr ʿAbd ar-Razzāq ibn Himām as-Sanaʿanī, *Mūsānnaf ʿAbd ar-Razzāq*, Al-Maktab al-Islāmī, 1403,

645 al-Bayhaqī , Aḥmad ibn al-Ḥusayn ʿAli ibn Mūsā Abū Bakr. *Shuʿab al-Imān*, #5359, Beirut: Dār al-Kutub al-ʿIlmīyyah, 1996.
and a similar narration in Aḥmad ibn Ḥanbal. *Al-Musnad*. 20 vols. Ed. Aḥmad Shākir and Hamza Aḥmad al-Zayn. Cairo: Dār al-Ḥadīth, 1995, #3838 without reference to "the people."

The Prophet ﷺ sent ʿAlī ؓ a manservant and said, "Do not beat him for indeed I have been prohibited from beating those who pray, and I have observed him praying."[646]

وفي المجتبى للدارقطني أن عمر بن الخطاب رضي الله عنه قال نهانا رسول الله صلى الله عليه وسلم عن ضرب المصلين .

ʿUmar ibn al-Khaṭṭāb related, "The Messenger of Allah prohibited us from beating any Muslim."[647]

Such clear statements by the Prophet are prohibitions to all Muslims, as every believer is obliged to obey the Prophet in his daily actions.

The personal example of the Prophet is also important, as it serves as a guide for all believers. The Prophet Muhammad's wife ʿĀʿishā said:

ما ضرب رسول الله صلى الله عليه وسلم امرأة له ولا خادما قط، ولا ضرب بيده شيئا قط إلا في سبيل الله أو تنتهك حرمات الله فينتقم لله

The Prophet never beat any of his wives or servants ... [648]

Because of this, even the classical commentators who used the meaning *ḍaraba* in the sense of striking, noted that that "it must not be mubarrih, where mubarrih is defined in *al-Mawrid* as 'violent, intense, severe, acute, sharp, excruciating.'"

---

[646] Khātib at-Tabrīzī. *Mishkāt al-masābiḥ,* Authenticated by al-Albānī, Maktabat al-Mishkāt al-Islāmī, and Aḥmad ibn Ḥanbal. *Al-Musnad.* 20 vols. Ed. Aḥmad Shākir and Hamza Aḥmad al-Zayn. Cairo: Dār al-Ḥadīth, 1995, #22208.

[647] Al-Dāraqutnī , ʿAlī b. ʿUmar (d. 385/955), *al-Sunan,* 4 volumes, Cairo. Also: Ed. Shams al-Ḥaqq ʿAzīmabādī,Delhi.

[648] Aḥmad ibn Shuʿayb Abū ʿAbdur-Raḥmān an-Nisāʾī, *Sunan al-Nisāʾī,* (authenticated by ʿAbdu 'l-Fattāḥ Abū Ghuddah), Aleppo: Maktab al-Matbuʿat al-Islāmīyya,1986.

وقد قال عليه الصلاة والسلام: " آضرِبوا النساء إذا عَصَينكم في معروفٍ ضَرْباً غيرَ مُبَرّحٍ " قال عطاء: قلت لابن عباس ما الضرب غيرُ المُبَرّحِ؟ قال بالسواك ونحوه وقال عطاء: قلت لابن عباس: ما الضرب غير المبرح؟ قال بالشراك ونحوه،

However, the greatest interpreter of the Holy Qur'ān and cousin of Prophet Muhammad ﷺ, ibn ʿAbbas, explained *"ghayr mubarriḥ"* as meaning "to use a twig (*siwāk*) or something like it." In another case he said, "with a shoelace or something like it." Thus, *ḍaraba* here means "to strike" with a twig or string to symbolize the husband's displeasure.

حدثني المثنى، قال: ثنا حبان، قال: ثنا ابن المبارك، قال: أخبرنا عبد الوارث بن سعيد، عن رجل، عن الحسن، قال: ضرباً غير مبرّح، غير مؤثر.

The Prophet's grandson al-Ḥasan, one of the highest jurist, second only to his father, ʿAlī ibn Abī Ṭālib, described *"ḍarban ghayra mubarriḥ"* as *"ghayru mu'atthir,"* "to strike without touching or without effect." This again shows *ḍaraba*'s purely symbolic nature, such as a wave of the hand or twig.

وَقِيلَ بِدِرَّةٍ أَوْ مِخْرَاقِ مِنْدِيلٍ مَلْفُوفٍ لَا بِسَوْطٍ وَلَا خَشَبٍ , فَإِنْ تَلِفَتْ مِنْ ذَلِكَ فَلَا ضَمَانَ عَلَيْهِ

Ibn ʿAbbas went even further saying the most a husband may do to indicate his displeasure, after first advising her, then separating from her in bed, is to "strike" her with a folded handkerchief (*mandīl malfūf*).[649]

---

649 Muḥammad bin Aḥmad as-Saffarīni al-Ḥanbalī, *Ghidā' al-albāb maṭlab fī ḍarb ar-rajul zawjatahu tā'dīban lahā* (Chapter: what is fournd regarding a man striking

The symbolic nature of *ḍaraba* is incontestable when one refers to another verse of the Holy Qur'ān which employs the same language as the verse in question. Here Ibn Kathīr, a prominent Qur'ānic exegete, relates:

> The Prophet Job, while suffering tremendous illness with patience, once became upset at something his wife had done, and swore a solemn oath that if God would heal him, he would punish her with a hundred stripes. But when God healed him, how could her service, mercy, compassion and kindness be repaid with a beating? So God showed him a way out, and finally having his health restored, was ordered by the Lord:
>
> وَخُذْ بِيَدِكَ ضِغْثًا فَاضْرِب بِّهِ وَلَا تَحْنَثْ إِنَّا وَجَدْنَاهُ صَابِرًا نِّعْمَ الْعَبْدُ إِنَّهُ أَوَّابٌ
>
> *Now take in thy hand a small bunch of grass, and strike therewith, and thou wilt not break thine oath!*[650]
>
> So Allah showed him a way out [from cruelly beating his wife], which was to take a bundle of thin grass with one hundred stems, and tap her with it one time. Thus, he fulfilled his oath and avoided breaking his vow. This was the solution and way out for one who had fear of God and turned to Him in repentance.[651]

---

his wife for the purposes of disciplining her"). Beirut: Dār al-Kutub al-'Ilmīyya, 1996.

[650] Sūrah Ṣād, 38:44

[651] Ibn Kathīr ad-Dimashqī, *Tafsīr ibn Kathīr,* 4:34, Beirut: Dār al-Kutub al-'Ilmīyya, 1996.

The Spiritual Meaning of the Verse

If we look at the purely spiritual interpretation of the verse in question, we can say that none of us has yet reached the level of manhood it describes when it says: "Men are the protectors and maintainers of women, because Allah has given the one more (strength) than the other, and because they support them from their means."

A "man" in the spiritual sense advanced by the great scholars of the science of self-realization, or Sufism, is a person – male or female – whose angelic self has conquered the lower self and achieved spiritual maturity. Such people are also known as saints (*awlīyāullāh*).

Taken in this light, it can be read: "Self-realized humans have taken charge of their selves, because of the superiority that Allah has bestowed on the soul over the self and in what they have given of their selves to Allah."

In this station, they have achieved a state of spiritual enlightenment by taking control of the lower promptings of desire and lust, and instead following the positive inspirations that come from the angelic self. For, as Allah said, He has:

$$فَأَلْهَمَهَا فُجُورَهَا وَتَقْوَاهَا$$

... inspired the self with what is wrong for it and what is right for it. [652]

At this time, the self becomes satisfied and content, a state referred to as the *nafs al-muṭma'inna*. About this state, the Successor al-Qatādah ؒ, said:

> It is the soul of the believer, made calm by what Allah has promised. Its owner is at rest and content with his knowledge of Allah's Names and Attributes.[653]

---

[652] Sūratu 'sh-Shams [The Sun], 91:8.

And Imām al-Baghāwī said:

> The *nafs al-muṭma'inna* has an angel to help, assist and guide it. The angel casts good promptings into the self so that it desires what is good and is aware of the excellence of good actions. The angel also keeps the self away from wrong action and shows it the ugliness of wrongdoing. All in all, whatever is for Allah and by Him, always comes from the Soul which is at Peace.[654]

So, when the lower self has been overcome by the angelic self, it become pure and righteous, and in that state the lower self becomes "devoutly obedient" to the angelic soul and guards itself from straying into transgression . If the angelic soul catches the lower aspects of the ego straying in selfish actions, it will "advise them," and failing this will "abstain from' desires by going into seclusion and asceticism, and finally, failing this, it will "beat" the self by taking on difficulties and discomfort, such as seclusions, fasts, vigils and other arduous tasks. At that time, when the lower self ceases its rebellion, it then becomes a vehicle by means of which the angelic self may ascend to the highest stations of Divine realities. At that time al-Qatadah said, "a believer such as this can almost see [realities of the afterlife] with his own eyes."

Thus, one sees in the life of the Prophet Muhammad ﷺ prior to receiving the Message from Allah how he used to seclude himself in the Cave of Hira for forty days every year, spending his time contemplating Allah's Creation, seeking the meaning of life, the reasons for mankind's difficulties and suffering, and subduing the ego by means of spiritual discipline. There the Prophet survived on salt, bread and vinegar, polishing his already faultless nature to perfection, thus preparing to receive the weight of Allah's Revealed Word, the Holy Qur'ān.

---

[653] al-Ṭabarī, *Jamiʿ al-Bayān fi Tafsīr al-Qur'ān*, vol. 13, Bulaq 1323.

[654] Imām Baghāwī's, *Lubab al-Tā'wīl fi Maʿalam at-Tanzīl*, 8 vols. Cairo, 1308.

THE IMPORTANCE OF PROPHET MUHAMMAD'S EXAMPLE IN MUSLIM LIFE

In conclusion, it is imperative that Muslims always look to the behavior of the Prophet Muhammad ﷺ for their example, for Allah said:

مَّنْ يُطِعِ الرَّسُولَ فَقَدْ أَطَاعَ اللّهَ وَمَن تَوَلَّى فَمَا أَرْسَلْنَاكَ عَلَيْهِمْ حَفِيظًا

Whoever obeys the Prophet indeed obeys Allah.[655]

Allah also said:

قُلْ إِن كُنتُمْ تُحِبُّونَ اللّهَ فَاتَّبِعُونِي يُحْبِبْكُمُ اللّهُ وَيَغْفِرْ لَكُمْ ذُنُوبَكُمْ وَاللّهُ غَفُورٌ رَّحِيمٌ

Say: "If ye do love Allah, Follow me: Allah will love you and forgive you your sins: For Allah is Oft-Forgiving, Most Merciful."[656]

Thus, obedience to the Prophet ﷺ and following his example is a must for all faithful Muslim. Allah's Messenger ﷺ never accepted and never allowed himself or any man in his community to raise a hand against anyone in his family. This is enough for all Muslims: to understand that if the Prophet ﷺ avoided something, the entire community must not do it either.

In light of this, there is no excuse for men to beat their wives and then seek religious means to justify their wrongdoing. Since Prophet Muhammad ﷺ did not do it, we must not do it. Laws,

---

[655] Sūratu 'n-Nisā [Women], 4:80.
[656] Sūrat Āli-'Imrān [The Family of 'Imrān], 3:31.

where they fail to do so, must be amended to prevent this kind of behavior.

Finally, it is essential in a time when tensions remain high that religious issues such as this not become a source of friction between communities. It is imperative that each community in our global society seek to understand the others, not through the eyes of extremist scholars, but through the knowledge, understanding and wisdom of moderate, open-minded scholars whose attitude is one of conciliation, not fanaticism and negativity.

Science and Technology

The Importance of Technology in the Development of Islamic Countries[657]

[657] Presented at a conference of Muslim scholars held by under the auspices of Nahdlatul Ulama in Indonesia, 2003.

What was the means by which the Prophet developed the Sahaba, their community and the entire Ummah? He taught them:

اطلب العلم و لو في الصين

Seek knowledge even if it be in China.[658]

It was through a cultural ethos informed by the Qur'ānic order to seek God's Signs in His creation and to ponder on them, that the sciences were built in Islam on the foundations of rational inquiry and logical thought while simultaneously seeking the philosophical and theological underpinnings to their observations. In this way, the Muslim world quickly surpassed its counterparts in developing science and research methodology, practical experimentation, and methods of confirming theory with observation - methods that are still followed today in modern laboratories and technical institutions.

The hadith:

طلب العلم فريضة على كل مسلم

Seeking knowledge is an obligation upon every Muslim[659]

---

[658] *Ḥadīth ḥasan mashhūr*. Narrated from Anas by al-Bayhaqī in *Shuʿab al-īmān* and *al-Madkhal*, Ibn ʿAbd al-Barr in *Jamiʿ Bayān al-ʿIlm*, and al-Khātib through three chains at the opening of his *al-Riḥla fī ṭalab al-ḥadīth* (p. 71-76 #1-3) where Shaykh Nūr al-Dīn ʿItr declares it weak (*daʿīf*). Also narrated from Ibn 'Umar, Ibn ʿAbbās, Ibn Masʿūd, Jābir, and Abū Saʿīd al-Khuḍrī, all through very weak chains. The Ḥadīth master al-Mizzī said it has so many chains that it deserves a grade of fair (*ḥasan*), as quoted by al-Sakhāwī in *al-Maqāsid al-ḥasana*. Al-ʿIraqī in his *Mughnī ʿanh ḥaml al-asfar* similarly stated that some scholars declared it sound (*saḥīḥ*) for that reason.

[659] A fair (*ḥasan*) narration in Ibn Mājah because of its many chains as stated by al-Mizzī, al-Ṭabarānī in *al-Kabīr*, ibn ʿAdī in *al-Kāmil*, al-Bayhaqī in *Shuʿab al-īmān*, while Dr. Muḥammad ʿAjāj al-Khātib in his notes on al-Khātib's *al-Jāmiʿ* (2:462-463) declared it "sound due to its witness-chains" (*saḥīḥ li ghayrih*).

was applied in every sphere of life from the religious to the most outwardly "secular," for in Islam nothing was considered outside the realm of God's Divine Command and thus every aspect of existence was considered addressed by the order "seek knowledge..."

Due to this zeal for knowledge inspired by the Prophet in the hearts of his followers literally millions of books such were authored and disseminated across the Muslim world.

It was such inspiration as provided by the Prophet through Sayyidina 'Alī ؉ and his school and the other Companions and their schools that evolved the sciences of astronomy, physics, chemistry, optics, pharmacology, botany, zoology, geology, mineralogy, medicine, dentistry, and surgery, as well as the more abstract fields like logic, mathematics and philosophy. From these schools came the likes of Jābir ibn Ḥayān, father of modern chemistry who studied under Jā'far aṣ-Ṣādiq; Muḥammad Ibn Mūsā al-Khawarizmī, who founded modern mathematics - including the fundamentals of algebra - in the early 800's, and studied the sciences of astronomy and geography with his renowned contemporary al-Kindī who did research as well in physics, music, psychology and medicine. Al-Birūnī is credited with founding the modern scientific method. Ibn Sīnā, known in the West as Avicenna, was renowned not only for his contributions to medical science, for which he was known as the 'doctor of doctors.' In particular his work the *Canon* (*al-Qānūn*) became the fountainhead of Western medicine in the early Renaissance, influencing the likes of Da Vinci and displacing Galen as the primary source of medical knowledge. Ibn Rushd (Averroes) was known for his tremendous contributions to the science of astronomy in the form of the book the *Almagest*, used by the Europeans long after Islamic civilization's twilight.

I could go on and on naming the great Muslim scientists and technologists but the point has been made – science, research and technology are a natural part of the Islamic value-system. And just as attention to matters of religion have declined in the last half-millennium, so too has the attention to these finer aspects of the faith. It is thus no wonder that with the decline in the religiosity of the Ummah as predicted by the Prophet, the material aspects have faded as well, so that today the Ummah is a mere shadow of its former greatness. We thank Allah that an illness once known can be treated, as the Prophet ﷺ informed us, "Allah has not made a disease without appointing a remedy for it, with the exception of one: old age,"[660] but misdiagnosis at this late stage will result in mistreatment and further degradation. For today, our Ummah is under an illness and only with inspiration from Allah and guidance from the Qur'ān and Sunnah can a remedy be found.

The scientists that developed in Islam's civilization knew the importance of knowledge and discovery. The Qur'ān repeatedly admonishes the believers to study Allah's Creation:

وَسَخَّرَ لَكُم مَّا فِي السَّمَاوَاتِ وَمَا فِي الْأَرْضِ جَمِيعًا مِّنْهُ إِنَّ فِي ذَٰلِكَ لَآيَاتٍ لِّقَوْمٍ يَتَفَكَّرُونَ

And He has subjected to you, as from Him, all that is in the heavens and on earth: Behold, in that are Signs indeed for those

[661]. who reflect

---

[660] Abū Dāwūd. Other similar narrations: "There is no disease that Allah has created except that He also has created a treatment" (*Saḥīḥ Al-Bukhārī,* 7:582) and "There is a remedy for every malady, and when the remedy is applied to the disease it is cured with the permission of Allah, the Exalted and Glorious" (*Saḥīḥ Muslim,* 5466) and "The one who sent down the disease sent down the remedy." (*Al-Muwaṭṭā,* 50:5:12).

[661] Sūratu 'l-Jāthīya [The Crouching], 45:13.

Whoever delves deeply into the understanding of many verses and *aḥādīth* that reveal information about today's discoveries cannot fail to understand that Islam builds up the nation and addresses the importance of stretching the boundaries of knowledge and its implementations.

We can see this in the teachings of the Prophet in Qur'ān and hadith regarding the importance of science and seeking knowledge. All such discoveries will eventually lead to the development of technology in its various forms directed towards building the well-being of the Nation and for use in promoting God-consciousness – *taqwā.*

For if we truly believe in Islam and in the Holy Qur'ān, we must follow the Prophet. Allah said:

قُلْ إِن كُنتُمْ تُحِبُّونَ اللّهَ فَاتَّبِعُونِي يُحْبِبْكُمُ اللّهُ وَيَغْفِرْ لَكُمْ ذُنُوبَكُمْ وَاللّهُ غَفُورٌ رَّحِيمٌ

Say: "If ye do love Allah, Follow me: Allah will love you and forgive you your sins: For Allah is Oft-Forgiving, Most Merciful."[662]

The Prophet left us his Sunnah - his way – and an essential part of that Sunnah is to encourage the development of science, research and technology. That is why, knowing as he did the importance of technology, he encouraged its development in many *aḥādīth.*

The *aḥādīth* which I intend to explain in the remainder of this paper demonstrate the importance of science and the importance of developing the Ummah. At the same time the Prophet's teachings related to the wealthy and their relationship with the poor are an essential component in the life of the Ummah.

---

[662] Sūrat Āli-'Imrān [The Family of 'Imrān], 3:31.

ZAKAT – OBLIGATION OF INDIVIDUALS, COMMUNITIES AND NATIONS

One of the principal teachings of Islam is the obligation of *zakāt* and the voluntary donations in the form of *ṣadaqah*. From this individual requirement for Muslims to help the poor, whether individually or collectively through the *Bayt al-Māl,* one can derived a societal requirement: the importance of wealthy "have" Muslim countries to support the poor "have not" ones in order to improve their conditions and raise their living standards. It is only through establishing such relationships, that the Ummah can be reconstituted after the fragmentation of the last century.

What better example of this than in the practice of the Prophet ﷺ and his Companions? What comes to mind is when as caliph, Sayyidina 'Umar ؓ used to go out at night in disguise, looking for those in need. He would take food and distribute it to the needy. One time he found poor woman late at night preparing 'stone' soup for her children who were crying for want of something to eat. Not realizing that the man she was speaking with was Sayyidina 'Umar ؓ, she complained about her condition and that the caliph was not doing his job. Immediately Sayyidina 'Umar ؓ brought her food and helped to prepare it for her hungry children.[663]

Such was the concern of the early Muslim leaders for their people: for them it was not the job of the state to help – rather it

---

[663] Many incidents of this nature were reported from the Khulaphā ar-rāshidīn, the four rightly-guided caliphs.
It is related that a blind old woman lived in a suburb of Madina and had no one to support her. 'Umar ؓ used to go in disguise to the house of the old woman, but was always surprised to find that someone else had anticipated him and had supplied the wants of the old woman. One night 'Umar ؓ went to the house of the old woman earlier than usual and hid himself to watch as to who attended to the wants of the old lady. He had not to wait long for soon a man arrived who attended to the needs of the old woman, and this man was Abū Bakr ؓ.

was a personal responsibility on them as the leader to see that each person was fed, sheltered and safe.

For this reason, Sayyidina Abū Bakr aṣ-Ṣiddīq ﷺ said, "The weak among you shall be strong with me till God willing his rights have been vindicated; and the strong among you shall be weak with me till, if the Lord wills, I have taken what is due from him."

Today we are fortunate to see such kind of leaders emerging from within the Ummah yet again. We see nations like Indonesia and Malaysia, where the leaders have a strong sense of civic duty and feel the obligation to help each and every individual to obtain a decent life.

It is the duty of the rich Muslim countries to help the poor ones to build civic society and to build their standard of living for having an excellent life. The Prophet ﷺ always sought refuge in Allah from poverty saying "O Lord I seek refuge in Thee from *kufr* (unbelief) and poverty,"[664] for according to another hadith, "Poverty, in all probability, leads to unbelief (*kufr*)."[665]

Allah has granted tremendous wealth to the Muslims. He gave them oil, gold, natural gas and minerals. Those possessed of such an overabundance of wealth cannot say to the poor nations, many of which consist of nothing but deserts and mountains and possess no resources whatsoever, and tell them, "Build yourselves!" Rather, it is the responsibility of the rich to assist the poor. The Qur'ān states categorically,

وَفِي أَمْوَالِهِمْ حَقٌّ لِلسَّائِلِ وَالْمَحْرُومِ

[664] Abū Dāwūd.

[665] Bayhaqī, al-Ṭabarānī.

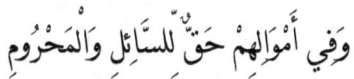

And in their wealth the beggar (or needy) and the deprived (who does not beg but nevertheless is needy) had due share.[666]

Simultaneously, Allah ordered *zakāt* as an obligation. Why is it then that the Muslim countries do not take *zakāt* from their money, at a minimum 2.5%, and give it to the poorer Muslim nations? How much oil and natural gas do the Muslim countries possess? Does it not have a *zakāt* on it? If there is 100 billion barrels of oil reserves, what is its *zakāt*?

We cannot cheat in Islam by saying, "It is in the earth." If you have gold in your possession, then from year to year you must pay *zakāt* on it - *min hawl ila al-hawl*. If you have gold in your house you know how much *zakāt* must be paid on it. On the other hand gold which is in the form of reserves requires a process for extraction because it is mixed within the soil and thus is not subject to *zakāt*. But oil is something that comes ready from the ground – it requires no extensive process to be used. It is therefore subject to *zakāt*.

A nation is analogous to a house controlled by a government, particularly if it is owned by certain people. And today by means of technology it is possible to ascertain exactly the quantity of oil present in reserve. *Zakāt* must be paid on that oil, just as with dates, with processed gold and with mines. Consider: the *zakāt* on the Muslim nations' oil reserves is more than sufficient to provide the entire Muslim world the wealth to build their nations to maturity and an advanced level of civilization and technology.

الناس شركاء في ثلاثة: الكلأ، والنار، والماء

The Prophet ﷺ said, "People are partners in three things: water, grazing and fire."[667]

---

[666] Sūratu 'dh-Dhāriyāt [The Winnowing Winds], 51:19.

[667] Arabic: الناس شركاء في ثلاثة: الكلأ، والنار، والماء, *Bukhārī*, Kitāb al-buyuʿ.

Fire here can be considered to represent all sources of fire, whether wood, oil or natural gas; and in these the people must be partners. Rich countries must share with the poor countries – it is not that Allah ﷻ gave it to one nation and it is not available for the others, who are in need. Allah ﷻ made the Ummah of Muhammad ﷺ one nation where He said:

إِنَّ هَذِهِ أُمَّتُكُمْ أُمَّةً وَاحِدَةً وَأَنَا رَبُّكُمْ فَاعْبُدُونِ

Verily, this community of yours is a single community, and I am your Lord and Cherisher: therefore serve Me.[668]

and thus regardless of which country it belongs to, the wealth of oil, gold and other valuables must be shared within the entire Ummah.

So we come to a poor nation and say "build yourself." The question is not should they, but how, for they have nothing. Allah ﷻ said:

وَاعْتَصِمُواْ بِحَبْلِ اللّهِ جَمِيعًا وَلاَ تَفَرَّقُواْ وَاذْكُرُواْ نِعْمَةَ اللّهِ عَلَيْكُمْ إِذْ كُنتُمْ أَعْدَاء فَأَلَّفَ بَيْنَ قُلُوبِكُمْ فَأَصْبَحْتُم بِنِعْمَتِهِ إِخْوَانًا

And hold fast, all together, by the rope which Allah (stretches out for you), and be not divided among yourselves. And remember the blessings which God has bestowed upon you…[669]

So this applies to the entire ummah. If all are holding tight to the rope of Allah ﷻ, it is a cause for unity. The Muslims are like one body, if one part is sick the whole is sick. The ummah is one body. If we have problems in one part the whole body becomes sick.

---

[668] Sūratu'l-Anbīyā [The Prophets], 21:92.

[669] Sūrat Āli-'Imrān [The Family of 'Imrān], 3:103.

And Muslims are brothers and sisters to one another. That is why it is the responsibility of the wealthy nations to help the poor countries to develop their technological bases.

But today we see the poor become poorer and the rich become richer. This is because there is no sincerity, except for a very small number who are helping the underdeveloped countries. It is the responsibility of the rich countries to help the underdeveloped ones. Instead of investing money with people and we are not taking benefit from the interest given on it, it is better to invest in Muslim countries and give the benefit to the poor ones.

RENOWNED SCHOLARS OF SCIENCE AND TECHNOLOGY

SCHOLAR	**Dates (CE)**	**Residence**	**Fields of Contribution**
JABIR IBN HAIYAN	Died 803	Kufa	Medicine, alchemy, chemistry,
YAQUB IBN ISHAQ AL-KINDI	800-873	Baghdad	philosophy, mathematics, physics, astronomy, medicine, geography, music.
MOHAMMAD BIN MUSA AL-KHAWARIZMI	D. 840	Baghdad	mathematics, astronomer and geographer
THABIT IBN QURRA	836-901	Baghdad	mathematics, astronomy and mechanics

ALI IBN RABBAN AL-TABARI	838-870	Merv	Medicine
MOHAMMAD IBN ZAKARIYA AL-RAZI	864-930	Ray, Baghdad	Music, mathematics, astronomy, chemistry, Philosophy,
ABU ABDULLAH AL-BATTANI	868-929	Raqqa, Iraq.	astronomer, mathematician and astrologer
ABU'L-ABBAS AHMAD IBN MUHAMMAD IBN KATHIR AL-FARGHANI	C. 860	Cairo, Samarra.	Astronomy, engineering.
ABU AL-NASR AL-FARABI	870-950	Baghdad, Damascus, Cairo, Aleppo.	science, philosophy, logic, sociology, medicine, mathematics, music
ABUL ḤASAN ALI AL-MASU'DI	D. 957	Traveled extensively, Cairo.	geographer, physicist, historian
ABU AL-QASIM KHALAF BIN 'ABBAS AL-ZAHRAWI	936-1013	Cordoba	Surgery, medicine, Ophthalmology, dentistry.
ABUL WAFA MUHAMMAD AL-BUZJANI	940-997	Baghdad	Astronomy, mathematics.

ABU ALI ḤASAN IBN AL-HAITHAM	965-1040	Cairo, Spain.	Physics (Optics), mathematics.
ABU AL-ḤASAN AL-MAWARDI	972-1058	Baghdad	political science and sociology
ABU RAIHAN AL-BIRUNI	973-1048	India	astronomy, trigonometry, mineralogy, geography, history.
IBN SINA	980-1037	Jurjan, Hamadan, Isfahan.	Medicine, physics, mathematics, music, geology, mineralogy metaphysics, philosophy, ethics, economics, politics.
ABU HAMID AL-GHAZALI	1058-1128	Baghdad, Damascus.	philosophy
ABU MARWAN IBN ZUHR	1091-1161	Seville	Physician, clinician.
AL-IDRISI	1099-1166	Palermo	Botany, geography, zoology.
OMAR AL-KHAYYAM	1044-1123	Nishapur	Algebra, general & analytical

			geometry, astronomy, medicine
IBN RUSHD	1128-1198 C.E	Morocco, Cordova.	Jurisprudence, medicine, zoology, astronomy, philosophy.
IBN AL-BAITAR	d. 1248	Malaga Spain. Constantinople, Tunis, Tripoli, Barqa, Adalia, Damascus.	Medicine, Botany, pharmacology.
IBN AL-NAFIS	1213-1288	Damascus, Cairo.	Medicine, diet, jurisprudence,.
IBN KHALDUN	1332-1395	Fez, Cairo.	philosophy of history, sociology, political science, education

THE QUR'AN'S MIRACULOUS ETERNAL RELEVANCE[670]

[670] A talk given to a conference in Sarawak, Malaysia, 2003.

'IJAZ AL-QUR'AN RELATES INFORMATION BEING DISCOVERED BY SCIENTISTS IN THE CURRENT ERA

INTRODUCTION

Islam comprises all of civilization. Within Islam's sources are to be found all that is of value – the ultimate treasure trove of intellectual knowledge, practical guidance and spiritual wisdom. Islam is the fount for all of civilization's achievements and the diadem of its crown.

Islam carries, like a treasure-laden ship, within its deep hold are every sort of store and provision. Its sails are the sciences of jurisprudence and spirituality, like two wings of a bird, both of which it needs to carry its precious cargo of humankind across the vast expanse of the ocean of this life. At the helm of this vessel is the Leader and Master of mankind, Sayyidina Muhammad ﷺ, under whose watchful eye and incalculable care it cuts through the depths of Allah's unsounded and uncharted Kingdom.

Its rudder is the inimitable Sunnah of the Messenger of Allah ﷺ and its compass is Qur'ān. Far above as it etches a glowing wake across the deep, the stars above, the companions of Allah's Messenger and His deputies among them shine forth as guiding lights, directing the vessel to her destination in the darkest nights. Within its deep hold are a storehouse of science, profound wisdom and practical instruction on right ways of living, which when followed carry the ship of salvation to its destination with facility to its crew and passengers, and when discarded or disregarded, cause it to languish in the doldrums of false teachings and error.

What drives the ship of Islam – is the wind from the Prophet ﷺ, for his every breath contained Allah's revelatory fragrance and each puff of the prophetic breeze wafts with the fragrant perfumes of Paradise's blooms. From each breath of the Prophet ﷺ came oceans of knowledge and from each of word which dropped, like a petal from vast rosebush, sprang a bouquet, a garden or a veritable forest, the branches of whose knowledge begin at his feet and extend into the heavens.

Every soul, behavior, discovery, invention, or aspect of life past, present, and future is mentioned in the Qur'ān.

وَلاَ رَطْبٍ وَلاَ يَابِسٍ إِلاَّ فِي كِتَابٍ مُّبِينٍ

(There is) naught of wet or dry but (it is noted) in a clear record.[671]

Allāh ﷻ is saying that everything living (wet) or non-living (dry) is mentioned in the Holy Qur'ān. That is, all scientific discoveries, regarding living or non-living things, are mentioned in the Qur'ān, but not everyone can discern them.

A lawyer cannot make scientific discoveries whereas a scientist can. To make discoveries, a scientist works with theories and tests them through experimentation until they are proven to be a fact, or reality. Because the lay person does not make scientific discoveries, it does not follow that these discoveries or realities do not exist. Rather they simply are not known, or accessible, to him.

To someone living in previous times it would have seemed impossible to think that water was composed of gases, but people now have the knowledge to understand this reality. Not everyone could see that ordinary water is composed of two hydrogen atoms and one oxygen atom, but after its composition was discovered it was known and accepted. In chemical symbolism: $2\ H_2 + O_2 \rightarrow 2\ H_2O$.

When it is said that everything is in the Qur'ān, this does not mean that everyone reading the Qur'ān will find what is in it.

---

[671] Sūratu 'l-Anʿam [Cattle], 6:59.

Depending on the reader's level of knowledge and understanding he may be able to identify the appropriate verse on a given subject, just as a scientist can identify a particular element or compound in a sample. However, **everything** is in the Qur'ān regardless of whether one can personally ascertain it or not.

Once a great scholar was asked to define internal knowledge as opposed to external knowledge (*ʿilm al-bāṭin* versus *ʿilm aẓ-ẓāhir*). He said:

> Whatever one cannot understand is hidden and seems esoteric but to the one who knows something it is external and plain. Internal knowledge cannot be perceived by some people but to us it is a reality. One may think there are two kinds of knowledge, but in actuality there is no difference between external and internal, it is only a question of perception.

The scientific process is the same. Before something is discovered, people deny its existence but then believe it when it becomes known. Nothing has changed, only the willingness and ability to accept the reality. Therefore, before one says that something does not exist one must consider that it may exist, but one does not yet know about it.

The hadith of the Prophet ﷺ are the second source of knowledge in Islam.

> The Prophet ﷺ said, "I have left among you two matters by holding fast to which, you shall never be misguided: Allāh's Book and the Sunnah of His Prophet."[672]

Thus the Sunnah is taken on a par with Allah's Revealed Book as a source of guidance.

---

[672] Narrated from Ibn ʿAbbās by al-Bayhaqī in *al-Sunan al-kubrā* (10:114 #20108) and—as part of a longer hadith—by al-Ḥākim (1:93=1990 ed. 1:171) who declared it *Saḥīḥ* and—without chain—by Mālik in his *Muwattā'*.

The Lord of Creation affirmed in the Qur'ān that each word spoken by the Prophet was neither by chance nor by mistake. The The Messenger of God ﷺ was inspired and divinely guided in every word and every action.:

وَمَا يَنطِقُ عَنِ الْهَوَى إِنْ هُوَ إِلا وَحْيٌ يُوحَى

Nor does he say (aught) of (his own) desire. It is naught but revelation that is revealed (to him).[673]

Every utterance, every movement, every breath of the Prophet ﷺ was, in fact, revelation from Allāh ﷻ and consequently of utmost value in the quest to understand and follow the Qur'ān and the religion of Islam.

The hadiths of the Prophet ﷺ are in fact essential to understand the Qur'ān. For every single event in his lifetime, Allāh ﷻ revealed to the Prophet's heart what to say and what to do. The Qur'ān and the hadiths both derive from revelation and are inseparable sources for understanding and implementing the divine message of Islam.[674]

---

[673] Sūratu 'n-Najm [The Star], 53:1-4.

[674] The Prophet said:

> Verily this Qur'ān is difficult and felt as a burden to anyone that hates it, but it is made easy to anyone that follows it. Verily my sayings are difficult and felt as a burden to anyone that hates them, but they are made easy to anyone that follows them. Whoever hears my saying and preserves it, putting it into practice, shall come forth together with the Qur'ān on the Day of Resurrection. Whoever dismisses my sayings dismisses the Qur'ān, and whoever dismisses the Qur'ān has lost this world and the next.

Narrated from al-Ḥakam ibn 'Umayr al-Thumalī by Khatīb in *al-Jāmiʿ li Akhlāq al-Rāwī* (1983 ed. 2:189), Qurṭubī in his *Tafsīr* (18:17), *Abū Nuʿaym, Abū al-Shaykh,* and *Daylamī.*

For the first millennium of Islamic civilization, the Muslims were favored by Allāh ﷻ with an advancement unparalleled before or since. Muslims were at the forefront of not only religious development, but were also the world's leading researchers, physicians, chemists, astronomers, botanists, philosophers, and architects. Muslims were the shining lights that illuminated Europe and touched off the Renaissance.

They demonstrated a remarkable awareness of scientific discoveries unknown until the contemporary scientific era.

حدثنا سعيد بن عفير حدثنا الليث حدثني عقيل عن ابن شهاب أخبرني سعيد بن المسيب أن أبا هريرة قال سمعت رسول الله صلى الله عليه وسلم يقول بعثت بجوامع الكلم...

> The Prophet ﷺ said, "I was sent with the pithiest expressions with the vastest meanings..."[675]

Examining the hadiths of the Prophet ﷺ today, many of these vast meanings are now being grasped by both Muslims and non-Muslims. It is not desirable for science to determine one's faith because Muslims believe in whatever is in the Qur'ān and hadiths regardless of what scientists say. However, today's researchers are discovering many realities previously unknown to them, but which were alluded to by Prophet Muhammad ﷺ and mentioned in the Holy Qur'ān and the hadiths fourteen hundred years ago.

These things were not elucidated by the Prophet ﷺ to the people of his time for two reasons. Firstly, they were not able to understand these discoveries. Secondly, the Prophet did not explain the meaning of these verses of the Qur'ān or these hadiths so they would exist as independent proofs for later days when scientists would discover them for themselves and verify their reality. They were left for future generations to appreciate the

---

[675] Narrated from Abū Hurayra in *Saḥīḥ Bukhārī*.

greatness of Prophet Muhammad ﷺ and the miraculous knowledge Allāh ﷻ gave him in the Qur'ān and hadith. When non-Muslim researchers make a "discovery" using today's advanced scientific knowledge and technology, it is a compelling testimonial to the Qur'ān and hadith, which mentioned them centuries before it was possible to know of such things.

If Muslims discovered these things, one might speculate they were merely trying to bolster their own faith. Yet it is non-Muslims who are independently corroborating these facts, verifying realities which were mentioned by the Prophet ﷺ fourteen hundred years ago. In this way Allāh ﷻ is guiding non-Muslims, through their own research, to realize that the Prophet ﷺ spoke the truth when he mentioned these things, and hopefully to infer that he also spoke the truth in conveying the message of Islam, Allāh's religion. Many things have been discovered and some things are still in process of unfolding. The Prophet ﷺ knew of discoveries on earth and beyond the earth, in space.

سَنُرِيهِمْ آيَاتِنَا فِي الْآفَاقِ وَفِي أَنفُسِهِمْ حَتَّىٰ يَتَبَيَّنَ لَهُمْ أَنَّهُ الْحَقُّ أَوَلَمْ يَكْفِ
بِرَبِّكَ أَنَّهُ عَلَىٰ كُلِّ شَيْءٍ شَهِيدٌ

We will soon show them Our signs in the Universe and in themselves, until it will become manifest to them that it is the truth.... [676]

The verse does not say, *"We are showing them,"* but *"We will show them Our signs in the horizons,"* i.e. the skies and space. Signs are not juristic rulings or legal verdicts based on historical precedents. Signs are the uncovering of realities. Allāh ﷻ said, "I will show them in the atmosphere." A discovery on earth may have somehow been discovered before. However, it is impossible

[676] Sūrah Fuṣṣilat [Explained in Detail], 41:53

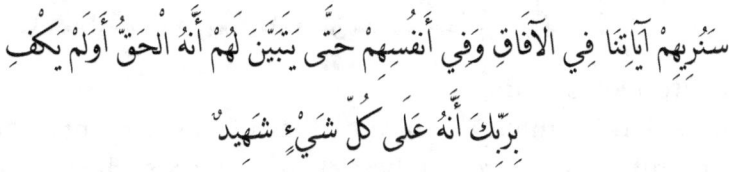

for someone fourteen hundred years ago to have known the discoveries made possible by space exploration. Islamic scholars who read this verse in the past were wondering what kind of signs Allāh ﷻ was going to show in the horizons. The Prophet ﷺ did not explain some aspects of the Qur'ān and hadith, but left them to be discovered later. That is why, up to today, there are many things that scientists are discovering in Qur'ān which were not understood, even recently.

Many things that are in the Qur'ān are not understood even today. Even today's scholars say that there are many secrets in the Qur'ān, and that is an aspect of its miraculous knowledge (*iʿjāz al-Qur'ān*). Those are secrets that were not even explained to the Companions, for they were not in a position to understand them.

نضر الله عبدا سمع مقالتي فواعها و حفظها و بلغها فربّ حامل فقه غير فقيه و ربّ

حامل فقه إلى من هو أفقه منه ثلاث لا يغل عليهن قلب مسلم إخلاص العمل لله منا

صحبة أئمة المسلمين و لزوم الجماعة فإن الدعوة تحيط من ورائهم

The Prophet ﷺ said:

> May Allāh brighten the face of that of His servants who hears my words, remembers them, guards them, and hands them on. Many a transmitter of knowledge does not himself understand it, and many may transmit knowledge to others who are more versed in it than they...[677]

Here the Prophet ﷺ foretold that the transmitters of hadith might not understand the import of a particular statement he uttered, but in order that later generations, more able to grasp their significance, would hear them correctly, urged the

---

[677] Narrated from Zayd ibn Thābit by*Tirmidhī* (*ḥasan*), *Abū Dāwūd*, *Ibn Mājah*, *Aḥmad*, *al-Dārimī*, and al-Shafi'ī in his *Risāla* (#1102). Al-Tirmidhī's version does not mention the last sentence. On the variant wordings of this important hadith see Shaykh ʿAbd al-Fattāḥ Abū Ghudda's *al-Rasūl al-Muʿallim* (p. 55-56).

transmitters of hadith to take utmost care in preserving their original wording.

The miraculous knowledge taught by the Prophet ﷺ comes to us today from two sources, the Holy Qur'ān and the hadith. Today, scientists are finding an amazing congruence between what is in Qur'ān and hadith and what science is discovering from the wonders of Allāh's creation. These discoveries cover a wide scientific spectrum, and reveal the divinely inspired levels of knowledge of the Prophet Muhammad ﷺ fourteen hundred years ago.

The astounding detailed foreknowledge of these realities could not have been independently discovered without the benefit of modern technology nor could they be happenstance or a lucky guess. Quite simply, the predictions made by Prophet Muhammad ﷺ are of unprecedented accuracy, detail, and content that did not come before him or after. These demonstrate the divine knowledge that the Prophet ﷺ brought that could only be known through revelation from Allāh ﷻ.

With the benefit of modern science people of today are in a unique position to appreciate the incredible and miraculous knowledge found in the message of Islam brought by Prophet Muhammad ﷺ in the Holy Qur'ān and hadiths. Before delving into the hadiths regarding the signs of the Last Days, a few verses of the Holy Qur'ān and their significance in light of recent scientific discoveries, will be examined. These verses illustrate the miraculous knowledge with which Allāh ﷻ favored the Prophet ﷺ, and are a compelling testimony to why everyone, both Muslim and non-Muslim, must examine the message of Prophet Muhammad ﷺ in its entirety and especially what he predicted was to come in the future.

THE DESCRIPTION OF IRON'S ORIGINS IN QUR'AN

Allāh said:

وَأَنْزَلْنَا الْحَدِيدَ فِيهِ بَأْسٌ شَدِيدٌ وَمَنَافِعُ لِلنَّاسِ

And We sent down Iron, wherein is mighty power, as well as many benefits for mankind.... [678]

Islamic scholars in the past, and even recently, explained *anzalnā* (We caused to descend, revealed) as *khalaqnā* (We created). They knew iron was mined out of the depths of the earth, and could not conceive that iron descended or was brought down from above the earth.

Scientists have uncovered that iron is found not only on earth but in the sun, in many types of stars, and throughout the universe. Moreover, the Muslim scholars learned that it is not possible for even a single atom of iron to be created on earth or even with the extremes of energy inside the earth. To produce one atom of iron (*ḥadīd*) requires energy greater than that of the sun. According to the theory of nucleosynthesis, the only place in the universe that is sufficiently hot to produce iron is in a supermassive star which then explodes, spreading the iron throughout the universe.[679] This confirms that iron was not

---

[678] Sūratu 'l-Ḥadīd [Iron], 57:25.

[679] Donald Clayton says:

> In a process known as nucleosynthesis, the most common type of stars, known as main-sequence stars, generate energy by converting hydrogen into helium through thermonuclear fusion. As stars use up their hydrogen fuel, they evolve off the main-sequence into what are known as giant or supergiant stars, whose energy given off may exceed one hundred times its original luminosity. During these stages stars will begin to "burn" helium or other even heavier elements as the core of the star reaches higher and higher temperatures and densities. How far this process proceeds depends on the initial mass of the star. The lowest mass stars will never go past burning hydrogen while the highest mass stars can produce elements all the way up to iron in their cores.

In the more massive stars as Hydrogen is converted into Helium and is used up, the pressure inside the star decreases allowing the core to collapse and heat up more. At some point, instead of fusing hydrogen into helium, the temperature will reach the point where helium begins to fuse into Carbon. The core will go through several such stages in which the product of thermonuclear fusion at one stage becomes the fuel for the next stage, with each succesive product being a heavier element in a series of evolutionary steps, depending on its mass, beginning with helium, then carbon, oxygen, silicon, and last being Iron.

With each change in fuel, there is an increase in core temperature and simultaneously the outer layers of the star heat up and begin to expand creating what are known as giant or supergiant stars. The most massive of these stars have an onion-skin structure -- an iron core surrounded by layers of the different elements which were "products" of previous stages, with the heaviest burning at the core to produce the star's energy output.

A start in the red giant stage will have expanded to about 40 times its normal radius, reaching 30 million km. and a temperature of 400 million degrees K.

The fusion of lighter elements produces a star's energy. However, once Iron becomes the fuel at the star's core, it no longer produces energy—instead it uses up energy. When this takes place, and this only occurs in extremely massive stars, at some point the star's core will collapse inward causing a massive explosion known as a supernova, in which all the outer layers are blasted into space at gigantic speeds. In the process, all kinds of nuclear reactions take place, synthesizing elements as high in the periodic table as plutonium or higher. It is this process which is believed by astrophysicists to have "seeded" the star clouds within galaxies with heavier elements—elements which at some point may condense during the formation of planets such as the earth, and from which life finally emerges.

After the supernova event, what remains of the original star is a tiny core, perhaps 100 km. in radius but burning at an incredible 100 billion degrees K. and spinning at 2000 rpm. Such stars are known as neutron stars, for the protons and electrons have joined together under the tremendous gravitational field to become neutrons.

created here on earth, but, as Allāh ﷻ said, descended or was sent down to the earth from above.[680] It was impossible for someone living fourteen hundred years ago to know that iron did not come from the earth but descended into the earth from space. This is an example of the miraculous knowledge with which Allāh ﷻ favored the Prophet Muhammad ﷺ in the Holy Qur'ān and the hadith.

There is the *iʿjāz al-ʿilmi* (astonishing or miraculous knowledge) and there is *iʿjāz al-raqamī* (or *iʿjāz al-ʿadadī*) the astonishing numerology in the Qur'ān. In the Qur'ān there are many instances of the numbers pointing to something that is later discovered by science.

The atomic number (number of protons in the nucleus) of iron is 26. There are four naturally occurring stable isotopes of iron with atomic weights of 54, 56, 57, and 58 (see Table 1). The isotope

---

> For even more massive stars, the result is more extraordinary. Gravitational forces are so strong that the star collapses inward forever, and becomes a point, with an infinite density. These are known as black holes. Not even light can escape the gravitational field of a black hole.

The Origin of Elements and Life of a Star, Clayton, Donald, Clayton University, 1999

680

> ...the numbers of naturally occurring atoms of the metals between atomic weights 45 and 65... are dominated, like a mountain, by four Abundant isotopes of iron. This is the sort of Abundance data that the theory of nucleosynthesis must consider. The scientific method has achieved a great triumph here, from the first argument half a century ago that iron is the natural product of the evolution of the stellar core, to the recent proof by detected gamma rays from supernovae that the iron isotopes were ejected as isotopes of radioactive nickel and cobalt, and in just the ratios found within a common hammer!... The calcium in our bones, the iron in our hemoglobin, all, all but the initial hydrogen and helium, are thermonuclear debris from exploding stars.

The Origin of Elements and Life of a Star, Clayton, Donald, Clayton University, 1999

iron 56 is the most abundant form of iron on earth.[681] The 57th *Sūrah* of the Qur'ān is named after iron, Sūratu 'l-Ḥadīd and iron 57 is possibly the most abundant isotopic form of iron in the universe.[682] In this *Sūrah* the word iron appears in the 25th verse. All of the chapters of the Qur'ān (except one) begin with the *basmala*[683] and it is considered by many scholars to be a verse. Counting the *basmala* as a verse brings us to the word iron (*hadīd)* in the 26th verse which is the same as the atomic number of iron, the number of protons. The *Sūrah* itself contains 29 verses, but with the *basmala* the total is 30, the number of neutrons in iron.

Isotope of Iron	Atomic mass (ma/u)	Natural abundance (atom %)
54Fe	53.9396127 (15)	5.845 (35)
56Fe	55.9349393 (16)	91.754 (36)
57Fe	56.9353958 (16)	2.119 (10)
58Fe	57.9332773 (16)	0.282 (4)

Table 1 Abundance of Iron Isotopes on Earth

NEUTRON BOMBS AND WARPLANES

Since all of us here believe in Allah and the Prophet (s), we accept the predictions of the Prophet. But it is extraordinary, when delving into the *sīrāh* of the Messenger, to find that many of the

[681] Commission on Atomic Weights and Isotopic Abundances report for the International Union of Pure and Applied Chemistry in Isotopic Compositions of the Elements 1989, Pure and Applied Chemistry, 1998, 70, 217. [Copyright 1998 IUPAC]

[682] 57 is the weight of the most Abundant stable isotope (variant nucleus) of iron seen in the solar neighborhood, according to measurements made by Charge, Element, Isotope Analysis System (CELIAS) on the SOHO spacecraft. It may be that in the entire universe, this is in fact the dominant isotope.
The Origin of the Elements and the Life of a Star, Clayton, Donald, Clayton University, 1999]

[683] *Bismillāh ir-Rahmān ir-Rahīm* in the Name of God, the Most-Merciful, the Mercy-Giving.

incidents that took place in his lifetime were like predictions of future scientific achievements and breakthroughs in technology.

One example comes from the time just prior to the birth of the Prophet, when the Abyssinian leader Abrāhah came to destroy the Ka`aba with a tremendous army accompanied by elephants. Confronted by such a huge and well-equipped army, what was `Abdul Muttalib, the Shaykh of the Quraysh able to do? He spoke to Abrāhah at a parley saying, "Does not the House have a Lord who will protect it?"

He asked only that Abrāhah return the camels that he had confiscated, for Abdul Muttalib had full faith that the Owner of the House was fully capable to defend it. And so it came to pass, as Allah said in Sūratu 'l-Fīl

أَلَمْ تَرَ كَيْفَ فَعَلَ رَبُّكَ بِأَصْحَابِ الْفِيلِ

Are you not aware of how your Lord dealt with the Army of the Elephant?[684]

Allah took care of that evil army and its leader and made their plans come to nought. It is written in *Durr al-manthūr*, the *tafsīr* of Imām Suyūtī, that these were "pebbles spinning at extremely high speed and red hot, and written on each pebble was the name of the person to be struck by it, and his father's name." As they flew through the air they left a glowing red trail in the darkness.

If we look at this event in the light of today's scientific understanding it is easy to understand that what was sent on Abrāhah's army were guided missiles, trailing red light like today's tracers. Imām Suyūtī quoting the Sahaba, described them as *banādir*. This word is used today for rifles - did they know about rifles at that time?

---

[684] Suratu'l-Fīl [The Elephant],105:1.

وَأَرْسَلَ عَلَيْهِمْ طَيْرًا أَبَابِيلَ

We sent against them birds [685]

Those were creatures that they never expected and we never saw creatures like those. Allah sent a normal creation, birds, but in a manner and with capabilities which made them what could be described in modern parlance as armed forces. Today they send airplanes. Allah's "warplanes" were these birds – and they were far more effective than the airplanes of today. What were they carrying? The Qur'ānic explanations describe *hijāratin min sijjīl* as pebbles – fiery pebbles. In fact "pebbles" does not convey the meaning of the term. If a pebble hits you it kills you. But Allah said,

فَجَعَلَهُمْ كَعَصْفٍ مَّأْكُولٍ

and caused them to become like a field of grain that has been eaten down to stubble. [686]

It no longer means simply pebbles. It is something that explodes inside them destroying them but not destroying the House of Allah.

Today they invented something that is similar to what is described in this sūrah – something which destroys without harming the physical surroundings. That is the neutron bomb. Allah eliminated the army sent to destroy the sacred House with an army of "warplanes" carrying guided missiles, each one tipped with something like a neutron bomb. With this tremendous weaponry Allah swt came against that army like a violent storm (*al-ʿasifa*).The result was they became like crops after the cattle

[685] Suratu'l-Fīl [The Elephant],105:3.
[686] Suratu'l-Fīl [The Elephant],105:5.

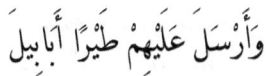

have passed over them - like something eaten. This storm of divine weaponry ate them - they disintegrated leaving nothing remaining.

STATISTICS AND PROBABILITY

The science of statistics is statistics is a reliable means of describing accurately the values of economic, political, social, psychological, biological, and physical data based on counting all members of a population or a sample of them and enumerating their characteristics. Allah swt said,

لَقَدْ أَحْصَاهُمْ وَعَدَّهُمْ عَدًّا

He does take an account of them (all), and hath numbered them (all) exactly.[687]

Aḥṣāhum means when you take an account of something, you assemble and put them next to one another and count them one by one. Allah swt knows the hairs of your head. He knows the drops of blood in your body.

وَكُلَّ شَيْءٍ أَحْصَيْنَاهُ فِي إِمَامٍ مُبِينٍ

and of all things have We taken account in a clear Book.[688]

Here Allah is stating that all things, in creation have been enumerated and taken into account, all their characteristics have been defined and described. This is not like human statistics – it is infinitely superior. For Allah's information about any of His creation is exact, precise and boundless.

---

[687] Sūrah Maryam, 19:94.
[688] Sūrah YāSīn, 36:12.

PROBABILITY OF EXTINCTION

Today's scientists say that there were once different species of huge creatures inhabiting the earth called dinosaurs. If one accepts that in the past dinosaurs lived on earth, then one must also ask, why are they no longer in existence today? Today one no longer sees dinosaurs on earth, so one must wonder what became of them. From an Islamic point of view, their time ended. Allāh ﷻ did away with them, and they became extinct. How Allāh ﷻ took them away is a topic of debate, even among scientists.

When dinosaurs roamed the earth, they may have thought themselves great and powerful, even though there was a probability that they would all be destroyed and made extinct. Even if the probability was small it still existed for them. Whatever event made them become extinct, eventually occurred. Although they were so magnificent in size and strength, they have now disappeared completely from the face of the earth. After them other species have come, also not expecting to be made extinct, although the probability exists for them to be rendered extinct just as it did for the dinosaurs.

Statistics and probability are empirical sciences, branches of mathematics, based on counting the occurrence of something over time. Zero probability means that there is no possibility whatsoever that something will ever happen. A probability of one means there is absolute certainty that something will definitely take place. For any possible event there is a probability between zero and one that it will occur. Someone can estimate or intelligently predict the probability of an event occurring by examining historical patterns. In the past, a certain event happened so many times which leads to the assumption that this will happen again in the future with a certain probability. This science is used in many areas of practical knowledge: quantum physics, chemistry, thermodynamics, weather, population, and even predicting the stock market. Probability is used for predicting the possibility of events for all things which cannot be precisely predicted by a mathematical formula.

If we want to take a scientific or probabilistic approach to the question of man's life on earth, we must admit that there is a chance that the human race will end. Dinosaurs also faced a probability of extinction and this came to pass. According to paleontologists, there were five massive extinctions throughout the history of the world. Moreover, biologists fear that as many as half of all living species will become extinct within the next century. A recent report of the United Nations predicts that within thirty years almost a quarter of the world's mammals will be in danger of becoming extinct.[689] If so many species are becoming extinct, who is to say that other mammals like human beings will not also face extinction one day? Using probability and logic we may infer that as dinosaurs and other species have came to an end, so too is there a probability that the human race will one day end.

Clear evidence of human existence on earth dates back to around five thousand to seven thousand years ago, and the oldest evidence of apparent human existence to about fifty thousand years ago. The creatures who existed fifty thousand years ago were different from today's humans, and there are no clearly human relics until the Stone Age five thousand to seven thousand years ago. Where are the relics from the creatures of fifty thousand years ago and why did they disappear so suddenly? Humans have lived on earth for a few thousand years, so our probability of disappearing is much higher than it was for the dinosaurs who survived for millions of years.

There is a distinct possibility that man will someday disappear. With extinction, either man will become nonexistent, as scientists and others believe, or as religions say, people are going

---

[689] Global Environment Outlook-3 (Geo-3) report of the United Nations Environment Programme (UNEP), Earthscan Publications Ltd, London, 2002.

to face an accounting. If we become extinct then we will be like others before us, but there is a probability that we will face an evaluation, a judgment. Let us take the two cases: either humankind will become extinct, with its existence finally and completely coming to an end, or humankind will come before the Creator and face an accounting. If these are the only two possibilities then all things being equal, the probability is one half, (½) or fifty percent that one or the other will take place.

If there is a chance that buying a certain stock would make one fabulously rich then many people would buy it, even if the probability was as low as twenty or thirty percent. At fifty percent people would even be willing to borrow money to take a chance on the stock skyrocketing in value. If people are this calculating and clever for the chance to succeed in a worldly venture in which one might lose or gain, then what about a prospect that is "out of this world." Statistically, given a fifty percent chance of the existence of an afterlife, why is no one investing? Even if one lives to be one hundred years old, it is but the blink of an eye compared to the millions and millions of years the earth has been in existence. Comparing one hundred years to eternity is beyond the mind's grasp. If there is no afterlife, one might say he "lost" one hundred years, but if there is an afterlife his gains are infinite. If the eternal afterlife is a reality (and we as Muslims know that it is), then the small investment of one hundred years is next to nothing.

There have been many inspired people throughout the ages who said, "We are messengers of the Creator, Allāh ﷻ," and who told people what was to come in the future and in the afterlife. In many religious traditions there were prophets and messengers who informed us of a coming evaluation, the Day of Judgment. The chance of so many thousands of prophets from different places all coming with the same message is minute. If they were correct and there is an appraisal to be given, one must prepare oneself for that most crucial examination.

Such a proposition of a coming Judgment and Afterlife is not farfetched. Something much more implausible is wholeheartedly accepted without question by most scientists. Today's scientists hold that via random chance and completely accidental occurrences, monkeys transformed into human beings. Using postulates based on purely haphazard events, they were able to elaborate a complex theory which they consider to be an actual fact, although its foundation is built upon sheer probability. Even if the basis for this theory was feasible, the number of mutations needed to randomly occur in an extremely short period of time is all but impossible. Darwin's original theory has been shredded by subsequent scientific discoveries but has been patched together by its proponents with a sort of blind faith that is ironically more consistent with religious belief than science.

Islam has sparked innumerable advances in the sciences and is not in the least antagonistic to scientific inquiry. In fact, Islam encompasses the knowledge of modern sciences and evidence of such was mentioned in the Qur'ān and by Prophet Muhammad ﷺ in hadiths many centuries before the scientific age. For example, scientists of today believe they invented probability, yet it was mentioned fourteen hundred years ago in the Holy Qur'ān:

وَمَا يُدْرِيكَ لَعَلَّ السَّاعَةَ قَرِيبٌ...

...And what will make you realize that perhaps the Hour is close at hand?[690]

The word used here in the Qur'ān, *La'alla* means "perhaps," indicating a possibility or a probability. In Allāh's ﷻ knowledge, the Hour's timing is known precisely, yet in the perfect eloquence of the Qur'ān, Allāh ﷻ uses "perhaps" here, as if to tell today's

[690] Sūratu 'sh-Shūra [Mutual Consultation] 42:17.

scientists, "Even if you don't accept it, there is still a possibility that the Judgment Day will occur and it may be very close." For Allāh ﷻ, there is no probability. Probability is an empirical tool used to measure the chance of something taking place for those lacking precise knowledge of a thing. For One who has perfect knowledge of what has passed and what is to come, there is no element of chance for it is already known. Allāh ﷻ is *al-'Alīm*, the Absolute Knower, and thus for Allāh ﷻ all things are known with perfect knowledge, precision and certainty.

اللّهُ يَعْلَمُ مَا تَحْمِلُ كُلُّ أُنْثَى وَمَا تَغِيضُ الأَرْحَامُ وَمَا تَزْدَادُ وَكُلُّ شَيْءٍ عِنْدَهُ بِمِقْدَارٍ

> *Allāh doth know what every female (womb) doth bear, by how much the wombs fall short (of their time or number) or do exceed. Everything is counted and is encompassed in His knowledge.*[691]

For those to whom Allāh ﷻ reveals these realities, there is also no probability, for they are acting according to certain knowledge. With certain knowledge from Allāh ﷻ, the probability of an event occurring is "one," definite and certain.

Believers know that when Allāh ﷻ says something it will inevitably come to pass, but for modern intellectuals predictions are based on assumptions, not belief. When Allāh ﷻ informed Nūḥ ؑ (Noah) that a flood would be coming and that he should prepare a ship in which to escape, he did so based on faith. Through this well-known story, Allāh ﷻ has created a paradigm for the people of later times, including the skeptics of today. Allāh ﷻ is showing them that even without faith, using empirical analysis, there is a chance that a flood would occur and water

---

[691] Sūratu 'r-R'ad [Thunder], 13:8.

would reach the ship Nūh ﷺ built. As if to say, "Let us go along with your system and rules of science and probability. Even though there is no way to imagine that the sea will reach that elevated area, probability states that there is a chance, no matter how miniscule, that rivers or springs might overflow and cause the ship to float." As is well-documented, the flood occurred and Nūh's predictions revealed to him by Allāh ﷻ came true.

Similarly for Mūsā ﷺ (Moses), who obeyed Allāh's ﷻ orders to flee towards the sea from Pharoah and his army. Despite knowing that he and the Children of Israel would be cut off by the sea, he put full faith in Allāh's Orders that he and his people would be saved. Viewing it within a scientific, probabilistic paradigm, Allāh ﷻ is again showing here that, "Yes, there is a probability, according to the laws of chance, that the sea would part and create a path of escape for Mūsā ﷺ and his people."

Life will not continue forever. As Nūh ﷺ prepared himself for the day of the flood, so must people prepare themselves for their passing from this life. Here Allāh ﷻ is addressing people using their own intellectual methodology demonstrating that there is a possibility of their destruction taking place. Similarly, there is a probability that a Judgment Day will transpire and people will become accountable for their actions in this life. Even if someone does not believe in Allāh ﷻ, statistical science and the laws of probability hold that there is a chance mankind may be brought for judgment. An unexpected event might occur and bring about the complete destruction of mankind who may then come before Allāh ﷻ to account for their actions. Who can say this is impossible when it is demonstrated frequently on a smaller scale by the action of earthquakes, volcanoes, floods and many other acts of God which take place without warning, taking away people, animals and homes. These occurrences are unpredictable, and as unlikely as they may be for a given person, people take out insurance against all these events, for just the same reason Nūh ﷺ

built the Ark, seeking protection and safety. If people have not prepared themselves for that day, there will be no escape from the doom that awaits them.

PREDICTIONS AND PROBABILITY

Another element of probability is found in the sayings and predictions of Prophet Muhammad ﷺ. We will describe many of these in greater detail in this book, but in relation to probability let us look at just one example.

وأن ترى الحفاة العراة العالة رعاء الشاء يتطاولون في البنيان

One of the signs of the Last Days that the Prophet ﷺ mentioned was:

> You will see the barefoot, naked, destitute bedouin shepherds competing in constructing tall buildings.[692]

If we wish to discuss this scientifically, then the probability for this to occur must be analyzed. The chance that someone fourteen hundred years ago would make such a prediction is very remote and the chance it would actually happen is even less likely. Even one hundred years ago such a prediction would have been rejected outright by scientists. How could it happen that barefooted, naked, primitive shepherds would build tall buildings? Yet the prediction was made long before the last century, when it was an even less likely occurrence. Nonetheless, the Prophet ﷺ predicted this implausible event with certainty, saying "you will see," not "you might see," and no matter how improbable at one time, this has come to pass, exactly as he foretold.

Believers accept these predictions on face value and simply wait for them to transpire. Believers who doubt that the Judgment is near, or say that it is yet far off, or whose faith in that event is

---

[692] *Saḥīḥ Bukhārī,* "Kitāb al-Īmān."

weak, should reconsider their expectations. Muslims must know and evaluate the current situation in light of what the Prophet ﷺ said about the signs of the Last Days. If one supposes that skyscrapers being built by bedouins is one of the signs of the Judgment Day, a sign which just took place, then one must admit that Judgment Day is near. Perhaps the remaining signs will take place very quickly, one after the other. Even the science of probability shows that it might happen and at any time. The law of probability says that anything can happen, but the chance of its happening is measured in terms of occurrences within a period of time; if not once in a hundred years, then once in a thousand years, or once in a million years. All people must take heed, and prepare for that Day. The existence of even the smallest probability that it will occur should be enough to make us take care for the future.

Telecommunications Predicted in Hadith

Abū Saʿīd ؓ related a long hadith, in part of which the Prophet ﷺ said:

> By Him in Whose hand is my soul, the Hour will not come until wild creatures talk to men, and a man speaks to the end of his whip and the straps of his sandals (shoes), and his thigh will tell him about what happened to his family after he left.[693]

This hadith signifies that people in the Last Days will talk about someone that they do not know. They will speak about someone they have only heard about somewhere and go into discussions about that person, or his family, or what he has or has not done.

"A man speaks to the end of his whip," indicates that people will speak into something with a cord like speaking into a telephone. Students of physics experiment by oscillating a string

---

[693] Aḥmad, *Musnad* (3:84 and 85). Ḥākim, *Mustadrak* (4:467).

to see the resultant waveforms. Also, when one shakes a whip it creates a waveform down the length of the whip. The Prophet ﷺ is showing through the motion of the whip that people in the Last Days will discover a technology using waveforms by which they will speak. This transmission using wavelengths includes all kinds of communications whether radio, television, or satellite. One's cellular telephone in his pocket next to "his thigh will tell him about what happened to his family after he left."

In some places there is a saying that "the walls have ears," i.e. whatever one says and does is known. In this hadith the Prophet ﷺ is saying that there is coming a time where everything one does will be exposed. Even as someone "speaks to his whip," or his shoe, people unknown and unseen will be aware of it. Telecommunications are monitored by computers and people, and every cellular telephone is able to pinpoint its user's location. One's cellular phone will relay information and signals or "speak about him" to unknown observers while he calls his family.

Shoes in this hadith represent what is needed to walk and move about and travel. Today's cars with GPS (global positioning satellite) technology are able to be located at the touch of a button. The location of one's plane high above the clouds is known to unknown air traffic controllers around the world. One's activities on the street are often recorded by security cameras on earth and satellites high in the sky. This hadith is also a warning to Muslims of the Last Days to be pious and virtuous because everything one does today is monitored by unknown people, and everything is exposed.

CUTTING TIES OF RELATIONSHIP

Imām Aḥmad narrated an authentic hadith that the Prophet ﷺ said:

> Verily with the Hour there will be: greetings offered only to acquaintances; an increase in trading and business to the

> extent that the wife will help her husband in working for money; the cutting of family relations; the bearing of false witness; the concealment of the truth; and the pre-eminence of the pen.[694]

This hadith mentions that there would be, qat'u ul-arhām—"cutting of family relationships." The close relationship between blood relatives is disappearing, between parents, brothers, sisters, uncles and aunts. Nowadays, children have problems with their parents and as soon as they grow up they leave the family home. One does not see the children anymore, and they do not visit their parents.

In this hadith "*qatʿu 'l-rḥām*" also means "to cut the means of continuing the family," namely fertility and childbirth. Today, contraception is widespread, abortions are commonplace, and both men and women are undergoing surgery to prevent fertility. The continuity of the family is being cut in all ways. People are severing the bonds of relationships already established and are failing to bring the next generation of relations, cutting off both past and future family ties.

Another literal manifestation of this hadith, "cutting of the womb—*qatʿul-arḥām*," is the actual cutting of the womb (uterus) that is occurring at an unprecedented pace. Routine births are commonly performed via caesarean section, surgically cutting into the uterus to deliver the baby abdominally, often to accommodate the busy schedule of the physician or even the mother. Hysterectomies, actual removal of the uterus, are commonly performed. Surgeries on the uterus are increasing, including intrauterine surgery on the fetus. Recently, in Saudi Arabia, the

---

[694] (*Saḥīḥ*). Aḥmad, *Musnad* (1:407, 408). Haythamī, *Majma' az-Zawā'id* (7:331). Ḥākim *Mustadrak* (4:445, 446). Albānī, #647 *Silsila Saḥīḥa*. He said al-Bazzār's men are *Saḥīḥ*.

first attempt at a uterine transplant took place.[695] The Prophet ﷺ foresaw all of these aspects of contemporary life and technology fourteen hundred years ago and foretold that during the end of time the "cutting of the womb" would become commonplace.

Another meaning which comes to mind for this term is the new technology of DNA-manipulation which while not yet applied to humans, is likely to be done in the near future. In this case, the ties of relationship are "cut" as the familially-transmitted DNA or chromosomes are modified, in much the same way that childbirth out of wedlock will cause a "cut" in the family lineage. Interestingly as well, the tools used to manipulate the gene sequences in essence cut linkages of the gene sequence from a lengthy strand which is then manipulated to be replaced by a similar strand from another source of genetic material.

THE COCCYX AND RECREATION OF MANKIND ON JUDGEMENT DAY

The Prophet ﷺ gave an indication about how people will be re-created at the Resurrection, and this has been confirmed with the help of modern technological advances.

حدثنا عمر بن حفص: حدثنا أبي قال: حدثنا الأعمش قال: سمعت أبا صالح قال: سمعت أبا هريرة، عن النبي صلى الله عليه وسلم قال: بين النفختين أربعون. قالوا يا أبا هريرة، أربعون يوما ؟ قال أبيت، قال أربعون سنة؟ قال أبيت، قال أربعون شهرا ؟ قال أبيت ويبلى كل شيء من الإنسان إلا عجب ذنبه، فيه يُركب الخلق (أخرجه البُخارِي في كتاب تَفْسيرِ القُرْآنِ)

Abū Hurayra ؓ related that the Prophet ﷺ said:

---

[695] W. Fageeh et. al. International Journal of Gynecology & Obstetrics 76 2002, pp. 245-251.

Between the two blasts of the Trumpet there will be forty. The people said, "O Abū Hurayra! Forty days?" He refused to reply. They said, "Forty years?" He refused to reply and added: "Everything of the human body will decay except the coccyx and from that bone Allāh will reconstruct the whole body."[696]

حدثنا عبد الله حدثني أبي حدثنا علي بن حفص أنبأنا ورقاء عن أبي الزناد عن الأعرج عن أبي هريرة قال قال رسول الله صلى الله عليه وسلم -كل ابن آدم تأكله الأرض إلا عجب الذنب فإنه منه خلق ومنه يركب. (أخرجه الإمام مالك في الجنائز و غيره)

Abū Hurayra ؓ also related that the Prophet ﷺ said:
The earth eats all of the human being except the coccyx. He was created from it, and on it he is built.[697]

Fourteen hundred years ago the Prophet ﷺ said that with death, the whole body is consumed by the earth, except for the coccyx. Muslim scientists could not understand this hadith in the past, because when a grave was opened they would not find the coccyx bone as all the remains were disintegrated. Scientists were finally able to unravel the secret behind this hadith of the Prophet ﷺ using the sophisticated techniques of DNA analysis. Scientists took a sample of the coccyx and subjected it to the most severe stresses imaginable. They crushed it under high pressure, boiled it, and even cremated it, yet no matter what they did it was impossible to destroy the DNA contained in the coccyx. Under conditions which annihilate all other bones and cells, the remnant of the coccyx somehow survived thereby preserving the DNA of that person. Each cell of the human body contains the entire

---

[696] *Saḥīḥ Bukhārī* (6:338).
[697] Imām Mālik's *Muwaṭṭa*, Book 16.

genetic blueprint for the whole body, and this microscopic remnant of the coccygeal DNA contains sufficient information to recreate the entire human being.

Such information, bestowed by Allāh on the Prophet so many centuries ago, show Allāh's Greatness, our smallness and are a powerful evidence to believers that their time would be better spent in seeking the benefit of the afterlife with the fervour most spend in pursuing the interests and pleasures of this temporary life.

THE COCCYX AND EMBRYOLOGY

The last hadith mentions that the human being is "constructed" from the coccyx, "He was created from it, and on it he is built." An examination of this in light of modern embryological findings is revealing. At approximately two weeks of age, the developing embryo separates from the placenta until there is no contact between the two except via a connecting stalk at the embryo's caudal-most end which is the future location of the coccyx.[698] This stalk is the precursor to the umbilical cord, which will connect the developing embryo to its nourishment from the placenta. Not only is the source of nutrition coming into the embryo from the caudal end (coccyx), but the embryo's formation also progresses from the starting point of the coccyx.

The embryo's orientation and subsequent development begins when a line called the "primitive streak" forms at the caudal end (coccyx) of the embryo and proceeds towards the cranial end (head). Development proceeds from this point, and the final phase of the neural tube closure is again at the caudal end—at the area of the coccyx—from whence it began. Fourten hundred years ago the

---

698 Early Embryogenesis. Dr. David Rapaport. UCSD Department of Surgery, Division of Anatomy.

Prophet ﷺ described the coccyx and human development, saying mankind "was created from it, and on it he is built."

Such discoveries are enough, O mankind, to realize the Glory of He Whose Greatness knows no bounds and Whose Superiority over His Creation is incomprehensible. It is sufficient as confirmation that we are endlessly in need of His forgiveness, His love and His tender mercy.

With the first trumpet blast Allāh ﷻ destroys everything, and with the second trumpet blast human beings and creation will be brought back to life. Then Allāh ﷻ will send a rain for forty days which reaches the height of seventy arm-lengths.

حدثنا أبو كريب، محمد بن العلاء . حدثنا أبو معاوية عن الأعمش، عن أبي صالح، عن أبي هريرة، قال: قال رسول الله صلى الله عليه وسلم ما بين النفختين أربعون قالوا يا أبا هريرة أربعون يوما ؟ قال أبيت .قالوا أربعون شهرا ؟ قال أبيت قالوا أربعون سنة ؟ قال أبيت ثم ينزل الله من السماء ماء فينبتون كما ينبت البقل ، قال وليس من الإنسان شيء إلا يبلى إلا عظما واحدا وهو عجب الذنب ومنه يركب الخلق يوم القيامة (أخْرَجه اليخاري في كتاب تفْسير و مسلم في كتاب الفتن)

Abū Hurayra ؓ related that the Prophet ﷺ said:

> ...Allāh will send down rain that makes the people grow like vegetables. Every part of the human body will be destroyed except the coccyx. By it Allāh will reconstruct the whole body.[699]

Every drop of that rain will be composed of sperm which will connect to the "egg" of each person—that being the remains of the coccyx—in order to re-create that person.

Allāh ﷻ said in the Holy Qur'ān:

---

[699] *Saḥīḥ Bukhārī. Saḥīḥ Muslim* (9:p. 92). *Riyāḍ as-sālihīn* #1836:

وَمِنْ آيَاتِهِ أَنَّكَ تَرَى الأَرْضَ خَاشِعَةً فَإِذَا أَنزَلْنَا عَلَيْهَا الْمَاء اهْتَزَّتْ وَرَبَتْ إِنَّ الَّذِي أَحْيَاهَا لَمُحْيِي الْمَوْتَى إِنَّهُ عَلَى كُلِّ شَيْءٍ قَدِيرٌ

And among His Signs is this: thou seest the earth barren and desolate; but when We send down rain to it, it is stirred to life and yields increase. Truly, He Who gives life to the (dead) earth can surely give life to (people) who are dead. For He has power over all things.[700]

Allāh ﷻ said:

إِذَا زُلْزِلَتِ الأَرْضُ زِلْزَالَهَا وَأَخْرَجَتِ الأَرْضُ أَثْقَالَهَا

When the earth is shaken to its (utmost) convulsion, and the earth brings forth its burdens (from within).... [701]

The way a sieve is shaken to separate different sized particles, the earth will shake and bring out the coccygeal remnants. Allāh ﷻ will bring out all these remnants by sifting the whole earth so that each one may meet its destined raindrop. Allāh ﷻ will recreate the earth and bring back each man, woman, and child as they were.

CONCLUSION

Allāh's Signs are evident in each creation, each atom, each subatomic particle. So too, Allāh's bestowing of miraculous knowledge on the Last Prophet Sayyidina Muhammad ﷺ is from His bounty, and we as human beings are most fortunate, for it is from our species of creatures that Allāh ﷻ chose to place the soul of His Beloved Prophet ﷺ. And it is through the Prophet's

[700] Sūrah Fuṣṣilat [Explained in Detail], 41:39.
[701] Sūratu 'l-l-Zalzala [The Earthquake], 99:1-2)

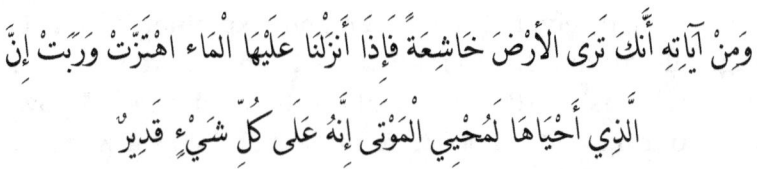

mediation, as receiver, transmitter and explainer of the Divine Message, al-Qur'ān, that mankind has been honored. We ask that Allāh ﷻ make us worthy recipients of this boundless knowledge and open our minds and hearts to understand it as it was meant to be understood, and make our actions, despite all the weakness in our capabilities, worthy of the Divine Presence.

Other Titles from the Islamic Supreme Council of America

Muhammad: The Messenger of Islam His Life and Prophecy

Hajjah Amina Adil
ISBN 1-930409-11-7, Paperback. 608 pp.

Since the 7th century, the sacred biography of Islam's Prophet Muhammad has shaped the perception of the religion and its place in world history. This book skillfully etches the personal portrait of a man of incomparable moral and spiritual stature, as seen through the eyes of Muslims around the world. Compiled from classical Ottoman Turkish sources and translated into English, this comprehensive biography is deeply rooted in the life example of its prophet.

In the Mystic Footsteps of Saints

Shaykh Muhammad Nazim Adil al-Haqqani
Volume 1 - ISBN 1-930409-05-2
Volume 2 – ISBN 1-930409-09-5
Volume 3 – ISBN 1-930409-13-3, Paperback. Ave. length 200 pp.

Narrated in a charming, old-world storytelling style, this highly spiritual series offers several volumes of practical guidance on how to establish serenity and peace in daily life, heal emotional and spiritual scars, and discover the role we are each destined to play in the universal scheme. Written by Shaykh Nazim Adil al-Haqqani, worldwide leader of the Naqshbandi-Haqqani Sufi Order and a descendant of best-selling poet and Sufi mystic Jalaluddin Rumi.

LIBERATING THE SOUL: A GUIDE FOR SPIRITUAL GROWTH

By Shaykh Muhammad Nazim Adil al-Haqqani
Volume 1 - ISBN 1-930409-14-1
Volume 2 – ISBN 1-930409-15-X
Volume 3 – ISBN 1-930409-16-8
Volume 4 – ISBN 1-930409-17-6, Paperback. Average length 300 pp.

This series focuses on classical Sufi teachings, which open the heart to receive life-altering spiritual powers. *Liberating the Soul* is based on coveted lectures of Shaykh Muhammad Nazim Adil al-Haqqani, the worldwide leader of the Naqshbandi Sufi Order and descendant of best-selling poet Jalaluddin Rumi.

CLASSICAL ISLAM AND THE NAQSHBANDI SUFI TRADITION

Shaykh Muhammad Hisham Kabbani
ISBN 1-930409-23-0, Hardback. 950 pp.
ISBN 1-930409-10-9, Paperback. 744 pp.

This esteemed work includes an unprecedented historical narrative of the forty saints of the renowned Naqshbandi Golden Chain, dating back to Prophet Muhammad in the early 7th century. With close personal ties to contemporary saints, the author has painstakingly compiled rare accounts of their miracles, disciplines, and how they have lent spiritual support throughout the world for fifteen centuries. The book outlines practical steps to manage stress, anger and time, and to identify and prioritize what is truly important in life, awakening the inner self to a higher dimension of spiritual consciousness. This book is a shining tribute to the power of spirituality to uplift humanity.

THE NAQSHBANDI SUFI TRADITION GUIDEBOOK OF DAILY PRACTICES AND DEVOTIONS

Shaykh Muhammad Hisham Kabbani
ISBN 1-930409-22-2, Paperback. 352 pp.

This book details the spiritual practices which have enabled devout seekers to awaken certainty of belief and to attain stations of nearness to the Divine Presence. The Naqshbandi Devotions are a source of light and energy, an oasis in a worldly desert. Through the manifestations of Divine Blessings bestowed on the practitioners of these magnificent rites, they will be granted the power of magnanimous healing, by which they seek to cure the hearts of mankind in this era of materialism.

This guidebook includes the daily personal *dhikr* as well as the rites performed with every obligatory prayer, rites for holy days and details of the pilgrimage to Makkah and the visit of Prophet Muhammad in Madinah.

NAQSHBANDI AWRAD OF MAWLANA SHAYKH MUHAMMAD NAZIM ADIL AL-HAQQANI

Compiled by Shaykh Muhammad Hisham Kabbani
ISBN 1-930409-06-0, Paperback. 334 pp.

This "pocket" book presents in detail, in both English, Arabic and transliteration, the daily, weekly and date-specific devotional rites of Naqshbandi practitioners, as prescribed by the world guide of the Naqshbandi-Haqqani Sufi Order, Mawlana Shaykh Muhammad Nazim Adil al-Haqqani.

THE HONOR OF WOMEN IN ISLAM

Professor Yusuf da Costa
ISBN 1-930409-06-0, Paperback. 104 pp.

Relying on Islamic source texts, this concise, scholarly work elucidates the true respect and love for women inherent in the Islamic faith. It examines the pre-Islamic state of women, highlights the unprecedented rights they received under Islamic Law, and addresses the prominent beliefs and prevailing cultures throughout the Muslim world regarding the roles of women in familial, social service and community development, business, academic, religious, and even judicial circles. In addition, brief case studies of historical figures such as Mary, mother of Jesus are presented within the Islamic tradition.

THE PRACTICE OF SUFI MEDITATION AND THE HEALING POWER OF DIVINE ENERGY

Dr. Hedieh Mirahmadi and Sayyid Nurjan Mirahmadi
ISBN: 1-930409-26-5, Paperback. 190 pp.

For those who have reached a level of understanding of the illusory nature of the world around us and seek to discern the reality that lies behind it, Sufi meditation - *muraqabah* - is the doorway through which we can pass from this realm of delusion into the realm of realities.

Through meditation the seeker has a means to return to his or her perfected original self. *Muraqabah* is the most effective method for advancing in spiritual degrees. It is in fact a migration from one's self to God. This book presents the spiritual background behind the practice of meditation, then takes the reader step-by-step, through the basics of spiritual connection based on the ancient teachings of the Naqshbandi Sufi masters of Central Asia.

KEYS TO THE DIVINE KINGDOM

Shaykh Muhammad Hisham Kabbani
ISBN 1-930409-28-1, Paperback. 140 pp.

God said, "We have created everything in pairs." This has to do with reality versus imitation. Our physical form here in this earthly life is only a reflection of our heavenly form. Like plastic fruit and real fruit, one is real, while the other is an imitation. This book looks at the nature of the physical world, the laws governing the universe and from this starting point, jumps into the realm of spiritual knowledge - Sufi teachings which must be "tasted" as opposed to read or spoken. It will serve to open up to the reader the mystical path of saints which takes human beings from the world of forms and senses to the world within the heart, the world of Gnosis and spirituality - a world filled with wonders and blessings.

---

www.ingramcontent.com/pod-product-compliance
Lightning Source LLC
Chambersburg PA
CBHW052006070526
44584CB00016B/1635
9781930409521